CRICKET, PUBLIC CULTURE AND THE MAKING OF POSTCOLONIAL CALCUTTA

Indian cricket mobilised a large and diverse popular following in the twentieth century. What was so special about cricket and why was it so important to a large number of people? In this book, the author tells the story of this banal humanity that historians tend to forget. Why do postcolonial Indians identify with the colonial game the way they do? Is the engagement with English culture a mechanism for empowering and modernising themselves? What does cricket tell us about the making of a public culture? *Cricket, Public Culture and the Making of Postcolonial Calcutta* uncovers the various modes through which the Indian public have been moulded as followers of cricket and examines the emergence of a postcolonial society through its lens.

Through thematic explorations of cricket's significance for the people of Calcutta, the book discusses the making of public culture in a postcolonial city. The six chapters survey long-term social, cultural and political processes through which cricket became an accessory to emerging identities and ideologies. By closely examining these processes the author analyses the discourses of postcolonialism, collective history and space-making in an urban context. The followers and critics of cricket in Calcutta are the protagonists in this book. A study of their entanglement offers two important insights into the making of postcolonial society. First, it enables us to understand how people attach symbolic values to cultural forms to reimagine and reinvent themselves. Second, it enhances the analytical value of cricket as a cultural tool that empowered, modernised and gave new meanings to its community.

Souvik Naha is Senior Lecturer in Imperial and Post-colonial History at the University of Glasgow. Prior to joining Glasgow, he held the Marie Skłodowska-Curie Actions fellowship at Durham University. He has published extensively in colonial and postcolonial history and has co-edited several journal special issues including *FIFA World Cup and Beyond: Sport, Culture, Media and Governance* (2017), *Global and Transnational Sport: Ambiguous Borders, Connected Domains* (2017), *Ethical Concerns in Sport Governance* (2018), *Moments, Metaphors, Memories: Defining Events in the History of Soccer* (2019), and *Cricket in the 21st Century* (2021).

Cricket, Public Culture and the Making of Postcolonial Calcutta

Souvik Naha

CAMBRIDGE
UNIVERSITY PRESS

CAMBRIDGE
UNIVERSITY PRESS

University Printing House, Cambridge CB2 8BS, United Kingdom

One Liberty Plaza, 20th Floor, New York, NY 10006, USA

477 Williamstown Road, Port Melbourne, vic 3207, Australia

314 to 321, 3rd Floor, Plot No.3, Splendor Forum, Jasola District Centre, New Delhi 110025, India

103 Penang Road, #05–06/07, Visioncrest Commercial, Singapore 238467

Cambridge University Press is part of the University of Cambridge.

It furthers the University's mission by disseminating knowledge in the pursuit of education, learning and research at the highest international levels of excellence.

www.cambridge.org
Information on this title: www.cambridge.org/9781108494588

© Souvik Naha 2022

First published 2022

Printed in India by Thomson Press India Ltd.

A catalogue record for this publication is available from the British Library

Library of Congress Cataloging-in-Publication Data

Names: Naha, Souvik, author.
Title: Cricket, public culture and the making of postcolonial Calcutta / Souvik Naha.
Description: New York, NY : Cambridge University Press, 2022. |
    Includes bibliographical references and index.
Identifiers: LCCN 2022038070 (print) | LCCN 2022038071 (ebook) |
    ISBN 9781108494588 (hardback) | ISBN 9781108781190 (ebook)
Subjects: LCSH: Cricket—India—Kolkata—History—20th century. | Cricket—Social
    aspects—India—Kolkata—History—20th century. | Popular culture—India—
    Kolkata—History—20th century. | Kolkata (India)—Social life and customs—
    History—20th century. | Kolkata (India)—Social conditions—History—20th century. |
    BISAC: SOCIAL SCIENCE / Sociology / General
Classification: LCC GV928.I4 N32 2022 (print) | LCC GV928.I4 (ebook) |
    DDC 306.4/830954147—dc23/eng/20220921
LC record available at https://lccn.loc.gov/2022038070
LC ebook record available at https://lccn.loc.gov/2022038071

ISBN 978-1-108-49458-8 Hardback

For Baba and Kaku

Sumit Naha and Partha Dutt

My horsemen in rain

Contents

Acknowledgements

This book carries the traces of uncountable hopes, bonds and debts. It started years before I enrolled as a student of history, in a suburban house trapped in a garden, where Dadu introduced me to the charm of cricket. A field replaced the garden, a balcony surrogated for the field, and desks substituted the balcony. I carried the curse those games with my family and friends and some of the nation's most influential by-lines on the sports pages wrote on me to Presidency College. I learnt the modes of historical critique from Kaushik Roy, had illuminating conversations with Subhas Ranjan Chakraborty and Sugata Nandi, and transformed my interest in history into a career choice with unstinting encouragement and warmth from Anasua Datta, Jayasree Mukhopadhyay and Paramita Maharatna.

Jawaharlal Nehru University offered an intellectually stimulating atmosphere that nurtured unconventional history-writing. Indivar Kamtekar let me write a seminar paper on the history of cricket in the first semester and sent it to Ramachandra Guha. My greatest debt is to Radhika Singha, whose supervision of my MA and MPhil dissertations has been my most vigorous training in interpreting sources. M. S. S. Pandian's robust interventions as MPhil co-supervisor stirred me to think about multiple explanations of events. Engaging with Arvind Sinha, Kaushik Bhaumik, Kunal Bhattacharya, Neeladri Bhattacharya, Ranabir Chakravarti and Tanika Sarkar profoundly shaped this book.

Large parts of the research for this book were undertaken during my PhD years at ETH Zurich, where Harald Fischer-Tiné sharpened this book's analytical edges with his cerebral insights. His appreciation for my research outputs outside the thesis and the experience of co-convening an international conference have been very rewarding. The kindness of Christian Koller, my co-supervisor, knew no bounds. Projit Bihari Mukharji, who examined my thesis, has remained a pillar of support.

The book owes a great deal to numerous academic collaborators, mentors and friends for their encouraging interest in my work. The experience of organising and taking part in conferences and workshops, editing journals and books, writing journal articles and book chapters has been immensely educative thanks to Annamaria Motrescu-Mayes, David Arnold, David Hassan, Dominic Malcolm, Raj Sekhar Basu, Rakesh Ramamoorthy, Stacey Pope, Stefan Huebner, Tom Fletcher and many other wonderful people. Prashant Kidambi and Simon Rofe have substantially enriched my academic life and this book. My deepest thanks go to Kay Schiller for being a capstone of support and generosity. Soumyen Mallick was unparalleled in his affection and knowledge of cricket. Conversations with Gopal Bose and Gautam Bhattacharya were immensely helpful. My colleagues at the West Bengal State University, Durham University and the University of Glasgow were ever accommodating.

I have been fortunate to receive several fellowships as I worked towards this book. The Swiss government graciously funded my doctoral research through its Excellence Scholarship scheme. Generous fellowships from the Design History Society, the Swiss Academy of Humanities and Social Sciences, St Chad's College Durham, the Institute of Advanced Studies at University College London and the Charles Wallace India Trust further supported my work. Although meant for a different project, the Marie Skłodowska-Curie Actions fellowship offered me invaluable time to reflect on the book's themes and revise the manuscript.

The dedicated and kind librarians and archivists at the ETH Zurich Library and the Zentralbibliothek Zurich; the Bodleian Libraries in Oxford; the British Library and the Marylebone Cricket Club Library in London; the Presidency College Library, the National Library, the Chaitanya Library, and the Bangiya Sahitya Parishad Library in Calcutta; and the JNU Central Library, the Central Secretariat Library, and the Nehru Memorial Museum and Library in New Delhi were a tremendous help. Sohini Ghosh at Cambridge University Press deserves special appreciation for seeing the book through to publication.

My terrific friends – Alex, Amrita, Aniket, Animeshda, Ankit, Anurag, Arghya, Arindam, Arnab, Aritra, Ashisda, Bosudhita, Bernhard, Bhubanesda, Debasmita, Debjanidi, Deepanjit, Hannah, Isha, Joyotidi, Madhurita, Manilata, Milindada, Paula, Philippe, Priyoshi, Ranada, Sabyasachida, Sarbajit, Sayoni, Sohinee, Subhransuda, Swapnanil and the dear ones in Calcutta, Durham, Gothenburg, London, New Delhi, Oxford and Zurich – thank you for your unremitting companionship. Yury always rocked, Soumik was the wellspring of fun, Borda (Aparup) supplied endless wit and wisdom, and Mejda (Avipshu) cured all of life's miseries. Kausik*da* never left my side. Anirban*da* was ever affectionate. Boria*da* unfailingly revived my spirit. Soumita did a wonderful job producing the cover photograph for this book.

I cannot adequately register the great personal cost Baba and Ma bore to ensure I stayed on course. I am much obliged to my relatives, especially Bulbul*jethu* (Manas Ray), and Baba's colleagues for their overwhelming support during my absence from India. The unconditional love of Mamma, Kaku, Kakima, Dida, Dadua and my extended family kept the wheels rolling. I would have happily given the book up to have Baba and Kaku back. Sandip is probably unaware of his immeasurable support over the years. Niranjan could not have been a better accessory to keeping sane and carrying on. A world with KK is the best in the multiverse. The highlight of the last decade has been seeing Chintu grow into an extraordinary brother. Manikarnika partnered me in every step and stumble. Our relationship has been the book we wrote to ourselves with characters cast from our dreams. Every time we look down its pages, it expands and enlivens.

Abbreviations

ABP	*Anandabazar Patrika*
AmBP	*Amrita Bazar Patrika*
BCCI	Board of Control for Cricket in India
BJP	Bharatiya Janata Party
CAB	Cricket Association of Bengal
CPI(M)	Communist Party of India (Marxist)
DB	*Dainik Basumati*
HT	*Hindustan Times*
ICC	International Cricket Council
IWI	*Illustrated Weekly of India*
KA	*Khelar Asar*
MCC	Marylebone Cricket Club
MLA	Member of Legislative Assembly
MP	Member of Parliament
ODI	One Day International
SKA	*Sharadiya Khelar Asar*
ST	*Sunday Times*
TG	*The Guardian*
TOI	*Times of India*
TS	*The Statesman*
TT	*The Telegraph*

Introduction

Australian Prime Minister Robert Menzies, in Calcutta (since renamed as Kolkata) on the way to London for the 1951 Commonwealth Prime Ministers' Conference, was taken by surprise seeing people playing cricket in a country ravaged by colonialism.[1] He said,

> When I was driven round Calcutta to my joy I found that on every piece of park lawn people were playing cricket. I pointed to this and said to the gentleman who was accompanying me, 'well, there you are. There is nothing wrong with this country from anybody's point of view. Everybody is playing cricket on the park lawns.[2]

What was so special about cricket and why was it so important to a large number of people? 'Is cricket a sport or a pastime?' asked an advertisement of the Central Tea Board in India in 1951.[3] There is no pithier one-line encapsulation of cricket's public history in India. A sport is defined as a structured, goal-oriented, competitive activity, whereas a pastime is a freewheeling indulgence, presumably devoid of conflict, politics and struggle.[4] A letter written by the schoolteacher O. H. T. Dudley to *The Times* in 1932 shows that Indians might have started to think of cricket as a way of life, more than a pastime, at the turn of the twentieth century. In the letter, Dudley wrote, 'Twenty-five years ago I went out to India to teach English. I have come back with a rich reward in the following sentence from an Indian schoolboy's essay on cricket: "Cricket is a very comfortable game: in it we disremember all our condition."'[5] In his analysis of the characteristics of Indian cricket in a 1946 book, journalist Berry Sarbadhikary wrote that cricket in India was 'more of a pastime than a grim science', referring to the ad hoc nature of the game's organisation at recreational level and the hybrid cultural attitudes resulting from the integration of Indian and British cultural traditions.[6] When a letter-writer introduced the India–England Test match in Calcutta in 1972–73 as the battle between the bat and the ball that had solved all of Bengal's socio-political problems, he did not come across as sarcastic but rather entranced by the impact an event spread over five days could have over the long term woes of a state of 45 million people.[7] For historian Sarvepalli Gopal, cricket was 'one of the few lasting and refreshing legacies of the *raj*'.[8] The journalist and author Khushwant Singh wrote in 1973 that the Indian's obsession with cricket needed to be psycho-analysed, adding that the cricket pitch had become the paradise of millions of Indians.[9] The journalist Soumya Bhattacharya recalled that cricket was a 'surefire conversational opener' during his student years in England in the 1990s. 'If you're Indian, you must be crazy about cricket', so went the assumption.[10] Reflecting on the attachment of Indians to cricket, Jonathan Rice, author and editor of several cricket books, unreservedly assumed in 2011 that cricket sat next to god and family for Indians.[11] Cricket, it seems from these accounts, is important for Indians. This book tells the story of this banal humanity that historians tend to forget.

Regardless of whether cricket has delivered radical social change or produced a sense of ethnic or cultural affiliation, the identities built around it have generated intense public conversations. It would be sheer naiveté to think of cricket in India as either a pastime or a sport, on account of the multiple meanings the sport has embodied since its introduction in 1721 by British seamen.[12] Over the next three centuries or so, cricket has built up a nationwide spread and mobilised a large and diverse popular following. Its networks have crisscrossed the dynamics and domains of colonialism, nationalism, economy, culture and various forms of identity. As an imperial game, a vehicle of colonial modernity and cultural hybridity, and a tool of nationalist resistance, cricket has simultaneously been a Western fetish and an indigenous cultural form in modern India. Why do postcolonial Indians identify with the colonial game the way they do? Is the engagement with English culture a mechanism for empowering and modernising themselves? What does cricket tell us about the making of a public culture? This book uncovers the various modes through which the public have been moulded as cricket followers and examines the emergence of a postcolonial society through the lens of cricket.

The public's diverse appreciation for elements such as skill, spectacle and tradition pluralised the culture of spectatorship. Hence, a study of cricket spectators need not defer to the somewhat limited historicist convention that the consumer necessarily represents a distinct social class and culture just as it generates inequality. Sport, and cricket in particular, resists division of class and culture. It blends human actions in all its cultural practices and aestheticism, leading to interpenetration of the class categories of subjects. The consumption patterns of the masses give sports new but no inferior meanings than those made by the highbrow cognoscenti. Why is cricket an appropriate device for understanding the life world of a postcolonial society? The game's palimpsest is layered with social, political and economic connotations that have produced a public culture in dialogue with historical contexts. The cycle of its production, circulation and consumption has defined much of the society's quotidian practices and beliefs. Various promotional activities have taken place as part of the widening sphere of cricket's commercialisation since the onset of international cricket in India in the 1930s. Two overseas Test series victories in 1971, an uninterrupted supply of excellent players throughout the 1970s, the World Cup victory in 1983 and the hosting of the tournament in 1987 gradually elevated India's status in world cricket. The proliferation of satellite television, internet and consumer culture in India added fresh dimensions to cricket's publicness, popularity and appropriation. More than cricket's success as a sport, this book argues, the beliefs and attitudes it has generated through media and other social practices have had an immense bearing on the making of a postcolonial society.

HISTORY, POSTCOLONIALISM AND CRICKET

The task of reinterpreting colonial history with greater agency to the indigene has taken historians of colonial India to unusual sites and practices – disease, insects, paperwork, punch houses, cricket, and so on. Paying attention to the vulnerabilities and collaborative nature of the British Empire, these works articulate a bottom-up version of how indigenous groups participated in colonial governance and in the nebulous process of *colonial modernity*.[13] A study of the interaction between British and Indian people, objects and practices enables one to understand colonisation and modernisation at both symbolic and institutional levels. This perspective has informed the studies of the emergence of Indian nationhood through colonial sport. The historians of colonial Indian cricket, Richard Cashman, Ashis Nandy, Ramachandra Guha, Boria Majumdar and Prashant Kidambi, in chronological order of the publication of their monographs, have all shown how little the British invested, materially and intellectually, in spreading cricket in India.[14] Their works do not explicitly engage with the colonial modernity framework, but they have used its tools to move beyond Eurocentric histories of sport and refuted the importance that British sports historians usually gave to cultural imperialism in the diffusion of sport. They have argued that since the mid-nineteenth century, Indians across class, caste, religious and gender divides have collectively, and sometimes in collaboration, shaped their identities around cricket. In the colonial period, participation through a number of ways – mimicry of the Victorian approach to team sports, resisting the British Empire through cricket, constructing identities and successful commercialisation – generated an indigenous cricket culture in which the British were more often than not uninvolved. In a way, their works echo historian C. A. Bayly's research in indigenous commercial and intellectual groups who appropriated certain colonial institutions for their own benefit.[15] Studies of cricket or sport in independent India, though relatively scarce, have addressed issues of identity, politics, communalism, caste, celebrity culture and the impact of media on leisure.

This book pursues two questions that this literature leaves unresolved. First, while these historians have convincingly refuted the primacy of cultural imperialism and established the process of a two-way transfer of culture, studies of how the vestiges of the colonial period shaped cricket in independent India are few. Second, they have not systematically considered cricket as a source of identity and popular culture in everyday postcolonial life. Through addressing these two questions, the book expands our 'historical understanding' of postcolonial India.[16] The game's postcolonial history, where I employ the term 'postcolonial' to denote both the temporal and ideological transition from the British Raj to an independent polity, raises a number of new questions in regard to the whys and hows of cricket's popularity.[17] In this book, postcolonialism is a process of reconstructing a region's political, social and cultural spaces, with emergent ideas and identities transforming, subsuming or replacing colonial institutions.

The book makes two key contributions: one, it decentres the nation as the fulcrum around which much of South Asian history and history of sport has been written; second, it interrogates popular attitudes and helps rethink the construction of postcolonial history outside conventional archives. It starts with the simple premise that cricket was important to at least some Indians and seeks to understand what this attachment meant for Indian society, mindful of cultural theorist Kwame Anthony Appiah's assertion about the pitfalls of assigning undue importance to historical actors and processes. As Appiah said, the bicycle was invented and taken across the globe by the white person, but the bicycle's popularity in Africa was not a by-product of colonial modernity and the civilising process. The machine won over Africans because of its usefulness rather than foreignness and modernising capacity.[18] In the same way, I contend that cricket thrived in India mainly because a large number of Indians liked it, and the impact of outside influences (such as gender divide, economic stagnation, overpopulation, and so on) on cricket provides a useful context for analysing Indian society.

CRICKET AS HISTORICAL NARRATIVE

Sport has been a blind spot for historians of postcolonial India. Historian Anne Firor Scott once argued that historians write about what they are willing to know and neglect what they personally consider unimportant, even if the subject in question is widely significant and richly documented.[19] Except in Swati Chattopadhyay's discussion of street cricket in Calcutta as an index of a public space's performative possibilities, sport finds little mention in monographs and anthologies that chart the making of a modern Indian city in the twentieth century.[20] The method of historians of Indian sport has been the structuralist use of sport as a component of the nation to fully or partially account for the nation's development. They tend to impose a national framework on regional characters often enough. Assigning a totalising explanatory potential to one sport can be problematic. While this book does not attempt any aggregated or comparative analysis, it recognises that a single sport can neither answer every question nor claim academic sanctimony on the exclusive strength of its visibility.

The Indian nation's long shadow across the playing field is manifest in the subtitles of two monographs on the history of cricket in India: 'An Indian History of a British Game' and 'A Social History of Indian Cricket'.[21] Although the authors, Ramachandra Guha and Boria Majumdar, respectively, demonstrate that there was scarcely anything 'Indian' about Indian cricket, they write histories of the nation through the lens of cricket. Prashant Kidambi too asks, 'How the idea of India took shape on the cricket pitch?'[22] Historian Paul Dimeo criticises the tendency of historians such as Guha to consider cricket as a mimetic text, saying this has resulted from a subconscious mythologisation of the sport as the pulse of the nation.[23] Satadru Sen questions the treatment of cricket in the prevalent historiography, contending that nationalism has been so deeply grafted onto Indian cricket that matches which did not convey overtly political messages of nationhood left no impression on popular memory, and, by extension, academic studies. This is why 'memorable' performances in regional tournaments are hardly remembered unlike even brief episodes from international matches.[24] The emphasis on the national model is a routine, one which Ranajit Guha terms the 'statist predicament of South Asian historiography' and exhorts historians to avoid.[25] Guha is uneasy about the uncritical acceptance and application of the state-centric models and methods of European history by many historians of India. This book moves away from the nation-state pattern, dwelling instead on a single site in which the local, the national and the global intermittently intermingled on the occasion of cricket matches. Even if Calcutta speaks for India, it uses its own vocabulary and not that of the nation.

India's independence in 1947, a watershed event in many histories, is not too important for this book, which straddles the late colonial and the postcolonial, repudiating the idea of a division based on the official end of imperial rule. The postcolonial in this book is a category of analysing tradition–modernity debates and the creation of difference. It conceptualises cricket as an allegory of colonialism and postcolonialism. It frames the identity of the postcolonial subject within a contentious exercise of mediation and collective inclination as exemplified by the public sphere around cricket in Calcutta. The identity cumulatively embodied by the actors in this book is simultaneously very local and global, across the worlds of ideology, occupation and ethnicity. Politics, both bureaucratic and cultural, plays a paramount role here in stringing together the beads of mediated public action.

It is noteworthy that historians of sport in India have not tailored 'pre-owned' sociological or anthropological concepts into history to give their texts the aura of interdisciplinary research, preferring instead the positivist historical method of rigorous assessment of sources.[26] Cashman, Guha and Majumdar established the history of Indian cricket as an inalienable aspect of political and social history, using the structuralist method of understanding a part of society in terms of its pertinence to a larger structure.[27] They have admirably engaged with a variety of sources, recovered little-known memories and debunked myths from a reconstructivist perspective. However, their writings often gloss over the textual nature of an event and the immense subjectivity of the administrative and press reports that are used as empirical evidence. This book appraises the nature of sources in addition to treating them as founts of knowledge. It does not deconstruct sources into narrative categories and analyse each of the constituent elements. However, it questions the privileging of one source over another as the authenticity of no text is beyond doubt.

A part of the book deals with a period in which I grew up to be a cricket follower, indulging in the rituals of spectatorship and readership that I explore here. A meaningful personal or anecdotal history incorporating one's personal experience into a larger context – from the neighbourhood to the nation or the globe – can possess great explanatory power.[28] The historian's position in the narrative can be both intimate and apathetic. One of the many problems of alloying oneself into a text is the trespassing of rhetoric and judgements. The presence of multiple and undifferentiated perspectives in a text demands very careful reading for one to decipher the meaning. It also brings into question the author's historical ethics, connections and function as a member of society.[29] I have not used autoethnography as a historical method in this book to avoid inconsistency with the rest of the chronology of which I have no lived experience. The historians of cricket in India who have incorporated personal experience into their writings have quite uncritically mingled presentism into interpretation of the past. Chronic appearances of the first person, such as Guha's conversation with Palwankar Baloo's descendants, effort to meet Alan Knott and the experience of watching the India–Pakistan match during the 1999 World Cup offer valuable perspectives about the context.[30] But as stray subjective impulses, these enrich only selected segments of history, sometimes without justification. It is unthinkable for a sport historian to have never watched the sport one writes about. Lived experience generates empathy and inclinations of plotting the narrative. Autoethnographical methods ought to be uniformly and rigorously applied to history-writing alongside other relevant sources; otherwise, the author is reduced to footnotes in one's own writing.

This book departs also from the focus on social formation and economic explanation as in the previous studies. Guha's analysis of the anti-Pentangular movement highlights contours of Hindu–Muslim relations and contemporary nationalist criticism of the tournament as a threat to communal harmony.[31] Majumdar has argued that the tournament's commercial viability so frustrated the organisers of the rival tournament, in this case, the Board of Control for Cricket in India (BCCI) and the Ranji Trophy, that they implicitly supported the campaign to eliminate this threat.[32] It has been argued that members of the national team do not represent the social demographics and that a conspiracy to exclude the scheduled castes from any level of cricket is afoot.[33] The release of *Lagaan* in 2000 stirred a debate about the film being a synecdoche of the present in its exhibition of the conditions of subalternity.[34] Additionally, scholars have reflected on the convergence of nationalist and communalist impulses in the theatre of cricket in postcolonial India.[35] This book refers to these social, political and economic aspects of cricket in connection with how these have been narrated in the media and analyses social relationships.

Finally, this book foregrounds the mediated discourses about cricket's position within the state, corporate and private patronage networks. It does not focus as much on infrastructure and operation. Historians have written about the introduction of the 'games ethic' through schools and colleges[36] and cross-cultural interactions such as the migration of foreign cricket professionals to the physically defined space of the nation.[37] While writing about the diffusion and resistance models, historians have barely considered the more complex processes of perception and translation of cultural codes. The accounts of the production of an indigenous brand of cricket among the upper-middle classes of colonial Bombay (now known as Mumbai) and Calcutta have elided the bridges of transfer, the conflicts in the ideational space mediated by agents of transfer, and the hypertexts of the transferred culture across social strata. Hence, they tend to advocate the logic of nearly identical group identities and mechanisms of appropriation across the nation. This book offers a corrective to this methodological problem by analysing the dilemma of cricket's appropriation in the light of the ambiguities of cultural transfer.

Scholars and dilettantes have mapped the transition from colonial patronage to post-independence sponsorship, stressing the advent of non-governmental enterprises, expansion of the media and creation of financial clusters around cricket. Cashman has written about the rise and fall of princely patronage and the subsequent seamless shift of cricket into a corporate structure that reflected the independent country's experiments with capitalist endeavours.[38] Among the works dealing exclusively with the post-independence years, Nalin Mehta and Boria Majumdar's articles explore the critical role of new media technologies such as satellite television in the proliferation of cricket's popularity.[39] The articles by Abilash Nalapat and Andrew Parker, Prashant Kidambi and Shamya Dasgupta have predicated the celebrity of Sachin Tendulkar on socio-economic transformations in contemporary India.[40] A number of studies have addressed the recent market economy and globalisation of Indian cricket.[41] The global business and cosmopolitan assemblage of sport cultures as ushered by the Indian Premier League has received probably the maximum attention from scholars.[42] Nearly all of these articles are fixated on administrative structures and thus overlook cricket's public dimension. This book shifts the spotlight away from the isolated domains of economy, spectacle and mass entertainment, turning it on to the ensemble arena of the sport's public culture.

POSTCOLONIAL CALCUTTA

The book studies the history of the cricket-loving people of Calcutta in the twentieth century, exploring cricket's place in the popular imagination from the beginning of international cricket in the city until a riot in 1999 spurred a reassessment of what cricket has meant to people. The game's entanglement with the city's everyday life, the sites of play and the audience metaphorically merged when Bengali poet Amitabho Dasgupta described the civic unrest in the 1960s–70s as:

> Calcutta is bowling fast. Play forward.
> Look carefully at the fielder at mid-on.
> Defend two balls, then jump out of the crease
> To hit a six over the bowler's head.[43]

The figurative translation here of the adversity of urban life as the aggression of a fast bowler that is to be countered with confident batting – a bold and straightforward mode of living – invested cricket with great symbolic capaciousness. The city did not live and breathe cricket round the year since international matches were hosted for a limited period. Football had a comparably mighty presence in Calcutta. Popular enthusiasm around local football far outscores the negligible attendance in domestic cricket matches. Yet this book explores the dynamics of cricket, arguing that popularity has many layers and football does not quite measure up to cricket's social significance on several levels.

Calcutta carved out a niche as the 'emotional headquarters' of this national obsession.[44] The city has represented cricket in Bengal, 'governing the game and making history' since long before the beginning of Test cricket at the Eden Gardens in 1934.[45] The combination of a ground considered by many as one of the most beautiful in the world, a crowd that considers silence heretical, and authors bent on establishing cricket as a metonymy for life has produced a unique sporting culture in the city. The polysemic nature of culture creates methodological problems, with value judgements enhancing the perplexity of what can be called culture. A veteran of three first-class matches for Bengal between 1964 and 1969 emphatically denied the existence of any 'culture' among local spectators in a personal interview with me.[46] On the contrary, Mike Denness, captain of England in 19 Test matches in the 1970s, considered the Test match 'atmosphere' created by spectators and the character of the stadium in Calcutta to have been rivalled only by Melbourne.[47] A correspondent of the Bengali sports periodical *Khelar Asar* wrote in 1979 that the spectacle appealed more to the spectators than the game itself. That is the reason why, he claimed, youth Test matches never generated the same degree of popular interest as would the ones involving the senior national team. He further argued that the decline in the number of knowledgeable spectators and the standard of play, both very subjective categories of assumption, in the 1970s discouraged many discerning cricket followers from going to the stadium.[48] These epistemic binaries about the routine of sport and spectatorship show how trivial empiricism can sometimes appear to cultural perceptions. Sport is one of the forms of culture whose public life is a 'dynamic field of competing voices forever commenting on each other'.[49] Sports media is the principal site of the coaction of these contending voices.

The history of football in Bengal began as a fin-de-siècle flag of unitary social identity, progressed as a short-lived emblem of nationalism, and culminated in social difference expressed through communal, ethnic and regional overtones.[50] The people of Calcutta spent the summer watching domestic football and the winter watching club and international cricket. A major reason for the lukewarm interest in domestic cricket was the lack of local cricket heroes. Only seven Bengali cricketers made it to the national team, playing between themselves 11 Test and 10 One Day International (ODI) matches, in the period between 1960, when Pankaj Roy retired, and 1992, when the talismanic Sourav Ganguly made his debut. Three others who played for India from the state were not ethnic Bengalis – Dilip Doshi, Ashok Malhotra and Arun Lal. The public would be more likely to watch local football teams, comprising players who won the national-level championship

27 times out of the 50 editions of the tournament played between 1947–48 and 1998–99. Unlike cricket, football mobilised an urban identity founded on localised group behaviour – a sense of cohesion usually missing from the mosaic of urban life. Cricket was more of an adoptive child that steadily became the parent's favourite. In the opinion of the novelist and literary critic Amit Chaudhuri, football spectatorship was reduced to a proletarian level in the 1980s, with the middle class decisively shifting their loyalty to cricket even before Ganguly's emergence as a star cricketer.[51] While Chaudhuri's division of cricket spectators into rigid social classes remains problematic, he offers a valid observation about the surge in support for cricket in the city.

Cricket reveals the city from a different perspective and degree of intricacy than football. First, cricket opened the city to a global network of personnel mobility and cultural circulation. As such, it offers a vantage point to observe transcultural encounters between the cosmopolitan and the provincial. If the local football derbies were intense, international cricket matches spawned collective frenzy. Second, cricket's clientele comprised a larger and more diverse cross-section of the society, a study of which vividly brings out the complexities of class formation, particularly the growth of the middle class. Third, the extent and variety of the literary attention given to football was minuscule compared to cricket. That in turn makes cricket's representation an ideal pathway to an understanding of what underpinned the acceptability and marketability of leisure, and how people thought, responded to and remembered its impact on society. At a symbolic level, cricket unfailingly conveys local, national and global expressions of Calcutta, however episodic. An interpretation of the grand convergence of the modernising impulses, political motivations and commercial initiatives in cricket illustrates the history of Calcutta in a way few other cultural enterprises can. Finally, adopting the cultural geographer Tim Edensor's contention that identity is a process and not an essence, it can be said that cricket in the city constructed a narrative of the interlacing of ambiguous identities far more potently than football did.[52] That precisely is why this book engages with the history of cricket, press narratives and the spectators in Calcutta in particular.

MEDIATED SPORT, PUBLICS AND HISTORY FROM THE MIDDLE

The indeterminacy of the production and reception of opinion in the sports media needs to be considered while examining cricket as a form of knowledge.

The materiality and meaning of knowledge are linked to their source, always open to appropriation by a surfeit of interpretative paradigms. The framing of a history of the public in terms of mediated opinions and actions calls for an understanding of, and not necessarily separating, the fiction–reality and production–consumption dyads. Historian Roger Chartier postulated cultural history as the ideal method of circumventing this dualism.[53] Cultural history focuses more on the modalities of representation than on the assembling of evidence to settle the truth value of statements; it often enough integrates the two approaches. From a cultural history perspective, journalists and readers cease to be producers and consumers of knowledge, respectively. Even reading can be cast as a creative strategy to interrogate conventional notions of high and low culture, something particularly evident by the public's appreciation of sport.[54]

The use of mediated texts or fiction as historical sources should involve an investigation of subjectivity. As Jeffrey Hill says, literary texts do not simply reproduce the widely held sense of a sport at any given time, but are capable of actively generating a 'reality' consistent with other historical evidences.[55] It is not easy to fathom the impact of a single novel on its readers as there is little possibility of those readers having recorded their response. Novels like *Tom Brown's Schooldays* are a few out of many that can be evidenced to have produced a 'social reality'.[56] The book, widely read, ostensibly inspired the modern public school system of cultivating sports as a character-building exercise. Sports literature of this sort is posterity's 'historical faith' par excellence, which, to quote Carlo Ginzburg, 'allows us to overcome incredulity, nourished by the recurring objections of scepticism, relating to an invisible past, through a series of opportune operations'.[57] In his analysis of a long unpublished dialogue written in Paris in 1647, Ginzburg counterposes two historical sensibilities: one favours the possibility of drawing out evidence from fiction, while the other denounces such trial of fiction as paradoxical due to the latter's inventedness. Ginzburg advocates the first perspective, suggesting (through selectively quoting the original dialogue) that fiction enables one to have 'emotive proximity' with historical actors.[58] The actors in the article think according to the philosophy available to them, while Ginzburg is careful not to extrapolate any stream of thought that might have been beyond their imagination. Hence, he is preoccupied with the question of reading history into fiction but only peripherally addresses the ancillary problematic of textual meanings being always in flux and contingent upon the reader's sensibility.[59]

Sport is full of symbols, the meanings of which vary and keep changing. In their introduction to the 'Sport and Literature' special issue of *Sport in History*, Hill and Jean Williams acknowledge that 'metaphor and semiology' underpin the representation of sport.[60] As a cultural text firmly entrenched in society, sport and its myriad manifestations might resist individuating fact and fiction. In addition to disseminating and acculturating sports codes, literary texts shape a sport's self-representation within the imagined communities of fans and other geopolitical entities.[61] This is why a close reading of sports fictions alongside everyday newspaper reports is particularly useful. Journalist N. S. Ramaswami was so enamoured of equal status for literature and cricket that he tried to pass personal opinion as universal truth, writing,

> Cricket criticism is often best expressed in terms of literary criticism. This is natural for the game, in its best deportment, is a phase of universal poetry. An innings by Borde seizes the senses by storm as if it were a book of Paradise Lost, while an hour of Baig is like reading an ode by Keats when it is twilight and all the world is still.[62]

Raymond Boyle and Richard Haynes warn against the perils of overemphasising the media as a lens for a study of social development, calling for attention to the political, economic and cultural pressures that often condition the parameters against which media-sport and its engagement with collective identities are framed.[63] It has been argued that historians often ignore the fact that on an everyday basis journalism is very conventional because too much focus on mega events or controversies may estrange the non-fan reader from the sports pages.[64] However, mediatised discourses of sport play an important part – at times more crucial than others – in reproducing, naturalising and even constructing values, attitudes and sometimes prejudices that circulate in the before society. There is a need to recognise that particular ideological formations of identity exist in and around sporting subcultures, such as the masculine culture which often surrounds wrestling and rugby football.[65] Cricket in India particularly illustrates the cultural dichotomy on a national scale owing to its conversion from the archetypal English sport to one of the country's main signifiers.

Mediatised versions may have reasons to ignore or amplify certain aspects of sports culture. Coverage of international sport, for instance, could sometimes be entangled with a broader political agenda, as evident in India–Pakistan cricket ties or England–Argentina football matches. The point remains just as valid at the national level, where sport and its attendant coverage often become a focal point for articulating a range of collective identities, as exemplified by the football rivalry between Barcelona and Real Madrid in Spain, or Mohun Bagan and East Bengal in India. This process calls into question the complex relationship between discourses that circulate in the media about sport and its appeal. Boyle and Haynes raise the pertinent point that the press, in a bid to sustain its symbiotic relationship with sport, rarely probes the internal politics of sporting institutions. It intervenes only when corruptions and scandals threaten to dismantle the extant structure.[66] The existing organisation, after all, signifies an arrangement designed to optimise the consumption of certain sport-mediated cultural artefacts.

To understand the consumption of mediatised sport, one ought to locate sports followers within their broader social context.[67] The experience of sport differs according to the audience's sense of tradition, community and place. The urge to capture the sense of belonging to class and community, and in some cases gender, has driven the sports media operations.[68] Much of the research into the interplay of sport, culture and society since the 1980s acknowledges the salience of a cultural politics that moves far beyond the concerns and confines of the nation-state. The 'trans-national cultural flow' around international sport has assigned a critical urgency involving cross-cultural explorations beyond unitary national contexts.[69] Regional comparisons within a country can be no less illuminating. The culture of cricket has developed very differently in Calcutta, Bombay and Delhi even though these cities were introduced to the sport in a more or less similar fashion. The difference owes to the social context of these sites and different approaches undertaken by the agents of mediation. It is necessary at this point to define this public and its culture, especially since media-sport is both for and about the audience.

The public in Jürgen Habermas' theory of the bourgeois, political public sphere is outwardly visible, opinionated, participatory, essentially male and transforms in consonance with drifts in capitalism and mass media.[70] The public nature of such a group is derived from the assembly and visibility of people connected by a common cause. The media, since it can create and manipulate public opinion, is critical to transforming the public sphere. The public sphere in the twentieth century is not primarily disposed to discussing the political aspect of public life. The proliferation of mass entertainment or mass culture has challenged, expanded and altered the mechanism of the Habermasian public sphere. The emergent cultural public sphere revolved not so much around literature and politics but new forms of communication which connected people to issues of everyday life.[71] According to Benedict Anderson, 'print-capitalist' authors and editors showed a trait of designing the narratives of events and ideas in a way that made sense only to their intended consumers, who in turn would imagine themselves as part of a shared community. Such imaginations transcended the need to physically meet or interact with other members of the 'imagined community'.[72] Although Anderson emphasised the national context, the plurality of Calcutta, and especially the post-independence primordialism of Bengal bearing a distinct and dissident identity as a cultural nation within the geopolitical entity of India, provide an appropriate context for examining his assumptions. The politics of production and transmission of information plays an inordinately critical role in structuring the contemporary public. The increasing national and global reach of mediating devices and other technological changes have diversified the process of intermediation by texts, allowing public debates to take place in impersonal, despatialised ways across geographical, ethnic and linguistic boundaries. People unknown to one another are thus categorised as following a common denominator of mass culture.

The commercial media's inclination towards profit and also its colossal presence as a social and political force have complicated the knowledge of how the media represents the public. Not only has active participation of the public been exceedingly substituted by abstract networks of encounters, but mediation is also known to produce so many interpretations of direct assemblies that it often becomes impossible to distinguish reality and perception, should that distinction be valid. The importance of texts in the formation of a public is evident in the sevenfold nominal features that Michael Warner has identified in the public of late modernity: (a) a public is self-organised; (b) a public is a relation among strangers; (c) the address of public speech is both personal and impersonal; (d) a public is constituted through mere attention; (e) a public is the social space created by the reflexive circulation of discourse; (f) publics act historically according to the temporality of their circulation; and (g) a public is poetic world-making.[73] Evidently, although the mass media largely determines the making of a public and one's engagement with the mediatised representation of sport, politics and other such consumables, the convergence of the media and the public always involves contestations of interest, consciousness and power. John Thompson analyses this reciprocal action in terms of a 'mediated publicness' – a creative and non-hegemonic space in which texts are circulated and appropriated with little restriction of visibility.[74] However, the operation of power is always discernible from within the process. The logic of exercise of power associates mediation closely with the other significant moderator of public life – spectacle.[75] Warner contradicts the open-ended nature of Thompson's publicness, giving priority to the work of purpose and pre-cognition in the circulation process. The duality of mediation reiterates the overall discursive nature of media content.

Sports followers are an affective community, one that bonds over sporting narratives, forming what Arjun Appadurai calls the 'communities of sentiment'.[76] The sociologist Cornel Sandvoss argues that interactions among followers often involve larger political debates around nationhood, citizenship, ethnicity, religion and gender. The discussions are sometimes very radical despite taking place outside the official political domain. Although appreciation of sport is essentially a private understanding of culture, public dialogue is an inescapable activity for sports fans. Interaction appends new symbols to popular culture and revises existing ones.[77] Hence, a cultural analysis of mediated sport ought to situate and investigate the binaries of the real and the imagined, agency and subjectivity, hegemony and subversion, and the hierarchy of participation. Media texts can be shown to have constructed cricket as a field representing the identities of subjects and framed the consuming society as agents whose acts are informed or determined by the discourses in circulation. These agents do not maintain a strict hierarchy mainly because their location in the production–consumption continuum is always in flux. The constitution of agency relies much upon the historical moment of interpretation just as it is given an identity by power differentials in the society.

STRUCTURE OF THE BOOK

The first chapter of this book analyses the observations of cricket as a foreign, imperial and English game in late colonial and postcolonial India. It explores the contradictory responses to the sport from the perspective of transcultural encounters, integrating the three fields that historians consider the most important in the context of Anglo-Indian cultural synthesis – politics, language and cricket.[78] Many Bengali authors and journalists justified cricket as an authentic Indian practice by showing its successful acculturation and intense bond with the local people. They connected Indian cricket to the sport's global order by appropriating its moral and pastoral aspects, a study of which enables this chapter to inspect the agenda, method and ramification of cultural transfer.

The second chapter explores the mediatisation and mediation of the public's attachment to cricket. It begins with an examination of the historicity of match reports, discussing the methods of reading them as historical sources and the appropriate questions to ask of them. The reading of narratives is an important part of understanding cricket's community of sentiment since the agenda of newspapers and periodicals changed with time, ownership, editorship and narrative agency of journalists. A study of radio commentary probes the method of circulating cricket to people who seldom read newspapers. The chaper leaves television out of the discussion since the technology came into force only in the 1980s and 1990s and its impact was only partially visible in the twentieth century.

The next chapter defines the public of cricket and ponders how reports constructed a public culture around the sport by promoting a sense of place and people. It then deliberates the mediated publicness of cricket with reference to the scamper for tickets to international matches. It traces the long history of how people acquired tickets for Test and ODI matches, showing the evolution of their taste, obligations and inclinations as constituted by the sports press. The mediation of the ticket crisis was a double bind for the press as its attention to detail was simultaneously admired by readers and accused of encouraging frenzied behaviour. Such descriptions of spectators, sedimented over the years in public memory, created a continuous narrative of public culture which this chapter examines.

The fourth chapter expands the theme of the making of public culture by taking into account the involvement of politicians as spectators and patrons, and the implication of regarding the selection of Bengali cricketers in the Indian national team as a political struggle. It analyses the ways in which politicians and the political public used cricket to improve self-image, create propaganda networks and leverage political goals in the open disguise of cultural benevolence. Bengal has contrived a complicated relationship with India, in which cultural dissension is amplified so much that it conceals the state's economic dependence on the nation. The next section studies the ways in which cricket was drawn into the prevalent resentment against a national conspiracy to upstage Bengal's lead in politics, economy and culture, demonstrating cricket's importance in the state's political life.

The fifth chapter is concerned with representation of gendered spectatorship, breaking away from the popular themes explored in relation to women's sport and media such as the representation of gendered bodies, identities and values in sport, particularly the use of the body in displays of sexuality. It travels through a period in which gender boundaries substantially shifted, and women's agency and the propriety of interaction between genders became topics of intense media discussion. It examines the mediatised negotiation of authenticity and legitimacy of female cricket followers in the stadium hierarchy, in terms of the perception of women's knowledge, sexuality and obsession, in order to survey the gendering of culture.

The final chapter delves into the specificities of the culture–politics nexus in the sports press by investigating representations of four incidents of crowd disturbance. It traces the impact of the political inclination of newspapers on the presentation of sports news from the 1960s to the 1990s, demonstrating the transformation of personal agency within the press. It studies three practical aspects of cricket's imagined community as manifest by the representation of entitlement and deprivation among spectators, the consequences of violence in collective history and the dilemma of defining the normative in the larger experiential context of spectatorship. A history of the interruption of what the press displayed as carnivalesque and hysteric explains the intersection of the imagined and the tangible aspects of public culture.

The main objective of this book is to show that sport has played more significant a part in the making of postcolonialism in India than historians have accorded to it. Although the role of television is well documented, it is relatively recent as a media outlet. Literature, news reports and radio broadcasts have served to transmit cricket for a longer period, and it is crucial to interrogate their producers as agents of history. The framework of culture in this book follows the social history approach that prioritises interactions between people and social relationships as a bottom-up historical perspective. It is informed by media texts that evoked canons, provided the sport with a sense of tradition and determined the protocols of its appropriation. The chapters argue that texts constructed the sport as an emotional and aspirational institution by asking rhetorical questions and producing knowledge for consumption by its followers. Although editorials, letters and articles on stadium riots, misogyny of spectatorship, dismal performances and scandals routinely expressed anti-cricket sentiments, a comprehensive analysis of every strand of opinion is necessary for understanding the making of the cricketing public. The book does not examine epistemological issues of the reading of texts in detail but emphasises the importance of mediation in the making of embedded audience and communities. From this premise, it claims to add a new dimension to the existing historiography of sport by integrating the histories of mediation, circulation and consumption.

NOTES

1. Not one to miss out on using cricket metaphors, Menzies wondered why India and Australia, two cricket-playing nations, could not have cordial diplomatic relations. The reasons were quite obviously the gulf of difference in how Australia and India saw their roles in the postwar world. Australia's empathy for Pakistan, South Africa and America, and Menzies's lack of respect for the Third World in particular, were not acceptable to India. Meg Gurry, 'Leadership and Bilateral Relations: Menzies and Nehru, Australia and India, 1949–1964', *Pacific Affairs* 65, no. 4 (Winter, 1992–1993): 510–26.
2. 'Common Bond of Cricket', *Times of India* (*TOI*), 28 December 1950, 1.
3. *Illustrated News* 16, no. 20 (25 October 1951), ii.
4. Barry D. McPherson, James E. Curtis and John W. Loy, *The Social Significance of Sport* (Champaign, IL: Human Kinetics, 1989), 15–17. Grant Jarvie has described the major characteristics of modern sport as: a ritual sacrifice of human energy, a common cultural currency between peoples, a means of compensating for deficiencies in life, a mechanism for the affirmation of identity and difference, a social product, and a contested arena shaped by struggles both on and off the field of play. See Grant Jarvie, *Sport, Culture and Society: An Introduction* (London and New York: Routledge, 2006), 3.
5. O.H.T. Dudley, 'An Indian Boy on Cricket', *The Times*, 5 July 1932, 15.
6. Berry Sarbadhikary, ed., *Presenting Indian Cricket* (Calcutta: A. Mukherjee, 1946), 1.
7. *Dainik Basumati* (*DB*), 1 January 1973, 5.
8. Sarvepalli Gopal, 'The Spell of Cricket', in *Imperialists, Nationalists, Democrats: The Collected Essays*, ed. Srinath Raghavan, 408–15 (Ranikhet: Permanent Black, 2013), 414.
9. Khushwant Singh, 'Cricket, Crazy Cricket!' *Illustrated Weekly of India* (*IWI*), 25 February 1973, 41.

10. Soumya Bhattacharya, *You Must Like Cricket? Memoirs of an Indian Cricket Fan* (London: Yellow Jersey Press, 2006), 24.

11. Jonathan Rice, ed., *Wisden on India: An Anthology* (New Delhi: Penguin, 2011), vii. He speculated that the future of this sport, in which 106 countries then participated, would be determined by events and decisions made in India. Gideon Haigh invoked the former US Secretary of State Dean Rusk's epigram about his country – 'the fat boy in the canoe' – to describe the global clout of Indian cricket: 'when it moves, everyone must adjust.' Gideon Haigh, 'Can the Centre Hold?' in *Spheres of Influence: Writings on Cricket and its Discontents* (London: Simon & Schuster, 2011 [2010]), 92.

12. The earliest reference to cricket in India comes from a war memoir by Clement Downing, naval officer and engineer with the East India Company. 'We lay here near a Fortnight …', writes Downing about an afternoon spent near the Bay of Cambay in 1721, "tho' all the Country round was inhabited by the Culeys, we everyday diverted ourselves with playing at Cricket and other Exercises, which they would come and be Spectators of.' Clement Downing, *A Compendious History of the Indian Wars* (London: T. Cooper, 1737), 229.

13. Tani Barlow defined colonial modernity as a 'speculative frame for investigating the infinitely pervasive discursive powers that increasingly connect at key points to the globalizing impulses of capitalism'. Tani E. Barlow, 'Introduction: On Colonial Modernity', in *Formations of Colonial Modernity in East Asia*, ed. Tani E. Barlow, 1–20 (Durham, NC: Duke University Press, 1997), 6. Some of the more important iterations of colonial modernity as a relativist ideological project with myriad trajectories and patterns rather than Eurocentric narratives of East–West synergy and progress include Antoinette Burton, ed., *Gender, Sexuality and Colonial Modernities* (London and New York: Routledge, 1999); Dilip Parmeshwar Gaonkar, ed., *Alternative Modernities* (Durham, NC: Duke University Press, 2001); Saurabh Dube and Ishita Banerjee-Dube, eds., *Unbecoming Modern: Colonialism, Modernity, Colonial Modernities* (New Delhi: Social Science Press, 2006); Michael Dodson and Brian Hatcher, eds., *Trans-Colonial Modernities in South Asia* (New York: Routledge, 2012).

14. Richard Cashman, *Patrons, Players and the Crowd: The Phenomenon of Indian Cricket* (New Delhi: Orient Longman, 1980); Ashis Nandy, *The Tao of Cricket: On Games of Destiny and the Destiny of Games* (New Delhi: Viking, 1989); Ramachandra Guha, *A Corner of a Foreign Field: The Indian History*

of a British Sport (London: Picador, 2002); Boria Majumdar, *Twenty-Two Yards to Freedom: A Social History of Indian Cricket* (New Delhi: Penguin, 2004); Prashant Kidambi, *Cricket Country: An Indian Odyssey in the Age of Empire* (Oxford: Oxford University Press, 2019).

15. C.A. Bayly, *Recovering Liberties: Indian Thought in the Age of Liberalism and Empire* (Cambridge: Cambridge University Press, 2012).

16. Stressed in the original chapter by David Washbrook in which he argues that with a few exceptions, historians have been lukewarm to the idea of examining the postcolonial period and have delegated the responsibility to social scientists and cultural theorists. The new directions in which postcolonial Indian society has moved along – rise of a middle class, Hindu nationalism, populism, technocracy, and so on – are arguably recent manifestations of long-term historical processes. Therefore, a 'history of the present' would enable historians to reappraise the historiography of the colonial period. David Washbrook, 'Towards a History of the Present: Southern Perspectives on the Nineteenth and Twentieth Centuries', in *From the Colonial to the Postcolonial: India and Pakistan in Transition*, ed. Dipesh Chakrabarty, Rochona Majumdar and Andrew Sartori, 332–57 (New Delhi: Oxford University Press, 2007).

17. Gyan Prakash, Michael Laffan and Nikhil Menon describe 'postcolonial' in the introduction to their edited volume as a 'condition produced by being worked over by colonialism – that is, as an aftermath, as an afterlife'. Gyan Prakash, Michael Laffan and Nikhil Menon, 'Introduction: The Postcolonial Moment', in *The Postcolonial Moment in South and Southeast Asia*, ed. Gyan Prakash, Michael Laffan, and Nikhil Menon, 1–10 (London: Bloomsbury, 2018), 1.

18. Kwame Anthony Appiah, 'Is the Post- in Postmodernism the Post- in Postcolonial?' *Critical Inquiry* 17, no. 2 (1991): 336–57.

19. Scott cited the example of the history of immigration and black people, saying they were visible to governments and social workers for the better part of the nineteenth and twentieth centuries before some scholars took notice of them as agents of history in the last quarter of the twentieth century in particular. Anne Firor Scott, 'On Seeing and Not Seeing: A Case of Historical Invisibility', *The Journal of American History* 71, no. 1 (1984): 7–21.

20. Swati Chattopadhyay, *Unlearning the City: Infrastructure in a New Optical Field* (Minneapolis and London: University of Minnesota Press, 2012), ch. 4.

21. Guha, *A Corner of a Foreign Field*; Majumdar, *Twenty-Two Yards to Freedom*.

22. Kidambi, *Cricket Country*, viii.

23. Dimeo also contends that elite patronage and financial promises contributed to the proliferation of cricket writings in twentieth-century India, enabling it to textually dominate other sports. Paul Dimeo, 'Cricket and the Misinterpretation of Indian Sports History', *Historical Studies* 24 (2005): 98–111.

24. Satadru Sen, 'History without a Past: Memory and Forgetting in Indian Cricket,' in *Cricket and National Identity in the Postcolonial Age: Following On*, ed. Stephen Wagg, 94–109 (London and New York: Routledge, 2005), 97–98.

25. Ranajit Guha, *History at the Limit of World-History* (New York: Columbia University Press, 2002), 74.

26. Alun Munslow, *The Routledge Companion to Historical Studies*, 2nd ed. (London and New York: Routledge, 2006), 64.

27. Cashman, *Patrons, Players and the Crowd*; Guha, *A Corner of a Foreign Field*; Majumdar, *Twenty-Two Yards to Freedom*.

28. An excellent example of such history would be Manas Ray's 'Growing Up Refugee'. Written in a first-person narrative, it takes the reader through the history of the development of refugee settlements in post-partition Calcutta with its networks of social bond, morality, violence, cosmopolitanism, governance and business, Ray, 'Growing Up Refugee', *History Workshop Journal* 53, no. 1 (2001): 149–79.

29. Robert Berkhofer, *Beyond the Great Story: History as Text and Discourse* (Cambridge, MA: Harvard University Press, 1995), ch. 9.

30. Guha, *A Corner of a Foreign Field*, 83–86, 355–59, 416–28.

31. The Bombay Pentangular started as the Presidency match in 1892 which was annually played between the Bombay Gymkhana and the Parsi Orient Club. The Hindu Gymkhana joined in 1907, the Muslims in 1912, and the Rest, comprising the Anglo-Indians and converted Indian Christians, came in 1937, effectively making the tournament a Pentangular. The teams were composed on communal lines, which led to frenzied protests against its very existence as inimical to national unity.

32. Majumdar, *Twenty-Two Yards to Freedom*, 226–61.

33. Sirivayan Anand, *Brahmans and Cricket: Lagaan's Millenial Purana and Other Myths* (Chennai: Navayana, 2003).

34. Nissim Mannathukkaren, 'Subalterns, Cricket and the "Nation": The Silences of "Lagaan", *Economic and Political Weekly* 36, no. 49 (2001):

4580–88; Chandrima Chakroborty, 'Subaltern Studies, Bollywood and Lagaan,' *Economic and Political Weekly* 38, no. 19 (2003): 1879–84; Grant Farred, 'The Double Temporality of Lagaan: Cultural Struggle and Postcolonialism', *Journal of Sport and Social Issues* 28, no. 2 (2004): 93–114; Nissim Mannathukkaren, 'Reading Cricket Fiction in the Times of Hindu Nationalism and Farmer Suicides: Fallacies of Textual Interpretation', *International Journal of the History of Sport* 24, no. 9 (2007): 1200–25.

35. Ian McDonald, 'Between Saleem and Shiva: The Politics of Cricket Nationalism in "Globalising India"', in *Sport in Divided Societies*, ed. John Sugden and Alan Bairner, 213–34 (Aachen: Meyer and Meyer Sport, 1999); Jishnu Dasgupta, 'Manufacturing Unison: Muslims, Hindus and Indians during the India–Pakistan Match', in *Sport in South Asian Society: Past and Present*, ed. Boria Majumdar and J.A. Mangan, 239–48 (London: Routledge, 2005).

36. J.A. Mangan, *The Games Ethic and Imperialism: Aspects of the Diffusion of an Ideal* (Harmondsworth: Viking, 1985), ch. 5.

37. Megan Ponsford, 'Frank and Bhupinder: The Odd Couple of Indian Cricket', *Sport in Society* 18, no. 5 (2015): 565–76.

38. Cashman, *Patrons, Players and the Crowd*.

39. Boria Majumdar, 'Soaps, Serials and the CPI(M), Cricket Beats Them All: Cricket and Television in Contemporary India', in *Television in India: Satellites, Politics and Cultural Change*, ed. Nalin Mehta, 124–39 (London and New York: Routledge, 2008); Nalin Mehta, 'Batting for the Flag: Cricket, Television and Globalization in India', *Sport in Society* 12, no. 4 (2009): 579–99; Nalin Mehta, 'The Great Indian Willow Trick: Cricket, Nationalism and India's TV News Revolution, 1998–2005', *International Journal of the History of Sport* 24, no. 9 (2007): 1187–99.

40. Abilash Nalapat and Andrew Parker, 'Sport, Celebrity and Popular Culture: Sachin Tendulkar, Cricket and Indian Nationalisms', *International Review for the Sociology of Sport* 40, no. 4 (2005): 433–46; Prashant Kidambi, 'Hero, Celebrity and Icon: Sachin Tendulkar and the Indian Public Culture', in *The Cambridge Companion to Cricket*, ed. Anthony Bateman and Jeffrey Hill, 187–202 (Cambridge: Cambridge University Press, 2011); Shamya Dasgupta, 'Sachin Almighty', *Sport in Society* 16, no. 1 (2013): 33–44.

41. Stephen Wagg and Sharda Ugra, 'Different Hats, Different Thinking? Technocracy, Globalization and the Indian Cricket Team', *Sport in Society* 12, nos. 4–5 (2009): 600–12; Souvik Naha, 'Cricket, Film, Glamour Industry

and Promotional Culture in India, 1913–2013', *Sport in History* 35, no. 3 (2015): 464–89.

42. Amit Gupta, 'The Globalization of Cricket: The Rise of the Non-West', *International Journal of the History of Sport* 21, no. 2 (2004): 257–76; Amit Gupta, 'India and the IPL: Cricket's Globalized Empire', *The Round Table* 98, no. 401 (2009): 201–11; Shakya Mitra, 'The IPL: India's Foray into World Sports Business', *Sport in Society* 13, no. 9 (2010): 1314–33; Amit Gupta, 'The IPL and the Indian Domination of Global Cricket', *Sport in Society* 14, no. 10 (2011): 1316–25; Shakya Mitra, 'The IPL Post-2010: An Uneasy Transition Phase?' *South Asian History and Culture* 3, no. 1 (2012): 116–25; Colin Agur, 'A Foreign Field No Longer: India, the IPL, and the Global Business of Cricket', *Journal of Asian and African Studies* 48, no. 5 (2013): 541–56.

43. Amitabho Dasgupta, 'Dalchhut Calcutta' (Unrivalled Calcutta), in *Bhalo Acho, Calcutta?* (How Are You, Calcutta?) (Calcutta: Dey's Publishing, 2000), 86. The poet, a slow left-arm bowler, played second division club cricket for two years at Baranagar club in the late 1950s, taking six wickets on debut. Dasgupta, 'Dombaganer Mathe' (In the Dombagan Fields), in *Bhalo Acho, Calcutta?* 141–44.

44. David McMahon, 'Jolly Roger', *Sportsworld* 8, no. 18 (25 February–3 March 1987), 16.

45. P. L. Mukherjee, 'Cricket in Calcutta: Its Growth and Development', in *Indian Cricket through the Ages: A Reader*, ed. Boria Majumdar, 275–81 (New Delhi: Oxford University Press, 2005), 275.

46. Personal interview with anonymous cricketer, 28 June 2013, Calcutta.

47. Mike Denness, *I Declare* (London: Arthur Barker, 1977), 109.

48. Pabitra Das, 'Cricket: Tela Mathae Tel' (Cricket: Ice to Eskimos), *Khelar Asar (KA)* 2, no. 38 (23 February 1979), 30–31.

49. Robert Hariman, 'Political Parody and Public Culture', *Quarterly Journal of Speech* 94, no. 3 (2008): 247–72, 257.

50. Important works on the history of football in India include Boria Majumdar and Kaushik Bandyopadhyay, *Goalless: The Story of a Unique Footballing Nation* (New Delhi: Penguin Viking, 2006); Kausik Bandyopadhyay, *Scoring Off the Field: Football Culture in Bengal 1911–80* (New Delhi: Routledge, 2011); Tony Mason, 'Football on the Maidan: Cultural Imperialism in Calcutta', *International Journal of the History of Sport* 7, no. 1 (1990): 85–96; Paul Dimeo, 'Football and Politics in Bengal: Colonialism, Nationalism, Communalism', *Soccer and Society* 2, no. 2 (2001): 57–74; Projit Bihari Mukharji, '"Feeble Bengalis" and "Big Africans": African Players in Bengali

Club Football', *Soccer and Society* 9, no. 2 (2008): 273–85; Souvik Naha, 'Of Magic and Mania: Reflections on the Fan Following of Brazilian Football and Pelé in Calcutta', *Soccer and Society* 15, no. 5 (2014): 803–19.

51. Amit Chaudhuri, 'Italians Abroad', in *Calcutta: Two Years in the City* (New York: Alfred A. Knopf, 2013), 218.

52. Tim Edensor, *National Identity, Popular Culture and Everyday Life* (Oxford and New York: Berg, 2002), 24.

53. Roger Chartier, *Cultural History: Between Practices and Representations*, trans. Lydia Cochrane (London: Polity, 1988), 44.

54. While flying back home from a trip to China, the music of Bismillah Khan gave Ramamchandra Guha a chance to ruminate the memories of watching Virender Sehwag bat. In his words, 'As my playlist went through "Nand Kedar", "Shyam Kalyan", "Yaman", "Durga" and the rest, I thought only of the maverick genius from Najafgarh, of his walk, his demeanour, the coloured cloth tied around his head, and, from time to time, of the range and subtlety of his strokeplay.' The convergence of Khan, a classical musician and recipient of India's highest civilian award, Bharat Ratna, and Sehwag, the mass hero with unconventional cricket skills, undermines the legitimacy of distinguishing between cultural forms. Ramachandra Guha, 'Memories of Virender', *espncricinfo.com*, 20 March 2013, http://www.espncricinfo.com/magazine/content/story/625814.html, accessed on 19 July 2016.

55. Jeffrey Hill, *Sport and the Literary Imagination: Essays in History, Literature, and Sport* (Oxford: Peter Lang, 2006), 27.

56. Andy Harvey, 'Team Work? Using Sporting Fiction as an Historical Archive and Source of Developing Theoretical Approaches to Sport History', *International Journal of the History of Sport* 30, no. 2 (2013): 136–37.

57. Carlo Ginzburg, *Threads and Traces: True False Fictive*, trans. Anne C. Tedeschi and John Tedeschi (Berkeley: University of California Press, 2012), 82.

58. Ibid., 81.

59. Louis O. Mink, 'The Autonomy of Historical Understanding', *History and Theory* 5, no. 1 (1966): 24–47.

60. Jeffrey Hill and Jean Williams, 'Introduction', *Sport in History* 29, no. 2 (2009): 129.

61. Anthony Bateman, *Cricket, Literature and Culture: Symbolising the Nation, Destabilising Empire* (Farnham: Ashgate, 2009), 12.

62. N. S. Ramaswami, *Winter of Content* (Madras: Swadesmitran Limited, 1967), 1.

63. Raymond Boyle and Richard Haynes, *Power Play: Sport, the Media and Popular Culture*, 2nd ed. (Edinburgh: Edinburgh University Press, 2009), 10–11.

64. Rod Brookes, *Representing Sport* (London: Arnold, 2002), 40.

65. Michael A. Messner, *Power at Play: Sports and the Problem of Masculinity* (Boston: Beacon Press, 1995); John Nauright and Timothy J. L. Chandler, *Making Men: Rugby and Masculine Identity* (London: Frank Cass, 1996).

66. Boyle and Haynes, *Power Play*, 29.

67. John Horne, *Sport in Consumer Culture* (Basingstoke: Palgrave Macmillan, 2006).

68. Boyle and Haynes, *Power Play*, 202.

69. Alan Tomlinson and Christopher Young, 'Sport in Modern European History: Trajectories, Constellations, Conjunctures', *Journal of Historical Sociology* 24, no. 4 (2011): 409–27, 414.

70. Jürgen Habermas, *The Structural Transformation of the Public Sphere: An Inquiry into a Category of Bourgeois Society*, trans. Thomas Burger (Cambridge, MA: The MIT Press, 1989).

71. John McGuigan, 'The Cultural Public Sphere', in *Festivals and the Cultural Public Sphere*, ed. Liana Giorgi, Monica Sassatelli and Gerard Delanty, 79–91 (London and New York: Routledge, 2011), 82–83.

72. Benedict Anderson, *Imagined Communities: Reflections on the Origins and Spread of Nationalism* (London: Verso, 1991).

73. Michael Warner, *Publics and Counterpublics* (New York: Zone Books, 2002), ch. 2.

74. John B. Thompson, *The Media and the Modernity: A Social Theory of the Media* (Cambridge: Polity Press, 1995).

75. Guy Debord, *The Society of the Spectacle*, trans. Donald Nicholson-Smith (New York: Zone Books, 1994).

76. Arjun Appadurai, 'Disjuncture and Difference in the Global Cultural Economy', *Public Culture* 2, no. 2 (1990): 1–23.

77. Cornel Sandvoss, 'Public Sphere and Publicness: Sport Audiences and Political Discourse', in *Media and Public Spheres*, ed. Richard Butsch, 58–70 (Basingstoke: Palgrave Macmillan, 2007).

78. Akbar S. Ahmed, *Postmodernism and Islam: Predicament and Promise* (London: Routledge, 2004), 122.

1 Cricket, Syndicated Englishness and Postcolonialism

What was wrong with cricket? On a Sunday morning sometime in 1960, this was discussed among a group of friends in a house on Khurut Road in Howrah, a town across the river Ganges from Calcutta. Three professors, two authors, two clerks, one schoolteacher, one lawyer, one businessman, one government officer and one engineer, aged from 20 to 45, vociferously debated if cricket was really worth its popularity. In the opinion of Sankar, a popular author in Bengali, cricket was an 'illegitimate, immoral, ill-conceived, illogical' English pursuit. The sight of 2 batsmen dominating 11 fielders reflected an obscene bureaucracy, and 11 fielders closing in on 2 batsmen resembled a slaughter. Cricket was a dreadful remnant of the British rule in India.[1] Sibnarayan Ray, a Marxist philosopher who taught at Calcutta University and was friends with Bertrand Russell, said that no progressive country in the world played cricket. He cited the examples of several countries that were not interested in cricket – Germany, the land of the greatest scientists and philosophers; France, the leader of pursuits of intellect and luxury; Russia, the rebellious redeemer of humanity; America, the champion of fast and consumerist living; and China, full of diligent, 'yellow-skinned' people.[2] The critics declared that cricket was merely a passive recreation for people of wealth and leisure, and cricket's cultural Englishness was deeply problematic for the postcolonial nation.[3] At this point, Sankariprasad Basu, a professor of Bengali at Calcutta University, launched a long polemic in cricket's favour. Basu made an a priori assumption that while the lack of faults was an admirable quality for a country, the absence of a certain excellence was not a merit or something to be praised. England was no less civilised or developed than the nations Ray had mentioned. Among the virtues to have contributed to England's rise to power were parliamentary democracy, drama and cricket.[4] It was shameful, Basu concluded, that other so-called developed countries did not play cricket.[5]

Sports followers can sometimes dislike aspects of the game, such as commercialism, but the sports press often marginalises such contradictions in the mythic quest for building an overwhelmingly popular image for the sport.[6] Historians of sport have also often overlooked critical responses to sport, and failed to offer a balanced perspective of sport's reception in society.[7] The historians of cricket in India have shown a similar inclination to ignoring anti-cricket sentiment in the country with the exception of narratives of the Congress-led anti-Pentangular movement in Bombay.[8] Ramachandra Guha's sketch of the Congress politician B. V. Keskar, a Sorbonne-educated nationalist who published an article entitled 'Will Cricket "Quit India" with the British?' in the *Blitz* magazine on 13 July 1946, shows cricket's path to popularity was fraught with ideological battles.[9] Keskar's was just an isolated case in the long-standing dispute that saw cricket lose its romantic innocence and become a bridgehead for different political approaches regarding making India a postcolonial nation-state. Just as several politicians wanted to abolish cricket, the sport did not have the people's unsparing support. Among cricket's ardent followers, some leading journalists presented cricket as everyone's favourite sport to the best of their abilities, burying the challenges to the sport's ideologies and dismissing anti-cricket sentiments as frivolous.

This chapter examines how cricket's print representations drew upon the sport's origin stories in England and yet conjured up an image consistent with India's decolonisation. Cricket had always been synonymised with the British Empire and Englishness. The sport's popularity in England seriously dwindled in the second half of the twentieth century, causing immense distress to its followers. In 1968, an infuriated D. M. Brittain from Aberdeen wrote to the editor of *The Times*, 'Now I know that this country is finished. On Saturday, with Australia playing, I asked a London cabby to take me to Lord's, and had to show him the way.'[10] His tone conveyed the sense that unfamiliarity with the country's premier cricket ground was a crime, and England's position in the world depended on how seriously its residents took cricket. In 1972, a reader named Shibdas Bandopadhyay wrote to the editor of the left-leaning newspaper *Dainik Basumati*, 'Cricket is not simply a game for the English; it is a symbol of principle and discipline, the life-force of the English character. Cricket runs in the blood of English cricketers.'[11] This testifies to the deep love of some Indians for cricket's moral values and connection with Englishness. The publication of such a letter in decidedly anti-West and anti-capitalism newspaper exemplified cricket's strange acclaim as a sport that brought together bourgeois and proletarian socialism.

Cricket followers like Bandopadhyay were bound by a culture of forgiveness, in which they were willing to forget Britain's imperial atrocities by fixating on the gift of cricket.[12]

I intend to call this selective admiration of English culture 'syndicated Englishness', inspired by David Hardiman's use of the term 'syndicated Ayurveda' and Romila Thapar's definition of 'syndicated Hinduism'. In Hardiman's words, syndicates of people seek, through 'combination, organisation, and publicity, to establish a particular, limited notion of their practice that set it apart from other forms of practice'.[13] This chapter argues that certain Indian authors created some derivative conventions by fusing Victorian paradigms of cricket and emergent forms of postcolonial nationalism. These conventions helped to set cricket apart from other despised vestiges of the British Empire. What does such respect for England's national game in a former colony with a long history of anti-colonial struggle suggest? To what extent was cricket's image as the 'life-force of England's character' a syndicated construct? How did followers defend cricket against criticisms of its foreignness and superfluity in the Indian context? This chapter, by looking into the debate over cricket's legitimacy in late colonial and postcolonial India, explores the dynamics of a form of culture's assimilation against imperial iconoclasm. It also adds cricket as a forgotten factor in India's transition from a colonial to a postcolonial state.[14]

CRICKET'S ENGLISHNESS AND ITS DISCONTENTS

Cricket had a special place in English educational institutions and politics from the mid-nineteenth century to the beginning of World War II, when it was mythologised as the ultimate lesson in 'ethics, morals, justice, religion and life itself'.[15] Invested with ideals of spirit and fair play, and promoted as an ideological template to strengthen one's moral and physical character, cricket was supposed to turn a player into an exemplary citizen and subject.[16] Cricket acquired a distinctive English imprint in the mid-to-late-nineteenth century, as the ethos of amateurism, fair play and rusticity were intricately woven into its history. A group of administrators and authors, eager to articulate their vision of a perfect society through cricket, developed desirable characteristics of the game and its players as well as several attractive origin myths that accompanied the spread of cricket. Many of these patrons resisted cricket's mutation with the changing times, trying to project the sport not as new and vague but as a time-honoured and binding social contract. The rich literature on English cricket, whose creators included several Nobel and Poet Laureates, synonymised cricket with what the idea of 'England' symbolised, almost without exception.[17]

The discourse of cricket as a morality tale and pastoral nostalgia was at its peak during the troubled interwar years.[18] The number of amateur and professional cricketers increased like never before during this period, often under the aegis of clubs and other leisure associations.[19] A cartoon published in *The Star* newspaper days before Christmas in 1920, titled 'The Relative Importance of Things', showed that cricket was discussed, even in the off-season, more than Christmas, the weather, the latest divorce, politics and other people's trouble.[20] The global economic and political trends in the interwar years and particularly after World War II, along with the surge of football fandom, increasingly trapped the dwindling constituency of 'English' cricket followers in a dungeon of history. In a world that kept pushing Test cricket to the brink of irrelevance, the game's followers needed to be shielded from the lure of other forms of leisure. The responsibility was taken up by writers who mediated the space between the sport and its followers. They constantly reminded cricket's audience of the sport's nineteenth-century tradition as 'England's lifeblood'[21] and not 'old imperial propaganda' as some commentators were to claim later.[22] Journalist Neville Cardus wanted his readers to believe that ideas, politics and strife were alien to cricket; the game was a world in itself.[23] He made a sweeping claim:

> If everything else in this nation of ours was lost but cricket – her constitution and the laws of England of Lord Halsbury – it would be possible to reconstruct from the theory and practice of cricket all the eternal Englishness which has gone to the establishment of that Constitution and the laws aforesaid.[24]

Test Match Special commentators on BBC Radio undertook a similar mission. As writer Mike Marqusee found out in the 1970s, they strove to convince listeners, without success in his own case, that cricket did not belong to the world of the welfare state, feminism, trade unions, sex, drugs and rock and roll. They reiterated the part cricket played in the lost, imperial 'world of deference and hierarchy, ruled by benevolent white men'.[25] Most British journalists at this time acknowledged the existence of un-English forms of playing and spectating, but strongly denied that these made or would ever make the game more attractive. The suggestion that cricket epitomised England's *belle époque* was largely incompatible with the occurrences in the 1970s, yet self-appointed custodians of the game's tradition continued to refer to its Englishness at every opportunity. Cricket, quipped Stephen Haseler, is the 'most exalted icon' in 'theme park heritage Englishness'.[26]

Englishness, according to Simon Gikandi, is a 'cultural and literary phenomenon produced in the ambivalent space that separated, but also conjoined, metropole and colony'.[27] The concept was undoubtedly created as a boundary separating the people of England from Britain and the rest of the world. As historian Linda Colley argues, the idea of a British identity was created on the back of the Act of Union of 1707 that combined England, Scotland, Wales and Ireland into a single geopolitical entity.[28] The British nation was thus a nation invented by politicians, appended by the monarchy, endorsed by participatory communities and ruptured along local identity and social class in the imperial project. A tendency to conflate Englishness with Britishness due to England's position of power in Britain was always present. The fractures of national identity were manifested time and again by the Irish and Scottish declarations of distinctiveness including their rejection of cricket.[29] Hence, on the one hand, Englishness was at the heart of the empire, by giving the colonisers from England a homogenous identity; on the other hand, the diversity within the empire and movement of people and ideas threatened to corrupt this imaginary ethno-linguistic similitude.[30] A national culture or collective consciousness can look homogenous, but it imperatively contains transcultural traces as it does not germinate in isolation. As philosopher Slavoj Žižek contends, an 'empirical Englishman' invariably assimilates something non-English to his deportment.[31] At the same time, Englishness was identified as an instantiation of the people of England and a bulwark against change in English society. Sociologist Dominic Malcolm suggests a literary class promoted the idea that the game and its players showed character traits that echoed the English national character. Practices fundamental to ideological Englishness, such as calling the break 'tea', the importance given to weather and environment, fascination with statistics, adhering to conventions, demarcating women and people from the Celtic fringe as the other, were perfectly enmeshed within cricket, making the sport, like English national character, an organic feature of the English people.[32]

Commenting on the non-negotiable nature of cricket's ideology of Englishness, anthropologist Arjun Appadurai remarked that cricket was a 'hard cultural form' that transformed its participants more than it changed itself.[33] As an inflexible belief system, cricket resisted questions, and any change in cricket's appearance would result in a sport that would not be 'cricket'. This was *one* and the most powerful discourse of cricket, which is replete with stories of actors clinging unwaveringly to their perception of cricket. Some of the early members of the Captain Scott Invitation XI, a village team put together by Harry Thompson, thought amateur cricket was non-serious and competitiveness against the spirit of cricket.[34] More often than not they deliberately underperformed and undermined the whole team's performance. Thompson himself understood amateurism to be a principle of playing hard and fair and enjoying doing so. His insistence on a good fight annoyed many of his teammates, who left, paving the way for more competitive players to join and ultimately make the club a respectable cricket team. Thus, contrary to the characterisation of cricket's form as innate and fixed, cricket did not cease to be cricket if its meanings were creatively interpreted. In his discussion of appropriation in his study of cricket's indigenisation in postcolonial India, Appadurai says that despite being a 'hard cultural form', cricket resonated well with Indian cultural values and emergent Indian nationhood, and cricket's moral and aesthetic world in the 1990s was nowhere close to its Victorian discourses.[35] Missing from his and other accounts of cricket's indigenisation is a discussion of syndicated Englishness – how the metaphors of Englishness were used to a greater extent than resisted, to make cricket popular in a postcolonial society.

CRICKET'S SYNDICATED ENGLISHNESS

In Mulk Raj Anand's novel *Two Leaves and a Bud*, Reggie Hunt, a British officer in a tea plantation in Assam, thinks 'cricket was a silly girl's game only fit for Nancy boys'.[36] Aggressive, violent and obsessed with male superiority, Hunt is a disruptive influence on the plantation culture and is later tried for sexual assault of Indian women. Hunt's character faults can very well be symbolically linked with his disdain for cricket and his inability to imbibe the finer life lessons the game offered. As alluded to in the novel, in some ways, cricket symbolised the British Empire's hegemonic experiment with the 'civilising mission'.[37] It was taken to the colonies and dominions, nested within the everyday activities of displaced, white Europeans. This international passage was not a triumphant march. Many Americans were earnest about cricket but most others rejected it, in some instances to articulate their dislike for English culture.[38] Non-English people did not uncritically accept the social relations spawned by cricket in England, but those who embraced cricket did so rather enthusiastically. As an anonymous reviewer of J. M. Framjee Patel's book *Stray Thoughts on Indian Cricket* wrote in 1905, 'in this country of sport indifferentism such a distinctly Anglo-Saxon pastime as cricket has secured the amazingly strong position that it holds today'.[39] Sir Robert Baden-Powell, founder of the Scout movement, remarked that cricket had taken deep roots in India, and Parsi cricketers were well known in England.[40] In the Indian press, 'English cricket' continued to be seen as a high-water mark of human civilisation throughout the twentieth century, so successfully was its positive image disseminated throughout the cricket world.[41]

Cricket's consecration as one of the most popular team sports in twentieth-century India, most historians agree, resulted from a successful domestication of a British imperial tradition. Richard Cashman draws attention to two interpretations of cricket's colonial spread: one, cricket was without doubt part of the British imperial agenda of indoctrinating colonial subjects; two, indigenous elements had a bigger role than colonial proselytisers in accepting and appropriating cricket. He asks a very pertinent question: 'Where does the promoting hand of the colonial master stop and where does the adapting and assimilating indigenous tradition start? ... was it that many colonial subjects chose to pursue a game, because of the ideology, or even in spite of it, because it suited them to take up cricket for their own reasons?' to which he offers no clear answer.[42] J. A. Mangan's studies of inculcation of the values of Western sport through colonial school curriculum, or 'moral training', suggest several discrepancies in the process of acculturation. These were most evident in the appreciation of Western sport in missionary schools and colleges in various countries. While Indians studying in these institutions were known to be sports lovers, African students preferred education to sport.[43] Mangan's conclusions, based upon ideology as an analytical tool and a broad-brush survey of a small number of institutions that were barely representative of the region, obfuscated and over-generalised colonial education.

Some of cricket's ideological verbiage, such as honesty and civility, struck a chord with many Indians. A deeper look at the domestication of the game's codes reveals some tensions between nationalist appropriation and colonial resentment. The Indian habit of playing football barefoot made Europeans wonder, but four Mohun Bagan players turning out in *dhotis* (a long cotton cloth wrapped around the legs and knotted at the waist) in a match in 1931 annoyed their opponent, the Calcutta Cricket Club.[44] The problem started when Calcutta Cricket Club's captain, R. B. Lagden, asked one of the fielders why he was wearing a *dhoti*. The person said it was more comfortable than trousers, after which Lagden allegedly threatened he would ensure Mohun Bagan would never play at the Eden Gardens. Afterwards, Mohun Bagan refused to have lunch and come out to bat in their turn. Lagden's comment came under a barrage of criticism from local sport clubs. He wrote a letter to *The Statesman* in denial and added that his intention was to evoke cricket's etiquette and approved costume. The *Times of India* correspondent felt that the letter did little to assuage Indians who viewed this incident as a racial affront.[45] Lagden's intervention transformed the dress of necessity into a political sign. British colonisers were not known to have enforced their clothing style on Indians; rather, Indians aspiring to emulate the British chose to dress like them in public. The nationalist movement's anti-foreign cloth propaganda caused a sartorial dilemma regarding the propriety of one's clothes and ensured the Europeanisation of Indian dress took place very slowly.[46] Cricket in Indian clothing probably gave Lagden a chilling premonition about the shrinking of English influence in the country. The decolonisation of cricket was underway.

Ashok Mitra, finance minister of West Bengal from 1977 to 1987, recalled in his autobiography the excitement in his politically conscious family, which had boycotted British clothes and entertainment, when a Marylebone Cricket Club (MCC) side led by Douglas Jardine played a Test match in Calcutta in 1933–34. Freedom fighter Binoy Bose, renowned for his daring attack on the Secretariat Building in Calcutta in 1930, was a good cricketer. Two of his younger brothers played cricket for Bihar in the 1940s–60s; one of them captained the team for a long time.[47] Cricket never lacked followers who were in awe of what the game represented to the English. Kiranlal Roy, High Court judge and cousin of international cricketer Pankaj Roy, was one to take the lesson of moral masculinity seriously enough. He played for East Bengal in Calcutta and then Edgware Club while he studied law in London. As a cricketer he would not dispute the umpire's call even when the latter got it wrong. A story goes that in a match against Mohun Bagan in 1938, he was at the crease with his team Town Club nine wickets down and staring at defeat. Birendra Kishore Ray Choudhury, Dhrupad style classical musician, not one to accept defeat, prematurely signalled end of play by ringing bells. When Roy found out about this trick, he led the teams back to the field so that the opposition got the victory they deserved. He later said that cricketers from colonial times respected senior cricketers like elder brothers and the captain as a leader. Cricket was both a blissful sport and a lesson in etiquette. He stopped watching Test cricket in the 1960s, the reason for which, as one of his relatives said, 'was not difficult to understand' – cricket was no longer cricket.[48]

While this story shows the positive influence of cricket's Englishness on character-building, novelist Salman Rushdie's sketch of Saladin Chamcha, one of the two protagonists in *The Satanic Verses*, exposed a bizarre appropriation of cricket. Saladin, in favour of preserving the sanctity of English culture, detested any attempt of emulation by Indians, afraid of people in the lower rung upsetting the hierarchy of civilisations. Contemptuous of India, in a fundamental fit of alienation, owing probably to his resolve to exorcise his minority status, he renounced his Indianness. His effort to eschew his Indian identity and graft himself onto a foreign culture had begun in his childhood. In his early teens in the 1950s, he cheered for English cricketers during Test matches at the Brabourne Stadium in Bombay. He wanted England to defeat 'the local upstarts, for the proper order of things to be maintained'.[49] Rushdie's characterisation of Anglophiles who lived with a fractured identity in a bid to establish cultural fidelity to the colonisers was grounded in colonial identity politics. Another assemblage of people selectively admired some aspects of English culture. In contrast, self-deracinating Indians such as Saladin were supposed to embody the worst of both cultures. Even after India's independence, England never ceased to be a part of India's everyday life, despite much opposition. As this chapter will show, the history of the relationship of Indians with cricket is essentially a history of this ambivalence.

Various groups of Indians were opposed to playing cricket. A week after India's independence, Marathi newspapers from Poona were full of articles and letters on the pros and cons of continuing to play cricket. One group argued that cricket should follow the departing British back to its country of origin. Another camp, led by Captain S. V. Damle from the Maharashtriya Physical Culture Institute, said cricket could stay but educational institutions must stop allocating maximum funds to cricket and should distribute their resources equally among sports. They provoked the students' organisations in some colleges to launch campaigns against cricket. They approached the authorities of a number of schools demanding a reduction of their cricket budget. Former cricketer D. B. Deodhar, who considered cricket to be an important connection to the Commonwealth, chastised this 'wanton vandalism'. He admitted that cricket was more expensive to organise than other sports, but if India were to continue playing international cricket, grassroots level cricket needed to be nurtured carefully as cricketers were reared through schools, colleges and Gymkhanas. He wrote, 'There is no other game as spectacular, as dignified, as glamourous as cricket, where even the best player can be turned into a nonentity by one single piece of bowling or fielding.'[50]

It is interesting to note that critics of cricket rarely complained against football and hockey, two other mass sports introduced to India by the English.[51] In their cynical judgement, cricket in independent India amounted to a perverted form of Anglophilia whereas football, hockey, tennis and badminton were not so abhorrent. As journalist N. S. Ramaswami pointed out, 'the austere and the killjoys' thought that cricket was an anathema because of its distinctive foreignness. The sport served the interests of the British Empire and would destroy India unless summarily abolished.[52] The former coloniser's signature sport was suspected to have the potential to push decolonised citizens towards the colonial culture Indians had worked so hard to dispel. The assimilation of Indians in the now officially defunct colonial project could alienate them from the task of building a postcolonial nation. This could undermine the very logic of the nationalist drive towards self-determination. Englishness and Anglophilia were not clearly defined at any moment by the proponents of anti-cricket sentiments. Cricket continued to flourish despite opposition and within decades of independence it became the most popular sport even in Calcutta, the capital of football. This chapter argues that deliberations over cricket's Englishness in the press and literature played a significant role in the rise of cricket.

THE EMPIRE WITHOUT COLONY AND THE AGENTS OF TRANSFER

Cricket lovers needed a strong justification for their fascination with cricket for the sport to survive. In Bengal, where football had a stronger presence than cricket, they found the instrument in cricket's Englishness – the same reason why a multitude of people were against the sport. The vernacular reproduction of their interpretation of this ideology enabled the formation of a large indigenous subculture with an English imprint. In many ways cricket writing in Bengali was a belated project. It started in earnest in the 1960s, more than half a century after a similar process had begun in England. The delay arguably afforded authors a useful critical distance. Theirs was a big leap forward from English writings in terms of subject and style of writing, if not in volume. It was the first time that Indian cricket writing moved beyond coaching guides, match reports and praise for fair play and gentlemanly behaviour to engage with complex cultural issues. The authors studied the value system etched into Anglo-Australian cricket writings and adapted those concepts to the local context. They acted as intermediaries who, according to historian Matthias Middell, 'select, translate, transport, and integrate seemingly foreign cultural elements'.[53] Episodes from nineteenth-century interwar and post-war cricket occupied the same imaginary time in this emerging literature. The invocation of cricket's past as a golden age was drawn from similar examples from English authors. As Anthony Bateman argues, the past was a popular trope when cricket began to be framed as a 'product of modernity' in late-nineteenth-century England.[54] The history of cricket in a postcolonial state was thus marked by both denunciation and admiration for colonial English culture. This sometimes led to anomalies such as the following mentioned by journalist Mukul Datta:

> We asked our children to stop playing and study. We claimed to be good sportsmen in job applications since the English loved sports. We never took sports seriously enough to inculcate true sportsmanship in us. That is why few sportspersons actually possess sporting spirit. Yet some people have learned the spirit and have prospered in their occupations by its successful application.[55]

Two novels by Shirshendu Mukhopadhyay comment on the contradiction between associating cricket-playing with people without work or studies and the mediatised elevation of cricket as the great Indian dream. In *Gosain Baganer Bhut* (Ghost of the Gosain Garden), the protagonist is in such a state of mind after failing his mathematics examination that he does not notice boys playing cricket in a winter afternoon.[56] Thereafter, having regained his confidence with help from a friendly ghost, he appears in a cricket match between teams of students who have either cleared or failed the previous annual examination. The better students are not too adept in cricket and are routed by the bunch of academic failures.[57] In the novel *Golmal* (Trouble) by the same author, the unsuccessful poet Haribabu does not approve of his sons playing cricket. Sport has no place in his scheme of aesthetics. He considers football to be an act of barbarity, exemplified by the legitimacy of violent physical contact in the sport. He despises the person who may have described cricket as poetry couched by willow, believing that cricket is the local game of *danguli* in disguise, glorified so much to satisfy the English ego.[58] Towards the end of the novel, he turns out to be a doting father by giving his sons a cricket ball, which is actually an advanced device that negates nearby sources of energy.[59] The contrasting opinion on cricket as an emblem of modern civilization and also a sheer waste of time was downplayed if not glossed over by sports journalists. These opinions appeared more frequently through literature and letters to editors.

In independent India, cricket's ideologies had two distinctive overtones: inherited (Englishness) and practised (which I consider syndicated rather than decolonised Englishness). The syndication enabled people, to draw upon Homi Bhabha's notion of the role of theory and writing, to 'interrupt the dominant and dominating strategies of generalization within a cultural or communicative or interpretational community'.[60] The nature of the anxiety of appropriating cricket changed with the political decolonisation of India. But the colonial denotations of cricket were ingrained too deeply in public life to be delinked in a short time. Cricket, therefore, created intermediate identities in the 1950s, and as this chapter will show, these identities were embedded in writings and formed the foundation of cricket's postcolonialism in India. Although several political parties demanded outright rejection of colonial traditions, cricket had become so commonplace and componential in society that it could not be separated from the growing sense of Indianness and yet retained its Englishness through literary tropes. The practice of cricket as a sport was hybridised as its extrinsic codes remained intact. The translation of cricket at various levels of appropriation, however, transformed the domain of its ideological codes.

One of the two aspects of this transformation was the vernacularisation project, that is, the translation of coaching instructions and the names of foreign players in indigenous scripts and syntax. According to Appadurai, this allowed a large number of Indians to participate in cricket in ways not so alien anymore, emancipating cricket from its English bonds.[61] Second, Englishness was recast within this vernacular public sphere as a dominant form of understanding cricket, contrary to what some of the proponents of indigenising cricket could have anticipated. Hence, the identity politics around cricket was always in flux, underlining the creation during transcultural encounters of what Parama Roy calls 'philosophical or epistemic secondariness'.[62] The phrase indicates the paradoxical situation in which a standardised code transferred from a different culture, such as nationalism, inhabits a threshold zone between the original and the derived. The love for cricket manifested a form of culturalism in which Raymond Williams's characterisations of culture as a 'way of life' and 'art' coexisted. For Williams, the common meanings of culture known to everyone were part of a 'way of life', whereas 'art' referred to the new meanings ascribed to existing forms through creative effort.[63] When brought together, the romanticism around cricket's English traditions and cricket's reshaping as a counter-cultural postcolonial modernity generated a syndicated Englishness that can be called an alternative postcolonial modernity. Mapping the translation and transmission of cricket's ideological codes in Bengali cricket writings illustrates this transcultural arbitration.

The amateurish and bucolic ideal of cricket sat well in the imagination of a number of Indians, while many others could not find any romance in such characterisations. Rusticity was an essential part of cricket's Englishness.[64] Among the things William Wordsworth considered English were 'the boys that in yon meadow ground/in white-sleev'd shirts …'[65] The game's literature perpetually evoked nostalgia among city-dwellers for a village green untarnished by modern civilisation.[66] Cardus considered cricket a mirror of English nature;[67] so did Edmund Blunden and E. V. Lucas, for whom cricket was 'the backyard, the garden, the playground, the school field, the club and college ground, and, above all, the village green'.[68] Stories from village cricket, mostly fictitious, involved a set of colourful characters who defied conventions and produced unforgettable, rollicking incidents. In a story about Rabindranath Tagore, winner of the Nobel Prize in literature in 1913, playing cricket, the authors chose the village of Gomoh as the site of action.[69] It was a direct tribute to the country meadows in pre-industrial England. Since Gomoh was the junction of three railway zones, there was a hint of the advent of modernity in the hinterland. Additionally, Gomoh was the place from which the great Bengali freedom fighter Subhas Chandra Bose took the train to Delhi on the way to his great escape from house arrest.

A fictional Bengali village cricketer, P. Chowdhury, whose first name is not given by his chronicler Sankariprasad Basu, was a purebred Indian follower of the English game. He had probably clashed with the colonial police as a freedom fighter and held strong nationalist opinions even after leaving politics.[70] He did not belong to the anglicised, transplanted and cosmopolitan classes of Indians that had absorbed European sport more eagerly. When asked why cricket was the only English thing he liked, he seldom had a concrete answer to offer. He spoke in a state of reverie about having 'dream-like visions' every time he had watched cricket since his childhood. He had seen himself 'standing on the cerulean ground of the sky, watching radiant figures play cricket'.[71] Evidently, for him, cricket was played on an existential plane in which he was not his Indian self, but a creedless person detached from reality. Chowdhury started an annual fixture around which was woven a very local folk culture.

The matches Chowdhury organised inscribed a vanishing folk culture onto an imaginary geography of modern West Bengal. This culture engaged in a foreign game and yet was authentically Bengali. In this transcultural world of selective mutation, the old man Sanyal takes the field with his *hookah* (tobacco pipe) in one hand and a bat in the other. The umpire holds his *hookah* while he takes stance. The decrepit Ghosh is helped to the crease by his grandson while spectators taunt him to ask his old wife for assistance. People play in local apparels like *vidyasagari choti* and *namaboli*; Chakraborty goes to bowl wearing a combination of *fatua* and full pants. Batsmen take wrong stances, which English cricket critics would have called oriental informality.[72] Although these incidents matched episodes from English village cricket in oddity, the purpose of these stories was to portray cricket as democratic and rankless. Journalist Shibdas Bandopadhyay replicated Basu's intention in a newspaper article, which commented on how the pull of the 'verdant field of gold, bathed in the shining winter sun' made people forget agonies. Cricket did not distinguish between the rich and the poor, and the ruler and the subject.[73] Cricketers recalled that the outfield at the Eden Gardens in the 1950s–60s was 'emerald green' and looked as serene as any English ground.[74] The public were shown to share an organic relationship with cricket.

In a piece about the cricket played at Natore Park in Calcutta, the first things the journalist Romesh Ganguli remembered were the 'delicious foliage', 'leafy trees', 'the pond by the side of the drive displaying the shadows of trees', 'the loving sunbeam', an ambience which taught him the 'poetry and philosophies of life'.[75] Nature was not just as important as cricket; it was inseparable from the sport. In a serialised column about famous cricketers in the periodical *Saptahik Basumati*, Santipriyo Bandopadhyay began his account of Lala Amarnath's performance in the inaugural Test match at the Eden Gardens (1933–34) with a description of not the teams but the bewitching landscape of trees, grass, dew and river.[76] The 'sylvan surroundings' charmed the cricketer Mushtaq Ali on his first visit.[77] The 'atmosphere' was lost by the early 1960s as the 'majestic' trees disappeared to make space for building concrete stands.[78] Many cricket enthusiasts were disgusted by the sacrifice of aesthetics. The incursion of football into the ground in 1967 made the journalist and radio commentator Ajay Basu wonder how the value of heritage.had fallen so low. How could one exchange the melody of cricket for the cacophony of football?[79] The rapport between place and people continued mainly on a ruminative mode in the 1970s, such as in the detailed panegyric Basu wrote in 1976:

> The people of Calcutta are quite sensitive about Eden. Nowhere else would one find a playground so charmingly adorned by a carpet of green grass. Once upon a time people went there just to inhale fresh air. The soaring pines encircling the ground swayed with the wind, and shades cast by the late afternoon sun produced a stunning, unforgettable light and shadow play ... Nature reigned supreme in the ground, beyond the boundary ropes, before repulsive brick and cement structure was raised ... The pavilion was a marvellous ode to British architecture. It dovetailed harmoniously with the calm surroundings. It still exists, hidden behind the tall, unspectacular galleries. There was a straw structure that the British called 'the hut', open on all sides with only a roof cover. Cricketers and other important persons used to watch play from under the 'hut'. Cricket is an English game. The English played in the suburbs, villages and sometimes in towns, with the intention to spend a few hours close to the nature. This is why they chose the 'village green' as the theatre of cricket. They built the straw hut here in Calcutta just to replicate the idyllic ambience of playing cricket ... Those were the days of bullock carts, peace of mind, abundant leisure and opportunities of amusement. We spent many a winter afternoon basking in the mild sun, sitting on the green carpet rolled out at Eden.[80]

The authors established the personal as the communal by remembering, resituating, reconstituting and re-instantiating an experience in the public press.[81] Such coupling of people, an environment tamed by cricket, and nostalgia for a lost and better past was homologous with the descriptions by English authors. Cricket was a lens for wistfully looking at a glorious and perfect past. In 1925, Justice Sidney Rowlatt, the person behind the infamous Rowlatt Act (1919) that enabled the British colonial police to make arrests on the basis of suspicion alone and detain people without trial for up to two years, was known to have remarked during an income tax case in the King's Bench Division, London: 'In the days when cricket was cricket, players did not trouble about averages. They went in to win for their side and then said, "Now that is done; let us get on with the next game.""[82] The fall from grace of cricketers and growing competitiveness were uniquely linked with the deterioration in social behaviour in cricket writings. In particular, cricket was seen as a barometer of morality and masculinity, which formed an important part of syndicated Englishness.

According to Keith Sandiford, the social and cultural leaders of the Victorian age found in cricket the answer to every psycho-social problem, including illness and illiteracy. The conviction that cricket was essential for health and character-building was expressed skilfully by the headmaster Dr George Ridding, who said, 'Give me a boy who is a cricketer and I can make something of him.'[83] The notion of the chivalrous cricketer was important for proponents of Muscular Christianity, aimed at reforming the middle class. Cricket was afforded a social and nation-building mission, with the image of the vigorous body signifying a healthy body politic and social harmony. The mission statement came from the novel *Tom Brown's Schooldays*, in which the teacher emphasised the discipline and interdependence among the team that merges the individual in the collective, so that one does not 'play so that he might win, but that his side may'.[84] Indians tailored the idea of moral masculinity to their liking, some of them expunging the ritual of drinking from the lives they envisaged for cricketers. Kartik Sinha, office superintendent at the Cricket Association of Bengal (CAB), recalled in an interview 25 years after the India–New Zealand Test series of 1954–55 that only the captain Bert Sutcliffe among the touring party drank alcohol, which he thought was not gentlemanly and praised the rest of his team for abstinence.[85] A change of generation had not interrupted Sinha's thought pattern. Cultural stability, though not symptomatic of postcolonial Bengali society, was emphasised by cricket writers as the quality need for a community's advancement.

In addition to being a symbol of class cohesion, cricket theoretically performed a humanising function as an antidote to many social evils. At the same time, Bengali authors added the contrasting possibility of the sport provoking crime. In 1960, a friend gave Sankariprasad Basu a ticket to the match against Australia with a warning that no one should know about it. Any ticket-holder could be murdered for possessing what the rest of the city fanatically craved.[86] That year, the felony rate in Calcutta was 446.6 crimes committed per 100,000 people, the third-highest among Indian cities after Bangalore (448.0) and Bombay (446.8), with a 50 per cent increase in the number of murders from the previous triennial.[87] The story thus makes a double gesture towards the lack of safety in the city and the absurdity of overestimating cricket's moral lessons on the vast number of moderately educated and unemployed youth. The shortage of urban space caused by the unregulated influx and settlement of refugees was imaginatively cast in an altercation among seven spectators over seating space. One of them considered it physically impossible, but others maintained that the problem could be spiritually solved by the willingness to share.[88] Basu provided shared empathy as an ad-hoc solution to the problem of habitation in the city. He read a rejection of India's pacifist policy in world politics in the jubilation of spectators when Ramakant Desai hit Australia's Ken Mackay on the chest.[89] Contemporary conflicts of values frequently appeared in his writings, planted within discussions about good versus bad, amateurism versus professionalism, style versus efficiency in matters of cricket-playing.

The unforgettable fictional character created by Moti Nandi, Nanida, captain and coach of the second division Hatkhola Cricket Club in Calcutta, blended romanticism with street-smartness, showing what cricket was like in the real world. The novel *Nanida Not Out* opens with a conversation between Nanida and the club's non-Bengali ground staff Durjodhon Mahapatra.[90] Durjodhon's lack of technical knowledge and the club's thin resources meant the pitches prepared over the years were always below standard. One of these years, he expected to finally satisfy Nanida, but his comment on how the pitch will behave met with terse remarks such as 'cricket is not a lorry-driver's game', 'cricket is not for washers' and 'cricket does not need peasants'. Exasperated, Durjodhon asked, 'So who plays cricket?' to which Nanida responded, 'Gentlemen.' Durjodhon, unaware of what 'gentlemen' meant in the context of cricket, thought his employer was referring to affluent and propertied people and asked to increase his salary if better service was expected of him. Nanida pulled out of the conversation, finding it unnecessary to explain the concept to someone outside the pale of cricket education. Showing no conciliatory effort, he denied Durjodhon any alternative approach to cricket and blocked his entry to cricket's discourses. The narrative shows that cricket bred a sense of cultural elitism among even the lower middle class. This elitism occupied an uneasy position among the dignities afforded by money and education. Nanida's utter disregard for the non-Bengali's capability of understanding cricket was evident when he turned his attention from Durjodhon to two persons wandering into the pitch. He did not try to explain why they should not walk across the newly laid pitch; he threw them off by saying they should not defile the place prepared for the cricket god's worship. He had a sense of

Bengali cultural superiority, and cricket was one of the reasons to afford him this perception.

Nandi revisited Nanida after 15 years in a short story entitled 'Shot, Cut, Ebong Nanida'.[91] Two of Nanida's devotees teamed up to make a television serial about a cricketer's romantic affair, and Nanida was offered the role of a mentor who had to deliver an impassioned speech about the hero's cricketing performance. Afraid that he might turn down the role if he realised this was just another commercial potboiler in which cricket was secondary, they initially told him that it was a documentary. It did not take Nanida long to know the truth but since his club needed money to stay afloat, he agreed to shoot and let the filmmakers use the club's facilities. He soon found out that the actor selected to play the cricketer was physically unconvincing and athletically deficient, the director was well read but lacked understanding of cricket's technicality, and the producer's goal was to exploit cricket's popularity. A dispute followed but the shooting team was somehow so convinced of Nanida's indispensability that they did everything to placate him until the end. However, Nanida refused to utter the scripted dialogue about the promise shown by the film's hero. Instead, he sermonised the crew on what made a cricketer great. Everybody listened with rapt attention as he brought back to life stories from cricket's golden age, a narrative in which form was more important than content and intent outplayed outcome. These values could not have been swapped for money. Bengali authors would not excuse famous cricketers if they failed to live up to these expectations. The poet Nirendranath Chakravarti memorialised Sunil Gavaskar's retirement in a poem called 'Apod Biday' (Good Riddance), describing the little master as an arrogant and selfish accumulator of records.[92] Many people did not share the infatuation of the likes of Basu, Nandi or Chakravarti, and took up the criticism of cricket as a duty.

FRACTURED ENGLISHNESS, CHALLENGED PURSUIT

The opposition to cricket had a long history in Britain. In a religious tract named *Terra Pacis*, published in Amsterdam in 1575, the author Hendrick Niclaes, a Westphalian Protestant monk who lived in England during Queen Mary's rule, criticised a foolish pastime called 'Kricket-Staves'. This was later proved to have been a mistranslation into English of the original Base-Almayn word *kolven*, meaning clubs, and hence not an accurate description of any malice against cricket.[93] The Anglican Church, however, objected to people skipping church prayers on Sabbath for playing cricket. A number of court records since the early seventeenth century shows that people were accused of 'playing at cricket in tyme of divine service'.[94] The attitude of the Church remarkably changed over time, and schools and churches became the primary channels of propagating cricket in the colonies in the nineteenth century.[95] In the twentieth century, David Sheppard, Bishop of Liverpool, played some of his 22 Test matches for England after he was ordained into priesthood. In 1966, the Vicar of Bognor, Dr William Snow, went a step further by receiving money from a local bookmaker for a bet placed on the batting performance of his son John Snow and donating it to church fund.[96] Temples and mosques in India did not quite perceive cricket as a threat. They rather encouraged fans to pray for their team to their respective gods, and often joined in the prayer by organising rituals. The Arya Pratinidhi Sabha of Punjab made some exceptional anti-cricket statements in the 1970s, using the familiar trope of the waste of time and money. Their secretary, Swami Agnivesh, cut a lone figure as a somewhat religious personage to have criticised cricket's imperialist character. He proposed its ban in a letter to the central government.[97] Probably cricket was inconsistent with the idea of social spirituality that he counterposed against the off-balance worlds of capitalism and communism.[98] His action was informed more by his anti-West political stance than religious conviction.

Among other dissenters, the socialist parties in India vacillated between pro- and anti-cricket stances, in ways the Labour Party in England probably never thought of. The reticent Prime Minister Clement Attlee would become 'positively garrulous' when cricket was mentioned.[99] One of his successors, Harold Wilson, played cricket behind the Iron Curtain on a visit as the president of the Board of Trade, watched over by two mounted Soviet riflemen.[100] C. L. R. James, dubbed 'cricket's philosopher king', put cricket, life and aesthetics in the same social space.[101] Jawaharlal Nehru followed this tradition. He took the initiative in establishing the Test stadium in Delhi and attended every match played there.[102] Author Achintya Kumar Sengupta lifts his stature as an exemplary person in a story about a charity match for the Madras flood relief fund between the Prime Minister's XI and the Vice-President's XI in 1953. Nehru formed a good batting partnership with the Communist leader A. K. Gopalan, surprising spectators with their mutual understanding while running between the wickets. The *Sunday Times* admired the fact that Nehru selected his parliamentary rival in his team in the

'British tradition of keeping sport and politics apart'.[103] It is said that Nehru was nearly run out trying to score briskly, but the wicketkeeper did not break the stumps, thinking about the people who had gathered to see their prime minister play well. W. G. Grace, the doyen of 'English' cricket, occasionally refused to walk when dismissed cheaply. Nehru, on the contrary, considered himself 'morally out' and threatened to declare the innings unless the umpires gave him out. As the umpires did not, he declared.[104] This was cricket in its glorious moral fortitude, Sengupta concludes: 'despise the sin but not the sinner, abolish empire but love the English'.[105] Dr Sarvepalli Radhakrishnan, captain of the Vice-President's XI, played in a *dhoti*, decolonising the English game very prominently. Nevertheless, cricket was not able to bring all ministers and parties together. Former Congress president Purshottamdas Tandon declined the invitation to play the match, reluctant to touch the cowhide leather ball.[106]

Probably under Nehru's influence, independent India's third minister of information and broadcasting, B. V. Keskar (1950–62), repealed the ban he had earlier imposed on broadcasts of cricket commentary and the other great obsession, Hindi film music. Keskar, a well-known opponent of cricket, was very confident until 1946 that 'with the fall of British power, it is bound to lose its place of honour and slowly grow out of date'.[107] Proven wrong soon enough, he prohibited cricket commentary on All India Radio to emend the misguided nation. A flurry of protest letters from disgruntled followers forced him to reconsider. On the contrary, speaking at a gathering organised to celebrate the BCCI's 25 years in 1954, Dr Radhakrishnan admitted that cricket symbolised the British civilisation, imbued the player with moral qualities, helped them to overcome race and colour bars, and developed 'national unity and international comity'.[108] The messages barely registered with a section of people who had developed the idea that cricket was a capitalist and English sport and should be discarded. The game became an object of hatred as part of a larger campaign to assert postcolonial freedom by replacing most things colonial about 'Indian' institutions – such as the substitution of English by Hindi as the main official language, removal of colonial statues and rebranding roads named after colonial administrators.[109] The anti-English movement was more apparent in northern India; politicians from other regions considered English to have been a better alternative to the northern language Hindi.[110] Socialist Party leader Dr Ram Manohar Lohia wanted cricket to be banned as it created a 'tremendous cultural link within the Commonwealth', an organisation he wanted India to leave.[111] Lohia might have been a covert cricket follower. As anecdotes go, after assailing Nehru, English language and cricket at a press conference during the 1960 Test match against Pakistan in Bombay, Lohia approached a betel-seller and asked if Hanif Mohammad was dismissed yet.[112] The postcolonial self may have had distinct public and private personas.

Several journalists counteracted the abolitionist efforts by Lohia and his associates by presenting the game as an integral part of national life. One correspondent to the *Illustrated Weekly of India* wrote in 1952, 'In the past, thousands packed the maidans to watch their favourites indulge in what was once described as the King of Sports. Cricket then was worth going a long distance to see ... Those in the centre of the pitch played it with real zest.'[113] Journalists chose to overlook the problems of race, caste, class and resources in colonial cricket. Instead, they highlighted a long history of cricket's peaceful coexistence with other forms of Indian culture, claiming that cricket was everywhere, played by everyone and was planted too deep into Indian society to be called foreign or superfluous. In 1953, describing the nation-wide zeal for cricket among the young generation, journalist T. S. Satyan wrote:

> To most of them, three lines drawn with a piece of charcoal on a compound wall or tree serve as stumps, a few pieces of discarded cloth rolled together make a ball, and the bat is shaped out of a scrap dealwood piece. But they are not less enthusiastic than India's Test players whom they hero-worship. If newspapers or magazines feature a cricket match with pictures of the country's celebrated sportsmen in action, the young lovers of the game will cut them out for their albums.[114]

A section of the press celebrated the effacing of cricket's elitism and formal extrinsic codes, but in the process of doing so, they also made the non-follower invisible. This section proved to be dominant in the long run. Cricket became *the* Indian game even though hockey was officially the national game. In parts of India, particularly the Northeast, people did not warm up to cricket as enthusiastically as the rest of the country. This is not surprising despite the dense network of missionary activities and consequent Anglomania in the region. There was no press to circulate cricket's gospel adequately enough to have impacted everyday life, creating and sustaining public interest. The national press treated the Northeast as the 'native' of Clifford Geertz, as people not entitled to a point of view for fear of them contradicting prevalent knowledge.[115] Hence, the region could not escape being classified as part of cricket-loving India. Cricket's reception had more contradictions in other parts of the country. The sport, so passionately categorised as a capitalist game, found a niche in the left-leaning West Bengal where anti-bourgeois and anti-English movements were mainstream public activities.

A majority of politicians considered English a former language of dominance, division and elitism.[116] English was irreplaceable as a common thread in the multilingual country. The elite intelligentsia looked upon the language as an insignia of the colonial concept of cosmopolitanism, the link between empires and civilisations.[117] S. K. Patil, the president of the Bombay State Congress and one of the politicians against banning English as the medium of academic instruction, called the language a 'national possession'.[118] After several protests and riots over the relative merits of giving weightage to various languages as the medium of learning and governance, the Official Languages Act of 1967 made English a permanent official language. All matters of administration were to be recorded in English alongside Hindi.[119] The usefulness of choosing English as the main foreign language was continuously debated in West Bengal. The author and polyglot Syed Mujtaba Ali wrote in an article that learning English was not too essential.[120] His opinion was supported by a few, and countered by some, such as Amita Roy and Rudrajit Dasgupta, who wrote back saying that learning two or more languages was always helpful. Academics in particular ought to learn more than one language, and compulsorily English, to remain updated with the latest research. Moreover, in a multilingual country like India, learning exclusively one's mother tongue would increase provincialism and constrain migrants working in other states.[121] In an effort to salvage his pride, Ali repudiated the claim that English was the most useful foreign language in the world.[122] Arguments against cricket were tied up with this malice towards the lingering traces of imperial Britain. These often referred to the English language and culture as corollary infestations by a regime of absurdity.

The India–England Test match in 1973, which was won by India, drew a flurry of exchanges about the ethics of playing cricket. A reader, under the name of Banga Chandra Pal, wrote to the *Anandabazar Patrika* that cricket was an unnecessary excess indulged by a nation plagued by unemployment, famine, inflation and other grave problems. He suspected a conspiracy hatched by the press in connivance with the government to promote cricket as the opiate of the masses, and appealed to readers to see through this corruption of socialist ideals.[123] Among other readers, Basanta Kumar Mukhopadhyay called cricket a virus. He suspected that the game might not qualify as a sport since not more than three–four countries played it. It generated grudge and hatred between the opponents, and was guided by the fear of being upstaged by the other.[124] In contrast, Ranjan Kumar Das argued that should cricket be banned on account of its foreignness, every other competitive national sport would have to be stopped too since all of them were transmitted from abroad. He was in favour of giving the country's half billion people the freedom to decide whether they would like cricket to continue. Progressive countries spent fortunes on sport as an essential part of nation-building, and India should follow a similar course.[125] In a retort against A. F. Qamruddin's letter that pitched the view that cricket should not be tolerated,[126] Ashok Mukhopadhyay suggested remedial action for those who had not yet learnt to appreciate cricket. He wanted bigger stadiums to be built and new grounds opened across the state in order to increase cricket literacy.[127] The argument continued for years without any consensus in sight.

On the occasion of the India–England Test match in 1977, a reader complained to the editor of *Dainik Basumati* about a million people wasting time after a nonsense sport. Three football matches could have been organised at the Eden Gardens instead of hosting a Test match. The government should consider taking legal measure to abolish England's legacy. Another reader was unhappy with cricket's slow pace and lack of intensity. He had found the previous week's national volleyball championship livelier.[128] A female reader, Sanghamitra Das, made a strange estimate that a total of 18,000,000 working hours were misused when a foreign team played a Test series in India.[129] Finally, Pranabesh Chakraborty expressed anti-cricket arguments the most precisely in a letter:

> The exploitative British imperialists and the local princes have historically indulged in extravagances such as playing cricket, which we continue to watch stupidly and burp with satisfaction. The British gifted cricket to the class of opportunist stooges, princes in the context of India, in each of their colonies … No socialist country has adopted this lazy and passive game that takes places over five days, four or five times in a complete series. How can we aim to be socialist unless we stop clinging to cricket …? It is like opium, with which people are poisoning themselves willingly. Such level of dedication can hardly be seen in other activities … We should not tolerate this farce that has bewitched a group of consumers … By watching cricket, people waste hours of productive labour. Test matches encourage dishonest social behaviour

such as giving one's superior in office a ticket as a form of bribe. Again, who other than hoarders of black money are able to purchase a 70-rupee ticket for 300? It has become necessary to flaunt tickets as a statement of one's social prestige. Cricket is as toxic as horseracing. World cricket operates under the logic that there should be a number of weak national teams in order for England to play and win.[130]

Several people tried to synthesise what they perceived as the good and bad aspects of cricket. The cricket follower Pratapchandra Jana wrote in a letter to the editor of *Jugantar* that language and cricket were the only positive legacies of the British Empire.[131] However, just as cricket was thought to be a tool of entertainment that masked everyday reality, he speculated if cricket was introduced as a plot to keep the colonial youth away from the freedom struggle.[132] A similar barrage of opinions appeared during every Test match at the Eden Gardens.

In the early 1970s, an argument that cricket's popularity undermined the development of all other sports started doing the rounds. As international performance in hockey and football declined, cricket was consolidated as the nation's favourite sport. Hockey player Prithipal Singh, winner of three Olympic medals for India, wrote in 1973, 'While we have been humbled, even humiliated, in international hockey competition, our cricketers have won laurels for the nation, having defeated renowned countries like the West Indies and England on their own soil. It would therefore be befitting if cricket, and not hockey, is now called our national game.'[133] Historian Satadru Sen, with a focus on how Sunil Gavaskar defined Indian masculinity through cricket in a way other athletes could not, has shed light on why cricket had a greater appeal than football and hockey.[134] Sen argued that excellence in international cricket was easier to achieve on account of the fewer number of teams involved than football. As a consequence, even moderate success in cricket looked better than performances in other sports, which were more competitive at the elite level. Many Indians, however, instead of fixating on improving performance in all sports, reckoned cricket to be at fault for the lack of success in other sports. Instead of properly addressing the obstacles to infrastructure and development, they branded cricket as the source of all evil, and the problem remained unresolved. The fascination with cricket upstaged the criticism. In the 1980s, one deputy commissioner supposedly told the travel-writer Alexander Frater while extending his visa:

Back in the days when Britain was rich and governed by Christians, was there any of this arguing with the umpire, hurling away the bat, tantrums on the field and so on? ... Britain was experiencing Fascism domestically so perhaps bodyline was a symptom of a general unease, a feeling that the old order was about to change for ever ... [Indian] economy is in a parlous state, our cricketers behave like a tribe of monkeys and the spectators are even worse. Once men played for India from a deep sense of national pride and commitment; it was like going into the priesthood. Today they play because it gives them access to money, overseas travel, hard liquor and fast foreign girls.[135]

Instances of contempt for a foreign game could be seen in other countries, and some of it was directed to football – 'the world's game'.[136] As an American correspondent found out during his travel to the subcontinent during the 2003 World Cup (played in South Africa), the few Indians who disliked cricket did so with the grit of fanatics. One of them told him that poor people wasted valuable hours watching cricket every day, thus reinforcing poverty. He thought that Americans did not indulge in such silliness, obviously unaware of the craze around the National Football League and the Major League Baseball.[137] More importantly, even after several decades of ideological opposition and its failure, some people's animosity to cricket remained unchanged. Cricket was still held responsible for India's problems. A winning streak muted the criticism, while a string of defeats helped raise voices. The cycle of drifts was condensed into four lines by poet K. V. V. Subrahmanyam,

Despite all the multitudes that throng the cricket field
Some do run down the game with comments veiled,
Talking of ennui and waste of time the spectacle does yield
But on the might of the game their lips are sealed.[138]

CONCLUSION

This chapter examined how cricket survived decades of ideological challenge and was canonised as Indian's ideal pursuit, and what it says about the braiding of England (not Britain) and India around transplanted cultural practices of Englishness. Cricket was India's intimate enemy in the years after independence. I deliberately invoke Ashis Nandy's assertion that colonialism did not stop after the colonisers left. Colonialism was coproduced by the coloniser and the colonised, and might have been reinforced after decolonisation.[139] In many other colonial contexts, such as in the American colony of Philippines, there was no tendency to return to indigenous games once the colonisers departed.[140] Resistance to colonial institutions provided a critical impetus to visions of nation-building, but so did Enlightenment values and Universalist dreams entrenched in sections of the civil society. The early history of the Indian nation-state is thus one of indecision and hybridity, in which cricket was an exemplar of postcolonial anxiety. The focus on cricket has also allowed this chapter to break free of the historiography of postcolonial state-building in India, in which the emphasis is squarely on what the state did and how the people responded. Cricket is a space the state could not dominate, but rather coproduced with the people. A study of cricket has thus enabled a fresh look into the people's programmatic agendas of postcolonial state-building.

The struggle between highly effective myths and implicit political polemics, featured in newspapers and political rallies, deterritorialised cricket from the station of its origin. The incomplete integration of cricket's Englishness to Indian society highlights the relevance of perception in transnational encounters. The constant debates surrounding cricket's ideological content, and the open possibility of both becoming and resisting the English through cricket, accorded the sport its formative role in public culture. It ceased to be just another sport as soon as the public started defining its character. Answers are more important than questions in postmodern criticism as they have the ability to reconstruct the question by shifting its meaning. Texts facilitated this negotiation by writing the answers given by a plethora of actors into concrete historical forms, and hence producing a visible and long-term account of similarity or difference.

This dilemma of appropriating a fundamentally English concept was not exceptionally Indian. Australian Aboriginals were never assimilated into the white pastime of cricket, for which the racist attitude of white settlers was to be held responsible. Cricket did not afford the Aboriginals any social mobility or selection in the national and state teams, so averse were the settlers to share power, provide moral tutelage or encourage advancement of the other.[141] Indians probably possessed greater social capital to be in control of their political life and resistance rhetoric compared to the Aboriginals. Although in the minority, critics of cricket in India have voiced dissent with an extraordinary liberty. A reason could be that these criticisms were not considered subversive enough to erode cricket's popularity. Moreover, critics provided the context within which cricket's ideologues could resolve the prejudices against the sport's alleged imperialist and capitalist substructure. The question of ethics left cricket hanging in an antithetical balance that continues to provide engrossing content for newspapers.

NOTES

1. Sankariprasad Basu, *Ramaniya Cricket* (Beautiful Cricket) (Calcutta: Karuna Prakashani, 1961), 1.
2. Ibid., 5.
3. For a treatment of the Marxist and neo-Marxist criticism of sport as an ideological tool for the bourgeois state and monopoly capitalists, see Jean-Marie Brohm, *Sport: A Prison of Measured Time*, trans. Ian Fraser (London: Ink Links, 1978). Brohm takes a dialectical materialist class analysis approach in his staunch, sometimes lopsided, critique of elite competitive sport as a tool of exploiting and manipulating the masses. Brohm's later works on sport, published in French, offer a more balanced view of the crisis in sport under late capitalism, fascism, and state capitalism. See Henri Vaugrand, 'Pierre Bourdieu and Jean-Marie Brohm: Their Schemes of Intelligibility and Issues towards a Theory of Knowledge in the Sociology of Sport', *International Review for the Sociology of Sport* 36, no. 2 (2001): 183–201.
4. In a book published more than half a century after Basu's, Niall Ferguson mentions 'representative assemblies', 'the English language' and 'team sports' as three of the eight cornerstones of the British Empire. Ferguson, *Empire: How Britain Made the Modern World* (New York: Penguin, 2004), 14.
5. Basu, *Ramaniya Cricket*, 6.
6. John Bale, *Anti-Sport Sentiments in Literature: Batting for the Opposition* (London and New York: Routledge, 2007).
7. G. K. Peatling, 'Rethinking the History of Criticism of Organized Sport', *Cultural and Social History* 2, no. 3 (2005): 353–71; John Bale, 'Anti-Sport: Victorian Examples from Oxbridge', *Sport in History* 34, no. 1 (2014): 34–48.
8. Ramachandra Guha, *A Corner of a Foreign Field: The Indian History of a British Sport* (London: Picador, 2002), ch. 11.
9. Ibid., ch. 14.
10. D. M. Brittain, 'The Way to Lord's', *The Times*, 25 June 1968, 11.
11. *DB*, 30 December 1972, 6.

12. Why is postcolonial international politics forgiving when it comes to matters of cricket? For introductory comments, see Richard M. Weintraub, 'Cricket Stirs Old British Empire', *Washington Post*, 8 November 1987, D18.

13. David Hardiman, 'Indian Medical Indigeneity: From Nationalist Assertion to the Global Market', *Social History* 34, no. 3 (2009): 263–83, 272; Romila Thapar, 'Syndicated *Moksha*', *Seminar* 313 (September 1985): 14–22.

14. There are numerous studies of the 'continuities and discontinuities between pre- and post-independence India', to quote Paul Brass's chapter title, but none mentions cricket. Paul Brass, *The Politics of India since Independence* (Cambridge: Cambridge University Press, 1990).

15. Keith Sandiford, 'Cricket and the Victorian Society', *Journal of Social History* 17, no. 2 (1983): 303–17, 310.

16. Jack Williams, *Cricket and England: A Cultural and Social History of the Inter-war Years* (London: Frank Cass, 1999), 1.

17. Derek Birley, *Land of Sport and Glory: Sport and British Society 1887–1910* (Manchester: Manchester University Press, 1995), 258.

18. Richard Holt, 'Cricket and Englishness: The Batsman as Hero', *International Journal of the History of Sport* 13, no. 1 (1996): 48–70.

19. Stefan Szymanski, 'A Theory of the Evolution of Modern Sport', *Journal of Sport History* 35, no. 1 (2008): 1–32, 5.

20. David Low, 'The Relative Importance of Things', *The Star*, 20 December 1920.

21. E. V. Lucas, 'The English Game', in *Cricket All His Life*, 213–15 (London: Pavilion Library, 1989 [1950]), 215.

22. Mike Marqusee, *Anyone but England: An Outsider Looks at English Cricket*, 3rd ed. (London: Aurum Press, 2005), 41.

23. Neville Cardus, *Autobiography* (London: Hamish Hamilton, 1984 [1947]), 142.

24. Neville Cardus, *Cardus on Cricket* (London: Souvenir Press, 1976), 20.

25. Marqusee, *Anyone but England*, 22. It was a world in which professional players, who played cricket for a livelihood, were compelled to address those who played for fun, the amateurs, as 'Mister' or 'Sir'. The professionals used different changing rooms, ate on separate tables and entered the ground through different gates. Any challenge to the order would see their contracts terminated for breach of etiquette. The team captain would be an amateur even if he were the worst player in the team. The system was so stringent in as late as 1937 that Wally Hammond was converted after 17 years of playing as a professional to an amateur by a monetary grant from Marsham Tyres, a subsidiary of Dunlop Tyres, so that he could lead the MCC in 1938. Stephen Wagg, '"Time Gentlemen Please": The Decline of Amateur Captaincy in

English County Cricket', in *Amateurs and Professionals in Post-War British Sport*, ed. Adrian Smith and Dilwyn Porter, 31–59 (London and New York: Routledge, 2000), 34–35. It was not before 1963 that the annual Gentlemen versus Players match was scrapped, and all first-class cricketers were declared professionals. Dissent against this class division was so fleeting that one could suspect that cricketers consented to inequality. Williams, *Cricket and England*, 188.

26. Stephen Haseler, *The English Tribe: Identity, Nation and Europe* (Basingstoke: Palgrave Macmillan, 1996), 59.

27. Simon Gikandi, *Maps of Englishness: Writing Identity in the Culture of Colonialism* (New York: Columbia University Press, 1996), xii–xiii.

28. Linda Colley, *Britons: Forging the Nation 1707–1837* (London: Pimlico, 1994), 16–17.

29. Krishan Kumar, 'Varieties of Nationalism', in *The Victorian World*, ed. Martin Hewitt, 160–74 (London and New York: Routledge, 2012), 167.

30. Wendy Webster, *English and Empire 1939–1965* (Oxford: Oxford University Press, 2005), 9.

31. Slavoj Žižek, *For They Know Not What They Do: Enjoyment as a Political Factor* (London: Verso, 1991), 110.

32. Dominic Malcolm, *Globalizing Cricket: Englishness, Empire and Identity* (London: Bloomsbury, 2013); Dominic Malcolm and Philippa Velija, 'Cricket: The Quintessential English Game?' in *Sport and English National Identity in a 'Disunited Kingdom'*, ed. Tom Gibbons and Dominic Malcolm, 19–33 (London: Routledge, 2017).

33. Arjun Appadurai, 'Playing with Modernity: The Decolonization of Cricket', in *Modernity at Large: Cultural Dimensions of Globalization*, 89–113 (Minneapolis: University of Minnesota Press, 1996), 90.

34. Harry Thompson, *Penguins Stopped Play: Eleven Village Cricketers Take on the World* (London: John Murray, 2006).

35. Appadurai, 'Playing with Modernity'.

36. Mulk Raj Anand, *Two Leaves and a Bud* (New Delhi: Arnold Associates, 1981[1937]), 174.

37. Paul Dimeo, 'Sporting and the "Civilizing Mission" in India', in *Colonialism and Civilising Mission: Cultural Ideology in British India*, ed. Harald Fischer-Tiné and Michael Mann, 165–78 (London: Anthem, 2004).

38. Boria Majumdar and Sean F. Brown, 'Why Baseball, Why Cricket? Differing Nationalisms, Differing Challenges', *International Journal of the History of Sport* 24, no. 2 (2007): 139–56.

39. 'Cricket in India: A History of the Game', *TOI*, 12 June 1905, 8.

40. Robert Baden-Powell, *Indian Memories* (London: Herbert Jenkins, 1915), 279.

41. Mihir Bose, 'An English Sporting Eden in India', in *The Magic of Indian Cricket: Cricket and Society in India*, 129–43 (London: Routledge, 2006).

42. Richard Cashman, 'Cricket and Colonialism: Colonial Hegemony and Indigenous Subversion?' in *Pleasure, Profit, and Proselytism: British Culture and Sport at Home and Abroad 1700–1914*, ed. J. A. Mangan, 258–72 (London: Frank Cass, 1988), 261.

43. J. A. Mangan, *The Games Ethic and Imperialism: Aspects of the Diffusion of an Ideal* (Harmondsworth: Penguin, 1985); J. A. Mangan, 'Ethics and Ethnocentricity: Imperial Education in British Tropical Africa', in *Sport in Africa: Essays in Social History*, ed. William J. Baker and J.A. Mangan, 138–71 (New York and London: Africana Publishing Co., 1987).

44. 'Abrupt End to Cricket Match,' *TOI*, 5 January 1931, 12.

45. 'Mr. R.B. Lagden Explains How the Dhoti Dispute Arose,' *TOI*, 28 August 1931, 3.

46. Emma Tarlo, *Clothing Matters: Dress and Identity in India* (Chicago: University of Chicago Press, 1996).

47. Ashok Mitra, *Apila Chapila* (A Prattler's Tale) (Calcutta: Ananda Publishers, 2003), 6–7.

48. Mukul, 'Kritir Krirabhumika' (The Achiever's Playground), *Desh* 37, no. 25 (18 April 1970), 1233.

49. Salman Rushdie, *The Satanic Verses* (London: Vintage, 1988), 37.

50. 'Crusade against Cricket', *TOI*, 31 August 1947, 13.

51. Narayan Gangopadhyay asked in his column why should hockey be India's national sport instead of football or cricket? Why was hockey exempt from the public's concern with the Englishness of other sports? Narayan Gangopadhyay, 'Cricket, Hockey, Ityadi' (Cricket, Hockey, Etc.), *Desh* 37, no. 3 (15 November 1969), 227–28.

52. N. S. Ramaswami, *Winter of Content* (Madras: Swadesmitran Limited, 1967), 4.

53. Matthias Middell, 'Is There a Timetable when Concepts Travel? On Synchronicity in the Emergence of New Concepts Dealing with Border-Crossing Phenomena', in *The Trans/National Study of Culture: A Transnational Perspective*, ed. Doris Bachmann-Medick, 137–54 (Berlin: De Gruyter, 2014), 146.

54. Anthony Bateman, *Cricket, Literature and Culture: Symbolising the Nation, Destabilising Empire* (Farmham: Ashgate, 2009), 23.

55. Mukul, 'Kritir Krirabhumika', *Desh* 37, no. 11 (10 January 1970), 1140.

56. Shirshendu Mukhopadhyay, *Gosain Baganer Bhut* (Calcutta: Ananda Publishers, 2005 [1979]), 13.

57. Ibid., 52.

58. Shirshendu Mukhopadhyay, *Golmal* (Calcutta: Dey's Publishing, 2002 [1989]), 30.

59. Ibid., 114.

60. Gary A. Olson and Lynn Worsham, 'Staging the Politics of Difference: Homi Bhabha's Critical Literacy', *JAC: A Journal of Composition Theory* 18, no. 3 (1998): 361–91, 368.

61. Appadurai, 'Playing with Modernity', 102.

62. Parama Roy, *Indian Traffic: Identities in Question in Colonial and Postcolonial India* (Berkeley: University of California Press, 1998), 2.

63. Raymond Williams, 'Culture Is Ordinary', in *Resources of Hope: Culture, Democracy, Socialism*, 3–18 (London: Verso, 1989).

64. Williams, *Cricket and England*, 8. Williams remarks that the pastoral dimension was an integral part of imagining the countryside in southern England.

65. William Wordsworth, 'Composed in the Valley, Near Dover, on the Day of Landing', *Poems II* (London: Longman, 1815), 208.

66. Claire Westall, 'What Should We Know of Cricket Who Only England Know? Cricket and Its Heroes in English and Caribbean Literature' (PhD thesis, Warwick University, 2007), 18.

67. Neville Cardus, *English Cricket* (London: Prion, 1997), 10.

68. Lucas, 'The English Game', 215.

69. Brahmanyabhusan and Kshama Bandopadhyay, 'Kabigurur Cricket Khela' (The Poet Laureate Plays Cricket), reprinted in Basu, *Cricket Omnibus II* (Calcutta: Mandal Book House, 1976), 370–75.

70. Sankariprasad Basu, 'P. Chowdhury'r Sesh Khela' (P. Chowdhury's Final Match), *Not Out*, in *Cricket Omnibus II* (Calcutta: Mandal Book House, 1976), 260.

71. Ibid., 255.

72. Ibid., 256.

73. *DB*, 30 December 1972, 6.

74. M. A. K. Pataudi, 'It Could Only Be a Draw', *Sportsworld* (7 November 1979), 20.

75. Romesh Ganguli, 'Romance of Sport', *Hindustan Standard Puja Annual 1959*, 185.
76. Santipriyo Bandopadhyay, 'Khelar Rajar Raja' (Kings of Cricket), *Saptahik Basumati* 75, no. 3 (9 July 1970), 124.
77. Mushtaq Ali, *Cricket Delightful* (New Delhi: Rupa, 1960), 21.
78. Berry Sarbadhikary, *My World of Cricket* (Calcutta: Cricket Library, 1964), 250.
79. Ajay Basu, 'Cricketer Nandankanane' (Cricket's Garden of Eden), in *Math Theke Bolchhi* (Calcutta: Ruprekha, 1968), 121–22.
80. Ajay Basu, 'Smritituku Shona Hoye Thak' (Golden Memories), *Amrita Krira Binodon Sankhya* (31 December 1976): 135–36.
81. Robert Rineart, 'Poetic Sensibilities and the Use of Fiction for Sport History: Map-making in Representation of the Past', in *Examining Sport Histories: Power, Paradigms, and Reflexivity*, ed. Richard Pringle and Murray Phillips, 184–201 (Morgantown, WV: Fitness Information Technology, 2013), 280.
82. 'When Cricket Was Cricket', *The Scotsman*, 19 June 1925, 6.
83. Sandiford, *Cricket and the Victorians*, 2.
84. Thomas Hughes, *Tom Brown's Schooldays* (Oxford: Oxford University Press, 1989), 354–55.
85. Subhas Dutta, 'IFA-r Kamal Dutta/CAB-r Kartik Sinha', *Sharadiya Khelar Asar (SKA)*, 1979, 161.
86. Sankariprasad Basu, *Edene Shiter Dupur* (Winter Afternoon at Eden) (Calcutta: Bookland, 1960), 106.
87. *Crime in India: 1960*, The National Crime Records Bureau, 2–4.
88. Ibid., 111.
89. Ibid., 150.
90. Moti Nandi, *Nanida Not Out*, in *Dashti Kishor Upanyas* (Ten Young Adult Novels), 9–49 (Calcutta: Ananda Publishers, 2000 [1973]), 11–12.
91. Moti Nandi, 'Shot, Cut, Ebong Nanida', *Saradiya Khela 1987*, 10–24.
92. Nirendranath Chakravarti, 'Apod Biday' (Good Riddance), *Saradiya Khela 1988*, 44.
93. John Major, *More Than a Game: The Story of Cricket's Early Years* (London: Harper, 2007), 20–21.
94. Ibid., 25.
95. Brian Stoddart, 'Sport, Cultural Imperialism, and Colonial Response in the British Empire', *Comparative Studies in Society and History* 30, no. 4 (1988): 649–73.

96. 'Snow's Test 59 Earns Church £34', *Daily Telegraph*, 22 August 1966, cited in *The Daily Telegraph Book of Cricket*, ed. Nick Hoult (London: Aurum Press, 2009), 173.
97. *Jugantar*, 17 January 1979, 3.
98. Rajesh Chakrabarti, 'Introduction', in *The Other India: Realities of an Emerging Power*, ed. Rajesh Chakrabarti (New Delhi: Sage, 2009), xvi.
99. Michael Jago, *Clement Attlee: The Inevitable Prime Minister* (London: Biteback, 2014), 6.
100. Hubert Preston, 'From Russia with a Dropped Catch', *Wisden Cricketers' Almanack 1951*, in *The Essential Wisden: An Anthology of 150 Years of Wisden Cricketers' Almanack*, ed. John Stern and Marcus Williams (London: Bloomsbury, 2013), 40.
101. Dave Renton, *C.L.R. James: Cricket's Philosopher King* (London: Haus, 2007).
102. Bose, *The Magic of Indian Cricket*, 73–74.
103. 'How's That', *Sunday Times* (*ST*), 13 September 1953, 6.
104. 'Morally Out', *The Guardian* (*TG*), 14 September 1953, 1.
105. Achintya Kumar Sengupta, *Mriga Nei Mrigaya* (*A Hunt Without Deer*) (Calcutta: Anandadhara, 1965), 126–27.
106. 'Nehru Bowls a Maiden in MP's Match', *ST*, 13 September 1953, 1.
107. Guha, *A Corner of a Foreign Field*, 322.
108. *TG*, 12 February 1954, 1.
109. Paul M. McGarr, '"The Viceroys are Disappearing from the Roundabouts in Delhi": British Symbols of Power in Post-colonial India', *Modern Asian Studies* 49, no. 3 (2015): 787–831; Sarah Ansari and William Gould, *Boundaries of Belonging: Localities, Citizenship and Rights in India and Pakistan* (Cambridge: Cambridge University Press, 2020), ch. 1.
110. Ramachandra Guha, ed., *Makers of Modern India* (New Delhi: Penguin Viking, 2010), 461. A concise account of the evolution of English from a 'tool of nationalism' to the 'career tongue' can be found in Nandan Nilekani, 'The Phoenix Tongue', in *Imagining India: Ideas for the New Century*, 83–102 (New Delhi: Penguin Allen Lane, 2008).
111. Taya Zinkin, 'Mutinous Thoughts in India: Socialists Not Playing Cricket', *TG*, 8 May 1957, 9. Lohia's arguments against English can be found in Rammanohar Lohia, *Language* (Hyderabad: Rammanohar Lohia Samata Vidyalaya Nyas, 1986). For an analysis of Lohia's socialist thoughts, see M. Arumugam, *Socialist Thought in India: The Contribution of Rammanohar Lohia* (New Delhi: Sterling Publications, 1978).

112. Guha, *A Corner of Foreign Field*, 439–40.

113. *IWI*, 6 January 1952, 45.

114. Ibid., 1 November 1953, 22.

115. Clifford Geertz, *Local Knowledge: Further Essays in Interpretive Anthropology* (New York: Basic Books, 1983).

116. Probal Dasgupta, *The Otherness of English: India's Auntie's Tongue Syndrome* (New Delhi: Sage, 1993).

117. At a more mundane level, English has been for the populace an avenue for upward mobility rather than a cultural bond, with 'new vernacular forces' promoted by the democratic nation perennially trying to marginalise the language with varying success. Vinay Lal and Ashis Nandy, 'Introduction', in *Fingerprinting Popular Culture: The Mythic and the Iconic in Indian Cinema*, ed. Vinay Lal and Ashis Nandy, xi–xxvii (New Delhi: Oxford University Press, 2006), xiii.

118. 'Permanent Fixtures in India', *TG*, 12 February 1954, 1.

119. Andreas Sedlatschek, *Contemporary Indian English: Variation and Change* (Amsterdam and Philadelphia: John Benjamins, 2009), 20.

120. Syed Mujtaba Ali, 'Panchatantra' (Five Treatises), *Desh* 35, no. 1 (1 November 1967), 35–36.

121. 'Alochona' (Discussion), *Desh* 35, no. 3 (18 November 1967), 293–95.

122. Syed Mujtaba Ali, 'Panchatantra', *Desh* 35, no. 4 (25 November 1967), 347–48.

123. Banga Chandra Pal, 'Cricketer Nabababublias' (The Dandies of Cricket), *Anandabazar Patrika* (*ABP*), 9 January 1973, 4.

124. *ABP*, 16 January 1973, 4.

125. Ibid.

126. Ibid.

127. Ibid.

128. *DB*, January 4, 1977, 7.

129. *KA* 2, no. 24 (20 October 1978), 15.

130. *DB*, 8 January 1977, 4.

131. 'West Indies: Cricket Jar Swatantra Shaili' (West Indies' Unique Style of Cricket), *Jugantar*, 28 December 1978, 3.

132. Lincoln Allison, 'Sport and Politics', in *The Politics of Sport*, ed. Lincoln Allison, 1–26 (Manchester: Manchester University Press, 1986), 14–15.

133. Prithipal Singh, 'Hockey: No Longer Our National Game', *IWI*, 12 August 1973, 55.

134. Satadru Sen, 'How Gavaskar Killed Indian Football', *Football Studies* 5, no. 2 (2002): 27–37. The issue has also been discussed by Somshankar Ray,

'"The Wood Magic"': Cricket in India – A Postcolonial Benediction', *The International Journal of the History of Sport* 25, no. 12 (2008): 1637–53.

135. Alexander Frater, *Chasing the Monsoon: A Modern Pilgrimage through India* (London: Picador, 2005), 266.

136. In a remote Egyptian village where Amitav Ghosh conducted the fieldwork for his doctoral research, at least one village elder loathed football. The person, Abu-Ali, screamed in anger from time to time, 'Isn't there work to do? Allah! Is the world going to live on soccer? What's going to become of …' Ghosh, *In an Antique Land* (London: Granta Books, 1992), 27.

137. Michael Y. Park, 'A Cricket Heathen in India', *New York Times*, 23 March 2003, 19.

138. K. V. V. Subrahmanyan, 'In Defence of Cricket', in *'A Breathless Hush …': The MCC Anthology of Cricket Verse*, ed. David Rayvern Allen, 143 (London: Methuen, 2004).

139. Ashis Nandy, *The Intimate Enemy: Loss and Recovery of Self under Colonialism* (Delhi: Oxford University Press, 1983).

140. Gerald Gems, *Sport and the American Occupation of the Philippines: Bats, Balls, and Bayonets* (Lanham: Lexington Books, 2016), 162.

141. Jon Gemmell, 'All White Male? Cricket and Race in Oz', in *Cricket, Race and the 2007 World Cup*, ed. Jon Gemmell and Boria Majumdar, 23–39 (London and New York: Routledge, 2008).

2 Narratives of Cricket and Collective History

The leisurely nature of Test cricket once made American comedian Groucho Marx remark, while watching England play during a trip to London in 1954, 'What a wonderful cure for insomnia. If you can't sleep here, you really need an analyst.'[1] Soviet tennis star Alex Metreveli once told journalist Moti Nandi that cricket was a tedious sport for a passive public.[2] Interestingly, an income-tax officer in Calcutta, who had received a season ticket as a bribe, remarked after a boring day of cricket, 'It is better to listen to radio commentary or read about cricket in the newspapers than to watch it for five hours.'[3] Indeed, in the 1950s, cricket journalism in Bengali developed from deadpan match reporting to an imaginative representation of both the play and the spectators. A major challenge for journalists in the 1950s–60s, the decades later criticised for uninspiring and slow play, was to enliven the day's proceedings to sustain the public's interest. This new direction in journalism as well as radio commentary nonetheless proved to be highly influential, just as the income-tax officer confessed. Later, the immediacy of radio and television challenged the belated impact of newspapers and magazines. In 1978, a satirical piece in the *Khelar Asar* addressed the growing apprehension that audio-visual media would change the fabric of journalism and recast the form and content of the knowledge of cricket. Narrating a fictitious meeting, the author articulated through the figure of the organiser that the information in match reports differed greatly from radio commentary, showing awareness of the complexity of representation.[4]

Any history of sport is to a large extent a history of mediatised and mediated sport. The constitutive role of authors and journalists in the emergence of sporting cultures is quite evident, if somewhat underexplored by historians. Sport and the media have shared an intimate bond for more than two centuries. The media has ensured that the twentieth-century public life becomes inconceivable without its componential 'sports chatter', a term Umberto Eco coined in his essay on the public dimensions of sport.[5] Eco writes, provocatively, that sport is a creation of the sports press, and 'at several removes there remains the actual sport, which might as well not even exist'.[6] Sports news delivers a large and loyal (mainly young male) readership to advertisers and contributes to the commercial viability of media organisations.[7] Sports journalism typically represents a large and almost autonomous department within the newspaper or news website, often with its own editor, sub-editors and reporters. It is the space in which the activities, selection, tactics and any information relevant to a sporting individual's or team's performance (injuries, attitude, commitment, and so on) are discussed at length. The work for sports journalists usually involves writing reports based on personal experience of a sport-related event, interviews, surveys or knowledge of past events and personalities. In addition, the press publishes the reader's perspectives and special interest books or booklets, holds stakes, organises or sponsors talks or meetings involving sports personnel, and distributes excellence awards. It is often claimed that modern sport and modern press flourished together.[8] The gradual expansion of the sports section did not only increase sport's popularity but also helped the print media earn more revenue and prosper.[9]

The public's widespread engagement has been reflected in sport's ubiquitous presence across all formats of discourse circulation. Sport has been inseparably tangled with various media and television in particular.[10] Mediatisation of sporting culture is entwined with the publicness and consumption of sport. Historian Eduardo Archetti categorises the participants in sport as 'the experts in knowledge, the central participants or players and the peripheral participants or audience', who mutually link the meanings, discourses and identities produced at various levels.[11] The content of sports media consists of a reality constructed out of interpretation of events by variously engaged authors.[12] By consuming media reports, the public creatively appropriate the sports event delivered to them by the organisers and mediators. Consumption techniques include both the institutionalised use of sport by a large group of fans and personal reading of media content. Sport has become increasingly allied to the consumption of goods and services through discourses about the modern consumer-citizen. In the second half of the twentieth century, the media has acted as a transforming force, turning sport into first a 'male soap opera' and then an all-gender phenomenon.[13] Sport has been promoted like other commodities as a consistent and quality product.[14]

Such promotion has added many dimensions to the appropriation of sport. It would be overambitious to assume that any sport is a true representation of society. The unlimited show of passion towards sport conceals the indifference of groups not taking interest in sport. Sports geographer John Bale believes that the latter almost always outnumbers sports followers but receives little or no attention since the influence exerted by even a small number of fans is asymmetrically enormous.[15] The spread and extent of consumption attach great academic importance to the mediatisation of categories of identity (class, gender, ethnic, cultural, national) and leisure, which have been extensively analysed from perspectives of sociology, history, gender studies, cultural studies, media studies, anthropology and leisure studies.[16]

The volumes edited by Lawrence A. Wenner were arguably the first serious attempts at studying the contours of media–sport relationship and its influence on social and cultural life.[17] Joseph Maguire expanded the collection's theoretical framework in his article on the 'media–sport production complex', while David Rowe introduced the 'media sports cultural complex'.[18] The major themes explored by scholars of mediatised sports include the economic and aesthetic drives in the sport–media complex, advertising, event planning, publicity and key figures.[19] Most of the studies on media–sport relationship have so far focused on television rather than the print media.[20] Recognition of the texts embedded within visuals is important for a study of television, whereas analysis of written narratives is at the core of studying the print media. Research has distinguished at least three aspects within both forms of communication, namely production, content and audience.[21] The production of media message involves hierarchisation, personalisation, narrativisation and framing of events for a particular audience. When treating these contents as sources (newspaper reports, magazine articles, photographs,[22] art,[23] newsreels,[24] films,[25] advertisements,[26] cartoons,[27] internet,[28] fiction,[29] biographical[30] and autobiographical[31] writings) of history-writing, one has to notice the agency of journalists, audiences, officials, sportspersons and other actors, the transactions among whom lead to alterity by the production of several versions of the same event.

Various scholars such as Walter Benjamin show awareness of the time-honoured role the press plays in making every follower an expert.[32] It helps stadium spectators to expand their understanding of the history they have helped to create and enable followers who were absent in the stadium to retrospectively engage with the event.[33] Words and images translate a sport into a form that followers consume and reciprocate. Recognising the function of this mediation is necessary to understand sporting culture.[34] A journalist is a spectator, interlocutor and mediator who produces knowledge of a stadium event. The person has access to sources of information other spectators do not. One is the (un)disputed authority on analysing sport events, the outcome of which is available for consumption before, during and after the event. Before the age of digital and social media, readers depended on the editor's discretion to publish their opinion. Spectators could interpret the reported events differently, but the press would mediate and determine the visibility and acceptability of their assessment. Journalists and editors could deliver an intellectual finality to their narratives. They had the institutional support to observe sport within a plenary context of its large community of sentiment. From minutes of administrative meetings to interviews with obscure acquaintances of players, the sports press serves everything deemed suitable for public consumption. Yet the meanings intended by journalists are often lost in transmission to readers of the present and particularly the future.

Apart from newspapers and periodicals, literature, film, photographs, and radio and television broadcasting have all had a profound effect on the popular and political culture of cricket. Journalists and radio and television commentators have creatively used non-sport imageries to embellish and enhance the appeal of sporting narratives. The chapter explores the extent to which these narratives constituted and derived their popular appeal from the social context of their production.[35] Multiple perspectives were bound to increase doubts about the exact meaning of texts glutted with rhetoric and polemics. Bengali print journalists devised certain methods of presenting news that were not replicable in other media, thereby clinching the contest in their favour. Through a study of the craft of print journalists and radio broadcasters, this chapter explores how cricket became popular in the state. I leave out television, which was no less important than other media in circulating cricket, as the time period studied in this book allows no more than a partial account of its growth. It will take another book to do justice to television's contribution to Indian cricket.

THE CRAFT OF RETELLING

When the MCC visited Calcutta in 1961–62, a correspondent of the *Anandabazar Patrika* remarked that nearly everybody in the city had become a cricket expert. A young man named Nyapla became a reporter for the

Honolulu Times and another person named Patla covered the match for the *Panama News Chronicle*. A boy tried to enter the stadium with an identity card issued by an Uttar Pradesh newspaper. A cricketer too was seen sporting a photographer's badge.[36] Twenty years later, in 1982, 20 people were booked during the India–England Test for sleeping in the gallery overnight. They tried to avoid the inconvenience of queuing very early for a day ticket by not leaving the stadium. A total of 140 spectators were arrested over five days, some for scaling the wall, some for carrying stolen or fake tickets, some for trying to enter without ticket, some for bringing alcohol and some for offering bribe to the police to let them in. Four tickets looked like counterfeit due to printing errors but were later found to be genuine.[37] In the next decade, in 1993, after Venkatpathy Raju took an English wicket, someone flashed a banner inscribed 'Raju Ban Gaya Gentleman', referring to the title of a recent blockbuster Hindi film. After Alec Stewart, Graham Gooch and Robin Smith were dismissed cheaply, one of the placards raised said: 'Today's menu, Gooch toast, Robin curry and Stewart stew'. The best placard on view was written by Abhishek Sikdar from Julien Day School, which read 'Azhar Kapil Bhai Bhai, Mandir Masjid Dui Chai' (Azhar and Kapil are kins/We want both temples and mosques), a relevant interjection in the times of communal cacophony. The famous singer Kumar Sanu was seen swaying to the Mexican wave, while the actor Anup Kumar watched the match attentively. Spectators sitting at the lower tier of the Club House asked Sunil Gavaskar's wife, Marshneil, to pass autograph books to Gundappa Vishwanath, who sat behind her.[38]

Some episodes from this medley of newspaper stories seemed to be sarcastic representations of cricket following while others conveyed a greater sense of possibility due to the manner in which they were written. Was there a newspaper called the *Panama News Chronicle* which deputed Patla to write about the match? Did someone write a witty banner connecting cricket and Bollywood? Did Marshneil pass autograph books to Vishwanath? Were these reports informed by direct observation or imagination? The number of arrests cannot be verified from official sources as the West Bengal police records from the 1980s are inaccessible. Whether or not Kumar Sanu casually danced during one of his many stadium visits in the 1990s has little practical value for understanding collective spectatorship. In the absence of supplementary sources – written text, memory, myth – to authenticate these incidents, one should be careful when rolling out these stories about spectators into the cauldron of history. The mediatised and mediated images of spectators are nearly all that there are. Use of interviews and autobiographies as historical sources presents the problem of verifiability and intensive subjectivity owing to personal choices and external pressures on writing (editorial preference, deadline, copyediting). People can misrepresent their beliefs even without social pressure, making historical evidence deceptive.[39] Umpires and cricketers are always critical of the journalists' tendency to judge the match situation better from the comfort of the press box. The umpire Swaroop Kishen once bantered with a journalist that during a Test match in Kanpur he read in the morning daily about the Australians opting for a heavy roller whereas no roller had been used.[40]

One needs to carefully approach the motivation of participants, which dovetails the Lévi-Straussian theory of competing systems of representation among historical actors and the historian.[41] According to historian Adrian Wilson, sources of history-writing can be alternatively seen as authoritative narration of the past, witness to the past, and effect of past events.[42] It is worthwhile to use this tripartite classification with qualifiers as press reports such as those mentioned earlier can embody all or none of these categories. A report can be an authoritative narration of a match, which the correspondent has preferably witnessed in person, and written about after the end of the day's play. Even without external interference, personal style of narration often blurs the boundary between witnessing an incident and being influenced in its wake. Writers such as Sankariprasad Basu were capable of influencing the perception of a match by aestheticising the most prosaic of events. Although one can interpret his works from a social history perspective, the quest for historical realism can be deeply troubling due to the reminiscing nature of his narrative. Hence, the effort to recreate a comprehensive history of what happened at the Eden Gardens may turn out to be fragmentary, a victim of subjectivities or the lack of archives. Is it possible to historicise the culture of spectatorship when the available sources are indeterminate? Douglas Booth encourages sports historians to apply postmodernist methods of discourse analysis when dealing with such sources, as Malcolm MacLean does in his re-reading of *Beyond a Boundary*.[43] Disparities do not really ease into coherence in a cultural history framework, nor is it fruitful to divide historical methods.[44] But recognition of blind spots allows one to rummage through evidence without having to sell them to the service of justifying an overarching argument.

Following the linguistic turn in history, assertions can no longer be evaluated for authenticity but deconstructed in order to understand the thoughts and actions of their authors.[45] Since a language is 'rather uncertain, partial, or inessential', meaning-making turns into a joint enterprise of the reader and the author.[46] The author does not seem to occupy journalistic texts so centrally as in literary texts since press reports, except for opinion pieces, are supposed to present facts as they happened. Nevertheless, journalists express opinions when they present an event, often in a style dramatic enough to draw new audience to the newspaper.[47] Any text is full of unwritten stories located within what is offered for public consumption. When considering media texts as primary sources, separating evidence from opinion often becomes impossible due to their 'constructedness'. For example, the charade of the *Panama News Chronicle* could be simply humorous as Panama the country had little enthusiasm for cricket, but it was possible that someone called Patla had indeed fabricated a false identity card and tried to fool an official into handing him a press card. It is more likely that the story referred to the high level of specialised cricket knowledge even among street urchins. The question is whether these statements described or represented the author's experience.[48] Hence, before trying to determine the truth value of the 'dense layer of signs' about spectators,[49] treating these signs as remnants of a time that help to formulate problems and explore knowledge production is more useful. Scholars have argued that historicising documents is no less important than documenting history.[50] This chapter does not delve into the context of the production of non-press cricket writings but considers research into the background essential for uncovering the cultural impulses precipitated by cricket.

Historians of sport have made copious use of newspapers as sources, not always taking note of the perspectives and language of correspondents. Historian Jeffrey Hill draws attention to this shortcoming in an article about the communal rituals around the Football Association Challenge Cup, or FA Cup, finals in the first half of the twentieth century.[51] The local press created local sentiments by stringing together popular feelings about *places* and *people*. When confronted with century-old news items that were more anecdotal than evidentiary, Hill decided to follow his colleagues in literary studies and Clifford Geertz.[52] He considered discourse analysis of the sentiments of journalists and readers with emphasis on the use of language and the interpretation of texts, concluding that all sources have certain 'fictive elements'.[53] A case in point is the *Illustrated Weekly of India*'s story about an Indian cricket follower offering one of his eyes to replace the eye M. A. K. Pataudi lost in a car accident. The story could have been culled from a dubious source, but it still articulates the journalist's conviction that his readers trusted the vagaries of fandom.[54] Spectators often gave cricketers unconventional gifts. Rusi Modi's double century against the Australian Services in 1945–46 was rewarded with five buns, an umbrella, a gold chain, three extemporised poetic eulogies, four fountain pens, a bottle of arrack, and a promise of a pup from an expected litter.[55] The president, Dr Rajendra Prasad, trumped everyone by gifting a stuffed tiger head to the West Indian batsman Rohan Kanhai after his epic 256 in Calcutta, and a tiger skin to the Indian bowler Subhas Gupte for taking 9 for 102 in an innings in Kanpur during the India–West Indies Test series in 1956–57.[56] The public recording made these unusual gifts spectacular and discussed by people, adding quirk to cricket's attractiveness.

In the absence of alternative sources, the newspaper turns cricket spectators into a 'people of history'. Disfranchised by the preference of scholars, sport spectators do not feature in any mainstream history of the Indian public. The history of consumption of culture in India has so far trained a cyclopean sight on cinema and manufactured goods.[57] Indian sport followers stand next to historical actors but outside written history itself as subjects having no or little impact on Indian society.[58] Hence, they have been a people without history, even though they are quite complex as a hierarchised, politicised, gendered community. According to the anthropologist Michel-Rolph Trouillot, people become historical in three distinct capacities as agents, actors and subjects.[59] Agents play out the role ascribed to their class, such as servants providing labour, mothers taking care of the household and journalists reporting events. Actors are not such a constrained category; they execute a plethora of activities depending upon situational specificities in time and space, such as individual resentment among fans snowballing into collective violence. Subjects are aware of their participation in making history, as journalists and some spectators do when experiencing a landmark performance. A typical example is the journalist Amitabha Choudhury's verbose outpour after India defeated England in 1973, 'I witnessed neither what transpired in Dhaka on 16 December 1971 nor the approach of Genghis Khan's victorious soldiers to Delhi, but the people's euphoric dash towards the pavilion gave me a visual impression.' Commenting on the spectator's agency, Choudhury added, 'Every spectator had then become one with India.'[60] While journalists were deputed to participate in and document history, the public found alternative ways to appropriate cricket.

Cricket has frequently featured in Bengali and English fiction based on Calcutta and Bengal as the site of the plot. The character of Paramhansa in

Samaresh Majumdar's novel *Kalpurush* (Orion), set in the late 1970s, who spoke in the language of cricket in everyday situations, reflected the fervour of many real-life cricket followers. Not a cricketer himself, he astutely substitutes 'you should not ask me that' with 'bowling bumpers to the no. 10 batsman is not allowed' or 'it is beyond believing' with 'it was a wide ball'.[61] Later, as Animesh deliberated if he should let other relatives visit his wife Madhabilata in the hospital first, Paramhansa asked him if he was afraid to open and would like to go two down.[62] Bengali fiction is replete with similar use of cricket as a signifier of an action. The solitary South Asian Nobel Laureate in literature, Rabindranath Tagore, referred to cricket in one of his poems, the only time that he has mentioned sport in his poetic oeuvre. Syed Mujtaba Ali wrote in a novel that the town Madhuganj accepted its new police inspector, David O'Reilly, 'like a cricket match', and did not drop their level of affection in the same way as the BCCI, which would unceremoniously sack talented cricketers.[63] In Sankar's debut novel *Kata Ajanare* (So Much Unknown), the barrister Noel Barwell asked Basudeb how many newspapers he had sold, 'with the zeal of asking about a Test match'.[64] Although many authors wrote cricket stories in special issues of periodicals that came out before international matches, cricket fiction did not systematically develop outside the works of Moti Nandi.

As a social process, cricket has been an important aspect for imagining, producing and understanding culture in Calcutta. Raymond Williams considered culture, especially art and literature, to have replaced religion in the twentieth century to have become 'the deepest record, the deepest impulse, and the deepest resource' of human society.[65] The near absence of sport in his works is not surprising given the propensity of scholars towards what they consider more pressing matters of concern, though it was paradoxical as in Williams' own formulation the distinction between high and popular culture was largely rhetorical. The recognition of sport as a complex cultural form, a problem of knowledge and a material component of history has since been noticed to have developed within global academia, fulfilling Williams' prophecy about the general drift of culture. Few things disrupt the false, derisive dichotomy between cultures as potently as sport. Nobel laureates write about plebeian heroes and operas are written and dramas staged about sport.[66] Bengal was no exception, as the major cricket writers had literary backgrounds and were winners of literary prizes for their others works. Their number was small enough for one to suspect that cricket might not have penetrated the intelligentsia to the extent claimed by the press. Footballer Amal Dutta was told by his sister-in-law that sport was not part of the bounded living of Bengalis, which is why it did not feature much in literature.[67] Exceptions are few. Author Vikram Seth referred to cricket many times in his novel A Suitable Boy and based an important part of the plot in the context of the third day of the Test match between India and England at the Eden Gardens in 1952. The suitors of Lata – Amit, Haresh and Kabir – met at the ground and bonded over cricket, still unaware of each other's affections for the same woman. In addition, Seth embeds a commentary on the spectacular ambience of the stadium and the behaviour of upper- and middle-class people in the conversations of the protagonists.[68] The Bengali context thus generally contradicts Alexis Tadié's argument that sport provides authors a tool of negotiating modernity, evidencing that sport's usefulness as a tool ultimately depends on the author's motivation to apply it.[69] Since both sport and politics were figurative battles, satirists and cartoonists often presented their political message through the vocabulary of sporting action.[70] To describe Bengal politics in 1969, journalist Gour Kishor Ghosh used the form of a dramatic dialogue between radio commentators Ajay Basu and Kamal Bhattacharjee.

> Bangla Congress is playing sensibly. The opening pair has weathered the threat posed by Pramod Dasgupta and Jyotibabu ... Judging by the way Ajoybabu hit Pramodbabu's inswinger 'Bengal Congress is the representative of jotdars and Ajoybabu is their agent' through extra-cover for four, do you not think, Kamalda, that Ajoybabu has mastered the pitch of the United Front? ... Even Sushil Dhara is hitting beautiful cover drives on the back foot off Pramodbabu...I could not understand why a crafty spinner like Jyotibabu keeps bowling flighted 'jotdar, jotdar' legbreaks ... Ajoybabu is belting him all over the park in an 'I am a jotdar despite not having a single property anywhere and the person who rents out houses in Calcutta claims to be a proletariat' attitude ...[71]

Ghosh was referring to Chief Minister Ajoy Mukherjee's hunger strike at Curzon Park, now renamed Surendranath Park, in protest against his disorderly United Front colleagues, which took place days before Australia arrived for the Test match in the winter of 1969–70. United Front, a coalition of democratic, socialist and communist parties with sharp differences in approach to politics, had displaced Congress to form the state government in 1967. The coalition ran into schism early on over managing the food crisis in the state. Bangla Congress, the leading member of the coalition presided over by Mukherjee, advocated collection of food grains given voluntarily by wealthy peasants (*jotdars*) and other donors. The communist parties accused Mukherjee of colluding with upper-caste *jotdars* and not forcing them to donate enough food. Bangla Congress faced the allegation of protecting class interest throughout the next two years as the dissension between political collaborators intensified.[72] While describing Mukherjee's hunger strike on the eve of the India–Australia Test match in 1969–70, Ghosh summarised the political conflicts taking place for months in the model of a cricket match. He concluded that the Test match between Bangla Congress and the Communist Party of India (Marxist), or CPI(M), had reached a stage in which Ajoy*babu* was uneasy against googlies symbolising 'if he considers this government uncivilised then he should resign from chief ministership of this uncivilised government', referring to Jyoti Basu's call for Mukherjee to resign.[73] Such imaginative representation of political news was a staple exercise among journalists across the country.[74]

Authors found numerous social plots in the narrative of cricket. Poet Falguni Roy supported the poor's chance of upward mobility and fractured the artificial correlation of wealth and elite taste by writing, 'A cobbler/Can watch Test cricket after making shoes.'[75] Poet Nirendranath Chakravarti discovered elements of class struggle in the strategy of encouraging tail-enders to go for quick runs or sending a lower-order batsman as nightwatchman when a wicket falls in the closing minutes of play. He mocked the team's lack of interest or faith in the lower-order batsman's ability to bat, encouraging the latter to break out of his shell and respond to the opposition's conspiracy all by himself. He writes,

> Come, my boy,
> Stride out at last.
> See where they stand in ambush, left and right,
> Before, behind:
> See how they're breathing down your spine:
> Smash their conspiracy with a few good strokes.
> Come, don't be so afraid.
> Take two firm steps ahead,
> And burn with a clear flame.[76]

To protect the more established batsmen, the nightwatchman ideally plays defensively in poor light, remains not out overnight, and plays out most of the next morning when conditions favour the bowlers. The responsibility of playing for the sake of others echoed with the socialist celebration of the working class which ensured the progress of civilisation from its obscure location in the fields and factories. Chakravarti writes,

> You'd better assume, my lad, this fading day
> We're sending you, for the team's good, to the crease
> Merely to be murdered.''

Other writers showed class consciousness, political commitment and cultural understanding in different ways. Sankariprasad Basu, better known for his books on the history of religion and religious institutions in colonial Bengal, was the pioneer of cricket literature in India. His contribution could be described in the same vein as John Arlott evaluated Neville Cardus – as 'the first writer to evoke cricket; to create a mythology out of the folk hero players; essentially to put the feelings of ordinary cricket watchers into words'.[78] He joined Shibpur Dinabandhu College as a lecturer in Bengali literature in 1953 and soon started coaching the college cricket team.[79] His next workplace was the University of Calcutta, where he taught 'Radhatattva, Krishnatattva, Sakhitattva' to graduate students at the same time as writing on 'Bradman, Larwood, Hall, Ramakant Desai, Subhas Gupte' for the *Anandabazar Patrika*.[80] Primarily he wrote reflexive reports on the lifeworlds of spectators around Test matches which were later anthologised into books, additionally containing personality sketches, fictional accounts and translation of stories from world cricket. He published a total of seven books between 1960 and 1975. As a matter of fact, the first six came out within eight years, and the final book was published not separately but as an addendum to complete the two-volume omnibus of his cricket writings. Thereafter, all he wrote about cricket was a pithy critique of commercialisation that was published in a special issue of the *Desh* magazine ahead of the 1996 World Cup. Recollecting the experience of reading Basu for the first time, Prasenjit Bandyopadhyay wrote:

> Bengalis appreciated cricket as the entertainment of civilised, educated people. But numerous cricket-loving kids like me, who could not visit the cricket ground at will, had to satisfy the craving by listening to radio commentary. There was no television. We received live news of cricket matches through Ajay*da*, Kamal*da*'s commentary the same way as the blind Dhritarashtra of the *Mahabharata* was kept abreast

of the Kurukshetra war by Sanjay. This was not enough. We earnestly waited for the morning newspaper, and finished reading the sports page breathlessly as soon as it arrived ... But this was not a mere journalist! The style of writing too was beyond what regular journalists were capable of. This was a new direction. This was the first time we realised that cricket could be literature.[81]

Basu shows a keen awareness of cricket's literary tradition. In the introduction to *Ramaniya Cricket* (Beautiful Cricket), he confessed to the inspiration behind the book: 'the best innings played in the long and glorious history of cricket has not come off a bat, but off a pen'.[82] This indeed evokes the famous line by E. V. Lucas, 'More mighty than the bat, the pen.'[83] He realised that cricket writings had to engage with society in order to be representative of the sport and life in general, since 'cricket is a great game because of the literature written on it. Literature develops out of life. If cricket has indeed inspired the greatest corpus of sport literature, it is only because cricket is vivacious like no other sport ... Had life been a sport, it would be cricket'.[84] The influence of Neville Cardus, Andrew Lang and Edmund Blunden is evident throughout his opus as Basu often referred to their writings and translated their phrases, within or without quotation marks. Nearly every page he wrote reflected his belief that cricket was not a game; it symbolised respectable behaviour.[85] Moreover, he attempted to resolve a number of the cultural and ideological tensions of the period, offering aesthetic solutions, which made his books a search for a morally ordered society against the background of social crisis in the 1960s. The contemporary conflict of values made recurring appearances in his writings in the form of discussions about good versus bad, amateurism versus professionalism and style versus efficiency in matters of cricket playing.

He closely watched and commented on spectators in his columns. He recognised that a Test match was an event around which a collective history was formed by public participation, though he was uncertain if the spectators themselves were aware of their agency in making history.[86] He mentioned elsewhere that an assembly with a common purpose made spectators historical characters.[87] Basu established the cricket lover as a *Homo Aestheticus* who approached cricket not as dispensable luxury, but as something essential for survival.[88] His sudden shift to writing on religion at the height of fame appears all too abrupt, which his readers interpreted variously. One of his aficionados, Prasenjit Bandyopadhyay, felt that he withdrew from cricket as cricketers became slave to money and less inclined to play their hearts out, thereby making the sport's traditions a mockery, and also because modern readers lacked the intellectual depth to understand cricket.[89] According to Nurul Anwar, his retirement was a protest against the usurpation of cricket's position by cheap forms of pleasure and its subservience to commercialism.[90] However, in an interview, Basu mundanely explained that he quit cricket writing as he felt the need to prioritise his research on the history of modern religion. Since his personality as a serious professor and researcher clashed with his other self that indulged in humour writing, he was compelled to select one over the other.[91] He stopped cricket writing as it was incompatible with the academic work that earned him a livelihood, but his reputation as a scholar of religion has not outweighed his popularity as a cricket writer.

Although Basu's discourses were derivative at their best, he expressed them with remarkable finesse in a highly accessible language. Letters from his readers bear testimony to the extent of his success. Sankar noted that the humorous pieces on cricket were the best among Basu's creations. He contends that while the works on Swami Vivekananda could be compared to the offerings of a devoted student to the goddess of learning, the cricket writings rendered prosaic realities as sheer delight, and hence possessed more cultural significance.[92] The success of his project of circulating cricket as a culture is evident from Jyotirmoy Ghosh's eulogy:

> You were the first author to realise, and practice, the truth that sport and life, in essence, embody one another. You taught us that one ought to play 'cricket' in the fields of education and culture – meaning that instead of surrendering to a principled, disciplined, honest, but tedious pedagogy, one ought to embrace those qualities with a buoyant attitude. In short, the message implicit in your cricket literature and philosophy, as I understand, is an appeal to regard sentience as one with sport as it is with human life.[93]

Following cricket was neither simply a ritual around sports nor a mirror of the society as the press alluded to, while unevenly recognising the fan's agency in history-making. Individual press narratives may come across as indeterminate representation but collective reading qualifies spectators as people with agenda whose aggregated action constitute history. There is also no denying the historical sensibility of some of the journalists, columnists, cartoonists and letter writers. The use of literature as a historical archive can evince the impact of creative writing on a public at a time when reading was considered essential for self-development. The number of reading public was sufficiently high to negate 'selection bias', which occurs when sources not statistically representative of the population are used.[94] Readers, listeners and spectators of cricket in Calcutta are categorically indistinguishable as the same people take on different roles. Although the publicness, mediated or otherwise, of reading is well acknowledged, these categories can be separated only by the notion of the interiority of reading practices. Spectatorship too was interiorised from the 1980s with the advent of television, and extremely personalised with the coming of the internet.[95] This chapter engages exclusively with the exterior, analysing the interplay of press, place and people.

CRICKET ON THE RADIO

In *Cricket Sundar Cricket* (Cricket Lovely Cricket), Basu tells the story of a person listening to an evening news bulletin on the radio. The news was full of reports of disasters such as ten thousand deaths in Bangladesh in a flood, nearly two hundred thousand people suffering from a famine in south India, an earthquake in Japan and scientists warning against nuclear fallout, which only mildly affected him. But as the news of Len Hutton's dismissal for his third consecutive score of zero was broken, he collapsed on the floor, unconscious.[96] Hutton indeed was universally idolised by cricket followers, including Nobel Laureate Harold Pinter who wrote in a strange ode, 'I saw Len Hutton in his prime/Another time/Another time.'[97] He scored three successive ducks for Yorkshire in June 1949, but the unusual string of failures did not coincide with the other catastrophes.[98] This proves that the story was imagined to show how deeply the fascination for cricket ploughed into Calcutta's mental landscape. It perfectly captured the mood around Test cricket at the time, accentuated by the radio.

In *The Long Revolution*, Raymond Williams commented on the need for sport and entertainment to be as 'real' as the need for art in the 1960s. Williams recognised the integration of art with public life in industrial societies as facilitated by the expanding mass media.[99] He acknowledged the significance of sport as an additional recreation regime, promoted largely by the television network with its regular quota of sport shows, serials and commercial advertisements, though not getting right the scale of its popularity compared to art. Radio was the only real-time provider of sports news in India in the 1960s. Unlike reading materials, radio commentary was a communal experience for most listeners, who gathered around a radio set in the house or in a public place. Such experiences validated Marshall McLuhan's description of the radio as the modern form of 'tribal horns and antique drums' which drew people together and intimately infused in them a single thought system that the recipients were free to interpret.[100] Arjun Appadurai stresses the emergence of vernacular radio commentary as the first stage of cricket's decolonisation. Running commentary started in English in 1933, delivered mostly by the maverick journalist A. F. S. Talyarkhan. The quality of English commentary declined following his retirement. Commentators in the 1950s left a lot to be desired. Every Test cricket centre appointed its own team of commentators with little regard for their knowledge and pronunciation, often resulting in disasters.

The blending of Indian linguistic idioms with English sporting vocabulary created 'a body of contact terms' and sporting, or more especially cricketing, 'pidgins', establishing a distinctively Indian position in matters of understanding the English game.[101] Commentators spoke in a language comprehensible to a constituency larger than before, increasing the public's cricket literacy, that is, competence to understand and practise the game. The socialisation of nonurban Indians into the cosmopolitan culture of cricket subverted the class dichotomy of cricket, unsettling and domesticating Englishness within an Indian cultural context. Berry Sarbadhikary recommended a panel of four commentators with good knowledge of cricket and English who would travel to every Test centre. Regular assignment would assist the commentators to master two skills necessary for fluency and accuracy – identification of players and the ability to discern every movement on the field of play.[102] The advice was never implemented, but the venues trialled commentary in the vernaculars – Hindi, Bengali and Tamil – beginning from the late 1950s.

Radio commentary in Bengali started during the Test match between India and Australia in 1959–60. It is not known whose brainchild the concept was. The idea was bold and incredulous when first proposed. Cricket's jargon had not been translated into any other language before, let alone be communicated to millions of listeners live over five days. When the programme executive of Akashvani Calcutta, Mr Mustafi, invited former cricketer Kamal Bhattacharjee to deliver cricket commentary in Bengali, the latter declined. Bhattacharjee was convinced that it was not possible to render certain cricket terms in other languages. Yet he discussed the proposal with the journalist Ajay Basu. They decided to go ahead with the idea. They practised doing commentary at the local Aryan (now Howrah Union) club ground a week before the Test match was to start. It was decided that Basu would introduce the match to listeners and speak about the ground, pitch, spectators, gallery and ambience, while Bhattacharjee would tackle the technical aspects of play. Pushpen Sarkar helped them with scores and statistics. He joined as a commentator during the Test match against Pakistan in 1960–61. All of them understood cricket very well and complemented one another.[103] The experiment was an instant success. Bengalis took to radio commentary so earnestly that they carried transistor sets into the stadium, for it helped them to understand the play.

The commentators were very different from one another. Bhattacharjee was so emotive, entertaining and confident that even his bloopers sounded incredibly humorous.[104] On the second day of the India–Pakistan Test match in 1960, a dog scampered into the field while M. L. Jaisimha and Abbas Ali Baig were at the wicket. Bhattacharjee speculated if Jaisimha had told the dog that it had shown them many tricks, and it was time to leave and let them show some.[105] Sometimes he locked himself in a mode of reminiscence, losing track of the match. His slip-ups have inspired legends such as failing to notice Ken Barrington's half-century and continuing with his story as if nothing had happened.[106] Incidentally, Barrington scored 14 and 3 in the only Test match he ever played in Calcutta, in 1961–62. On the contrary, Sarkar was effortless and precise in description. If Bhattacharjee said there had been a lot of rain on the ground, Sarkar would say,

> It has been raining since the morning. The sky has cleared but the cloud cover not dispersed, so rain is still a possibility. Desai starts his run-up, now he bowls. It is pitched outside off stump and Hanif leaves it. No run taken. The score remains unchanged. 104 for 2.[107]

The extent of their success can be estimated from anecdotes. Biplab Dasgupta and Pradeep Roy met an Assamese couple on their way to Darjeeling. The man said that they enjoyed Bengali commentary. Pahari Sanyal once told Kamal Bhattacharjee that he was not going to the ground, so Kamal was the hope.[108] Spectators often took a radio inside to listen to the expert analysis of what they had observed, eliciting criticism from journalists about their knowledge and understanding of cricket.[109] When New Zealand played a Test match in Calcutta in 1965, one journalist wrote that Ajay Basu's voice sounded like an oracle in its gravity and depth.[110] In the 1970s the public started demanding radio commentary of the matches played abroad, and were joined by several newspapers which hoped that the authorities would arrange for commentary.[111] Moloy Bose and Chayan Mitra profusely admired the quality of Bengali commentary in their letters to the editor of *Jugantar*.[112] Yet the CAB seemed to have little regard for the Bengali commentators whom they initially allocated a small space inside the scoreboard. Basu and his colleagues would climb up a ladder to get inside the tiny seating space. There would be no washroom and water. The situation slightly improved when they were shifted to the top tier of the B. C. Roy Club House in the 1970s. Exposed to the wind blowing from the north, directly under the sun for the better part of the day and full of the gallery's noise, this space was very uncomfortable too. People at the stadium listening to the commentary shouted if they noticed any mistake from the commentators. Their remarks were often caught on the microphone along with the usual profanities.[113] The matches played in other Indian cities were broadcast from Delhi on the Calcutta B channel.

Bhattacharjee and Basu successfully translated much of cricket's glossary into Bengali. They coined phrases such as *jhuliye bawl* (swing), *khato lengther bawl* (short-pitched delivery), *mapa lengther bawl* (good-length delivery) and *jhnata mar* (sweep), which became popular with listeners. They often fumbled for the appropriate word and made inane mistakes but recovered quickly to adapt to the requirements. They were selective about the words to be translated. Nouns for fielding positions, most of the batting strokes and bowling techniques were not changed; only the adjectives were. Bengali listeners would be confused with the names of fielding positions such as gully, which was the Bengali word for a narrow lane. A puzzled woman, listening to radio commentary while watching the match at the Eden Gardens, asked her husband, 'They are saying that someone is standing in the gully, but where is the gully in the field?' The husband replied nonchalantly, 'Must be somewhere. Watch the play, leave the gully alone.'[114] Ten-year-old Tulumani was shocked to find out that even Test cricketers played in the gully, just as the Bulbuls, Jhunjhuns and Tuntuns of the neighbourhood did.[115] Notwithstanding the linguistic aberrations, commentaries enabled millions of Bengalis, including two aunts of the sport journalist Mihir Bose, to learn their cricket entirely from the radio.[116] Commenting on the early impact of vernacular radio commentary, Ajay Basu wrote in 1979 that Akashvani merely channelled the interest for cricket into the right course, having little idea of the emerging wave of enthusiasm for cricket on the radio.[117]

The fascination with radio commentary received a new lease of life as Berngali authors joined the admiration of the radio's reach and influence on private lives. In his column for the *Desh* magazine, Narayan Gangopadhyay wrote about his alter ego Sunanda's brush with radio commentary at the house of his cricket-loving cousins. Sunanda, a terrible cricketer in his childhood and an enthusiastic spectator afterwards, happened to visit his once-nerd cousin Bhaju*da* and his family during the India–West Indies Test match in 1966–67.[118] He found Bhaju*da*, his cardigan-knitting wife and their 12-year-old son listening intently to the radio commentary. As Sunanda applauded a four hit by Rohan Kanhai, Bhaju*da* and his wife joined in explaining that the hit was rather unconventional and risky and chiding his failure to visualise the shot. The sister-in-law's knowledge of cricket absolutely shocked Sunanda. The new, postcolonial household was significantly more liberal towards allowing women to evolve beyond their traditional roles as silent consumers. The liberalism was arguably complemented by the fact that listening to the radio or reading newspapers increased women's knowledge without them having to shed domestic inhibitions and go out in the public. The embargo on public appearance was to change soon, which was foretold by the sister-in-law's daughter storming into the room, yelling about the bet she and her friend had wagered on the outcome of the match. At one stroke, the male privilege of public gambling over sport crumbled. The family's aggressive passion for cricket led Sunanda to wonder how the commentators managed to instil in listeners such bloodlust while talking about a boring contest. Such occurrences of a family bonding over a sport or girls' freedom to use money were not too unfamiliar but were being articulated for the first time.

The high degree of Bengali translation of cricket vocabulary and other ancillary issues of delivery came under criticism from various quarters. Ajay Basu was afraid that if he made mistakes, even his wife would criticise him, saying, 'Huh, relay in Bengali! Listen to English commentary, so fluently they speak.'[119] Basu might have faced criticism from the Anglophiles among Bengalis. He describes this fictitious scenario of a household in *Akashe Cricket Bani* (Cricket on the Radio), in which an Anglicised Bengali, who stayed in India perhaps out of pity for his motherland, was so irritated by the Bengali commentary coming out of the kitchen that he asked his wife, 'How often have I told you, that betrays taste, for heaven's sake tune it to English! *Mapalength, khato-length, soja char, chakka, jhulonto ball, thuke diyechen*, oh intolerable! Stop that *jhyata mar*, sweep them out of here.'[120] Other people asked him, 'So which sari have you draped around outswing and square cut?'[121] In *Phire Phire Chai* (Looking Back), an anthology of his articles, the comment was attributed to a football spectator who asked about the colour of the sari covering terms such as goal and free kick.[122] Still, Basu noted with an air of relief that the tendency among some of the English-educated Bengalis to despise their mother tongue was on the wane.

People more sympathetic to experiments, such as Sujit Mukherjee, offered alternative models of translation. He criticised the non-translation of English nouns, asking for vernacularisation of every term, including 'batsman' and 'bowler'. He admitted that people would laugh at the translation of 'batsman' as *batpurush* or *taktamanush*, but urged journalists to try using such words, hoping that continuous application would regularise use. Marathi and Hindi commentators experimented with such overall translation, which did not sound as funny as the Bengali derivative.[123] His ideas were called ludicrous by two readers of the magazine.[124] Mukherjee disliked the use of honorific inflections when talking about cricketers, contrary to the use of far more informal salutation when people spoke about cricket at an everyday level.[125]

The supremacy of the radio subsided with the advent of television in the mid-1970s. The government instituted a community telecast system to enable school and college students to watch the Test match between India and West Indies in 1974–75. The Electronics Corporation of India loaned 250 television sets free of cost to the state government. Twelve sets were returned, six due to poor connectivity as their locations fell in 'shadow' areas and six as the organisers failed to control the crowd. The largest gathering was around the television set at the Press Club tent. The information and technology minister, Subrata Mukherjee, stated that 40,000 people thus watched the match.[126] At the same time, the lack of innovation in radio commentary and the use of the same rhetorical devices by the same team for over a decade bored the public. They started to find Kamal Bhattacharjee's chitchats irrelevant to the match and an attempt to conceal his shortcomings in ball-by-ball commentary. During India's tour of Pakistan in 1978, he exclaimed in horror as the corpulent Bishen Bedi took the ball after a thrashing from Zaheer Abbas, saying, 'Here comes Bedi again. Is this a bowler, or a road-roller?'[127] The commentators often missed important events as they were busy in gossiping. Their selective translation of cricket's glossary and inclination to use literary motifs to describe match situations were now considered illogical.

Moreover, people complained that they made shocking mistakes that anybody listening to commentary at the stadium would understand. The commentators confused square cut with square drive, changed a batsman's forward glance to sweep and once described a genuine outside edge from Sunil Gavaskar as a skilful deflection towards third man.[128] Cricketers such as Shute Banerjee made surprisingly inane mistakes while commentating. It was said that he did not pay sufficient attention to the proceedings. Once, as Jim Higgs resumed his unfinished over from the last day's play, Banerjee wondered why the captain started the morning with him, having forgotten that the bowler was in the middle of an over.[129] The new generation of commentators, Dilip Roy and Rathin Mitra, made numerous mistakes such as stating India's score as 187 when it was 127, and failing to notice that Yashpal Sharma was bowled and instead declaring a four when the ball, deflected after hitting the stumps, raced to the boundary.[130]

The standard of commentary generally fell throughout India in the late 1970s. English commentary was under perennial criticism for poor pronunciation and inaccurate description of cricket's techniques. In a letter to *Sportsworld*, Dr Ratnakar Behera from Berhampore singled out Madras's Balu Alaganan and Parthasarathy, Bangalore's P. Anand Rao, Delhi's Raj Singh and Bombay's Vijay Merchant for criticism. V. Ramakrishnan from Madras (now known as Chennai) mentioned commentators using wrong phrases such as 'first debut' and 'returned back to the pavilion', wondering if a team comprising the more competent Dicky Rutnagar, Pearson Surita, Narottam Puri and Anand Setalvad for an entire Test series would be too much to ask. Subroto Chatterjee from Calcutta pointed out several inconsistencies in Bengali commentary such as 'extra cover drive' and 'extra cover boundary', terms which did not exist in cricket vocabulary, and not announcing the score sometimes for up to 10 minutes at a stretch. Delhi's Amit Agarwal thought that the Hindi commentators were the worst; they spoke nonsense and presented a lopsided view of the events. Idiosyncratic commentary inspired Prakash Iyer from Bombay to write:

> It's hockey they imagine when cricketers bowl
> A wicket falls, and they seem to shout 'goal'!
> The English folks are double as bad
> The dreary expert drives me mad
> In the absence of eloquence these statistics they show off
> They can't even distinguish midwicket from midoff![131]

The appeal of radio commentary grew stronger throughout the 1980s despite the public's reservations about its quality. The access to televised cricket was circumscribed by the whims of officials until satellite television proliferated in the 1990s. Even then people on the move had no alternative to radio to keep in touch with the match's progress. Strangers interacted to know cricket news, students listened to commentary between classes, and communities bonded over radio sets. Bengali radio commentary was started with the aim to initiate people into the cult of cricket, stoking their interest in the game's intricacies. Although it developed new consumers and anchored the circulation of cricket, its legacy is the production of a public attuned to collective behaviour. Forms of socialisation through the radio did not readily disappear after it was discontinued in the 2000s; its form changed as the tradition was kept alive by community television and later by online forums.

CONCLUSION

The chapter explored the setting and structure of press writings and radio commentary on cricket, especially of the sport's significance in the life of the author, the reader and the listener. To unpack cricket's place in everyday life, it draws out the mundane interplay of cricket and society outside the context of international cricket matches. As a cultural text firmly entrenched in society, cricket and its myriad manifestations shaped the sport's self-representation within the imagined communities of followers and other geopolitical entities. Arguing that these texts did not simply reproduce the widely held sense of cricket at a given time, but actively generated a reality, this chapter counterposes two historical sensibilities – the one that favours the possibility of finding evidence in fiction and the one that maintains fiction's inventedness. It addresses the ancillary problematic of textual meanings being always in flux and contingent upon the reader's cognitive ability. Through an interpretation of the organisation, function and performance of language, this chapter examined the importance of the media in the formation of sporting culture.

The chapter considered a small section of cricket writings in the press and in popular literature. The key figure of this domain was undoubtedly Moti Nandi. He broke new ground in sports journalism through a pioneering harmonisation of technical analysis and literary flair in match reporting, breaking away from Sankariprasad Basu's intense lituratisation and the mundane descriptive style of most other journalists. He is better known for his sport novels for young readers. I discussed *Nanida Not Out* in the earlier chapter. His other cricket-related novels such as *Jibon Ananta, Buro Ghora, Aloukik Dilu* and the ones with the schoolgirl cricketer Kalabati as the protagonist are rich in his reflections on the Bengali society's idiosyncratic attachment to the English game. Besides, these project cricket as a site in which class and gender relations were redefined and reshaped. Cricket gave the upper and middle classes a powerful resource to consolidate their social and cultural hegemony, take ownership of their class identity, and spread their social philosophy. Nandi's cricket writings were part of an eclectic oeuvre of novels based on football, atheletics, boxing, tennis and many other sports, all of which need to be considered for unpacking his aesthetic examination of the ideological foundations of modern Bengal. Therefore, the chapter did not delve into an analysis of Nandi's cricket writings in isolation.

NOTES

1. John M. Gale and Michael Davie, 'An Afternoon at Lord's', *The Observer*, 27 June 1954, 3.
2. Moti Nandi, 'Cricket Ke Mukti Dewa Hok' (Liberate Cricket), *Betar Jagat* (1–15 January 1975), reprinted in *Khelasangraha* (Calcutta: Deep Prakashan, 2015), 38.
3. Sankariprasad Basu, *Not Out*, in *Cricket Omnibus II*, 84–262 (Calcutta: Mandal Book House, 1976), 173.
4. Oshtabokro, 'Anyo Chokkhe' (Different Angle), *KA* 2, no. 8 (16 June 1978): 11.
5. Umberto Eco, 'Sports Chatter', in *Travels in Hyperreality: Essays*, trans. William Weaver, 159–65 (San Diego: Harcourt, Inc: 1986).
6. Ibid., 162.
7. Rod Brookes, *Representing Sport* (London: Arnold, 2002), 38.
8. Tony Mason, 'All the Winners and the Half Times ...', *Sport in History* 13, no. 1 (1993): 3–13, 3.
9. Michael Oriard, *Reading Football* (Chapel Hill: University of North Carolina Press, 1993), 59–60.
10. The impact of media on sport started to be explored in the 1970s. A. Famaney-Lamon and F. Van Loon, 'Mass Media and Sports Practice', *International Review for the Sociology of Sport* 13, no. 4 (1978): 37–45; Susan Birrell and John W. Loy, 'Media Sport: Hot and Cool', *International Review*

for the Sociology of Sport 14, no. 5 (1979): 5–18. Sut Jhally's work in the 1980s initiated the 'sport/media complex' debate, which rapidly grew into a vast body of literature on the dynamics of textual circulation in sporting culture. Jhally, 'The Spectacle of Accumulation: Material and Cultural Factors in the Evolution of the Sports/Media Complex', *Insurgent Sociologist* 12, no. 3 (1984): 41–57.

11. Eduardo P. Archetti, 'The Meaning of Sport in Anthropology: A View from Latin America', *European Review of Latin American and Caribbean Studies* 65 (1998): 91–103, 93.

12. Oriard, *Reading Football*, 17.

13. Richard Holt and Tony Mason, *Sport in Britain 1945–2000* (Oxford: Blackwell, 2000), 94.

14. Ibid., 177.

15. John Bale, *Sport, Space and the City* (London and New York: Routledge, 1993), 59–64.

16. Alina Bernstein and Neil Blain, eds., *Sport, Media and Culture: Global and Local Dimensions* (London: Routledge, 2002), 1.

17. Lawrence A. Wenner, ed., *Media, Sports, and Society* (Newbury Park, CA: Sage, 1989); Lawrence A. Wenner, ed., *MediaSport* (London and New York: Routledge, 1998).

18. Joseph Maguire, 'The Global *Media-Sport* Complex', in *Global Sport: Identities, Societies, Civilizations*, 144–75 (Cambridge: Polity Press, 1999); David Rowe, *Sport, Culture and the Media: The Unruly Trinity*, 2nd ed. (Maidenhead: Open University Press, 2004), 4.

19. Neil Blain, Raymond Boyle and Hugh O'Donnell, eds., *Sport and National Identity in the European Media* (Leicester: Leicester University Press, 1993); Richard Haynes, *The Football Imagination: The Rise of Football Fanzine Culture* (Aldershot: Arena, 1995); Aaron Baker and Todd Boyd, eds., *Out of Bounds: Sport, Media and the Politics of Identity* (Bloomington: Indian University Press, 1997); Mark Lowes, *Inside the Sports Pages: Work Routines, Professional Ideologies, and the Manufacture of Sports News* (Toronto, Ont.: University of Toronto Press, 1999); David Rowe, ed., *Critical Readings: Sport, Culture and the Media* (Maidenhead: Open University Press, 2003); Arthur Raney and Jennings Bryant, eds., *Handbook of Sports and Media* (Hillsdale, NJ: Lawrence Erlbaum, 2006); Matthew Nicholson, *Sport and the Media: Managing the Nexus* (Oxford: Elsevier, 2007); Heather Hundley and Andrew Billings eds., *Examining Identity in Sports Media* (Thousand Oaks, CA: Sage, 2010); Cornel Sandvoss, Michael Real and Alina Bernstein, eds.,

Bodies of Discourse: Sports Stars, Media, and the Global Public (New York: Peter Lang, 2012).

20. John Goldlust, *Playing for Keeps: Sport, the Media and Society* (Melbourne: Longman Cheshire, 1987); Garry Whannel, *Fields of Vision: Television Sport and Cultural Transformation* (London: Routledge, 1992).

21. Garry Whannel, *Media Sport Stars: Masculinities and Moralities* (London and New York: Routledge, 2002).

22. Joyce Woolridge, 'Cover Stories: English Football Magazine Cover Portrait Photographs 1950–1975', *Sport in History* 30, no. 4 (2010): 523–46; Susann Baller, Giorgio Miescher and Ciraj Rassool, eds., *Global Perspectives on Football in Africa: Visualising the Game* (London and New York: Routledge, 2013).

23. Mike Huggins, 'The Sporting Gaze: Towards a Visual Turn in Sports History: Documenting Art and Sport', *Journal of Sport History* 35, no. 2 (2008): 311–29; John Hughson, 'The Cultural Legacy of Olympic Posters', *Sport in Society* 13, no. 5 (2010): 749–59; Iain Adams and John Hughson, '"The First Ever Anti-football Painting"? A Consideration of the Soccer Match in John Singer's *Gassed*', *Sport in Society* 14, no. 4 (2013): 501–14; Mike Huggins and Mark O'Mahony, eds., *The Visual in Sport* (London and New York: Routledge, 2012).

24. Michael Oriard, *King Football: Sport and Spectacle in the Golden Age of Radio and Newsreels, Movies and Magazines, the Weekly and the Daily Press* (Chapel Hill, NC: The University of North Carolina Press, 2001).

25. C. Richard King and David J. Leonard, eds., *Visual Economies of/in Motion: Sport and Film* (New York: Peter Lang, 2006); Aaron Baker, *Contesting Identities: Sports in American Film* (Urbana, IL: University of Illinois Press, 2006); Emma Poulton and Martin Roderick, eds., *Sport in Film* (London and New York: Routledge, 2009); Seán Crosson, *Sport and Film* (London and New York: Routledge, 2013).

26. Jackson and Andrews, *Sport, Culture and Advertising.*

27. Souvik Naha, 'Visually Playing Politics: Use of Sports as Political Critique in Newspaper Cartoons', in *Visual Histories of India: New Methodologies and Perspectives on South-Asian History*, ed. Annamaria Motrescu-Mayes and Marcus Banks, 209–29 (New Delhi: Primus, 2018).

28. Brett Hutchins and David Rowe, *Sport Beyond Television: The Internet, Digital Media and the Rise of Networked Media Sport* (London and New York: Routledge, 2012); Gary Osmond and Murray G. Phillips, eds., *Sport*

History in the Digital Era (Urbana, Chicago, and Springfield: University of Illinois Press, 2015).

29. Christian K. Messenger, *Sport and the Spirit of Play in American Fiction: Hawthorne to Faulkner* (New York: Columbia University Press, 1981); Michael Oriard, *Dreaming of Heroes: American Sports Fiction, 1868–1980* (Chicago: Nelson-Hall, 1982); Christian K. Messenger, *Sport and the Spirit of Play in Contemporary American Fiction* (New York: Columbia University Press, 1990); Alexis Tadié, J. A. Mangan and Supriya Chaudhuri, eds., *Sport, Literature, Society: Cultural Historical Studies* (London and New York: Routledge, 2013).

30. John Bale, Mette Krogh Christensen and Gertrud Pfister, eds., *Writing Lives in Sport: Biographies, Life-Histories and Methods* (Aarhus: Aarhus University Press, 2004); Dave Day, ed., *Sporting Lives* (Crewe: MMU Institute for Performance Research, 2011); Emmanuel Bayle and Patrick Clastres, eds., *Leaders of International Sport Organisations* (Basingstoke: Palgrave Macmillan, 2018).

31. James Pipkin, *Sporting Lives: Metaphor and Myth in American Sports Autobiographies* (Columbia, MO: University of Missouri Press, 2008).

32. Walter Benjamin, 'The Work of Art in the Age of Mechanical Reproduction', in *Illuminations*, trans. Harry Zohn, 217–51 (New York: Schocken Books, 1968), 231.

33. Chris Gaffney and John Bale, 'Sensing the Stadium', in *Sites of Sport: Space, Place, Experience*, ed. Patricia A. Vertinsky and John Bale, 25–38 (London: Routledge, 2004), 37–38.

34. Eileen Kennedy and Laura Hills, *Sport, Media and Society* (Oxford and New York: Berg, 2009), 120.

35. See Roger Chartier, 'Intellectual History or Sociocultural History? The French Trajectories', in *Modern European Intellectual History: Reappraisals and New Perspectives*, ed. Dominick LaCapra and Steven L. Kaplan, 13–46 (Ithaca, NY: Cornell University Press, 1982), 30.

36. *ABP*, 2 January 1962, 6.

37. Ibid., 6 January 1982, 1.

38. Ibid., 31 January 1993, 8.

39. Stephen Greenblatt, 'Invisible Bullets', in *The Greenblatt Reader*, ed. Michael Payne, 121–60 (Malden, MA: Blackwell, 2005), 122.

40. *KA* 3, no. 25 (9 November 1979): 18.

41. Claude Lévi-Strauss, *Structural Anthropology*, trans. Claire Jacobson and Brooke Grundfest Schoepf (New York: Basic Books, 1963), 16.

42. Adrian Wilson, 'Foundations of an Integrated Historiography', in *Rethinking Social History: English Society 1570–1920 and Its Interpretation*, ed. Adrian Wilson, 293–335 (Manchester and New York: Manchester University Press, 1993), 305.

43. Douglas Booth, 'Sport History: Modern and Postmodern', in *Making Sport History: Disciplines, Identities and the Historiography of Sport*, ed. Pascal Delheye, 71–99 (London and New York: Routledge, 2014), 76; Malcolm MacLean, 'Ambiguity within the Boundary: Re-reading C.L.R. James's *Beyond a Boundary*', *Journal of Sport History* 37, no. 1 (2010): 99–117.

44. John Hughson takes Booth to task for his unqualified criticism of 'modernist theory' and failure to situate postmodernism in the tradition of intellectual history of the twentieth century. Hughson, 'The Postmodernist Always Rings Twice: Reflections on the "New" Cultural Turn in Sports History', *International Journal of the History of Sport* 30, no. 1 (2013): 35–45.

45. The claim of historical objectivity has been demolished step by step by cultural theorists since Roland Barthes and Jacques Derrida called into question the idea of authorship, language, writing and intertextuality, and Hayden White blurred the dichotomy of fact and fiction, symbolic and actual. Historians have either accepted or rejected this sacrilege of narrative and archives, an annoyed Keith Windschuttle even giving his rebuttal the title *The Killing of History: How Literary Critics and Social Theorists Are Murdering Our Past* (New York and London: Encounter Books, 1996).

46. Jacques Derrida, *Writing and Difference*, trans. Alan Bass (London: Routledge and Kegan Paul, 1978), 2.

47. Richard Gruneau and David Whitson, *Hockey Night in Canada: Sport, Identities, and Cultural Politics* (Toronto: Garamond Press, 1993), 85.

48. According to Frank Ankersmit, a true statement's logical form contains a fixed set of properties, identifying which holds the key to understanding the accuracy of what it describes. Understanding the meaning of representation is more difficult since objects of statement and attribution are implicated in a web of language too complex to be disentangled. Frank Ankersmit, *Meaning, Truth, and Reference in Historical Representation* (Ithaca, NY: Cornell University Press, 2012), 65–66.

49. Michel Foucault, *The Order of Things: An Archaeology of the Human Sciences* (London and Routledge: 2002), 44.

50. The meaning of history depends on the historian's interpretation. Primary sources are often invested with a plethora of intentions to appear in a

particular way, which the historian needs to see through. For example, Sam Kaplan has written about how French military officials sought to construe and preserve their documentation of African ethnology as credible. Kaplan, 'Documenting History, Historicizing Documentation: French Military Officials' Ethnological Reports on Cilicia,' *Comparative Studies in Society and History* 44, no. 2 (2002): 344–69.

51. Jeffrey Hill, 'Rite of Spring: Cup Finals and Community in the North of England', in *Sport and Identity in the North of England*, ed. Jeffrey Hill and Jack Williams, 85–111 (Keele: Keele University Press, 1996), 86.

52. Jeffrey Hill, 'Anecdotal Evidence: Sport, the Newspaper Press, and History', in *Deconstructing Sport History: A Postmodern Analysis*, ed. Murray G. Phillips, 117–30 (Albany: State University of New York Press, 2006), 124.

53. Ibid., 127.

54. *IWI*, 20 August 1961, 51.

55. *Daily Mercury*, 19 January 1946, 4.

56. Rohan Kanhai, *Blasting for Runs* (Calcutta: Rupa, 1977), 27.

57. Douglas Haynes, Abigail McGowan, Tirthankar Roy and Haruka Yanagisawa, eds., *Towards a History of Consumption in South Asia* (New Delhi: Oxford University Press, 2010).

58. This should not be confused with either Albert Camus' characterisation of Meursault as an 'outsider' because he refused to lie or the anthropological concept of people and culture located 'outside of history', in which societies marginalised in the traditional high histories written by the so-called Western academic elites were described as a people with no history. This notion has come under challenge since the 1980s as anthropologists turned their attention to doing ethnography 'from below', thus giving more voice to people from the historical backwaters. Albert Camus, *The Outsider* (Harmondsworth: Penguin, 2000 [1942]), 118; Johannes Fabian, *Time and the Other: How Anthropology Makes Its Objects* (New York: Columbia University Press, 1983); George E. Marcus and Michael F. Fischer, *Anthropology as Cultural Critique: An Experimental Moment in the Human Sciences* (Chicago: University of Chicago Press, 1986).

59. Michel-Rolph Trouillot, *Silencing the Past: Power and Production in History* (Boston: Beacon Press, 1995), 23.

60. Amitabha Choudhury, 'Lokaranye Aloukik' (Miracle in the Crowd), *ABP*, 5 January 1973, 1.

61. Samaresh Majumdar, *Kalpurush* (Calcutta: Ananda Publishers, 1985), 133.

62. Ibid., 321.

63. Syed Mujtaba Ali, *Obishyashya* (Incredible), in *Syed Mujtaba Ali Rachanabali V*, 1–107 (Calcutta: Mitra O Ghosh, 1954), 9.

64. Sankar, *Kata Ajanare* (Calcutta: New Age, 1954), 299.

65. Raymond Williams, *Marxism and Literature* (Oxford: Oxford University Press, 1977), 15.

66. David Rowe, *Popular Cultures: Rock Music, Sport and the Politics of Pleasure* (London: Sage, 1995).

67. Amal Dutta, *Ghera Math Chharano Gallery* (Enclosed Ground, Unbound Gallery) (Calcutta: Bishwabani Prakashan, 1972), 91.

68. Vikram Seth, *A Suitable Boy* (London: Phoenix House, 1993), 1138–43.

69. Alexis Tadié, 'Heroes, Fans and the Nation: Exploring Football in Contemporary Fiction', *International Journal of the History of Sport* 29, no. 12 (2012): 1774–90.

70. Naha, 'Visually Playing Politics'.

71. Gour Kishor Ghosh, 'Rupdarshir Sangbad-Bhasya' (Rupdarshi's News Bulletin), *Desh* 37, no. 8 (20 December 1969), 743.

72. Bhowani Sen, *CPM's Fight against United Front in West Bengal* (New Delhi: Communist Party Publication, 1969).

73. Ghosh, 'Rupdarshir Sangbad-Bhasya', 743.

74. A report in the *Times of India* described the Rajya Sabha session during the India–Pakistan ODI match in 1987, beginning with 'the two seamers Mr Madhu Dandavate (Janata) and Mr Dinesh Goswami (AGP) kept pegging away through the week, maintaining their line and length and were occasionally relieved by spinners, Mr Jaipal Reddy (Janata) and Mr Amal Dutta and Mr Saifuddin Chowdhury (both CPM).' *TOI*, 30 March 1987, 21. Another report towards the end of the year said, 'Cricket is not the only glorious game of uncertainty popularised by Union Jackwallahs. Parliamentary democracy is another ... Now, who could believe that Mr L. K. Advani and his boys in the Rajya Sabha would emerge on the top by sunset, when in the afternoon his batsmen seemed to be struggling against the rather clever bowling of Mr N. K. P. Salve, the deputy leader of the Congress party?' *TOI*, 7 December 1987, 6.

75. Falguni Roy, 'Tinti Kabita' (Three Poems), in *Hungry Generationer Srastader Khudhartha Sankalan* (The Hungry Collection of Hungry Generation Creators), ed. Saileshwar Ghosh, 551–52 (New Delhi: Sahitya Academy, 1995), 551.

76. Nirendranath Chakravarti, 'Tail-ender', in *The King without Clothes*, trans. Sukanta Chaudhuri (New Delhi: Sahitya Akademi, 2010 [1989]), 41–42.

77. Nirendranath Chakravarti, 'Bloodshed at Dusk', in ibid., 43.

78. Christopher Brookes, *His Own Man: The Life of Neville Cardus* (London: Methuen, 1985), 6.

79. Sushanto Chattapadhyay, 'Shraddhashpadeshu' (The Honourable), in *Sankariprasad: Byakti O Sristi* (Sankariprasad: The Person and His Creation), ed. Sujata Raha et al. (Calcutta: Sankariprasad Basu Sambardhana Samiti, 2000), 67.

80. Rabindranath Bandopadhyay, 'Amar Mastermoshai' (My Teacher), in ibid., 40.

81. Prasenjit Bandyopadhyay, 'Sankari Prasad Theke Sankarida' (From Sankari Prasad to Sankarida), in ibid., 96.

82. Sankariprasad Basu, *Ramaniya Cricket* (Calcutta: Karuna Prakashani, 1961), ii.

83. E. V. Lucas, *Cricket All His Life: The Cricket Writings of E.V. Lucas* (London: Pavilion Library, 1989), 219.

84. Basu, *Ramaniya Cricket*, 15.

85. Ibid., 36.

86. Basu, *Edene Shiter Dupur*, 80.

87. Basu, *Not Out*, 172.

88. Ellen Dissanayake, *Homo Aestheticus* (New York: Free Press, 1992).

89. Prasenjit Bandyopadhyay, 'Sankari Prasad Theke Sankarida', in *Sankariprasad*, ed. Raha et al., 99.

90. Nurul Anwar, 'Sankari Prasad Basu'r Cricket Sahiya' (Sankari Prasad Basu's Cricket Writings), in ibid., 258–59.

91. Sujata Raha, 'Sakkhatkar' (Interview), in ibid., 182–83.

92. Sankar, 'Sankarida', in ibid., 6.

93. Jyotirmoy Ghosh, 'Tarun Ek Not Out Obhijatri' (A Young Undefeated Explorer), in ibid., 31.

94. David Collier, 'Translating Quantitative Methods for Qualitative Researchers: The Case of Selection Bias', *American Political Science Review* 89, no. 2 (1995): 461–66, 462.

95. Walter Benjamin draws attention to the growing compartmentalisation of bourgeois life into public and private in nineteenth-century Paris. The interior was a safe, sanitised space shorn of the everyday hassles of occupation and commerce. Benjamin, 'Paris, Capital of the Nineteenth Century', in *The Arcades Project*, trans. Howard Eiland and Kevin McLaughlin (Cambridge, MA: Belknapp Press, 1999), 8–9. The distinction collapsed in Naples, where the private was entrapped in the public, existence

was collective. Benjamin, *Reflections: Essays, Aphorisms, Autobiographical Writings*, trans. Edmund Jephcott (New York: Schocken Books, 1986), 171. Indian interiors can be somewhat understood as a mingling of the Parisian and Neapolitan interiors, straddling the internal and the external with a fair amount of colonial mimicry, but they have been always anachronistic with European notions of the domestic. The interior plays a constructive role in an individual's life. Historians of India have explored this function in connection with women's place, drawing rooms and eating in the colonial household and the consumption of television in postcolonial times, with little attention given to the materiality of reading, indoor games, gossiping and such. Rosinka Chaudhuri, 'Modernity at Home: The Nationalization of the Indian Drawing Room, 1830–1930', in *Interpreting Homes in South Asian Literature*, ed. Malashri Lal and Sukrita Paul Kumar, 221–40 (New Delhi: Pearson Longman, 2007); Utsa Ray, *Culinary Culture in Colonial India: A Cosmopolitan Platter and the Middle-Class* (New Delhi: Cambridge University Press, 2015).

96. Sankariprasad Basu, *Cricket Sundar Cricket*, in *Cricket Omnibus II* (Calcutta: Mandal Book House, 1976 [1963]), 62.

97. Harold Pinter, *Collected Poems and Prose* (New York: Grove Press, 1996), 51.

98. Gerald Howat, *Len Hutton: A Biography* (London: Kingswood Press, 1988).

99. Raymond Williams, *The Long Revolution* (Harmondsworth: Penguin, 1965 [1961]), 364.

100. Marshall McLuhan, *Understanding Media: The Extensions of Man* (New York: McGraw-Hill), 261.

101. Arjun Appadurai, 'Playing with Modernity: The Decolonization of Cricket', in *Modernity at Large: Cultural Dimensions of Globalization*, 89–113 (Minneapolis: University of Minnesota Press, 1996), 100–02.

102. Berry Sarbadhikary, *My World of Cricket* (Calcutta: Cricket Library, 1964), 240–41.

103. Biplab Dasgupta, 'Tin Kingbadanti' (Three Legends), in *Kolkata Betar, 1927–1977* (Kolkata Radio, 1927–1977), ed. Bhabesh Das and Prabhatkumar Das, 487–94 (Calcutta: Purbanchal Sanskriti Kendra, 2011), 487.

104. Ibid., 488.

105. Ibid., 489.

106. Shibaji Dasgupta, 'Tafat Onek' (Very Different), *Saradiya Khela 1997*, 70.

107. Dasgupta, 'Tin Kingbadanti', 491.

108. Ibid., 489.

109. *ABP*, 4 February 1964, 7.

110. *Jugantar*, 6 March 1965, 6.
111. Ibid., 24 February 1971, 6.
112. Ibid., 5 March 1971, 6.
113. Pushpen Sarkar, 'Bangla Khelar Dharabibaran: Onek Badha', *KA* 3, no. 28 (30 November 1979): 34.
114. *ABP*, 4 February 1964, 7.
115. Ajay Basu, *Akashe Cricket Bani* (Calcutta: Falguni Prakashani, 1971), 2–3.
116. Mihir Bose, *A History of Indian Cricket* (New Delhi: Rupa, 1990), 219.
117. *Jugantar*, supplementary, 25 October 1979, 1.
118. Narayan Gangopadhyay, 'Paribarik Cricket' ('Cricket in the Family'), in *Sunandor Journal* (Calcutta: Mitra O Ghosh, 2002), 487–88.
119. Basu, *Akashe Cricket Bani*, 1.
120. Ibid., 8.
121. Ibid., 8–9.
122. Ajay Basu, 'Chhai Felte Bhanga Kulo' (Broken Winnow to Dispose Ash), in *Phire Phire Chai* (Calcutta: Aajkal, 2005), 54.
123. Sujit Mukharji, 'Byater Ami Baller Tumi' (The ABC of Cricket), *KA* 3, no. 47 (11 April 1980): 22–23.
124. Ibid., 4, no. 2 (8 May 1980): 16.
125. Sujit Mukherjee, *Between Indian Wickets* (New Delhi: Orient Paperbacks, 1976), 138–39.
126. *ABP*, 3 January 1975, 6.
127. Abheek Barman, 'Before Cricket Became WWE', *TOI*, 8 February 2015, 8.
128. *KA* 3, no. 32 (28 December 1979): 39.
129. Ibid., 3, no. 27 (23 November 1979): 11.
130. Ibid., 3, no. 28 (30 November 1979): 36.
131. 'Letters to the Editor', *Sportsworld* (5 December 1979), 3–4.

3 The Making of a City of Cricket

Last month [November 1974], there was a debate on the food situation in the state Assembly – a listless debate … The quorum was frequently lacking when the discussion on the food position was on. Immediately following the debate on food, someone raised the issue of allocating a quota of test match tickets for the MLAs; the Food Minister, who is also the Sports Minister, rose once more to speak on the question in his latter capacity; suddenly, there was a rush of incoming members; the Assembly was brimming to the full. The Sports-cum-Food Minister, kindly soul, unable though he is to provide food to the poor who die in their thousands, was generosity unbound. Per MLA he was prepared to allot a quota of five tickets. Pandemonium in the House; no, no, we demand justice, we must have at least 25 to 30 tickets each; the members of the Assembly could not be more conscious of their prerogatives – and of their social responsibilities. Their constituents may die for lack of food; that is no matter; ticket for the cricket test match is an altogether different proposition, truly a matter of life and death. They must be given at least 25 tickets, each one of them, or else West Bengal would once more be brought to the brink of revolution. The Food-cum-Sports Minister, ever responsive to the stirrings of emotions at the grassroots, pacifies them: he relents, and straightaway assures them an initial quota of 10 tickets; he also promises to talk to the Cricket Association of Bengal so that the MLAs could get some more tickets before the test match starts. The revolution is averted, the MLAs cheer the Sports-cum-Food Minister, they chair him, wish him long life.[1]

This magic realist tale of tickets recounted by CPI(M) politician Ashok Mitra in his 'Calcutta Diary' column for the *Economic and Political Weekly* was bizarre and yet too familiar. Exaggerating the hunt for tickets to the India–West Indies Test match in 1974–75, Mitra mocked the habit of ministers to request, cajole, pressurise or threaten people to obtain those articles of prestige. West Indies had routed India in Bangalore and Delhi to go 2–0 up in the series. Interest in the match was high as people expected India to win and reduce the deficit just as they did against England in 1972–73. Organising the match was so important for the Congress-led West Bengal government that Chief Minister Siddhartha Sankar Ray, a former club cricketer, asked three ministers to camp at the stadium and supervise the preparation for the match.[2] In the end, Food and Sport Minister Prafullakanti Ghosh appeared to break the promise of tickets. He might not, however, have made the promise, as the Assembly Proceedings did not record the exchange mentioned by Mitra.[3] West Bengal was going through a food crisis at the time; 2.5 million people were on dry dole, 300,000 were served through gruel kitchens and 250,000 survived on cheap canteens.[4] Managing his responsibilities as ministers for sport and food could not have been easy for Ghosh. As the Centre had repeatedly rejected requests for assistance, the state had to dig deep into its resources.[5]

When the Test match began, as a result of Ghosh's 'betrayal', a minister turned up at the gate with just one ticket and demanded admission for both himself and his wife. As the guard at the pavilion gates refused to admit two persons on one ticket, the furious minister threatened to summon his strongmen. The President of India, Fakhruddin Ali Ahmed, showed more responsibility by returning the 33 complimentary passes given to his companions.[6] Many people bought counterfeited lottery coupons from black marketeers, and about 350 of them were caught and denied tickets. A demonstration was staged in front of the CAB office and later a four-member delegation sent to Chief Minister Ray's office in protest. Five persons were arrested for selling forged lottery coupons before the match.[7] The price of tickets was increased by 20–75 per cent from the previous Test match. The correspondent of the *Desh* magazine felt that the state government should not have approved the hike considering the CAB was financially stable and the Centre had kept commodity prices fixed for several years.[8] The police arrested a total of 86 persons for selling counterfeit tickets.[9] As newspapers would report, most people in the state were vying for a precious ticket. For people in power such as politicians and high-ranking civil servants, the ability to obtain, distribute or gift tickets was also a demonstration of prestige. The way one obtained a ticket showed one's character. In 1996, to malign Police

Commissioner Tushar Talukdar, former Deputy Commissioner of Police Runu Guha Neyogi alleged that Talukdar used to watch cricket without valid passes in the 1970s. Once, when then Police Commissioner Nirupam Som asked him to check Talukdar's pass, Neyogi obtained a pass from Congress Member of Legislative Assembly (MLA) Ambika Banerjee to save his colleague.[10] He brought up the issue of tickets after two decades to remind people how corrupt his former colleague was.

Through a study of the creation of cricket and the city's main cricket stadium as a niche for emotions, entertainment and commerce, this chapter probes the making of a community based on ties of leisure. The idea of such an emotional community is unique and helps us to think beyond the extensive scholarship on communities built around village, caste or religion. It will also enable us to reassess the traditional identifiers of community-feeling, such as 'bonds of territoriality, language, culture, tradition and religion' and, as Gyan Prakash argues in the Indian context, 'a common essence', 'a shared substance' or 'an inherent togetherness' articulated chiefly through nationalist political discourses of nationhood.[11] The research on community-building in India has followed two major trajectories. On the one hand, scholars such as Sudipto Kaviraj, Partha Chatterjee, Dipesh Chakraborty, Nicholas Dirks, Prakash, and so on, have explored the political constitution of colonial communities showing how they drew strength from their own cultural distinctiveness and created collective identities and traditions both in opposition to and appropriating coercive Western norms of community and history.[12] On the other hand, Douglas Haynes's 'moral community' approach to understanding a society divided among a set of individuals who judged one another through a shared vocabulary, or Sandria Freitag's work on the cultural roots of political violence between Hindu and Muslim communities and Rajat Kanta Ray's analysis of Indian communities of sentiment highlight the historical role of emotions in shaping communities outside the intervention of modern nation-states.[13] This chapter expands this extensive literature by introducing cricket – a nascent and strange foreign import that few Indians were very familiar with until the 1950s – as an emotion generating complex cultural and personal engagements with the spaces of the sport. The previous chapters have discussed some of the shared substances such as bonds of culture and language that assembled people around cricket. This chapter analyses territoriality and tradition, mainly through examining how people watched cricket, built a connection with the space of play, communicated and kept alive their sense of belonging to a built environment and, finally, how the gradual decentring of their commitment to the Eden Gardens reflect the transition in how people consumed leisure.

CRICKETSCAPE

The journalist Berry Sarbadhikary called the Eden Gardens the 'Worcester of the East,' probably because of the comparable greenery, riverside location and high spires of the Calcutta High Court and the Worcester Cathedral in the background. Established in 1864, the Eden Gardens is the second oldest cricket ground in the world with a record of continuous play.[14] It is the only international cricket stadium in West Bengal and was the only venue in Eastern India until the Keenan Stadium in Jamshedpur hosted an India–West Indies ODI on 7 December 1983 and the Nehru Stadium in Guwahati another on 17 December 1983 as part of the BCCI's expansion plan. Colonial Calcutta had two other notable cricket grounds. One was Natore Park in Ballygunge, where the team of Jagadindra Nath Roy, the Maharaja of Natore, practised and played against invited teams. At the time Ballygunge was difficult to reach from the 'native' quarters of North Calcutta, with little public transport link aside from an infrequent train service from Sealdah. The remoteness meant elite people with private vehicles were the main spectators at the ground, which existed for 14 years before being sold after the end of the First World War. The other ground was Woodlands in Alipore, maintained by the Maharajas of Cooch Behar – Nripendra Narayan Bhup Bahadur, his sons Victor Narayan and Hitendra Narayan, and grandson Jagaddipendra Narayan – until princely states were abolished after independence.[15] This is where the Bengal Gymkhana played its first match in 1911 against the Maharaja of Kashmir's team. These were the grounds frequented by Indians in Calcutta for watching cricket, as cricket in the *maidan* was mostly an affair for Europeans.[16]

From its humble beginning at a corner of the vast expanse of the *maidan*, the Eden Gardens developed into a concrete bowl in the centre of the city, reflecting the evolving organisation of local leisure. It represents the characteristics of modern stadiums, which geographer Chris Gaffney identifies as 'monuments, places for community interaction, repositories of collective memory, loci of strong identities, sites for ritualised conflict, political battlefields, and nodes in global systems of sport'.[17] Some academics consider a stadium a non-ideological space separated from the real world, inside which athletes are identified by their physical performance and the audience becomes a hyperactive body of gestures.[18] On the contrary, years of active participation mould spectators' unique logic of practice. A stadium visit often takes the form of pilgrimage. Frequent visits become part of a spectator's sense of routine and pride, encapsulating one in the process of making history. An individual spectator is often part of a larger group of friends, club mates or people met during the match. The norm of spectatorship is one of unity of purpose among the crowd, emotional bonding with the players representing the crowd and the sport space. Tales of people's association with the ground test the elasticity of belief sometimes, such as the story of Amar Chatterjee.

Chatterjee played football for Bali Dakkhinpara Sammilani and Howrah Pragati Sangha before the famous scout Bhutnath Biswas had him join the first division club Khidirpore in 1967. After two years with the club, he took up a job with the state government's physical education department on sports quota. He was posted as a security guard at the Eden Gardens. He stayed in staff quarters beneath the gallery with his wife and three daughters. He fell so much in love with the stadium that he could not live outside it for more than one or two days, so he stopped taking holidays. He patrolled the roads running along the boundary until late night, often striking his baton on the road to announce that he was awake. Not one to be distracted from his mission, he refused job offers made by the Bihar cricketer Daljit Singh for TATA and Sailen Manna for the Geological Survey of India.[19] This is extreme, topophilia – a deep love of place, as Yi-Fu Tuan notes – generated by participation.[20] Intense love for sport and its venue drives much of the appeal for spectator sport. Repeated participation fosters the sense of belonging to a place, inducing one to create history rather than just be a witness. The crowd thus created is a 'historic product' with its own rationale of action and volition.[21] A space for the mediated public to enact their subjecthood was contingent on the practice of creating the public.

The first chapter showed how Bengali authors designed a pastoral identity for the Eden Gardens to bring Indian cricket closer to its English roots. The social relations generated in a stadium depend very much on how spectators perceive the place, a process in which the press comes into play. Perception largely influences action, or practice, which according to Michel de Certeau reinvent a place as a space.[22] The Eden Gardens became a 'space' when spectators periodically appropriate the system of watching, replete with the rituals of reading reports, buying tickets, going to the ground, watching the match and/with fellow spectators, and leaving for home. Interruption in the order, such as shortage of ticket, created a panoply of possibilities for spectators to individually or collectively organise the normative, such as buying a ticket from the black market and taking seats elsewhere than are allocated to them. The existing order having been disrupted, which happened too frequently, spectators could inscribe their own experience-driven sense of space onto the stadium place. Such re-contextualisation transcribed the physical, inanimate, fixed place of the Eden Gardens into a cultural, lived, mobile space for cricket watchers A concatenation of spatial encounters over time, full of memories and symbolic meanings, engaged spectators and the press in the production of identities of both the people and the stadium.

Events create followers who socially construct and maintain a normative sense of public space while trying to accommodate fellow spectators in its realm of the stadium. The cricket spectators of Calcutta have remade the landscape of the Eden Gardens as a 'sportscape', a space devoted to sport and its followers, vibrant with the impact of their participation.[23] Since spectatorship is very much ideological as it is practised, perception plays a significant role in the overall experience. Perception is tied too affectingly to a civic context to have a national, let alone global, explanation. Alan Bairner contends that sport supports and draws meanings from national landscapes, which are a combination of the real and the imaginary sense of place.[24] The concept of national landscapes is not valid for a complex country such as India where a number of culturally distinct sporting spaces coexist. The relationship between individual and collective spaces both inside and outside the stadium follows its own logic. As Tuan says, spectators share a camaraderie despite the discomforts and anonymity of the stadium whereas a congested highway is infuriating despite the lower density of people.[25] He disregards the problems of stadium violence, but shared activities such as chanting sometimes generate rapport among strangers.

The Calcutta spectators employed two chants to unnerve the opposition – 'Baba Taraknather Chorone Seba Lagi', denoting wholehearted submission to the god Shiva for a boon, and 'Bolo Hori Hori Bol', usually uttered while taking the deceased to a crematorium. The first chant started in the 1950s to accompany Putu Chowdhury's run-up and deliveries during Bengal's domestic fixtures.[26] Later it became the official incantation to get foreign batsmen out. Sometimes spectators rang bells to break the concentration of foreign batsmen when Indian bowlers failed to dislodge them. Sankariprasad Basu notes the sparing use of this tactic, not allowing opponents to get accustomed. At 1.38 p.m. on the third day of the 1960 Test match against

Australia, he writes, the crowd rang bells, causing Ray Lindwall to startle and get out to Ramakant Desai. They did not repeat the tactic for the rest of the day, saving it for the next emergency.[27] The chanting spectators were seen to have formed a counterpublic to the knowledgeable and restrained patrons. Basu addresses the cultural pluralism rather sympathetically, never once showing any disrespect for the alternative behaviour so frequently considered 'uncultured' for cricket.

The tame end to the 1960 Test match, brought about by defensive batting by the touring team, made Basu wonder if he would return for the next match.[28] He quickly realised that the sentiment of participating in a stadium event was too strong and binding to be repressed. His fictional creation P. Chowdhury was very attached to the landscape of an array of Deodar and Jhau trees that had witnessed cricket matches alongside human spectators. Personified trees became an inexorable companion to his winter afternoons. So deep was their bond that the plan of cutting down the trees to make space for more seats severely disturbed him, making him wish for death before it happened.[29] The Statesman reported in 1961, 'On the idyllic banks of the lily pool where the flowers are in bloom, or in cars parked nearby, entire families make the most of the lunch breaks.'[30] A report from 1979 noted that people missed the long shadows cast by trees in the late afternoon. The older generations told stories of beautiful trees. Although birds scurried across the grass and flew away when spectators loudly clapped or a ball raced towards them, the natural beauty of the stadium was already a thing of the past.[31] Grandfathers were often seen explaining cricket to their grandsons, making correspondents wonder if they were handing the stadium's legacy over to the future generation of cricket lovers.[32]

In his first book on cricket, journalist Soumya Bhattacharya summarised the attitude of three kinds of spectators, each of whom was the self-appointed solitary and rightful proprietor of cricket. The aristocrats occupied the members' gallery on either side of the pavilion, while the adjacent stands were for the annual and associate members. They received tickets without having to queue, and therefore were a permanent presence within the stadium and its collective history. The bourgeoisie were the public sector and corporate elites who filled the more expensive seats and hospitality boxes. They were the least respected among spectators as they used money and power to buy privilege. The working class populated the rest of the gallery, always shouting, dancing and claiming to be the most authentic fans for having to endure the hardship of queuing for tickets.[33] Much of the sports press had stopped subscribing to this tripartite division long before Bhattacharya came up with it. No specific class was ever dominant enough to define the parameters of consumption.

My encounters with several knowledgeable and long-standing spectators suggested a bourgeois drive towards self-differentiating one's class position from that of the people undervalued in highbrow society. Nevertheless, the long history of the stadium's public culture conformed to Ashis Nandy's remark that the inability of much of India's upper-middle class to dissociate from the cultural preferences of the lower-middle class led to a class indistinction in modern India, whereby the upper-middle class was a comparatively affluent lower-middle class.[34] The members' gallery, in particular, lost its sanctimony from the 1970s as people from all walks of life began to acquire tickets to the Club House and the nearby stands. The press dissented this invasion of poor taste, brought upon by the indiscretion of some of the so-called elites who sold or gifted their tickets to an illegitimate public. The criticism of 'miscreants', such as the 161 people arrested during the two semi-finals of the Hero Cup in 1993 for throwing crackers onto the field, drunken revelry and lighting a torch in the gallery, consistently referred to the erosion of culture.[35] The press appeared to gratify the incompatible appetences of various categories of spectators.

In the 1960s, people without tickets could be seen loitering around the stadium, lunching on the fruit slices and other snacks sold near the gates and approaching the spectators coming out of the gates to know the latest scores and relevant details. They listened to the shouts breaking through the wooden pavilion. Some of them claimed expertise in being able to understand from the intensity whether a boundary had been scored or a wicket had fallen.[36] Radio commentators generously acknowledged the public's emotional attachment to cricket. While delivering the news of India's win against England in 1962, the radio commentator Ajay Basu's voice choked with joy as he gushed about being part of the emotional crowd on the 'auspicious occasion'.[37] The nature of the public changed, sometimes in complete apathy to and with little regard for the rest of society that was not involved in the event. Sunil Gavaskar, not part of the team against West Indies during the 1974–75 match, noticed a singular lack of interest among doctors – who were busy watching the match – to treat his injured finger, compelling him to return to Bombay for treatment.[38] During the Test match against Pakistan in 1980, employees at five branches of the Municipal Corporation did not receive the salary for January as only one of the accountants was at work.[39] The father of the protagonist of Amit Chaudhuri's novel *A New World* complained to his son that bank employees were more interested in trade union memberships than doing their job properly and seemed to perpetually talk about cricket (or a relative's wedding) among themselves, keeping customers waiting.[40] The press was often blamed for promoting an excitement that bordered on insanity. A reader complained to the *Khelar Asar* about the damage the periodical was doing to the youth by sensationalising cricket.[41] On a different note, journalist Arijit Sen attacked inexperienced and ignorant authors for creating a hedonistic world of cricket that enthralled young people. He asked fellow journalists to behave more responsibly.[42] However, when cricket produced episodes of fanatical involvement of people, sometimes even an accurate description seemed sensationalised.

Cricket's narrative was not only about captivation. In addition to the deaths and injuries sustained during stadium violence, cricket turned out to be devastating for domestic circumstances as it usurped the mantle of the nation's destiny. The India–Pakistan ODI match in 1987 turned out to be fatal for several people. A 16-year-old student at St. Xavier's School in Burdwan committed suicide as his parents refused to let him go to the match.[43] Bimal Ghosh, executive committee member of Wari club, slumped on his way back to the club tent with fellow members and died before he could be taken to the nearest hospital. Seventy-year-old Makhan Majumdar from Chinsurah had a stroke while watching the match on television.[44] A 72-year-old social worker in Midnapore, Ganapati Basu, died of a heart attack at 9.20 p.m. when the Pakistan wicketkeeper Rashid Latif started attacking Indian bowlers during the India–Pakistan quarter-final match of the 1996 World Cup. Many of the shops were closed for business as a mark of respect. In Agartala, retired government employee Nikunja Deb suffered a heart attack when Saeed Anwar and Aamir Sohail put Indian bowlers to the sword. 'We have to win at any cost,' he said before collapsing.[45] Imbued with a patriotic energy, such deaths became resilient and even heroic, elevating the victim to a faithful champion of the nation. Patriotism offered a meaningful justification for avoidable deaths. As most victims were men, a subtext of the masculine quality of defending the nation pervaded newspaper reports, though traces of the feminine traits of care and affection for the nation were often snuck into the content. The deaths were not desirable, but commanded respect in a society where the project of the self was seldom externalised to the care for others.

In other newspaper reports, some of the fundamental problems caused by cricket for the nation's development was set apart in a binary relation to the affinity for the sport. One of these concerns was the wastefulness indulged by spectators and consumers in general. An interesting reference to consumption in the 1960s comes from an ironical estimate of the time and money people spent on the India–England Test match in 1964. According to the report, about 25 per cent of the spectators were unemployed. Over the five days, about 185,500 people skipped office and wasted 1,312,000 work-hours by going to the Eden Gardens. In addition to the eggs, *rotis*, chops, cutlets, oranges and bananas taken from home, a total of 50,000 people bought food at the stadium at a cost of no less than 2.50 rupees. Ninety per cent of the spectators drank tea, amounting to a minimum of 450,000 cups worth 67,500 rupees. Snacks of 125,000 rupees were devoured. Considering 5,000 cars were parked daily, 25,000 parking tickets were issued throughout the match. Seventy-five per cent of the spectators used trams and buses. Based on the average ticket price of 20 paisa, the transport sector could be said to have acquired 187,500 rupees over five days. Assuming 60 per cent of the spectators smoked one packet of cigarettes daily, 1,500,000 cigarettes worth 93,000 rupees were exhausted. If 25,000 people chewed two betel leaves at 20 paisa each, 25,000 rupees were spent on betel. Journalists sent telegrams compassing 116,000 words, among which 27,500 words were transmitted inside the country. Fifty thousand phone calls were made daily, making the service providers richer by 39,000 rupees. The CAB received 950,000 rupees from the sale of tickets and sponsorship, out of which 350,000 rupees were profit. In every hour 21,800 rupees and in every minute 364 rupees were spent. Forty-five thousand rupees were dispensed for the meals of the police, ticket checkers and volunteers. The Tea Board daily sponsored 500 cups of tea. Doctors profited by mending arms and legs broken in the melee, and mechanics made a killing by repairing radio sets for commentary listeners.[46] The witty narrative was both an ironic reproach to cricket enthusiasm, particularly its consumerist aspect, and an approval of the game's growth.

The options for lunch expanded in the 1970s as new eateries were set up and the number of vendors' passes increased. Newspapers would report the eating preference of people from different classes and localities. For instance, during the 1977 Test match against England, the *Amrita Bazar Patrika* reported that a bank employee from Bandel, a town 30 kilometres north of Calcutta, brought bread, butter, boiled egg, a pair of bananas and sweet. A housewife accompanying her family from Bowbazar gorged on *luchi* and *halwa*. An engineer from Regent Park in Tollygunge and his wife ate at a restaurant with a French name. Several thousand people ate at the club canteens in which prices were cheaper than at the temporary stadium stalls. The Mohun Bagan canteen daily served 2,000 spectators. Some of the posh restaurants put up stalls in which food was very expensive.[47] In 1987 the police were accused of illegally demanded food packets from vendors and beating them if they refused.[48] The quality of food inside the stadium was never satisfactory, but restrictions on bringing fruits and water bottles in the 1990s forced the public to rely more on vendors. The prohibition on bringing fruits ended the culture of throwing oranges at cricketers, which was observed as a ritual, except during the Test match against Australia in October 1979 when the seasonal fruit was not available in the market.[49] Azharuddin's century on debut in 1985 was celebrated with a barrage of oranges on the field.[50] It is surprising that the authorities took so long to realise the nuisance caused by the fruit-hurling spectators. Aside from an impressionistic criticism of public behaviour, the reports on food represented the transition in commercialising the stadium. People's growing acceptance of buying food and drink in the stadium reflected a change in their budget and ways of enjoying themselves. The earlier strictures on eating out was slackening as people gradually tended to ignore whether the preparation and storage of provisions were appropriate for their religion or class. In this way, the treatment of food betokens the emerging sociabilities in the city.

Narratives of cricket's pull became grander with the suggestion that cricket did not simply turn government employees or students away from their work, but led to a breakdown of law and order in the city. Robberies were common during cricket matches when a substantial part of the city's police force was deployed to secure the Eden Gardens, leaving many areas of the city relatively unprotected. The issue received massive coverage when, on the opening day of the India–Australia Test match in 1969, a group of robbers carried out a meticoluously planned and daring heist of the State Bank of India branch at the intersection of Park Street and Russell Street, stituated fewer than 2 kilometres in walking distance from the Eden Gardens. The timing and sheer audacity of the robbers shook the police department. As police officer Runu Guha Neyogi, infamous for illegal custodial torture of members of left-wing extremist groups, recollected in his autobiography, the entire detective department was at the ground, some on duty but most as spectators, when the public announcement system broadcast a message for them to report to the police headquarters immediately.[51] The robbers were identified as members of the Revolutionary Communist Council of India and arrested, but acquitted after years of trial for lack of evidence. Guha Neyogi's story suggests that police personnel thronged the stadium as cricket followers shirking their responsibilities. The pattern repeated itself year after year. As Calcutta watched Kris Srikkanth blitz his way to 123 against Pakistan in an ODI match in 1987, gangs of masked men robbed the Bank of India's Salt Lake branch and the United Bank of India's Mayfair Road branch taking an estimated 1.2–2.1 million rupees in cash. Most of the staff and armed guards were away watching cricket. The police suspected that the robbers took advantage of relaxed security in the city.[52] Instances of thieves using the cover of a match to break into households and shops, when people were not attentive to security, were regularly reported in newspapers. International cricket made the city unsafe.

Besides reflecting the ongoing anxieties around subsistence and security, the cricket stadium became an arena for articulating and contensting contemporary cultural practices. Tradition was an important part in the making of the cricket culture in the city. As we have seen before, cricket had generated a sense of decorum consistent with a Bengali patrimonial notion of permissible behaviour that should remain unchanged. In 1979, when the ground staff took the field in blue trousers and khaki shirts instead of the customary short *dhoti*, most journalists rued the change as a decline of tradition. While the Westernisation of Bengali clothing was increasingly accepted in the wider society, cricket remained a citadel of people who thought culture was immutable.[53] They found the 'Calypso Nights' organised by the CAB as a closing ceremony of the Asia Cup in 1991 embarrassing. The CAB eventually stopped the programme when two scantily clad young women beckoned onlookers to throw oranges while they danced. They blamed the sponsor, Videocon, for hiring this calypso group that reneged the contract of performing cricket songs set to simple tunes and clever lyrics, and did a mixture of circus, belly dance, juggling and impromptu capers backed by guitars and drums. While reporting the incident in a disapproving tone, the *Anandabazar Patrika* mentioned a Bengali person telling his wife how the dance performance ruined the excitement of the win and diminished the Eden Gardens.[54] Journalists always commented on how consistent cricket was with Bengali cultural tastes and practices. In one instance, they used the game as a siginifier of how Bengali liberalism promoted religious integration in Calcutta. The India–West Indies match in 1994 was played a day after the Bengali Hindu festival of Bhai Phonta (in which sisters put a dot of sandalwood paste on the forehead of their brothers and pray for each other's well-being). The *Anandabazar Patrika* billed the match as a celebration of the stadium giving Bhai Phonta to her brother Azharuddin.[55] A century-old stadium played the sister to a 31-year-old Muslim with a phenomenal batting record at the venue. Azhar's Test scores of 110, 141, 60 and 182 marked a special bond between the cricketer and the ground. Apart from giving a topophilic resonance to the connection, the personification of the ground pushed ahead the metaphorical perimeter of the lived world of Calcutta cricket.

Although the cricketscape outside the stadium became more complex as years passed, spectators could not take control of their field of dreams in the long run. The Eden Gardens embodied how the city's public spaces were governed and perceived, and new attributes given by a multitude of actors enriched its symbolism over the years. As a lived space, however, the stadium displayed characteristics of Henri Lefebvre's conceptualisation of a dominated space more than an appropriated space, since the CAB, sponsors and the media determined the visual imageries of the struggles and conflicts over its use.[56] Following the two riots at the Eden Gardens in the 1990s, the CAB reserved the right to search every spectator, expel one without refund, and confiscate every food and drink item, bottle, can, cigarette, lighter, musical instrument, firecrackers, heavy bags, laptop and sometimes even camera and coins. The Indian Premier League convenors increased the restriction on what could be brought inside, which included any poster or banner of a brand that competes with any of the tournament sponsors. The ground is fenced to prevent unauthorised entry, the disciplinary architecture increasing territorialisation of the arena, putting the organiser more in control.[57] A hierarchy of power has clearly developed, and social inequalities materialised as organisers and public policies sought to maintain the wider and elitist urban ideology of class. However, the Eden Gardens retained its spaceness in press narratives that functioned outside the ambit of sports governance. Both Lefebvre and de Certeau conceptualised the public as users and transformers of place, omitting from their narratives the constructive role the press might have played in mobilising a public into action. The shift of focus from the corporeal to the ideational dimensions of the stadium offers an insight into how the press understood and influenced some of the experiences of spectating.

TICKETS

Atul Mukherji, the editor of the *Khelar Asar*, was a first division cricketer when West Indies came to play a Test series in 1948–49. Equipped with 20 rupees given by his maternal aunt, he went to CAB Secretary Amarendranath Ghosh's (A. N. Ghosh) house at Mango Lane in central Calcutta where Ghosh personally sold tickets. The ticket covered both the Test and the match against the Governor's XI. Mukherji bought one. He was told before leaving, 'come back should you need more tickets'.[58] Twenty years later, during the India–Australia Test match in 1969, around 20,000 people queued before daybreak for the 7,000 day-tickets on sale, leading to a stampede, six deaths, infamy for the city's cricket administrators and end of the practice of selling day-tickets until 1993. The press mourned the deceased and expressed shock about the public's morality considering that the tragedy was quickly forgotten and the match continued without any homage to the departed.[59] What was it about cricket that made the people of Calcutta scamper for ticket, giving new meanings to the Eden Gardens as a space and writing a new handbook of collective behaviour?

In terms of the quality and breadth of content, the late 1950s represent a watershed for media attention to cricket, in which Rohan Kanhai's innings of 256 runs in a single day in 1958–59 can be claimed to have been a turning point. As international cricket piqued people's interest in attending matches, the press began pondering, sometimes amplifying, what cricket meant to them. The pot started simmering when Pakistan played in Calcutta in 1960–61. It was the first time newspapers reported people clashing with the police and queueing for tickets.[60] The pot came to a full boil as India faced England in 1961–62. Ticket distribution was now politicised so much that the editor of the *Anandabazar Patrika* compared the method of acquiring match tickets with the dismal culture of people using influential patrons, usually politicians, to ensure success in school admission, government job or hospital admittance. Cartoons reflected the desperation of watching the match by showing, for example, a person asking an acquaintance, who was carrying a large holdall, if he was travelling out of Calcutta. The second person responded that he was going to queue outside the Eden Gardens. Another cartoon showed two cold passers-by enjoying the heat generated by a scuffle for tickets. In a third cartoon, a trader sold tickets for seats on the branches of a tree next to the ground, implying the stadium was sold out. Journalist Santosh Kumar Ghosh wrote satirically that police constables left no stone unturned to be assigned duty at the stadium.[61]

The hilarity was supplemented by serious reports on surveillance and black marketing of tickets, which is considered the traditional barometer of cricket's appeal.[62] A total of 116 persons, mostly students, were fined 2 rupees each for trespassing into the stadium without a ticket. Forty-two people were taken into custody, among whom 12 were fined for entering with counterfeit tickets.[63] The black marketeers N. I. Kanjariwala, Ramanand Agarwal, Radheshyam Chhedia and Maqsood Alam were fined 100 rupees each.[64] Twenty tickets were seized from three vendors, Chandreswar Prasad, Mahendra Prasad and Ramjatan Shaw, who were charged with selling vendor's passes. Ramesh Kander was fined 5 rupees for trying to pass his ticket to a friend through a gate.[65] Since all the people named in connection with the crimes were non-Bengalis, it can be presumed that immigrant workers controlled the informal ticket economy. The reference to non-Bengalis as culprits matched the growing sentiment against their intrusion into Calcutta's economic life. As India won the match, an old man was seen distributing sweets in the evening, who admitted having relived the feeling of Mohun Bagan winning the IFA Shield in 1911. Finally, the report of a number of missing children having been traced outside the Eden Gardens provided an encore to the concert of spectatorship.[66]

The enthusiasm bubbled over the pot in 1964 with the return of MCC.[67] To give more people the chance to watch cricket, the CAB reduced the number of season tickets and released daily tickets, 6,000 priced at 5 rupees and another 1,200 at 10 rupees. Massive queues formed in front of the ticket counters every morning. People started to queue up to 30 hours in advance to buy the first day's ticket; the first in line was a student from Bengal Engineering College.[68] Fifty black marketeers were arrested even before the match began. As the police baton-charged the thousands assembled to see foreign cricketers practise, the people pelted stones.[69] The press reported double-booked seats, overcrowded galleries, and brawls with fellow spectators and the police. The situation became so outrageous by the third day that spectators set fire to the canopy 10 minutes before the end of the day's play. The *Dainik Basumati* editorialised that the incident was not an abrupt outburst, but 'written on the wall'.[70] The police force in 1964 was neither properly trained nor numerically strong to control crowd disturbance. According to a satirical report in the *Anandabazar Patrika*, in the second tier of the gallery, a spectator so fiercely and skilfully spun a stick in a circular motion that the police did not dare to get close and apprehend him. Ten young men hurled earthen teacups at constables, which must have been an inexhaustible barrage considering around 10,000 people bought tea at the stadium that day. The police arrested a number of spectators, claiming that throwing cups was illegal. The first aid personnel were happy to have become useful. As two injured spectators were carried out on stretchers, someone who presumably was never ferried on a stretcher before chased one as if running after a rush-hour bus.[71]

The press was unequivocally supportive of spectators despite their poor behaviour and critical of the police and the administration, who were unprepared to handle crowd pressure. The sports journalist Santipriya Bandopadhyay wrote that after all the trouble of acquiring tickets, the public did not deserve to find their seats occupied by others bearing the same ticket, with no way to know whose ticket was counterfeit.[72] Readers were not so forgiving, as is evident from the letter Nabakumar Shil wrote to the *Jugantar* about how sections of spectators 'heroically' fought with sticks, set fire to the awning and pelted one another with fruit skins and teacups. He deplored how unsporting the spectators were, having little inclination to abide by the dedication and discipline of cricket and cricketers. The public earned no right to call themselves sports lovers simply by watching cricket in droves or displaying elite tastes and knowledge; their behaviour should be worthy of being ranked alongside that of cricketers.[73] With little compulsion of supporting the fledgling run of international sports in the city, readers were primed to show more chagrin than journalists.

When Australia visited Calcutta later in 1964, A. N. Ghosh, the secretary who personally sold tickets from his house 15 years ago, was the most sought-after man in the city. He announced in a press conference that the CAB had added 4,000 seats and the stadium would now be able to accommodate 43,500 spectators.[74] The 10,600 season tickets issued were reserved as complimentary passes, the public had to vie for the 7,300 day-tickets, a meagre increase of 100 from the last match.[75] The decision to reserve more tickets backfired as bundles of season tickets lay unused in the CAB office on the first day. Afraid of substantial loss of gate money, on the second day the CAB officials peddled season tickets to people lingering after failing to buy day-tickets. Another lack of foresight was to accommodate holders of the 100-rupee season ticket in the new press box. In addition to disturbing journalists with loud cheers and shouts, these ticket-holders fought among themselves on several occasions as the number of chairs was fewer than the number of people.[76] The day-ticket-holders set fire to the canopy four times. In an atmosphere of political and economic crisis, a murmur against cricket being a saboteur of Indian morality and economy started to be heard. Shedding its previous unobtrusive character, the press reported the palimpsest of the scamper for tickets from a variety of angles, all interrogating the boundary between sense and nonsense.

Some journalists were critical of taking leisure too seriously; some praised the public's commitment to cricket.

West Indies postponed its 1964–65 tour as India went to war with Pakistan. They visited Calcutta in 1966–67 amidst high expectations. Watching the enthusiasm with which West Indian cricketers were greeted once out of the aeroplane, author Narayan Gangopadhyay was certain that in his next birth, he wanted to be a cricketer and not a politician, an author, a singer or an actor as they did not come close to the unreserved adulation for cricketers.[77] The riot on 1 January 1967 led many people to blame newspapers and radio for fomenting cricket frenzy in the state. In self-defence, journalists said that the problems in organised sport reflected a pervasive social malaise, which could be possibly redeemed by indulging the philosophy of cricket. The author Chanakya wrote in the *Desh* that cricket was a real art, and the public should plunge into cricket instead of setting busses on fire. With India's decline in international football, cricket and hockey were the only alternatives to claim a foothold in world sports. The public must have seen something great in cricket as sheer craze would not have made thousands queue for tickets for hours year after year. People without ticket, instead of returning home in despair, often convened outside the Eden Gardens and listened to radio and the occasional cries of jubilation coming out of the ground.[78] Although the riot tarnished Calcutta's image and the press was critical of the lumpenisation of spectatorship, the public were in no mood to be discouraged. The rising need for tickets substantiated the theory of scarcity driving up consumption.[79] Women were frequently accused of blocking seats of male cricket lovers. Well-connected and financially solvent upper-middle class women, who could afford the high price, went to the stadium in droves. People without tickets earnestly read match reports and consumed the cynical portrayal of these women whose presence was suspected to have made tickets scarce, depriving them of the tactile enjoyment of cricket.[80]

Accounts of the craze for tickets continued to be published despite the criticism that the press commercially exploited cricket to garner readership and adversely affected the sport. On the eve of the Test match against Australia in 1969, a cartoon in the *Amrita Bazar Patrika* showed one person in possession of a ticket pompously strutting towards the stadium, whereas two of the ticketless passers-by hid their faces in shame.[81] Newspapers continued to present black marketing as a non-Bengali enterprise as a person named Anwar Singh was arrested.[82] Narayan Gangopadhyay imagined to have acquired the rare gem of a ticket for which people could have surrendered a kingdom. As he decided to give it to a deserving candidate, he started reflecting on the available choices in a biting commentary on the public. Excluded from his list of probable recipients were a budding cricketer from the neighbourhood, the captain of a college team, a knowledgeable professor and an enthusiastic schoolboy, for the first two could one day attend matches on their merit as cricketers and exposure to cricket could distract the latter two from learning. After careful consideration, he shortlisted the overweight female neighbour who could finish in five days the cardigan she had been knitting for three months, an executive who needed a cricket break in the soothing green expanse to breathe life into his dreary routine, the sport administrator who had run out of tickets but needed to gift one to his brother-in-law and the business magnate who could clinch a million-rupee deal by interacting with important people at the stadium.[83] The selection evinces the type of spectators he did not want in the stadium.

The ticket crisis revealed the debate in the press over the entitlements and legitimacy of spectators. Although watching Test cricket at any Indian stadium in the 1960s was not comfortable, cricket followers would do their best to attend the match and do anything for a ticket.[84] In his autobiography, Sujit Mukherjee shares a story about a friend who, unable to acquire a ticket, left Calcutta for a fortnight to escape being ridiculed by his friends.[85] In Moti Nandi's novel *Nanida Not Out*, the fictitious trader Chandmohan Srimani donated 1,500 rupees and the attorney Makhan Dutta sponsored 30 kilograms of potatoes, 10 kilograms of chicken, 50 pounds of bread and 5 kilograms of mustard oil for Hatkhola Cricket Club team in exchange for five and two Test tickets respectively from the club's quota.[86] It was suspected that students participated in inter-college cricket tournaments just to stake their claim to tickets from the student-cricketer quota.[87] The lure of a season ticket motivated Shyam Sundar Ghosh to join the *Dainik Basumati* as a sports journalist while studying law at Calcutta University in 1962, thus stepping into his 50-year career in journalism.[88] Even after scaling the hurdles, several people would be turned away from the gates as ticket inspectors suspected their tickets to be duplicated due to printing errors on the part of the CAB. Several hundred would find their seats to have been occupied by people bearing tickets with the same numbers; some would find that the seat number punched on their tickets did not exist; some would be unable to plod through the congestion to go near their seats; while those who would manage to sit had an average space of 8 inches or less to perch on, less than the dimension of a paperback book.[89] Even the Australian cricketer Ashley Mallett, who witnessed a riot in Bombay and six deaths in a stampede in Calcutta in 1969, recognised the problem before Indian authorities did. He wrote:

> In India, many fans would spend an entire year saving their money for the price of a Test match ticket, then walk for days on end to gain admission – standing room only – to watch the game. Little wonder they get upset when they cannot get into the ground or, if they manage to get a reasonable vantage point, a decision goes against the Indian side… During the Bombay Test match about 5,000 tickets in one stand were duplicated by a gang of forgers, and sold out. Can you imagine how anyone would react having to share one seat between two people, each thinking he had the correct or legitimate pass.[90]

The six deaths put the boiling pot to its melting point. The CAB reformed the model of ticket distribution after the debacle. It started a lottery for tickets, the results of which were published in a book and sold in bookstalls. The new system was an ideal conduit for the press to generate exciting stories. It published the names, addresses and reactions of some of the lucky winners, particularly of schoolchildren and housewives. The winners were asked to collect the reserved tickets from the Mohammedan Sporting Club ground.[91] Tickets were priced at 45 rupees and 20 rupees for the 1972–73 Test match against England, which were sold in the black market for as high as 200 rupees.[92] Cricket followers devised ingenious ways to watch matches. As the MCC team arrived at their hotel, one of the security guards introduced himself to the captain, Tony Lewis. He asked Lewis to sign a piece of card and write 'Captain, MCC and England'. Later, as the Test match began, the journalist E. W. Swanton found a card on one of the tables in the area for dignitaries, written 'Please admit bearer to the VIP area,' undersigned Tony Lewis. The security guard beat a million other aspirants to the coveted place in the stadium, that too in the special enclosure, while 70,000 people thronged the gallery.[93]

Newspapers published funny stories and cartoons about the craze for tickets. A cartoon in the *Amrita Bazar Patrika* in 1977 showed two robbers disappointed at finding money instead of tickets for the upcoming Test match against England in the safe they had broken open.[94] In a sequel cartoon, an employee flamboyantly walked into his director's room with a ticket in hand, and strode out dressed as the director, apparently having swapped the ticket for the position.[95] These cartoons annoyed some readers who thought they aggrandised cricket. In 1979, Dipakranjan Maity complaied to the *Jugantar* that the press had articificially created the demand for tickets. He wanted resumption of the sale of day-tickets so that only the people willing to go through the hardship for their favourite sport would be able to attend, and not the ones who watched cricket for mere entertainment and social prestige.[96] Journalists and photographers were reprimanded for selling or gifting their work passes to relatives and friends. The *Khelar Asar* commented in 1980 that while the sports editor of the *Amrita Bazar Patrika*, Sunil Bose, and his colleague Bishnu Mishra did not get work passes because of the CAB's inefficiency, several compositors, proof readers and clerks of press houses sat in the press box. The *Sunday* magazine's editor was alleged to have given a press pass to his wife.[97] The state government too failed to regulate the use of tickets. Even though the press celebrated a record average of 100,000 spectators daily watching the Test match between India and England in 1982, it just barely referred to the disappearance of a bundle of 20,000 lottery coupons, out of which 2,000 had yielded valid tickets, from the Writers' Building.[98]

Just before the Test match against West Indies in 1983–84, a gang of thieves raided the ticket distribution centre in Narkeldanga's Gurudas Institute, killed the guard, and broke into the office room looking for 250 tickets. They found none as the tickets had been shifted elsewhere earlier during the day.[99] However, the demand for Test match tickets had declined after India's victory in the 1983 World Cup, which was evident on the opening day as black marketeers were seen loitering around the big banyan tree with unsold tickets. Members of several cricket clubs had little luck selling their extra tickets. Even the CAB officials were keen to sell extra tickets at throwaway prices. For the first time a number of life members, associated clubs and regional associations did not collect their allocated tickets.[100] A reason for the indifference could have been the non-selection of Kapil Dev for the match. Some cricket followers fixed 'No Kapil, No Test' posters on the Club House and Akashvani walls. The situation worsened in 1984–85 during the Test match against England. Many black marketeers were seen to be begging people to buy tickets. Although tickets were sold at less than the printed price, a few seats were still empty.[101] Journalists showed concern about the logic of distributing the Club House and complimentary tickets as numerous complaints were lodged about these tickets going to people without much knowledge of cricket. They wrote that unlike in London or Melbourne where only members could sit in the Club House, in Calcutta the life members and former cricketers were often seen perched in the gallery while people needing the aid of radio commentary to understand the proceedings occupied the Club House seats.[102]

The decline in interest in Test cricket became very apparent in 1987 when tickets for the ODI match against Pakistan far outsold the tickets for the Test match against the same opponent in the same month.[103] Although the CAB officials were in denial of the downturn, black marketeers confessed to their first loss since the trade began in 1956.[104] However, stories of ticket swindlers did not cease to be reported. When a police officer showed his ticket for inspection at one of the gates, the ticket inspector asked him to wait and handed it to his colleague who went inside to watch the match. On return to his office, fooled, the officer complained to the Police Association and threatened to go on fast. The ticket, numbered 003873, was confiscated but no charge was filed due to lack of evidence.[105] The scurry for tickets reached a new height as soon as Calcutta was chosen to host the 1987 World Cup final, but the next Test series reverted to the new pattern of declining interest.

In an interview given to the journalist Jayanta Chakraborty during the Test series against West Indies in 1987–88, the black marketeer Sheikh Kallu, whose trade began during the Test match against Pakistan in 1960–61, revealed the open secrets of his career. He recalled having done the maximum business in the Test match against West Indies in 1974–75. The 1987–88 serieswas disastrous for cricket associations throughout India, mainly due to the people's preference to watch matches on television. Merely 300 spectators witnessed the start of play in Delhi, and 33 journalists were joined by a meagre 27 spectators in Bombay when the first ball was bowled, whereas in Calcutta the figure was still about 50,000.[106] The idea of a partly filled gallery at the start of the match was still unthinkable. A spectator who had watched every Test match in Calcutta since 1934 confirmed that this was the lowest attendance ever. The advent of ODI cricket was blamed for the public's lukewarm response to Test cricket.[107] The CAB Joint Secretary, Jagmohan Dalmiya, announced that tickets for the ODI match raised 1,500,000 rupees, more than that of the five-day aggregate of the Test match. Ninety thousand tickets were put on sale, out of which 25,000 were given to the CAB members, 2,000 to the National Cricket Club (NCC) members, 3,500 were reserved for Club House patrons and 10,000 for the state government. Forty-nine thousand and five hundred tickets were distributed among the public, a huge leap compared to the 7,000 day-tickets of the 1960s.[108]

The stories of people doing daring things for a ticket almost disappeared from press reports in the 1990s. In 1993, the hundredth Test match for Graham Gooch and the chance to watch Tendulkar for the first time drew around 60,000 people to the stadium with a capacity of 92,200. Day-ticket was reintroduced in the hope of having at least 70 per cent of the galleries full but no block was congested as before.[109] Many of the 31,000 complimentary tickets given to life, annual and associate members were not used. Officials blamed the dwindling spectatorship on the scheduling of matches over the last week of a month, sometimes starting on the last day, when the public had spent most of the month's earnings and were cautious about expending on leisure. This was a wrong logic as Test matches in the heydays of ticket craving would mostly start in the last week of December, so the real reason was the people's preference for watching the match on television or going elsewhere. The match referee, Cammie Smith, a former West Indies cricketer, admitted that people had lost the patience to watch Test cricket. Although the CAB Joint Secretary, Prashanta Gayen, stated that the stadium looked emptier because the number of seats was increased by 11,000 from the last Test match in 1987, and the CAB's profit trebled in comparison to the previous match, the press unanimously agreed to the waning of public interest in Test cricket.[110] The high demand for tickets for the Hero Cup tournament later that year, resurgence of black marketing and increase in police vigilance vindicated the impression of the ascendency of ODI cricket.[111]

Matches were organised less frequently at a particular venue in the 1990s with the construction of new cricket stadiums in every state Cricket started to be shown on satellite television beginning with the Hero Cup, which was an instant success. The coverage, replete with replays, highlights, commentaries and reviews, was far better than the fare offered by the state-run Doordarshan that had so far monopolised cricket telecast in India. People in the urban areas with access to satellite channels were now reported to have preferred watching televised cricket. The 1996 World Cup resurrected some of the old enthusiasm and brought the city to a standstill on match days. During the quarter-final match against Pakistan in the 1996 World Cup, the emptiness of the city's usually congested thoroughfares looked like an optical illusion. Most of the street hawkers reported no business; some of them were still strangely unperturbed so long as India were playing well.[112] Over the three days preceding the semi-final match between India and Sri Lanka in Calcutta, 32 persons including a Delhi-based cricketer, one groundstaff each from Mohammedan Sporting and Central Excise clubs, and a CAB member,

Dip Kumar Dasgupta, were arrested for selling tickets on the black market.[113] The India–Australia Test match in 1998 coincided with the state board examinations, so the ground was not full.[114] The Test match against Pakistan in 1999 was better attended but the enthusiasm of the early 1980s was never to return.

This thick description of the scamper for tickets, initially for Test cricket and later for ODI cricket, unfolds several aspects of the sociocultural practices concerning built environment and the sports press's space-constituting role in Calcutta. Journalists had a prominent position in the press's part in assigning social norms to cricket, reflecting the wider society's changing attitude to the consumption of leisure. In the dialogic relationship among sport, reporting and readership, cricket followers were secondary actors in the production of knowledge. Their letters to the editor regarding cricket, ticket and access to the Eden Gardens commented on the sport and its mediation, fragmenting and opening up new understandings of cricket's discourses. Editors who screened these letters before their publication were in control of the content and likely impact of the public's self-observation and understanding of the symbolic and social order of the stadium. In the field of reports and the responses of readers to the Eden Gardens's spaceness, the space was not simply a product of their perspectives but played a significant role in structuring their sense of organised leisure. Media houses authorised journalists to produce opinions on the space of cricket. However, an assessment of the knowledge collectively disseminated by the sports press, here in the context of the distribution of tickets, reveals the agents of knowledge production were involved rather discursively in space-building. No definitive approach to cricket emerged as every opinion was contested, sometimes from within the same publication. This postmodernist logic of the decentred authority dismantles the hierarchy of journalists and readers as producers and consumers respectively, merging their identities as cricket followers. Journalists could still be primary producers of knowledge as they had greater collective visibility and capacity for publicising opinions in comparison with the public whose ambit of articulation was far more individual.

The spectrum of figurative speech used for reporting the people's experience of procuring tickets ranged from irony to pathos. Every newspaper followed a different rhetoric policy depending on its readership and not always being consistent with its editorial ideology. The *Anandabazar Patrika* started the hyperbolic description of the hardship people went through for tickets in the early 1960s, followed by other newspapers. The responsibility of reporting would be divided among a group of journalists who would reproduce the preparation for the match and the day's play using various methods such as blending fact and fiction in reports about spectators and doing technical analysis of cricket. The presentation raised debates over the acceptability and aesthetics of dramatising contrary to the banalising of events. Not only did the meaning of reflection, opinion and reporting change in accordance with authorship and circumstances, the subjective use of language often set the context of writing. This was evident in the late 1960s as the journalists who aggrandised the rush for tickets as a template of the city's love for cricket before the 1967 riot described the culture as dreadful following the 1969 stampede. Journalists were very critical of the ethics of ticket distribution in the 1970s as black marketing increased and people without 'credentials' occupied the Club House. They launched a re-evaluation of the acumen of spectators in the 1980s when ODI cricket replaced Test cricket as the meridian of the sporting public sphere.

The history of buying tickets highlights the transformation of the leisure economy. The evolution of participation from the stressful queuing for tickets in the 1960s to the comfortable leisure space of televisual experience in the 1990s illustrates the shifts in the public's attachment to cricket. In the 1950s and 1960s, Test matches were one of the few international experiences of the people of Calcutta. Attending matches raised one's status specifically as it was difficult to obtain tickets. Those without connections to the right people braved the challenges of weather, inefficient administration and peer pressure to buy tickets. The changes in leisure choices were more responsible than the coming of television in easing the burden of participation in the second half. The usual explanation of people becoming more occupied with work in the 1990s and hence unable to attend cricket consecutively for five days is ludicrous considering office hours and regulation for leave of absence have not changed in the state since India's independence. A more plausible explanation would be that the public were no longer topophilic enough to take leave on the pretext of a relative's death or wife's illness.[115] They started to feel that Test cricket had outlived its original neaning as a test of character in a leisurely setting and should be replaced with a shorter and faster version. Although the sports press reflected this change, an examination of its contents does not indicate any connivance in bringing about this shift, but rather an inclination to resist by playing up the virtues of Test cricket. Its limited success indicates that the ceiling of its power to incite public frenzy was not as high as was alleged. Rather, the public's willingness to cultivate self-behaviour was stronger than journalists usually acknowledged.

CONCLUSION

The chapter traced the collective history of cricket watching since the beginning of international cricket in Calcutta, using the mediation of the traditional publicness of spectators as the rubric of interpretation. While addressing cricket as a text, it pondered the systems of cultural mediation. The representation of participation indicated that journalists tended to dramatise incidents and people. It also refers to how multiple perspectives and hybrid identities were practised and unevenly assimilated into a dominant form of culture. The cricketing public sphere has been a non-hegemonic space, under neither the state nor the media's control, but at the latter's mercy for expressing itself in the twentieth century. The people without tickets relied on the press and radio to know the score, hence using mediated experience as the tether to their favourite sport. Ticket-holders too were dependent on journalists for expanding their knowledge of cricket, and many among them accepted their group representation as a gospel. However much they discussed cricket with each other and devised new models of group participation, in the absence of institutionalised preservation of sporting memory in India the press provides the only systematic compilation of cricket culture in the twentieth century alongside ethnographic bargains. Hence, in spite of the event-driven and episodic nature of its coverage of international matches, the press played a very important role in manufacturing a long-standing profile for spectators.

NOTES

1. A.M., 'Calcutta Diary', *Economic and Political Weekly* 9, no. 50 (14 December 1974): 2041–42, 2041.
2. *TOI*, 25 December 1974, 9.
3. Ghosh promised every member of the council two tickets. He mentioned that before the Test match in 1972–73 at least eight friends of the members had come to collect tickets on behalf of the members showing him forged letters. The members had then feigned ignorance of the deception and

demanded their due tickets. *Proceedings of the West Bengal Legislative Assembly* 57 (November 1974), 220.

4. To his credit, Ghosh urged the chief minister to declare a holiday after India won the match, *Amrita Bazar Patrika* (*AmBP*), 2 February 1975, 6.

5. *TOI*, 2 November 1974, 5.

6. *Jugantar*, 30 December 1974, 1. His clean image was later irrevocably tainted when he signed the Emergency declaration without Cabinet approval in 1975.

7. *TOI*, 25 December 1974, 9.

8. 'Khelar Mathe' (From the Ground), *Desh* 42, no. 5 (1974), 386.

9. *AmBP*, January 1, 1975, 6.

10. *TOI*, 16 June 1996, 7.

11. Gyan Prakash, 'The Colonial Genealogy of Society: Community and Political Modernity in India', in *The Social in Question: New Bearings in History and the Social Sciences*, ed. Patrick Joyce, 81–96 (London and New York: Routledge, 2002), 90.

12. Sudipto Kaviraj, 'The Imaginary Institution of India', in Subaltern Studies VII, ed. Partha Chatterjee and Gyanendra Pandey, 1–39 (New Delhi: Oxford University Press, 1992); Partha Chatterjee, *The Nation and Its Fragments: Colonial and Postcolonial Histories* (Princeton: Princeton University Press, 1993); Dipesh Chakrabarty, 'Modernity and Ethnicity in India: A History for the Present', *Economic and Political Weekly* 30, no. 52 (1995): 3373–80; Nicholas Dirks, *Castes of Mind: Colonialism and the Making of Modern India* (Princeton: Princeton University Press, 2001); Gyan Prakash, 'Civil Society, Community, and the Nation in Colonial India', *Etnográfica* 6, no. 1 (2002): 27–39.

13. Douglas E. Haynes, *Rhetoric and Ritual in Colonial India: The Shaping of a Public Sphere in Surat City, 1852–1928* (Berkeley: University of California Press, 1991); Sandria Freitag, *Action and Community: Public Arenas and the Emergence of Communalism in North India* (Berkeley: University of California Press, 1989); Rajat Kanta Ray, *The Felt Community: Commonalty and Mentality before the Emergence of Indian Nationalism* (New Delhi: Oxford University Press, 2003).

14. Berry Sarbadhikary, *My World of Cricket: A Century of Tests* (Calcutta: Cricket Library, 1964), 20. The oldest, the Vine Ground in Seven Oaks, Kent, has not staged any Test match.

15. Sachin Sen, 'Edener Baireo Kolkatar Duti Mathe Ekada Akarshaniya Cricket Dekha Jeto' (We Could Watch Attractive Cricket at Two Grounds in Calcutta Besides Eden), *SKA*, 1980, 125–29.

16. Partha Chatterjee writes that since European sporting clubs monopolized the use of vast swathes of the *maidan*, Indians were not allowed to freely roam there. Indians were probably thrilled to be breaching the 'protected zone of power' when they watched football and other sports involving Indian clubs in the *maidan*. Partha Chatterjee, *The Black Hole of Empire: History of a Global Practice of Power* (Princeton and Oxford: Princeton University Press, 2012), 293.

17. Christopher Gaffney, *Temples of the Earthbound Gods: Stadiums in the Cultural Landscapes of Rio de Janeiro and Buenos Aires* (Austin: University of Texas Press, 2008), 4.

18. Marc Perelman, *Barbaric Sport: A Global Plague*, trans. John Howe (London and New York: Verso, 2012), 49–50.

19. Jayanta Chakraborty, 'Edener Noishoprohori' (The Nightwatchman of Eden), *Amrita* 17, no. 26 (11 November 1977), 56.

20. Yi-Fu Tuan, *Topophilia: A Study of Environmental Perception, Attitudes and Values* (Englewood Cliffs, NJ: Prentice-Hall, 1974).

21. Niels K. Nielsen, 'The Stadium in the City', in *The Stadium and the City*, ed. John Bale and Olof Moen, 21–44 (Keele: Keele University Press, 1995), 34.

22. Michel de Certeau, *The Practice of Everyday Life*, trans. Steven Rendall (Berkeley: University of California Press, 1984), 117–18.

23. John Bale introduced the concept of 'sportscape' to describe the synergy of modern sport with other social practices, starting from the late nineteenth century, resulting in redistribution of particular landscapes into spaces devoted to sport. Bale, *Sports Geography*, 2nd ed. (London and New York: Routledge, 2003), 4.

24. Alan Bairner, 'National Sports and National Landscapes: In Defence of Primordialism', *National Identities* 11, no. 3 (2009): 223–39.

25. Yi-Fu Tuan, *Space and Place: The Perspective of Experience* (Minneapolis, MN: University of Minnesota Press, 1997), 64.

26. Rakhal Bhattacharya, 'Banglar Cricketer Adijug, Adikatha' (The Early Years of Cricket in Bengal), *SKA*, 1983, 160.

27. Basu, *Edene Shiter Dupur*, 152–53.

28. Ibid., 173.

29. Ibid., 176–77.

30. *The Statesman* (*TS*), 2 January 1961, 12.

31. *KA* 2, no. 42 (23 March 1979), 5.

32. Prafulla Roy, 'Joubone Bujhi Kichu Furoe Na' (Nothing Expires in Youth), *Jugantar*, 3 January 1979, 4.

33. Soumya Bhattacharya, *You Must Like Cricket? Memoirs of an Indian Cricket Fan* (London: Yellow Jersey Press, 2006), 148–50.

34. Ashis Nandy, 'Introduction: Indian Popular Cinema as a Slum's Eye View of Politics', in *The Secret Politics of Our Desires: Innocence, Culpability and Indian Popular Cinema*, ed. Ashis Nandy, 1–18 (New Delhi: Oxford University Press, 1998), 5.

35. *ABP*, 26 November 1993, 11.

36. 'The Lighter Side of Test Cricket', *TS*, 2 January 1961, 12.

37. Ajay Basu, *Hater Bat Hatiyar* (Bat Becomes A Weapon) (Calcutta: Ruprekha, 1969), 33.

38. Sunil Gavaskar, *Sunny Days* (Calcutta: Rupa, 1976), 165.

39. *Jugantar*, February 3, 1980, 1.

40. Amit Chaudhuri, *A New World* (London: Picador, 2000), 28.

41. *KA* 3, no. 14 (10 August 1979), 28.

42. Arijit Sen, 'Bharater Khelar Man Konodin Unnata Habe Ki?' (Will Indian Cricket Ever Improve?), *SKA*, 1977, 81.

43. 'Cricketer Karone Atmahatya' (Cricket Leads to Suicide), *Jugantar*, 21 February 1987, 7.

44. *ABP*, 26 November 1993, 11.

45. *The Telegraph* (*TT*), March 11, 1996, 1.

46. Kanailal Bose, 'Rajar Khelar Rajosik Khoroch' (The Princely Cost of Cricket), *ABP*, 7 February 1964, 4.

47. *AmBP*, 4 January 1977, 10.

48. 'Edene Lathi' (Fight at Eden), *Jugantar*, 17 February 1987, 8.

49. 'Sidelights', *Sportsworld* (7 November 1979), 14.

50. Swapan Mishra, 'Edene Birpuja' (Hero Worship at Eden), *Jugantar*, 4 January 1985, 7.

51. Runu Guha Neyogi, *Sada Ami Kalo Ami* (Myself in Black and White) (Calcutta: Jinia Publishers, 1997), 84.

52. *TS*, 19 February 1987, 1.

53. *KA* 3, no. 25 (9 November 1979), 46.

54. *ABP*, 5 January 1991, 8.

55. 'Ajju Bhai Ke Phonta Debe Eden' (Eden Will Pray for Ajju Brother), *ABP*, 4 November 1994, 1.

56. Henri Lefebvre, *The Production of Space*, trans. Donald Nicholson-Smith (Oxford: Blackwell, 1991), 164–68.

57. John Bale, *Landscapes of Modern Sport* (Leicester: Leicester University Press, 1994), 82.

58. Alok Dasgupta, 'Test Crickete Edener Darshak' (The Eden Spectators and Test Cricket), *SKA*, 1984, 138.

59. Narayan Gangopadhyay, 'Atitheyota' (Hospitality), *Desh* 37, no. 10 (3 January 1970), 963–64.

60. *DB*, 30 December 1960, 6.

61. Sankariprasad Basu, *Ball Pore Bat Nare* (The Clash of Ball and Bat) (Calcutta: Karuna Prakashani, 1962), 106.

62. David McMahon, 'Cricket Moods', *Sportsworld* 8, no. 19 (4–11 March 1987), 26.

63. *Hindustan Standard*, 5 January 1962, 1.

64. 'Test Matcher Ticketer Chorakarbar Koyekjoner Arthodondo' (People Fined for Black Market of Test Match Tickets), *DB*, 3 January 1962, 5.

65. *TS*, 3 January 1962, 1.

66. Ibid., 5 January 1962, 1.

67. In Delhi, the local water board cut the supply of water to the English dressing room in protest against not receiving their allocated quota of free tickets. With the Delhi cricket organisers not complying, it was up to the English manager David Clark to collect all the complimentary tickets he could from the English players and assuage the water authorities. The taps sprang to life as soon as Clark handed over the tickets. Colin Cowdrey, *MCC: The Autobiography of a Cricketer* (London: Hodder & Stoughton, 1976), 152–53.

68. 'Khela Dekhar Utkot Basona' (The Terrible Urge of Watching Cricket), *DB*, 29 January 1964, 6.

69. 'Jal Ticket Bikroyer Obhijoge 50 Jon Greptar' (50 Arrested for Selling Counterfeit Tickets), *DB*, 29 January 1964, 6.

70. 'Dorshoker Pran Rakhte Prananto' (Risking Lives to Watch Cricket), *DB*, 31 January 1964, 6.

71. *ABP*, 3 February 1964, 6.

72. Santipriyo Bandopadhyay, 'Dorshoker Gallery Theke Edener Kanna' (Eden Weeps from the Galleries), *DB*, 4 February 1964, 6.

73. *Jugantar*, 19 February 1964, 8.

74. *DB*, 11 October 1964, 6.

75. Ibid., 17 October 1964, 6.

76. Ibid., 18 October 1964, 6.

77. Narayan Gangopadhyay, 'Jonopriyotar Mandande' (A Measure of Popularity), *Desh* 34, no. 10 (7 January 1967), 957–58.

78. Chanakya, 'Kolkatar Diary', *Desh* 34, no. 11 (14 January 1967), 1073–74.

79. Daniel Wann, Christina Bayens and Allison Driver, 'Likelihood of Attending a Sporting Event as a Function of Ticket Scarcity and Team Identification', *Sport Marketing Quarterly* 13, no. 4 (2004): 209–14.

80. Sankariprasad Basu sympathises with a friend who spent a high amount of money every year to buy his wife tickets from the black market, *Ramaniya Cricket*, 62.

81. *AmBP*, 13 December 1969, 1.

82. *DB*, 11 December 1969, 8.

83. Narayan Gangopadhyay, 'Amar Atmatyag' (My Sacrifice), *Desh* 37, no. 8 (20 December 1969), 747–48.

84. N. Sunderasan reviewed the stadiums during the 1969 Test series against Australia, saying, 'While the galleries were jampacked – only at Madras one could discern a sense of comfort among the spectators in almost all the stands – many more clamoured for admission, with a nasty stampede in Calcutta even resulting in loss of lives. There is an urgent need to put up stadia to accommodate the growing number of enthusiasts', in 'A Close Series', in *Indian Cricket 1970* (Madras: Kasturi & Sons Limited, 1970), 38.

85. Sujit Mukherjee, *Autobiography of an Unknown Cricketer* (New Delhi: Ravi Dayal, 1996), 161.

86. Moti Nandi, *Nanida Not Out*, in *Dashti Kishor Upanyas*, 9–49 (Calcutta: Ananda Publishers, 2000 [1973]), 24.

87. 'Calcutta Biswabidyalayer Cricketer Eto Gondogol Keno?' (The Trouble with Cricket at the University of Calcutta), *KA* 2, no. 2 (5 May 1978), 28.

88. Shyam Sundar Ghosh, 'Smritir Sarani Beye' (Down Memory Lane), *Sharadiya Dainik Statesman*, 2011, 187.

89. *ABP*, 2 January 1967, 1.

90. Ashley Mallet, *Rowdy* (Blackwood: Lynton, 1973), 49.

91. *DB*, 22 December 1972, 6.

92. Ibid., 25 December 1972, 6.

93. Mike Denness, *I Declare* (London: Arthur Barker, 1977), 50.

94. *DB*, 1 January 1977, 1.

95. Ibid., 2 January 1977, 1.

96. *Jugantar*, 19 October 1979, 4.

97. *KA* 3, no. 39 (15 February 1980), 36.

98. *Jugantar*, 1 January 1982, 6.

99. 'Test Ticket Niye Khun' (Test Ticket Leads to Murder), *Jugantar*, 7 December 1983, 1.

100. 'Aj Edene Bharat–Englander Tritiyo Test Match Shuru Hoche: Kalobajarider Mathaye Hat' (India–England Third Test Starts Today: Black Marketeers Distraught), *DB*, 31 December 1984, 3.

101. 'Prothom Diner Khelae Pran Chhilo Na' (Boring Play on the First Day), *DB*, 1 January 1985, 3.

102. Ashis Roy, 'Club Houser Ticket Pan Kara' (Who Receives Club House Tickets), *ABP*, 1 January 1985, 8.

103. 'Test Ticketer Chahida Nei' (Little Demand for Test Ticket), *DB*, 9 February 1987, 3.

104. *ABP*, 11 February 1987, 8.

105. 'Ticket Keteo Police Officerer Birombona' (The Police Officer's Embarrassment Despite a Valid Ticket), *DB*, 19 February 1987, 1, 6.

106. *Jugantar*, 26 December 1987, 8.

107. Ibid., 27 December 1987, 8.

108. 'Teste Ebar Ticket Bikri Hoyeche Ponero Lakh Takar' (Test Ticket Worth 15 Lakh Sold), *DB*, 28 December 1987, 3.

109. *TS*, 29 January 1993, 14.

110. *ABP*, 30 January 1993, 12.

111. Ibid., 23 November 1993, 12.

112. *TS*, 10 March 1996, 3.

113. *TT*, 12 February 1996, 15.

114. *Bartaman*, 18 March 1998, 1.

115. The *Times of India* reported that attendance in many offices in Bombay was poor on the day of the 1996 World Cup semi-final match played in Calcutta. Male employees suddenly reported ill whereas female employees were all present. The manager of a firm regretted not having a half day as those who turned up stopped work after lunch and watched the match on television. Televised Test cricket did not arouse the same passion anymore. *TOI*, 14 March 1996, 5.

4 Politicians, Patronage and Centre–State Relations

In February 1959, after the West Indies had trampled India 3–0 in a five-Test match series in India, some parliamentarians in the lower house discussed how to improve the national team's performance.[1] Jaipal Singh, former hockey captain, was against touting these defeats as a 'national catastrophe', as defeats should be taken sportingly.[2] Yet, he added, to the elation of communist members, that sportspersons were the country's best ambassadors and corruption in sport administration must not be tolerated. In particular, most parliamentarians opposed the corrupt ad hoc committee appointed by the Ministry of Education to review the cricket board's operation. Finally, Singh suggested that parliamentary cricket teams should play a healing role in troubled areas since cricket seemed to have a 'mellowing effect' on the political atmosphere. The two-hour discussion revealed how important politicians thought cricket was for India's national prestige, and also the personal attachment of several politicians with cricket. Members of parliament (MPs) are known to have requested declaration of holidays during cricket matches. Congress leader H. P. Saksena asked the chairperson, in vain, for a holiday on the first day of the India–New Zealand Test match in Delhi in 1955.[3] In 1972, several MPs demanded the installation of a television set in the Central Hall of the parliament for the India–England Test match.[4] Politicians have appeared at receptions, distributed prizes, mingled with cricketers and delivered speeches on the contributions of cricket to the nation. Some of them were quick to exploit the sport's political potential by being involved in sports administration.

Leveraging sport for political purpose was not uniquely Indian. British monarch George V started attending FA Cup finals in 1914, showing his empathy with the event that historian Eric Hobsbawm called the 'festival of the proletariat'. This ritual presence integrated the political commonplace with the field of public culture, helping to portray the ruler as one of the public and legitimise the state as the public's representative.[5] Attending sports events henceforth became a part of the royal and political itinerary.[6] The imperial tradition was continued by democratic and dictatorial governments whose appetite for organising and participating in sports events became increasingly insatiable. Historians have extensively written on how states exploit the public's attachment to sport. In his introduction to *The Changing Politics of Sport*, published in 1993, political scientist Lincoln Allison referred to a disposition among historians to conceptualise politics as a struggle between class and ideology over the distribution of resources. This materialist paradigm trivialised the politics of culture, religion, arts and sport as peripheral to the study of human society. As the study of culture gained currency among political historians, they started evaluating sport as part of mainstream politics.[7] Some of their studies have noted how sport has served diplomatic purposes and fostered international cooperation.[8] Others have examined specific national case studies to show the intimate connection between sport and nationalist politics, and also politicians aggrandising their image of benevolence, creating propaganda networks and informally communicating with potential voters through sport.[9] The same processes have unfolded, but not replicated in India. How is the Indian story different?

This chapter's contribution is in its emphasis on the malleability of ideology owing to the personal preference of politicians rather than political or electoral necessity. In Bengal, political parties seldom produced sport; they rather framed sport in accordance with their personal choice. After India's independence, the Congress government in Bengal in the 1950s and 1960s had little to do with organising cricket, other than providing security, even when the Congress at the Centre under Jawaharlal Nehru's leadership were intent on building the nation through physical education and sport.[10] As Congress chief minister in the 1970s, Siddhartha Sankar Ray took a personal interest in cricket and left his indelible mark on the game's organisation. From the late 1970s to the late 1990s, where our discussion ends, the CPI(M) government and its office-bearers, in utter contradiction to the communist stand against bourgeois culture, showed much personal appreciation for cricket and patronised the sport as a medium of reaching out to the people. This study of politics driven more by personal choice than tyrannical ideology recentres the global historiography of sport and politics, instead of producing yet another national or regional variation on the well-trodden genre of sport and politics. The final section of the chapter shows how the press capitalised on the public's attachment with cricket by framing the non-inclusion of Bengali players in the Indian team in terms of the central government's perceived longstanding antagonism towards Bengal.[11] Centre–state relations in the federal republic of India have been bitter owing to parochial politics. This chapter makes an original contribution to postcolonial Indian history by studying Centre–state relations through the lens of cricket.

CRICKET AND POLITICS IN BENGAL

Bengal faced a massive political crisis in the 1950s–60s owing to a shortage of employment, food, housing, electricity, and so on, but the problems rarely spilled onto the cricket field before the mid-1960s. In this period, the left parties had adopted demonstration and strike as forms of political protest on their way up to electoral power. The brigade parade ground and the *maidan* staged political rallies and public meetings with thousands of people, turning Calcutta into a city of processions.[12] Much like the Chinese under communist regime, people of Calcutta under left influence believed that they were a very progressive society and responsible towards anti-capitalist and anti-imperialist forces at work elsewhere in the world.[13] There is no evidence that Indian politicians grasped the significance of the structural similarity of work and labour with modern sport. The universal principles of workers' sport, contrary to bourgeois sport, were inclusivity and altruism. It served as an alternative to the commercialised, chauvinistic and statistics-obsessed sports culture bred by capitalist societies.[14] Sport was supposed to play more than a recreational role in workers' movements. It was expected to develop an anti-bourgeois character in the proletariat so that they could in turn protect sport from a possible corruption by bourgeois allures.[15] In interwar Europe, the workers' sport movement harshly, though unwisely, criticised sensation-seeking spectators for being undisciplined and violent and prioritising bourgeois spirit over educational benefit.[16] Although cricket was termed a bourgeois sport par excellence, it lent itself to a brand of respectable and rational recreation like workers' sport. It shared the ideals of the workers' sport movement about spectatorship. The class and cultural underpinnings of cricket seemed to have little impact on Indian politicians, as their connections with the sport were mostly self-serving and populist.

The growing left influence in Bengal in the 1960s led to intense confrontations between socialist and non-socialist ideals, which was asserted more than demonstrated due to the inconclusive debates on what counted as socialism among the party ideologues. Commenting on the CPI(M)'s political philosophy, Atul Kohli has said the party was 'communist in name and organisation but "social democratic" in ideology and practice'.[17] The party had created strong peasant and working-class associations, marking a break from the *bhadralok* politics of the Congress. It has been criticised for investing its energy on electoral politics, instead of developing proper anti-capitalist and anti-imperialist programmes and shaping peasants and workers into a revolutionary force against bourgeois politics. The CPI(M)'s tactics failed to confront the question of class power.[18] Unlike Kerala, where the party was more concerned with grassroots organisations, the Bengal branch was embedded more in demonstrations than social movements.[19] Some of the more radical members left the party in 1969 following the Marxist–Maoist ideological split. The new inductees, though more moderate in their political outlook, did not spare any opportunity for demonstrating their discontent with other political systems.

In the politically charged atmosphere of 1969–70, a group of people besieged the Great Eastern Hotel where the Australia team were put up. Cricketer Ashley Mallett referred to them as 'a large crowd' in a 1973 book and 'a 10,000-strong crowd' in a 2008 book. They waved placards that said 'Doug Walters Go Home', in protest against the cricketer's suspected participation in the Vietnam War.[20] Bengal communists shared a long-term bond with fellow comrades from Vietnam, empathising with their anti-colonial resistance and mounting symbolic solidarity by staging Vietnam Days (21 January 1945, 8 April 1965, 20 November 1968) and Vietnam Week (7–14 July 1968), distributing pamphlets and staging dramas. Calcutta reverberated with slogans of 'Tomar nam amar nam Vietnam Vietnam' (Your name, my name, Vietnam, Vietnam). The city's mayor, Prashanta Shur, declared, 'May our Ganges and your Mekong unite and may Ho Chi Minh's last wishes be fulfilled through that union.'[21] A rumour circulated that Doug Walters was part of the Australian Task Force which fought in Vietnam from March 1968. Walters was indeed conscripted into the army in 1966 to the resentment of Australians. Journalists wanted the next great batting hope to be exempted from national service.[22] The pleas fell to deaf ears; Walters underwent two years of military training. When given the choice to list three preferences for postings, Walters chose the battalion that was currently serving in Vietnam, expecting that he would not be sent to the front as he was still inexperienced, and would have served his mandatory period and left by the time the battalion would be required to return to Vietnam after the present stint.[23] Walters thus cleverly avoided going to war, and did not even leave Australia. Yet the irate mob rushed into the hotel's foyer, broke doors and windows, and fought with the police to make their point.

Beyond these mass level protests, the state's politicians astutely used cricket as a tactic in broader politics. Ram Chatterji of the Forward Bloc (Marxist) was appointed West Bengal's first sports minister in 1969. He made headlines by raiding the Calcutta Swimming Club with a retinue of hundred-odd Adivasis and plunging into the pool all together, ending the elitism of private clubs.[24] He decided to distribute free tickets among reporters for the 1969 Test match. The intention took Jyoti Basu by surprise. He did not understand why every reporter and not just sports correspondents should be given tickets, and where the additional tickets would come from. Chatterji replied, 'I would give tickets to only those who come to the Writers', publish nice reports about you and circulate them across London, America and Moscow.'[25] Basu was still sceptical about the policy of payoff but permitted him to go ahead. It is not known if extra tickets were indeed distributed among left-leaning journalists, but CPI(M) leaders Basu, Land and Revenue Minister Harekrishna Konar and Public Works Minister Subodh Banerjee refused their complimentary tickets for the same Test match in protest against the state government. Basu went to meet the cricketers but left once the match was about to begin.[26] Tickets had now become a tool of politics. Later, in 1980, Governor Tribhuvan Narain Singh refused to attend the match, feeling insulted by the CAB's failure to send him complimentary tickets alongside the invitation letter for his family.[27] However, the inclination to refuse free tickets was few and far between.

We know that sport has served as sites of ideological battles between socialist and non-socialist states.[28] This did not happen in India. The communists in India did not comply with the philosophy of sport in the Soviet Union or China. The Soviet state had denounced the capitalist world of sport in which spectators were easy converts to consumers. It wanted its citizens to improve their health and efficiency by watching elite athletes exhibit the benefits of exercise, learning 'values of honesty, obedience, discipline, culture, sexual equality, and selflessness'.[29] The spectators instead treated sports venues as sites of pleasure, male bonding and hero worship, not quite acknowledging the state's purpose of developing sport for 'glorifying the state, enhancing the efficiency of production, and improving the condition of the military'.[30] The Bengali leftists expected no such edifying benefit, probably because they had no intention of modifying the existing culture of spectatorship. All of their anti-capitalist and anti-globalisation rhetoric disappeared when dealing with cricket.

After coming to power in 1977, the CPI(M) followed a policy of development through reform rather than revolution. Many detractors of cricket were now emboldened, thinking the party's socialist goals might help curb the enthusiasm for cricket in the state. In 1980, as the Pakistan team arrived in Calcutta, one Nandalal Mukhopadhyay wrote to a newspaper that cricket should not be organised in a poor country. He cited examples of socialist countries that did not play cricket because the sport reduced industrial production and hampered learning.[31] Other readers such as Kumar Chattopadhyay and Samar Chakraborty supported him, complaining against so much interest in matters of bat and ball when millions of young people were unemployed and insufficient healthcare claimed innumerable lives.[32] A predictable counter-letter, from Bibhutibhusan Dutta, attacked this judgement as irrational, asking why similar forms of entertainment such as Rabindranath Tagore's birth anniversary, the Olympic Games and film festivals would be exempt from criticism.[33] This stream of debate declined after India's World Cup win in 1983 as no other sport vyed with cricket for popularity. Most significantly, a party that celebrated dignity of labour declared holidays on most match days from the very beginning of their rule. They probably recognised how hard cricketers worked to make the masses proud.

POLITICIANS AND CRICKET BEFORE 1977

Indian spectators have always been intensely political. In 1946, after scoring a double century against Australian Services in Madras, Rusi Modi was presented with an umbrella with 'Vote for Congress' and 'Down with Britain' written on the canopy.[34] At least a few among the crowd had no doubt that sport and politics were inseparable aspects of social life. In Bengal, where political fervour had been the lay of the land since the late nineteenth century, cricket was a site for the demonstration of political power and protests. The halt of play during the match against Australian Services in 1945 was probably the first instance of a long list of incidents in which cricket was imbricated in state politics.[35] The 1950s were surprisingly free of such incidents. The Congress-led government took an interest in constructing a proper stadium at the

Eden Gardens. It was instrumental in the foundation of the National Cricket Club (NCC) in 1948 that leased the ground from the Calcutta Cricket Club. The state was responsible for security at international cricket matches and investigating complaints of misbehaviour in sport, which gave government officials an opportunity to expand their zone of influence in sport.

A significant aspect of spectator sport is the presence of influential people during events.[36] In his narration of the 1960 Test match against Australia, Sankariprasad Basu noted the presence of Chief Secretary Satyendra Roy, Justice J. P. Mitra, Police Minister Kalipada Mukherjee, Police Commissioner Harisadhan Ghosh Chaudhuri, Inspector General Hiren Sarkar, communist leader Jatin Chakravorty, and the Maharajas of Baroda and several other defunct states during the fourth day. He remarked that so many important people were present at the ground that a single bomb could have wiped out the ruling elite of West Bengal and a few other parts of India.[37] Ministers and civil servants made beelines for Test match tickets during the heyday of the format and later for ODI matches. In 1962, one could see officers from the Writers' Building in the BCCI box alongside film directors, actors and businesspeople from the Royal Exchange.[38] CAB administrator Bechu Dutta Ray was against political interference in sports administration. Once he received a letter informing him about the state government's decision to form a committee to probe misconduct in the cricket field and to include in the stadium subcommittee a representative of the Police Commissioner. Unwilling to allow the government to impede the autonomy of sports associations, he refused to admit any state representative to the subcommittee, saying that the police was supposed to maintain order and not decide sports policy. He was soon summoned to a meeting attended by Chief Minister Bidhan Chandra Roy, the Police Commissioner, the Chief Secretary and the barristers Hem Sanyal and Ranadeb Choudhury. Roy accepted Dutta Ray's distrust of politicians and cancelled the Police Commissioner's proposal.

On a different occasion, Dutta Ray received a phone call from an excited Siddhartha Sankar Ray, then the law and tribal welfare minister in Bidhan Chandra Roy's cabinet, informing him of the bill passed in the legislative assembly for constructing a stadium for both cricket and football at the Eden Gardens. He opposed the plan despite political pressure. He contacted the Congress leaders Bijay Singh Nahar, Tarun Kanti Ghosh and Jagannath Kolay, only to be told that the bill could not be overturned. Nihar Mallick told him that Roy was leaving for Delhi the next day to discuss the plan with the Centre. They met him immediately, asking him to reconsider as it would not be possible to stage both sports at the Eden Gardens. Different soil, ground dimension, seating arrangement, illumination and scheduling of matches were needed for cricket and football fields. Roy accepted his logic and annulled the bill.[39] The CAB later named its Club House after him.

Roy's successors were not so flexible. Football started at the ground in 1967 as Calcutta had no large football stadium. Every match severely damaged the turf. In 1970 the United Front government decided to build a composite stadium at the Eden Gardens. Sports journalists vociferously opposed the decision, arguing that it was undemocratic for the state to ignore public opinion against such construction. The government claimed that it was not possible to set up a separate stadium for every sport and the Eden Gardens was the only centrally located space available. Hence, the stadium would be a combined arena for cricket, football and hockey. One journalist caustically remarked that the presence of one or two persons with knowledge of sports and stadiums across the world would have greatly benefitted a stadium committee otherwise peopled by politicians.[40] Finally, the decision to construct the stadium in Bidhannagar was taken during a conference of the Congress government which came to power in 1972, a late-night discussion among Siddhartha Sankar Ray, now chief minister, and Public Works Minister Bhola Roy and Youth Congress president Priyaranjan Dasmunshi. The resolution was finalised in 1973. Work did not progress as planned as the government's attention shifted to building an indoor stadium next to the Eden Gardens as a venue for the World Table Tennis Championship in 1975.[41] The delay resulted in football continuing to be played at the cricket ground.

Siddhartha Shankar Ray was probably the best cricketer among Bengali politicians, who captained the cricket and football teams of Presidency College.[42] He led the college to its ninth and final Elliot Shield and Hardinge Birthday Shield in 1939. He joined the cricket squad of Kalighat, which was then captained by Berry Sarbadhikary. He achieved the 1,000 runs landmark in three consecutive seasons between 1940 and 1942, with four double centuries. In Sarbadhikary's opinion, Ray could have excelled in cricket had he played just one sport. Ray represented Law College in cricket, football, hockey and tennis from 1941 to 1943, played inter-university football and cricket for Calcutta University, and cricket for the Indian Gymkhana in London. His father, Sudhir Ray, was a Sporting Union cricketer and maternal grandfather, Chittaranjan Das, played cricket too.[43] As the central Education Minister in 1971, he specially flew to Bombay to receive the cricketers returning from the Caribbean tour on behalf of the Union government.[44] He tried to organise cricket matches to raise funds for the victims of Bangladesh's war of liberation.[45]

Ray took an active interest in organising Test matches during his chief ministership between 1972 and 1977. At his behest, Home Minister Subrata Mukherjee set aside his personal apathy to cricket and temporarily shifted his office to the Eden Gardens to supervise law and order.[46] In 1972, Sports Minister Prafullakanti Ghosh chose not to follow suit, to avoid any suspicion of the government's interference in the CAB's activities. There were complaints that about 180 young members of Youth Congress and Chhatra Parishad asked the CAB to entrust them with gate keeping. The CAB, afraid that these people might misuse the privilege and let party workers enter without passes, requested Ghosh to bring the incident to the notice of Ray and Youth Congress president Priyaranjan Dasmunshi.[47] Ray duly put an end to the students' enthusiasm. He regularly interacted with cricketers and was known to develop cordial relationships with many of them. He once suggested that all Indian players should marry Bengali women, as the state's sons-in-law (Pataudi Junior and Erapalli Prasanna) turned out be outstanding cricketers.[48] In 1976, he laid the foundation stone of the CAB's new office building. Unhappy with the BCCI not scheduling any of the Test matches against New Zealand in 1976 due to its rotation policy, he asked the CAB president A. N. Ghose to write a letter stating that 'Bengal refuses to be bypassed in this manner.'[49] He was elected president of the CAB in 1982 and for another term between 1983 and 1985. Later, he worked as Sourav Ganguly's lawyer twice, once overturning the sentence of a two-Test ban imposed by the match referee Clive Lloyd in 2004 and next reducing a six-ODI suspension by the match referee Chris Broad for a repeat offence in 2005 to four matches.[50]

The efforts made by politicians and public officials to attend matches or listen to radio commentary, often malingering, elicited humorous responses. As part of the press, cartoonists referred to sport to communicate their political misgivings. In a cartoon in the *Jugantar*, a parrot informed a telephone caller that the minister had gone to the Eden Gardens to watch the Test match.[51] A cartoon in the *Hindustan Times* displayed the guilty impulse of watching sport by showing a minister at a tennis match whispering to another that he was supposed to be at the Planning Commission and should not be photographed watching tennis.[52] Another cartoon in the same newspaper depicted a minister listening to radio commentary inside his chamber while his personal assistant refused appointments to visitors, telling them how busy the minister was.[53] As a recurring criticism of political culture, these cartoons warned readers against trusting current politicians and civil servants with the task of developing the country, given their negligence of administrative responsibilities. Such criticisms proved to have little effect on the people concerned. When England visited Calcutta in 1977, one television set each was installed in the canteen and the room of the Deputy Secretary for Information and Public Relations at the Writers' Building. Ministers could be seen disposing of files at the office and returning to the stadium.[54] Evidently, the lampoons were no longer embarrassing. The nation's success in cricket made the cricket field an extension of political offices.

POLITICIANS AND CRICKET AFTER 1977

A Left Front led by the CPI(M) came to power in West Bengal in 1977. Chief Minister Jyoti Basu, a competent footballer in his student days in Calcutta and London, believed that sport was above politics. When he was the United Front government's deputy chief minister during the tumultuous late 1960s, one journalist asked him if sporting spirit could resolve the conflict of interest within the government. He had responded that fair play would not work in politics where too many vested interests intersected.[55] The CAB pleaded to the Left Front government not to stage football matches at the Eden Gardens but Basu took a populist stance and rejected the plea.[56] He managed the office of the sports minister for a few years after coming to power. In 1978, he presented awards at the CAB's annual prize distribution ceremony and inaugurated the Pankaj Gupta Sports Library. The library had 700 books and every edition of the *Wisden* almanac between 1895 and 1957.[57] He pledged support for the development of sport across the state, beginning with the installation of four fully covered practice pitches at the Eden Gardens.[58] Sanghamitra Das, a regular writer of letters to the *Khelar Asar*, criticised Basu's act of patronage as surrender to cricket for cheap popularity.[59] Her allegation of Basu's deviation from socialist principles was not taken kindly by other readers. At least two of the latter chastised her for bringing politics into cricket and the double standard of appreciating the former Congress chief minister for constructing an indoor stadium but condemning Basu for providing better practice facilities for cricketers.[60] Political opponents missed no chance to exploit an organisational blunder against his ministerial position. Prafullakanti Ghosh, now president of the Aryan club, demanded Basu's resignation after 16 people were killed in a stampede during the East Bengal–Mohun Bagan match on 16

August 1980, criticising excessive state interference in managing sport and politically motivated distribution of tickets.[61]

The growing indignation of cricket followers with football in the Eden Gardens compelled the government to soon end its support for a composite stadium and plan a new stadium at Bidhannagar. One reader had complained to the *Sportsworld* editor that the ravaging of the Eden Gardens' 'chastity and elegance' needed to be condemned and stopped.[62] The government's plan for the new stadium caused fresh controversies. On 22 November 1979, the Society for Sports and Stadium was founded under Basu's chieftainship. They did not consult the CAB, the Indian Football Association (IFA) or the three major clubs, East Bengal, Mohun Bagan and Mohammedan Sporting. The society's governing body consisted of high-ranking government officials and a number of CPI(M) members. Politicians from other communist parties were ignored, giving the CPI(M) full control over the society. Despite the snub, the CAB continued to ingratiate itself with Basu for future favours. In 1982, they presented him with a souvenir, a badge, a tie and a bunch of red roses on the occasion of the India–England match. Since he was unable to attend the function, CAB vice-president Biswanath Dutt requested Public Works Minister Jatin Chakaravorty to convey the gifts.[63]

The society's members remained in office until the general election of 1982, after which the defeated Finance Minister Ashok Mitra was replaced by S. Venkatraman. The society organised a small meeting with journalists in April 1982 in which Jyoti Basu formally accorded it the responsibility of stadium building. It was disclosed that the society would raise 10–12 crore rupees from life memberships of 10,000 rupees and institutional memberships of 25,000 rupees. The members would be able to watch sports at the Bidhannagar stadium and the Eden Gardens. The society demanded the construction of 10,000 new seats at the Eden Gardens for its members. This would mean reserving a large part of the gallery for people affluent enough to buy life memberships. If no new stands were built, these seats were to be reserved in the existing gallery. A *Khelar Asar* correspondent wrote that this membership plan would enable rich people to receive tickets throughout their lives, and restrict the chances of middle- and lower-income people of watching sport.[64] The society's chairperson, Kamal Bose, argued that some cricket followers might feel slighted, but this arrangement would allow 110,000 people to watch every other sport at the new stadium. Sport and Youth Affairs Minister Subhas Chakraborty too was in favour of general cricket spectators giving up space for the greater good. The CAB remained silent as its president,

Snehangshu Acharya, was also the society's vice-president. The next CAB president, Siddhartha Sankar Ray, now the opposition leader, objected and had the proposition shelved.[65]

During the left rule, political issues haunted the cricket field more than ever. The frictions within Assamese politics during the ethnonationalist movement starting in 1979 put the CAB in an uncomfortable situation. The movement aimed to secure the rights of people who identified as ethnic Assamese, against Bengali immigrants from Bangladesh. It soon became very violent and needed the Centre's intervention for law and order, resulting in the imposition of President's Rule several times over the next decade.[66] Probably in solidarity with and to emphasise the movement's anti-Bengali rhetoric, the Assam Cricket Association decided to boycott the India–Pakistan Test match in Calcutta and returned its quota of 500-odd tickets. The Cachar District Sports Association, a representative of a Bengali-majority district in Assam, opposed this boycott. Its secretary telegrammed the CAB for tickets to its representatives who had already left for Calcutta. The CAB could not help as they had already returned the tickets allocated for Assam to the BCCI, and the match was sold out. An MP from Silchar wrote to the CAB president about buying two season tickets. He was told that Assam has forfeited its quota and hence the right to claim anything.[67] The match reflected the fault lines in political exchanges between the Centre and states.

The England team's tour of India in 1981–82 tested the CPI(M)'s cohesion. The team included Geoff Cook and Geoff Boycott, two cricketers who had played in apartheid South Africa. The CPI(M) politburo demanded the tour's cancellation unless the cricketers were excluded from the team. The Bengal communists were concerned more about the backlash if the Test match was cancelled on an ideological pretext months before the assembly elections. The CAB and the State Sport Council president, Snehangshu Acharya, wanted the match to take place and received support from other political stalwarts in the state.[68] The state government, unable to decide between populism and ideology, tried to find an excuse for not organising the cricket match, saying that they lacked the resources to provide security to both cricket and the international film festival coinciding with the match. They projected the film festival as more important because of the participation of people from more than two countries, unlike the cricket match.[69] The CPI(M) eventually decided to support the match but asked its ministers not to attend. Their communist allies did not even pretend to boycott the match. Five Revolutionary Communist Party of India and four Forward

Bloc ministers collected their pool of tickets.[70] For some members of the Left Front parties, the apartheid controversy was a reminder of the Doug Walters incident in a new decade.

As the English team marched into the team hotel on 1 January 1982, 50–60 members of the Indian Students Association demonstrated for 30 minutes in front of building, starting at 5 p.m. They left a memorandum, addressed to the English team manager, with the officer-in-charge of Taltala police station. They alleged baton charge by the police on the peaceful demonstration, which the police later denied.[71] England's physiotherapist Bernard Thomas received the memorandum but nothing more was known of it. English cricketers Ian Botham, Graham Gooch, John Emburey and Bob Willis spent time at the racecourse without any incident of harassment.[72] CPI(M) ministers tried to assuage their central command by avoiding the match.[73] For the first time in many years, the state's chief minister was not present on the opening day. Jatin Chakravorty welcomed the governor and his wife to the ground, saying 'good luck' to them for some unknown reason, but did not once go to the VIP box. He watched the match on television on the ground floor of the Club House.[74] India drew the match, but the CPI(M) won over both its voters and the politburo. Political partisans found another shot at protest when Sunil Gavaskar pulled out of the Test match against Pakistan in 1987.

Gavaskar decided against playing at the Eden Gardens as a result of untoward incidents during the Test match against England in 1984–85. The mercurial all-rounder Kapil Dev was dropped from the Indian side as a punishment for playing an irresponsible stroke during the previous Test match in New Delhi and throwing tantrums when confronted. Kapil was a crowd favourite, and also a counterweight to captain Gavaskar in the team. Calcutta spectators resented Kapil's exclusion and put up 'No Kapil, no Test' posters around the stadium. Slow batting by both India and England dashed any hope of an outcome. Gavaskar's decision to prolong India's first innings into the third day particularly irritated the crowd. Even a police officer felt compelled to ask Gavaskar to declare and show some urgency to win. Finally, when Gavaskar led the team onto the field for the England innings, a section of spectators pelted him with fruits and abused his wife. The police arrested nine people for attacking Gavaskar.[75] Incensed by the insult to his wife, he swore never to play in Calcutta again.

A section of the press sympathised with Gavaskar; another section would have liked him to transcend personal troubles for the sake of the nation.

Among the well-known Bengali people annoyed with the decision were authors Atin Bandyopadhyay and Baren Gangopadhyay and sportspersons Prakash Poddar, Samir Chakbabarty, Samar Banerji, Sukumar Samajpati, Probir Mukherjee and Prasun Banerjee.[76] Journalists such as Kunal Kanti Ghosh doubted Gavaskar's professionalism.[77] A reader wrote to the editor of *Sportsworld*, 'Gavaskar may have reached the sky as a cricketer, but he does not even reach up to his physical height as a sportsman.'[78] Journalist Amitabha Chowdhury would have preferred Gavsakar to rise above personal grievances, but empathised with the cricketer's anguish at the disrespect towards his wife by a section of spectators.[79] The Students Federation of India suspected that Gavaskar's unavailability was a ploy to disgrace the state government. Other youth and students' organisations planned demonstrations. The stadium was consequently full of anti-Gavaskar posters, one of which read: 'Little Master Is Too Little for Eden Gardens'.[80] Another brand of posters said, 'Gavaskar is now the burden of Eden'. The batsman was so much at the centre of attention that the public overlooked Younis Ahmed, a Pakistani team member, who had also played in apartheid South Africa.[81]

Subhas Chakraborty sent a radiogram requesting Gavaskar to play in the upcoming ODI match, arguing that a great cricketer should respect the will of millions of sports lovers and not base a decision on the behaviour of a few miscreants. Congress politician Rajesh Khaitan asked the chief minister to intervene and ensure Gavaskar played. He told journalists that it might be too late to convince the batsman to play in the Test match, but he must play in the ODI match or face the consequences. He warned that Congress members would gherao BCCI members if they were to forget Gavaskar's disregard for cricket and country and select him for the next Test match.[82] The West Bengal Cultural Association general secretary, Anjan Nag, went on a hunger strike along with other members from his association in front of the footballer Gostho Paul's statue in the *maidan*, demanding the sacking of Gavaskar.[83] Former Sports Minister Prafullakanti Ghosh ridiculed the excesses, exonerating the cricketer.[84] The 'little master' salvaged some of the lost reputation by telexing Chakraborty from Bombay,

> Thank you for your message. The sentiment expressed is much appreciated. Even if the circumstances for my unavailability were to change it would be unfair of me to deprive a player of his place since the side has already been selected. My sincere and best wishes to you and the people of Calcutta.[85]

During the 1987 Test match against Pakistan, the press revelled at the opportunity to fill political gossip columns because of the attendance of many politicians. One of the reports exclaimed, 'If the presence of Jyoti Basu, Jatin Chakravorty, Prasanta Shur, Subhas Chakbaborty and other painted the VIP box red before lunch, the likes of Ashok Sen and Priyaranjan Dasmunshi brought in Congress colours after lunch.'[86] Journalists sometimes generalised politicians as cricket fans, partly in a bid to curry favour and partly owing to ignorance of the person's intention and interests. The *Amrita Bazar Patrika* thought that Subrata Mukherjee must be a true cricket lover since he was watching the India–West Indies Test match in New Delhi in 1987.[87] Congress politicians were not so visible during the Test match against England 1993, probably as Somen Mitra and Tapas Roy had accused the CAB of putting tickets on the black market and called for a boycott.[88] The reporter was unaware that Mukherjee thought cricket reflected feudalism, and took his presence alongside Sudip Bandopadhyay and Sushovan Bose as an assured sign of affection for the game rather than a political gesture.

The demand for tickets reached its crescendo before the final match during the 1987 World Cup. Certain that the defending champion India would brush aside every challenge and lift the trophy, politicians and government officers of all denominations demanded tickets to the match. As many as 148 councillors from across parties united in the demand for one complimentary and two paid tickets for the final. Congress leader Rathin Ghosh announced that Congress and CPI(M) councillors and aldermen would depute Mayor Kamal Bose to send a proposal to CAB secretary Jagmohan Dalmiya. The mayor said that councillors were given tickets until 1976. When asked why so many councillors should get complimentary tickets, one of them retorted that he would otherwise dump ten truckloads of garbage in front of the stadium. A CAB member responded that Calcutta need not be disgraced any further; the condition of the streets, lights and garbage disposals were dismal enough. Dalmiya said he would forward the proposal to a committee for the final decision.[89]

The councillors urged the organisers to offer the city's mayor, deputy mayor, chairperson of the municipal council and the leader of the opposition the same privileges as ministers got during these matches. They also asked to be given as many tickets as MLAs received. Shiv Kumar Sharma, leader of the opposition, asked the mayor to boycott World Cup matches should the CAB refuse to issue free tickets. The Indian National Trade Union Congress–affiliated Calcutta Corporation Employees' and Workers' Union threatened to organise a demonstration unless Dalmiya apologised for his remarks about the mayor and the councillors.[90] It should be noted that Dalmiya fiercely resisted political interference in sports administration all his life. He and the CAB president, Biswanath Dutt, asked Prime Minister Rajiv Gandhi to waive the 400,000 rupees tax imposed on the roller and mower imported from Australia on the occasion of the World Cup, but he did not want to involve politicians in administration.[91] When the central government threatened to take over the BCCI in 1999, he was said to have told the Secretary for Sports, N. N. Khanna, 'We have not come here to listen to trash from you.'[92] He practised the same confrontational policy in his home state, antagonising the government.

The Labour Union Association protested the spend on embellishing Calcutta for the World Cup, asking the government to construct housing with proper drainage and water supply for the poor instead. They submitted a memorandum addressed to the central Public Works Minister to Urban Development Minister Buddhadeb Bhattacharjee, also a passionate cricket follower. Members of the association sat for an eight-hour strike at Esplanade East.[93] Secretary-ranked officials received two final tickets each, one for free and the other to be purchased for 400 rupees. Joint and deputy secretaries were not eligible.[94] Four councillors, Prakash Ranjan Pal, Amal Dutta, Rajkishor Gupta and Sanjay Bakshi, wrote a letter to the Union sports minister, Margaret Alva, complaining about the laundering of tickets to business houses with no connection to cricket and deprivation of general cricket lovers. The letter ended with the demand for tickets to the final as their right as councillors.[95] Political matters were so intricately related to cricketing performance that after India's loss to England in the semi-final, one politician shouted within earshot of Prime Minister Rajiv Gandhi, 'What do you expect with that guy in charge?'[96] The stadium continued to be a political theatre. In 1999, Rupak Saha estimated that politicians and civil servants occupied two-thirds of the 3,200 Club House seats.[97] The blatant use of privilege to watch important matches and assertion of power through political demonstrations entangled the vocation and fanhood of politicians. The political and personal selves collapsed in varying degrees among politicians. Some politicians such as Jatin Chakravorty came across as genuine cricket lovers in a manner Jyoti Basu did not. The popular image of politicians as untrustworthy power-mongers continued to influence the press to distinguish the motivation of politicians from other spectators despite their common crave for tickets.

CENTRE–STATE RELATIONS AND CRICKET

Raj Singh Dungarpur, a former chairperson of the national selection committee, remarked in 1992, 'An Indian Prime Minister can be dishonest while choosing a cabinet. But you cannot be dishonest while selecting the national cricket team. The public will not allow it. You feel the weight of the country's expectations every time you sit down to select the best to represent the country.'[98] The method of selecting eleven players for the national team in a country divided along race, ethnicity, language, religion and politics was bound to rile some section of the public. Every state resented national selectors ignoring its coterie of India probables. Regional stereotypes such as batsmen from Bombay or bowlers from the south were embedded so deeply in the selection process that selectors were often accused of ignoring excellent bowlers from Bombay or batsmen from the south.[99] Bengal rarely had a player in the national team. The people of Bengal went beyond a distrust of selectors to uniquely blaming Indian federalism and the Centre's discriminatory attitude towards Bengal for having influenced the BCCI to neglect their cricketers. Many scholars have studied Centre–state collaborations in administration, legislation and policy development, which have shown the existence of political disputes and bargaining even during Congress rule at both central and state levels.[100] In the CPI(M) era, mobilisations around a strong subnational Bengali identity, regionalism and sentiments against the Congress's alleged betrayal of the state strengthened the anti-Centre outlook of the people.[101] This also further entrenched the rhetoric of the BCCI's discriminatory attitude towards Bengal cricketers as a concerted attempt by the Centre to humiliate the state.

The press in Calcutta has historically attributed the non-selection of Bengali cricketers in the Indian team to a conspiracy to slander the achievements of Bengalis. Sujit Mukherjee, a regular reader of the *Desh*, the state's premier literary periodical, reportedly told Ramachandra Guha that the magazine was so infatuated with the theory that every year it would carry at least one cover story or major article entitled 'Aar koto din ei enyayi ...' (For how much longer this injustice).[102] Bengalis have alleged that the Centre has blatantly discriminated against the state in terms of resource allocation since the capital of British India was shifted from Calcutta to Delhi in 1911. This narrative of deprivation, rooted in colonial and postcolonial India's political economy, is so deep-seated in the Bengali psyche that they hold this prejudiced character of the nation-state responsible for national selectors overlooking Bengali cricketers for the Indian team. Selection politics could be behind some of these decisions, but the link made between cricket and national politics in the press provided the locals yet another course of venting their dissatisfaction with the nation.

Bengali journalists brought unrelated political issues into the cricket selection controversy, creating a comprehensive lived practice of being the victim of favouritism and injustice. In general, they like to project the idea that other provinces were jealous of Bengal's lead in politics and culture in colonial India. Bengal's decline began with the shifting of the imperial capital to Delhi and the ascendancy of Gandhian nationalism over Bengali revolutionary strategy as the more accepted method of anti-colonial struggle in the early twentieth century. Author Nirad C. Chaudhuri aptly summarised the power relation between Indian states in the 1930s saying, 'What the Englishman was to the Bengali, the Bengali was to the Hindustani.'[103] Other states gradually challenged and dismantled this internal hierarchy, and the failure to recuperate from the downfall apparently made the Bengalis desperate to clasp on to the lost world of pride. The community took shelter behind the shield of cultural arrogance, yearning the command that dwindled every passing year.

The clamour of a national cricket conspiracy against Bengal started in the 1930s as Shute Banerjee was denied an India cap during the 1936 tour of England for refusing to insult C. K. Nayudu at the breakfast table.[104] In his autobiography, Mushtaq Ali mentioned two other cricketers who should have been selected in the 1930s – the 'great Bengal all-rounder' Kamal Bhattacharya and 'that delightful stroke-maker' Nirmal Chatterjee.[105] The public would have expected better treatment of local talents once Bengal's Bechu Datta Ray became powerful in the cricket board in the 1940s. However, the situation turned for the worse as Datta Ray seemed to be committed to promoting only players from Sporting Union.[106] One of the first victims of Datta Ray's regime was Sudhangshu Sekhar Banerjee, better known by his nickname Mantu. A medium pacer with the ability to swing the ball both ways, Banerjee came into contention for a position in the Bengal cricket team in 1941. His performance in a match between Calcutta Cricket Club and the Cooch Behar XI was to decide his inclusion in the state team. A rumour spread before the match that someone influential had asked the Maharaja of Cooch Behar, better known as Bhaya, not to open the bowling with Banerjee to reduce the bowler's chances of getting wickets. The Maharaja was no person to take orders; he opened the bowling with Banerjee and the bowler took seven wickets, making a compelling case for his selection.

Mantu Banerjee was called up to the Indian team to play against West Indies in Calcutta in 1948 after taking the first and till date the only first-class hat-trick at the Brabourne Stadium in Bombay. He bowled well and took five wickets, but at Datta Ray's behest the Mohun Bagan club's Putu Chowdhury replaced him for the next match.[107] Chowdhury played only one more match for India, and Banerjee never again. Chowdhury made way for the veteran Shute Banerjee in the final Test match, which was the latter's only international appearance, made memorable by a haul of five wickets. The resolute Maharaja of Cooch Behar became more amenable to suggestions within two years. Anil Dasgupta recalled having been involved in an unpleasant incident during a trial match at the Kalighat ground which was used for selecting the Bengal team for the 1942–43 season. Bhaya declared the innings before Dasgupta had a chance to bat. After Dasgupta took three wickets, one of the selectors spoke to Bhaya during a drink break. Dasgupta was taken off from the attack at once and missed selection for Bengal. Bhaya went on to captain the Ranji team which lost to Western India in the final in 1943–44.[108]

Probir Sen represented India between 1948 and 1952 when West Bengal was swamped with problems arising from India's independence and partition. The state's territory was truncated by more than half, much of its natural resources went to the province now controlled by Pakistan, and the influx of Hindu refugees from the avowedly Islamic East Pakistan caused a massive demographic crisis. The political muscle of the Bengali leadership in the central government was now a shadow of its strength in the 1920s. The allegation that Bengal cricket officials paid 5,000 rupees to the national selectors Lala Amarnath, Phiroze Palia and Datta Ray for Sen's inclusion, necessary probably as Sen played for Kalighat and not Sporting Union, was largely buried under the debris of predicaments.[109] The local press in the 1950s were not sufficiently supportive of Premangshu Chatterjee and Durga Shankar Mukherjee, swing bowlers with extraordinary first-class bowling averages, who were overlooked in favour of cricketers with worse statistics. It was more concerned with the state's financial stake which declined rapidly after 1947 following the withdrawal of colonial European capital.

The wheels of the economic discrimination theory started to roll in 1956 as the Centre's policy of freight equalisation worked against the interest of the industrial belt in eastern India. The brainchild of Union Finance Minister T. T. Krishnamachari, the new policy subsidised the cost of transporting iron ore and coal anywhere in the country to foster new industries. Most of the investors in heavy industry were based in western and southern India, who were now able to import minerals from eastern India at a cheap rate and develop industries in their home states. Industries in eastern India stagnated as they no longer enjoyed the advantage of local resources, and fresh investments did not come up. All that West Bengal received from the Centre in this decade was a steel plant in Durgapur. None of the eastern states, led mostly by Congress governments, realised the long-term consequence of this policy despite cautionary editorial pieces by Sachin Chaudhuri and the like. The prosperous jute industry in West Bengal suffered from the Centre's plan of minimum support prices of buying fibres.[110] Complaints of discrimination mounted in the 1960s as the state became a political muddle. The Centre's apparently lukewarm response to aid refugee resettlement, grant industrial and business licence, and share a larger amount of annual revenue fuelled countless editorials and opinion pieces. The sports press too became intent on criticising the cricket board for systematically ignoring the state's sporting capabilities.

The prolific batsman Shyam Sundar Mitra was purportedly denied the India cap as he refused Datta Ray's invitation to play for Sporting Union. Amidst the chorus of discrimination, the non-selection of the Bengali medium pacer Subrata Guha in the Test team catalysed a riot in 1966–67. The United Front came into power in the state government a month after the riot, displacing the 20-year Congress rule. The coalition government faced the challenges of internal bickering and law and order situation. The Centre, unhappy with the state's failure to resolve the escalating problems, dismissed the legislative assembly and imposed President's Rule, which Bengal saw as an undue intervention. Chief Minister Ajoy Mukherjee vowed to resist the Centre's effort to cripple the state. An idea of the Centre depriving the state of its constitutional right sprouted across social strata. The pervasive sense of victimisation made the Centre an easy scapegoat for politicians. Planning Minister Somnath Lahiri alleged that the Centre's intention to interfere in the state's administration was clear from how it denied United Front ministers priority in the allocation of office telephones.[111] While the state tottered on the brink of civil unrest in the autumn of 1969, Guha received the India call-up against Australia in Bombay. However, the selection committee chairperson, Vijay Merchant, asked Guha to step down minutes before the toss so that Srinivas Venkataraghavan could be played. Merchant issued a statement lauding Guha's great sportsmanship, mentioning what Guha told him: 'If the selection committee and the captain feel that Venkataraghavan would be more useful to the side to have a chance of winning the Test match, I would gladly sit out and give him my place. To me, my country comes first.'[112] Surprisingly, none of the Calcutta dailies raised storm over Guha's non-selection. The feature writer Ajay Home praised Guha's attitude towards the devastating decision and consideration for the greater interest of the nation.[113]

The talking heads in the media seemed never to stop debating the decline of Calcutta. Editorial pages were always full of estimations if the city had reached its saturation point and the possible ways forward.[114] Bengalis were now so averse to non-Bengalis that even the Calcutta Municipal Development Authority was once suspected to be involved in an anti-Bengali conspiracy.[115] Pakistani businessperson Afzal Rasheed reminisced in an interview with Mudar Patherya how his college classmate Dilip Doshi, who later played in 33 Test and 15 ODI matches, always complained during the 1970s that selection politics would keep him out of the national team forever.[116] Doshi himself lamented in his autobiography about the lack of a godfather, attacking Gavaskar and Kapil Dev for promoting Ravi Shastri and Maninder Singh to replace him as the first choice left-arm spinner.[117] The press was now so obsessed with the theory of conspiracy that even allocation of space for English radio commentators directly behind the wicket and for Bengali commentators at an adverse angle from the pitch became a component of the plot. A correspondent of the *Jugantar* declared that nobody cared about the inconvenience of Bengali commentators because of their ethnicity and residence in Calcutta.[118] The most unfortunate Bengali cricketer from the 1970s was perhaps Gopal Bose. A steady opening batsman, considered by many to be the perfect foil to Sunil Gavaskar, Bose went in and out of the 14-member squad without ever given a shot at playing. He had a spat with team captain Mansur Ali Khan Pataudi during a train ride and refused to apologise to a board official for an offence he did not cause. This could have antagonised the decision-makers during his purple patch in 1974–75.[119] Bose was very critical of the dissension among Bengali officials that frustrated local talents and handicapped cricket in the state.

The CPI(M) significantly consolidated its hold over the state's electoral politics and voters in the early 1970s before forming the state government as the major player of the Left Front in 1977.[120] The party was seen as a 'regionally rooted opposition' to Congress hegemony in national politics for the rest of its 34 years in power.[121] It suggested radical changes to the Centre's constitutional powers, including sending security forces to a state, the president's authority to suspend a state government, and rejecting any bill passed by the state legislature. It asked for a bigger share of revenues generated by income tax, excise duties, corporation tax and customs duties to ease the massive financial burden imposed by increasing expenditure on agriculture, irrigation, education, public health and justice.[122] In 1980, it accused the Centre of providing only half of the amount of the state's allocated share of food grain, sitting on 14 important bills and unlawfully delaying election without consulting the state government – in short showing no interest to develop a state not ruled by the Congress.[123] The Congress maintained throughout the 1980s that the anti-Centre diatribe was a cloak for the communists' own inefficiency. They piled up facts in favour of their argument against those posited by West Bengal. Although cricket was not yet one of the areas the CPI(M) was invested in, Ramachandra Guha, based on his experience of studying in Calcutta in the decade, poses a conundrum to ponder:

> Here indeed is a fit topic for a Ph.D. thesis in political science: would the communist-dominated Left Front have ever come to power if the Indian cricket selectors had not so cruelly treated Ambar Roy, Subroto Guha, Gopal Bose, D.S. Mukherjee and Dipankar Sarkar? This is indeed a dissertation topic that even lends itself to postdoctoral research – for would the Left Front have stayed in power so long if Robin Mukherjee, Barun Barman, Amitava Roy, Sambaran Banerjee, and Utpal Chatterjee had got their just desserts?[124]

The confrontation escalated after the Left Front won its second term in West Bengal in 1982.[125] Finance Minister Ashok Mitra accused the Centre of trying to unseat the CPI(M) from power by systematic financial deprivation of over 700 crore rupees.[126] In a public meeting organised by the Democratic Youth Federation to discuss the Centre's conspiracies, Jyoti Basu resented the Centre's decision to implement the Finance Commission's recommendations in the Congress-governed states and postpone it until the next year for West Bengal. He called it a policy of 'economic belligerence against a constituent of the Indian union.'[127] Several observers affirmed the Centre's attempt to weaken the state government's political support by obstructing economic growth and the latter's criticism of the Centre and demand for changing the Union–state relations throughout the decade.[128] Others refuted the state's discrimination claims as largely unfounded since revenues seemed to be evenly disbursed across states.[129] With their election promise of emancipating the downtrodden fast dissipating, all that remained for the CPI(M) towards the late 1980s was to play the blame game and, to quote Günter Grass, 'live off advance payments of hope'.[130] In 1988 Basu forged political capital out of the Centre's refusal to clear the Haldia petro-chemical and Bakreshwar thermal power projects for 11 years, calling a strike in protest against the injustice.[131] However, the state's former prestige irreconcilably declined during the left rule, which author Amit Chaudhuri describes as a spiralling decrepitude:

> Within India itself, Calcutta had become a butt of jokes. This slow turn was fascinating; the former centre of 'culture', once admired for its eccentricity and waywardness being ridiculed by other uppity cities like Delhi and Bombay for being obsolete and out of joint; for its unionised workplace, its permanent go-slow work ethic, its oppositional politics. Resistance to change and, eventually, to globalisation came to be seen as Bengali traits. It was a mood encouraged by the Left Front government …[132]

Alongside these political interdictions, the press was particularly attentive to what it perceived as a methodical omission of Bengalis from every major national honour. The fact that only 3 out of the 27 Jnanpith awardees between 1965 and 1990 were Bengalis was hurtful to a people proud of their culture above every other sphere of life. Reports of the mistreatment of cricketers reinforced the sentiment of victimisation. Bengal's stock in the Indian team collapsed drastically after the brief stints of Subrata Guha and Ambar Roy in the late 1960s. Wicket-keeper Sambaran Banerjee raised hopes of Test selection in 1976 as the selectors were looking to replace Syed Kirmani. It was rumoured that a former Test cricketer had asked Banerjee to shift to his club, promising his selection among the Test probables, thus giving him a platform to prove his worth. At the same time, Banerjee declined Bedi's offer to join the Mohan Meakins Company in Delhi and Ashok Mankad's invitation to go to Bombay, choosing to stay with his family and play for the East Bengal club. These decisions might have gone against him.[133]

Impressed with Banerjee's performance in a West Zone–East Zone Duleep Trophy match in Ahmedabad in 1976, selector Vijay Mehra hinted at his selection for the upcoming Test match against New Zealand. Karsan Ghavri congratulated Banerjee during the tea break on the last day, saying the latter and Parthasarathi Sharma would be in the team. When the team was announced at 8 p.m., Bharat Reddy was found to have been selected as the wicket-keeper ahead of Banerjee.[134] The lost opportunity turned out to be the last as Banerjee was never in the hunt again; he was not invited even to the trial camp before the Pakistan tour in 1978. The telling absence of Bengalis in the national team prompted author Prafulla Roy to wonder that if the 10 million youth out of the 50 million people in West Bengal could not yield a single international cricketer, would it take long for Bengalis to go out of contention in every other field![135] His premonition was supported by the decline in the state's success at the national engineering, medicine and civil service examinations, and of course cricket.

Raju Mukharji's non-selection in the East Zone that played Australia in 1979 provided the press another excuse to lament discrimination.[136] The *Sportsworld* correspondent began the match report with an assertion about the stepmotherly attitude of national selectors.[137] A letter writer complained against one Hindi commentator abusing Pankaj Roy and Bengalis on live television.[138] During the 1980 Test match against Pakistan, Alok Bhattacharya substituted the ill Sunil Gavaskar and fielded for two full days. Yet he received the twelfth man's fee of 1,500 rupees instead of the full match allowance of 10,600 rupees, no place in the team hotel and arranged his own transport from his home in Howrah to the stadium. One day he had to depend on a former Test cricketer to drop him home after the end of play. Neither he nor the other Bengali cricketer in the squad, Barun Burman, was invited to the party organised for the Test cricketers. In contrast with Dilip Vengasarkar being provided all the facilities including accommodation in the team hotel and full match fee despite not playing in the match, the board's apathy towards Bhattacharya shocked the press. The locals were convinced that Bhattacharya was not taken seriously because he was a Bengali.[139]

Local sports periodicals kept supporting Banerjee and Burman. Alok Dasgupta wrote in the *Khelar Asar* about how selectors from other zones forced their preferred players into the national team. Talented East Zone players received scant opportunities.[140] The clamour to have Burman in the national team reached such a high decibel that a selector was said to have woken up a colleague at 5 a.m., asking the latter to include Burman and save him from the wrath of Bengal officials.[141] An interview-based life sketch of the sport administrator A. N. Ghosh published in the *Khelar Asar* was entitled 'Injustice to Bengali Cricketers Continues'.[142] The article traced Ghosh's journey from a cricketer with Albert Sporting, whose career never took off due to a knee injury, to the president of the BCCI between 1969 and 1972. Ghosh spoke about the contest between the English-dominated Calcutta Cricket Club and the Bengali-controlled Bengal Gymkhana over cricket administration in colonial Bengal, prevalence of the latter in the

CAB, acquisition of the lease of the Eden Gardens after independence, and formation of the NCC. It was while speaking about his term with the BCCI that he admitted the policy of discrimination against Bengali cricketers. A statement by no measure central to the article was made the headline. The intensity of such reports during the early 1980s diminished towards the end of the decade as the state seemed to have given up hope of watching a local play regularly for the national team. Spectators would shout 'Bangali Jago' (Rise, Bengalis) as Arun Lal, a Delhite who played for Bengal, went out to bat in a Test match.[143] A century by Sourav Ganguly against England in 1996 reopened the fissures in interstate relations.

A review of the journalistic output during Ganguly's career reflects a mass-mediated primordial sentiment of maintaining a communal bond against the pressure of assimilating into the national mainstream. Ganguly's achievements were framed as a revival of the fortune that politicians and industrialists had failed to deliver. Barely months after Ganguly's Test debut against England, the CPI(M) rejected a chance to join the coalition government at the Centre. It received 9.10 per cent of votes, a good result considering it was right after the Congress and the Bharatiya Janata Party (BJP) in terms of the number of seats won. Basu, offered the post of the prime minister, was in favour of joining the government. However, the party's central committee chose to stay out of power, arguing that it did not have sufficient MPs and ministers to command policy changes. Ganguly alleviated the pains of this 'historic blunder' with a long career full of memorable performances, stoking the Bengali ego into an all-consuming fire of parochial pride that relentless journalists ensured was never put out. A poster boy for West Bengal and the CPI(M), Ganguly never promoted undeserving local players and supported talents from every state. The way he conducted himself elevated his iconic city, which according to Ramachandra Guha was tantamount to the honour given to Satyajit Ray and a little below the veneration received by Rabindranath Tagore and Subhas Chandra Bose.[144] The mediated expressions of the self and the other with regards to Bengali identity as mobilised by Ganguly's career can be used as conceptual tools for examining the internal dynamics of state-making and the place of a state widely mistaken as culturally compact within a heterogeneous nation.

Bengalis found in Ganguly an opportunity to advocate some of their favourable stereotypes and repudiate the damaging conventions. His elegant, sublimely effortless batting affirmed the very elitist but spectacularly popular image of the Bengali gentlemen's modern, creative, artistic, cultured character. The second distinction was negative, symptomatic of the state's steady decline. The team management had bitterly complained about Ganguly's laziness and arrogance at the time of his international debut in 1992. When selectors floated his name for the team again in 1996, the former cricketer Ravi Shastri wrote it off as a gimmick doomed to fail, comparing Ganguly with the famous soft, spongy local sweet called *rosogolla*. The national press threatened to expose the BCCI secretary Jagmohan Dalmiya's complicity in forcing into the team a player from his state.[145] Reflecting the colonial reification of non-martial Bengalis in the national public's conception, cricketers and coaches from other states objectified Ganguly in the traditional mould of cricketers from Bengal – talented but timid, and hence unsuited for the highest level of competition. The tenacity and aggression Ganguly subsequently displayed was made to symbolise in the local press what author Dominique Lapierre claimed to have brought his novel recognition from the West Bengal government, for portraying 'the virtues of courage, vitality, and hope' of the city's people.[146] Basu often made international phone calls to encourage and congratulate the cricketer. When asked to comment on Ganguly's score of 183 against Sri Lanka during the 1999 World Cup, the politician known for his terse remarks made an uncharacteristically long statement to Gautam Bhattacharya, speaking as if he was an affectionate grandfather.[147] Urban Development Minister Ashok Bhattacharjee and Culture and Information Minister Buddhadeb Bhattacharjee were said to be very close to him.

Ganguly consolidated his position in the team by the end of 1997, was the leading run-scorer in ODI cricket in 1999 and was appointed the captain in 2000. Media narratives of his early career leading to the captaincy consistently engaged with the spatialised self–other conflict manifest in the political discrimination stories. Ganguly was said to have rued not getting the kind of support from Bengali press corps that Tendulkar received from the Bombay lobby.[148] Experienced journalists and former cricketers soon launched a concerted effort to develop his persona. After he scored 173 against Sri Lanka in December 1997, Pankaj Roy reminded readers of the discriminations against Ganguly – the futile efforts to demolish his morale by changing his batting position too often.[149] When the team management wanted him to open the batting, the *Aajkal*'s Partho Rudra compared the move to that of sending one's adversary on a tiger hunt. The board could either take credit if Ganguly succeeded or easily discard him if he failed.[150] As soon as Ganguly completed his century, which put him ahead of Roy in the number of Test centuries made by a Bengali, Apu Das, secretary of the Maharaj Fan Club, organised a procession with colourful cut-outs of the cricketer, which was only one of the many parades to have taken place that day.[151] The press highlighted such events as an index of Ganguly's popularity among Bengalis. The title of Sabyasachi Sarkar's book *Sobar Sachin Amader Sourav* (Everybody's Sachin, Our Sourav) epitomised the cultural insularity woven around the cricketer's linguistic identity.[152] Every time he went out to bat, he reportedly battled the combined force of the opposition, some of his teammates, the national selectors and the press from the rest of India.

Ganguly's success looked more spectacular as no other Bengal cricketer was able to replicate his performance. Laxmi Ratan Shukla came close to a Test cap in Colombo in 1999. He even had his name displayed on the scoreboard at the ground as part of the final eleven but then Ashis Nehra was instead seen to take the field. The Bengali media blamed Azharuddin, who was claimed to have objected to Shukla's inclusion during the bus ride to the venue in the morning, much the same way as he had replaced Arun Lal with Venkatpathy Raju minutes before the Test match against Sri Lanka in Chandigarh in 1990.[153] The left-arm spinner Utpal Chatterjee complained that Azharuddin would hardly allow him to have proper practice during the ODI series against New Zealand in 1995, let alone think of playing him in the match. Rupak Saha fulminated against what he perceived as Azhar's method of hurting the sentiments of Bengalis.[154] Most Bengali newspapers conceived the incident as yet another conspiracy, and declared that it made the state seethe with rage.[155]

In the introduction to an anthology of his articles on Ganguly, the *Anandabazar Patrika*'s sports editor Gautam Bhattacharya heralded him as the iceberg of collective Bengali emotion. The abiding wave of deprivation and discontent surged so high that even accomplished Bengalis had started to suspect that the world was up against their community. Ganguly was the weapon for them to scythe through this universal antagonism.[156] He repositioned a state long thought to be gasping for glory into one that breathed normally and approached its task efficiently.[157] Ganguly was so successfully packaged into a community icon that the public would confront journalists for making any critical comment, sometimes uncharitably asking if the latter were paid for such treachery. On the contrary, a number of Bengalis disliked the adulation heaped on Ganguly. Two persons from Chinsurah, listed in Bhattacharya's mobile phone as 'Leave It 1' and 'Leave It 2', taunted his devotion towards Ganguly as scandalously parochial. Many unnamed letter writers wanted to know if the cricketer's rich parents paid journalists for their obedience; some of them asked if his failure would be highlighted more than India's defeat.[158] The excesses of the press resulted in this duality, which intensified as Ganguly's career progressed. The editorials and reports about Ganguly in the 2000s present a site of contested identities, specifically of an indexed battle between the local and the national press, engaging at one level the politics of interstate relations and at another the contradictions within Bengal.

CONCLUSION

This chapter traced the history of how politicians in Bengal capitalised on cricket's appeal to the masses for personal gains and political ascendency. CPI(M) leaders occupied a special place in this oligarchy as their patronage of cricket countermanded the communist party's distrust of the sport as the ultimate bourgeois pastime. The top brass of CPI(M) leaders were an educated middle class whom the author Amit Chaudhuri aptly terms 'orphans of bhadralok history' – a people who found a family in their party and let political allegiance rather than family ties define their identity.[159] In the first 20 years of their rule, the CPI(M) flaunted the left's historical antipathy to capitalism, liberal democracy, globalisation and the like, except Western professional sport. In the 1980s, when South-East Asia realised the importance of technology and the services sector, West Bengal conceded its advantage of a significantly longer history of Western education, middle class and industrialisation by resisting the development of industry and computers, and abolishing English in government primary schools.[160] Cricket not just escaped the state's list of proscriptions, it commanded a pride of place among the party's achievements. A distinctive intellectual strain circled round the party's leadership and publications. Cricket with all its cerebral pastiches was consistent with what the party thought of leisure in theory. They exploited the mass media's growing reach to promote a rhetoric that cricket was in decline during Congress rule and had a resurgence during theirs.

Both politicians and journalists narrativised the non-selection of Bengal cricketers in the national team as symptomatic of the larger malaise of provincialism and discrimination since before independence. This chapter navigated the political patronage of cricket and the mediatised jeremiads against the politicisation of cricket in the context of West Bengal to probe the shadow of politics across the playing field and the mediated intermingling of sporting and political sentiments. The press formulated cricketers as embodiments of West Bengal's contentious identity of a dissident state within a hostile nation. Cricketers were a critical part of the media's protest against the discrimination against Bengalis in every walk of life. Unable to reconcile with other ethnic and language groups who purportedly threatened and superseded Bengal's intellectual excellence and economic prosperity, often working from within the state, the locals sensed a larger conspiracy to undermine the state's leadership in national life. The grudge, over-politicised and institutionalised by the media, questioned the lineage of the modern Indian nation, aggravating annually as the instances of denying financial grants and 'depriving' cricketers increased.

The discontent culminated in a strange furore in the 1990s as Ganguly battled his way into becoming one of the legends of Indian cricket. Bengali sentiments were rallied into opposing camps that either blindly supported him or despised the carousel around him as scandalous. Ganguly's fall from grace in the 2000s, once from the national team and next from his Indian Premier League franchise, exhibited another aspect of group motivation. When personal choices of cricket spectators prevail over the narrative order produced by the press, the spectators and readers start contesting the idioms of mediatised group identities at a fundamental, quotidian level. The public's uneasy understanding of Ganguly's identity as a Bengali cricketer and an Indian captain aptly testified to the fluidity of mediated identity.

NOTES

1. Taya Zinkin, 'Indian Parliamentarians Worried: Cricket Thicker Than Politics', *TG*, 21 February 1959, 1.
2. Ronojoy Sen discusses Jaipal Singh's life in sport and politics in 'Divided Loyalty: Jaipal Singh and His Many Journeys', *Sport in Society* 12, no. 6 (2009): 765–75.
3. *TOI*, 16 December 1955, 13.
4. Ibid., 20 December 1972, 11.
5. Eric Hobsbawm, *The Age of Empire 1875–1914* (New York: Vintage, 1989), 107.
6. Richard Holt, *Sport and the British: A Modern History* (Oxford: Clarendon, 1989), 269.

7. Lincoln Allison, 'The Changing Context of Sporting Life', in *The Changing Politics of Sport*, ed. Lincoln Allison, 1–14 (Manchester: Manchester University Press, 1993), 4.

8. Victor Peppard and James Riordan, *Playing Politics: Soviet Sport Diplomacy to 1992* (Greenwich, CT: JAI Press, 1993); Donald Macintosh and Michael Hawes, *Sport and Canadian Diplomacy* (Montreal: McGill-Queen's University Press, 1994); Peter J. Beck, *Scoring for Britain: International Football and International Politics, 1900–1939* (London and New York: Routledge, 1999); Barbara J. Keys, *Globalizing Sport: National Rivalry and International Community in the 1930s* (Cambridge, MA: Harvard University Press, 2006); Stephen Wagg and David L. Andrews, eds., *East Plays West: Sport and the Cold War* (London and New York: Routledge, 2007); Kevin Jefferys, *Sport and Politics in Modern Britain: The Road to 2012* (Basingstoke: Palgrave Macmillan, 2012); Heather L. Dichter and Andrew L. Johns, eds., *Diplomatic Games: Sport, Statecraft, and International Relations since 1945* (Lexington: University Press of Kentucky, 2014); Craig Esherick, Robert Baker, Steven Jackson and Michael Sam, eds., *Case Studies in Sport Diplomacy* (Morganstown: FiT Publishing, 2017); Philippe Vonnard, Gregory Quin and Nicola Sbetti, eds., *Beyond Boycotts: Sport during the Cold War in Europe* (Oldenburg: De Gruyter, 2018); J. Simon Rofe, ed., *Sport and Diplomacy: Games Within Games* (Manchester: Manchester University Press, 2018); Heather L. Dichter, ed., *Soccer Diplomacy: International Relations and Football Since 1914* (Lexington: University Press of Kentucky, 2020).

9. James Riordan, *Sport in Soviet Society: The Development of Sport and Physical Education in Russia and the USSR* (Cambridge: Cambridge University Press, 1977); James Riordan, *Sport, Politics and Communism* (Manchester: Manchester University Sport, 1991); Teresa González Aja, 'Spanish Sports Policy in Republican and Fascist Spain', in *Sport and International Politics*, ed. Pierre Arnaud and James Riordan, 97–113 (London and New York: E & FN Spon, 1998); Angela Teja, 'Italian Sport and International Relations under Fascism', in *Sport and International Politics*, ed. Pierre Arnaud and James Riordan, 147–70 (London and New York: E & FN Spon, 1998); James Riordan and Robin Jones, eds., *Sport and Physical Education in China* (London and New York: Routledge, 1999); Vic Duke and Liz Crolley, '*Fútbol*, Politicians and the People: Populism and Politics in Argentina', in *Sport in Latin American Society: Past and Present*, ed. J. A. Mangan and Lamartine P. DaCosta, 93–116 (London: Frank Cass, 2002); Arnd Krüger and William Murray eds., *The Nazi Olympics: Sport, Politics,*

and Appeasement in the 1930s (Urbana and Chicago: University of Illinois Press, 2003); Simon Martin, *Football and Fascism: The National Game under Mussolini* (Oxford: Berg, 2004); Mike Dennis and Jonathan Grix, *Sport under Communism: Behind the East German 'Miracle'* (Basingstoke: Palgrave Macmillan, 2012); Fan Hong and Lu Zhouxiang, *The Politicisation of Sport in Modern China: Communists and Champions* (London and New York: Routledge, 2013); Susan Grant, *Physical Culture and Sport in Soviet Society: Propaganda, Acculturation, and Transformation in the 1920s and 1930s* (London and New York: Routledge, 2013); Toby Rider, *Cold War Games: Propaganda, the Olympics, and US Foreign Policy* (Champaign, IL: University of Illinois Press, 2016); Robert Edelman and Christopher Young, eds., *The Whole World Was Watching: Sport in the Cold War* (Stanford, CA: Stanford University Press, 2019).

10. Souvik Naha, 'No One Plays with Nehru: Sport, Games Ethic and Postcolonial Nationhood in India' (unpublished article).

11. For studies on Centre–state relations in India, see Asok Kumar Chanda, *Federalism in India: A Study of Union–State Relations* (London: Allen & Unwin, 1965); Anwarul Haque Haqqi, *Union–State Relations in India* (Meerut: Meenakshi Prakashan, 1967); K. Matthew Kurian and P. N. Varughese, eds., *Centre–State Relations* (New Delhi: Macmillan, 1981); Sati Sahni, ed., *Centre–State Relations* (New Delhi: Vikas Publishing House, 1984); Anirudh Prasad, *Centre–State Relations in India* (New Delhi: Deep and Deep Publications, 1985); Hari Hara Das and Sanjukta Mohaptra, *Centre–State Relations in India (A Study of Sub-national Aspirations)* (New Delhi: Ashish Publishing House, 1986); and Sumitra Kumar Jain, *Party Politics and Centre–State Relations in India* (New Delhi: Abhinav Publications, 1994).

12. Raka Ray, *Fields of Protest: Women's Movements in India* (Minneapolis: University of Minnesota Press, 1999), 57.

13. Once past the delusion of their high standard as China opened up to the world in the late 1970s, the Chinese developed a 'new nationalism' to revive their status. International sporting events became a stage to demonstrate the strength of the nation. This tendency did not catch up with Bengal. Lu Zhouxiang and Fan Hong, *Sport and Nationalism in China* (London and New York: Routledge, 2014), 130.

14. James Riordan, *Sport, Politics and Communism* (Manchester: Manchester University Press, 1991), 35. The rich literature on the socialist/workers' sport includes Stephen G. Jones, *Workers at Play: A Social and Economic History of Leisure, 1918–1939* (London: Routledge & Kegan Paul, 1986);

Stephen G. Jones, *Sports, Politics and the Working Class: Organised Labour and Sport in Inter-War Britain* (Manchester: Manchester University Press, 1988); and Arnd Krüger and James Riordan, eds., *The Story of Worker Sport* (Champaign, Ill.: Human Kinetics, 1996).

15. Bero Rigauer, 'Marxist Theories', in *Handbook of Sports Studies*, ed. Jay Coakley and Eric Dunning, 28–47 (London: Sage, 2002), 37.

16. Jones, *Sport, Politics and the Working Class*, 168.

17. Atul Kohli, *The State and Poverty in India: The Politics of Reform* (Cambridge: Cambridge University Press, 1987), 7.

18. Premen Addy and Ibne Azad, 'Politics and Culture in Bengal', *New Left Review* 1, no. 79 (May–June 1973): 71–112.

19. See Manali Desai, 'Party Formation, Political Power, and the Capacity for Reform: Comparing Left Parties in Kerala and West Bengal, India', *Social Forces* 80, no.1 (2001): 37–60; Kheya Bag, 'Red Bengal's Rise and Fall', *New Left Review* 70 (2011): 69–98.

20. Ashley Mallett, *Rowdy* (Blackwood: Lynton, 1973), 54; Ashley Mallett, *One of a Kind: The Doug Walters Story* (Crows Nest, NSW: Allen & Unwin, 2008), 171.

21. Abin Chakraborty, 'The Peasant Armed: Bengal, Vietnam and Transnational Solidarities in Utpal Dutt's *Invincible Vietnam*', in *Cultures of Decolonisation: Transnational Productions and Practices, 1945–70*, ed. Ruth Cragge and Claire Wintle, 109–25 (Manchester; Manchester University Press, 2016), 115.

22. Kevin Blackburn, *War, Sport and the Anzac Tradition* (Basingstoke: Palgrave Macmillan, 2016), 101.

23. Doug Walters, *The Doug Walters Story* (Adelaide: Rigby, 1981), 44.

24. Swapan Dasgupta, 'An Exile's View', *Seminar* (March 2006), http://www.india-seminar.com/2006/559/ 559%20 swapan%20dasgupta.htm, accessed on 5 March 2015.

25. Chiranjib, 'Pratham Kriramantri Ram Chatterji, Mohun Baganer Ekti Sabha Ebong …' (First Sports Minister Ram Chatterji, a Mohun Bagan Meeting, and …), *SKA*, 1983, 34.

26. *TOI*, 13 December 1969, 12.

27. *AmBP*, 1 February 1980, 1.

28. John Hoberman, *Sport and Political Ideology* (London: Heinemann, 1984), 6.

29. Robert Edelman, *Serious Fun: A History of Spectator Sports in the USSR* (New York: Oxford University Press, 1993), 6.

30. Ibid., 9.

31. *Jugantar*, 31 January 1980, 4.

32. Ibid., 7 February 1980, 4.

33. Ibid.

34. *Daily Mercury*, 19 January 1946, 4.

35. Denis Compton, *End of an Innings* (Calcutta: Rupa, 1962), 21.

36. The Bombay gangsters show a peculiar penchant for cricket. Dawood Ibrahim married his daughter with Javed Miandad's son. In Suketu Mehta's novel about life in the city's underbelly, Chhota Rajan asked a tea boy to shoot the assassin of his mentor Bada Rajan during a cricket match, which the boy did in front of hundreds of spectators (*Maximum City: Bombay Lost and Found* [New York: Vintage, 2005], 135). Mohsin killed the gangster Husain Vastara at a cricket match too, with his bodyguards having relaxed their attention (ibid., 195).

37. Sankariprasad Basu, *Edene Shiter Dupur* (Calcutta: Bookland, 1960), 167.

38. *ABP*, 2 January 1962, 6.

39. Alok Dasgupta, 'M Dutta Ray: The Kingmaker', *SKA*, 1978, 139–40.

40. Santipriyo Bandopadhyay, 'Composite Stadium', *Saptahik Basumati* 74, no. 29 (15 January 1970), 1854.

41. Pabitra Das, 'Bidhannagare Stadium O Golden Card', *KA* 6, no. 26 (5 November 1982), 24.

42. Many of the Indian politicians were active cricket players. Goa's first chief minister, Dayanand Bandodkar, was a regular face at the Brabourne Stadium during international matches. He attended even the local Kanga League matches in Bombay on political visits. *TOI*, 26 September 1968, 14.

43. Mukul, 'Kritir Krira-Bhumika', *Desh* 37, no. 19 (7 March 1970), 608.

44. *TOI*, 26 April 1971, 1.

45. Ibid., 15 September 1971, 10.

46. Subrata Mukherjee considered cricket a very feudal system, replete with socio-economic discrepancies, and hence was against its promotion. *KA* 6, no. 36 (14 January 1983), 5.

47. *TOI*, 20 December 1972, 16.

48. *AmBP*, 16 January 1975, 1.

49. *TOI*, 28 May 1976, 14.

50. Ibid., 24 July 2006, 25.

51. *Jugantar*, 3 January 1973, 6.

52. *Hindustan Times* (*HT*), 31 July 1971, 1.

53. *HT*, 17 January 1973, 1.

54. *AmBP*, 4 January 1977, 10.

55. Mukul, 'Kritir Krira-Bhumika', *Desh* 37, no. 16 (14 February 1970), 296.

56. *TOI*, 22 June 1977, 14.

57. The library was shifted to the first floor of the CAB Club House in 2005 as part of the Centre for Excellence in Cricket. The centre was shut down following Jagmohan Dalmiya's fall from grace in 2006. The room was used as a kitchen during the India–South Africa Test match in 2010 and afterwards as the seating place for the Third and Fourth Umpires and Match Referee when the Club House was renovated prior to the 2011 World Cup.

58. 'Sara Kolkatae Khola Mather Obhab' (Calcutta Lacks Open Space), *KA* 2, no. 16 (11 August 1978), 19.

59. Ibid., 3, no. 19 (21 September 1979), 10.

60. Ibid., 3, no. 24 (2 November 1979), 12.

61. *TOI*, 18 August 1980, 11.

62. Salil Banerjee, 'Spare the Gardens', *Sportsworld* 2, no. 15 (30 January 1980), 1.

63. *ABP*, 9 January 1982, 1.

64. Das, 'Bidhannagarer Stadium O Golden Card', 24–26.

65. Atul Mukharji, 'Edener Asol Malik Ke?' (Who Really Owns Eden?), *KA* 6, no. 26 (5 November 1982), 27.

66. See Sanjib Baruah, *India against Itself: Assam and the Politics of Nationality* (Philadelphia: University of Pennsylvania Press, 1999), ch. 6.

67. Alok Dasgupta, 'Sidelights', *Sportsworld* (6 February 1980), 16.

68. *TOI*, 13 November 1981, 11.

69. *KA* 5, no. 30 (27 November 1981), 41–42.

70. *Jugantar*, 1 January 1982, 1.

71. *TS*, 1 January 1982, 9.

72. *Jugantar*, 1 January 1982, 7.

73. Ibid., 2 January 1982, 6.

74. *ABP*, 3 January 1982, 12.

75. *Aajkal*, 6 January 1985, 6.

76. *Jugantar*, 8 February 1987, 5.

77. *AmBP*, 11 February 1987, 10.

78. *Sportsworld* 8, no. 19 (4–11 March 1987), 4.

79. Amitabha Chowdhury, 'Samajhdari Kake Bole' (What Is Understanding), *Jugantar*, 15 February 1987, 1.

80. Ibid., 3 February 1987, 7.

81. *TOI*, 10 February 1987, 13.

82. *ABP*, 11 February 1987, 1.

83. Ibid., 11 February 1987, 8.

84. *Jugantar*, 11 February 1987, 8.

85. *AmBP*, 15 February 1987, 11.
86. *Jugantar*, 12 February 1987, 1.
87. *AmBP*, 29 November 1987, 12.
88. *TT*, 28 November 1993, 15.
89. *ABP*, 10 October 1987, 7.
90. *TS*, 14 October 1987, 10.
91. Ibid., 2 October 1987, 14.
92. Jaywant Y. Lele, *I Was There: Memoirs of a Cricket Administrator* (Mumbai: Marine Sports, 2011), 12.
93. *ABP*, 10 October 1987, 7.
94. Ibid., 11 October 1987, 8.
95. *ABP*, 13 October 1987, 12.
96. Richard M. Weintraub, 'Cricket Stirs Old British Empire,' *Washington Post*, 8 November 1987, D18.
97. *ABP*, 19 February 1999, 11.
98. Rajdeep Sardesai, 'All's Fair and Foul', *TOI*, 27 September 1992, 15.
99. Rajan Bala writes a balanced account of these regional grievances in 'When Players Become Pawn', in *The Covers Are Off: A Socio-Historical Study of Indian Cricket*, 234–60 (New Delhi: Rupa, 2004).
100. Marcus F. Franda, *West Bengal and the Federalizing Process in India* (Princeton, NJ: Princeton University Press, 1968).
101. Atul Kohli, *Democracy and Discontent: India's Growing Crisis of Governability* (Cambridge: Cambridge University Press, 1990); Aseema Sinha, *The Regional Roots of Developmental Politics in India: A Divided Leviathan* (Bloomington and Indianapolis: Indiana University Press, 2005).
102. Ramachandra Guha, 'The Gentleman Scholar: Sujit Mukherjee', in *The Last Liberal and Other Essays*, 229–36 (Ranikhet: Permanent Black, 2003), 229.
103. Nirad C. Chaudhuri, *Thy Hand, Great Anarch! India, 1921–1952* (London: Hogarth Press, 1990), 331.
104. Ramachandra Guha, *The States of Indian Cricket: Anecdotal Histories* (Ranikhet: Black Kite, 2005), 24.
105. Mushtaq Ali, *Cricket Delightful* (Calcutta: Rupa, 1960), 168.
106. Sporting Union was founded by Sarada Ranjan Roy and Hemanga Bose in 1896. Its cricket team was one of the strongest in Calcutta throughout the twentieth century.
107. Soumya Bandopadhyay, 'Edene Goddarder Team: Dinti Ajo Smaraniyo' (Goddard's Team at Eden: Still Remarkable), *KA* 3, no. 2 (11 May 1979), 18–20.
108. Anil Dasgupta, 'The War Years II', *TT*, press clipping in author's collection.

109. Boria Majumdar, *Lost Histories of Indian Cricket: Battles Off the Pitch* (London and New York: Routledge, 2006), 55.

110. A.M., 'Fragments of Other Facts', *TT*, 12 January 2016, 8.

111. *TOI*, 19 March 1969, 9.

112. *AmBP*, 5 November 1969, 8.

113. Amal Home, 'Krira Jagat' (Sports World), *Sandesh* 9, no. 8 (December 1969), 602.

114. Pankaj De, 'Calcutta: A Dead City?' *AmBP*, 20 December 1969, 6.

115. *Jugantar*, 12 February 1971, 1.

116. 'The View from the Top of a Hill', *Telegraph Magazine*, 9 January 1983, 7.

117. Dilip Doshi, *Spin Punch* (Calcutta: Rupa, 1991).

118. *Jugantar*, 29 December 1972, 8.

119. Gopal Bose, *Soja Byate* (Straight Bat), (Calcutta: Sristi, 2001), 23–25.

120. Kohli, *Democracy and Discontent*, 285.

121. Sumantra Bose, *Transforming India: Challenges to the World's Largest Democracy* (Cambridge, MA: Harvard University Press. 2013), 119.

122. *TOI*, 8 September 1977, 6.

123. Ibid., 26 November 1980, 1.

124. Guha, *The States of Indian Cricket*, 26.

125. *TOI*, 14 October 1983, 1.

126. Ibid., 21 August 1984, 5.

127. Ibid., 2 September 1984, 9.

128. Rajani Ranjan Jha and Bhavana Mishra, 'Centre–State Relations, 1980–90: The Experience of West Bengal', *Indian Journal of Political Science* 54, no. 2 (1993): 209–37, 230.

129. Ross Mallick, *Development Policy of a Communist Government: West Bengal since 1977* (Cambridge: Cambridge University Press, 1993), 100.

130. Günter Grass, *Show Your Tongue*, trans. John E. Woods (London: Secker & Warburg, 1989), 94.

131. *TOI*, 19 May 1988, 7.

132. Amit Chaudhuri, *Calcutta: Two Years in the City* (New York: Alfred A. Knopf, 2013), 87–88.

133. Special correspondent, 'Sambaran Banerjee K Trial E Daka Holo Na Keno?' (Why Was Sambaran Banerjee Not Called to Trial), *KA* 2, no. 21 (15 September 1978), 32–33.

134. Alok Dasgupta, 'Bharat-Roger Sujog Pele Barun-Sambaran Pabe Na Keno?' (If Bharat-Roger Play, Why Not Barun-Sambaran), *KA* 5, no. 19 (4 September 1981), 40.

135. Prafulla Roy, 'Joubone Bujhi Kichu Furoe Na', *Jugantar*, 3 January 1979, 4.
136. Santipriya Bandopadhyay, 'Banchana Ebar Anchalik Daleo' (Deprivation in the Regional Team), *Amrita* 19, no. 19 (19 October 1979), 58–59.
137. 'Was Bad Pitch Only Cause of Defeat?' *Sportsworld* 2, no. 2 (31 October 1979), 20.
138. 'Comments on Commentaries', *Sportsworld* 2, no. 7 (5 December 1979), 4.
139. Alok Dasgupta, 'Sidelights', *Sportsworld* 2, no 16 (6 February 1980), 16.
140. Dasgupta, 'Bharat-Roger Sujog Pele Barun-Sambaran Pabe Na Keno?' 40–41.
141. Sardesai, 'All's Fair and Foul'.
142. 'Banglar Cricketerder Prati Abicharer Dhara Ajo Abyahata' (The Tradition of Injustice against Bengal Cricketers Continues), *KA* 6, no. 26 (5 November 1982), 29–31.
143. *Jugantar*, 12 February 1987, 1.
144. Guha, *The States of Indian Cricket*, 38.
145. Sabyasachi Sarkar, *Lords Theke Taunton* (Lord's to Taunton) (Calcutta: Ananda Publishers, 2000), 11.
146. Dominique Lapierre, 'Afterword', in *City of Joy* (London: Arrow, 1992 [1986]), 517.
147. *ABP*, 27 May 1999, 8.
148. Gautam Bhattacharya, 'Guyana Tei Hoyto Jiboner Sera Shikkha Peye Gelen Sourav' (Sourav Probably Learnt His Biggest Lesson in Guyana), *ABP*, 18 April 1997, 8.
149. Pankaj Roy, 'Sarbakaler Sera Bangali Cricketer' (Greatest Ever Bengali Cricketer), *Aajkal*, 5 December 1997, 1.
150. Partho Rudra, 'Open Korano Niye Natok' (The Drama Round Opening), *Aajkal*, 3 December 1997, 8.
151. *Aajkal*, 5 December 1997, 8.
152. Sabyasachi Sarkar, *Sobar Sachin Amader Sourav* (Everyone's Sachin, Our Sourav) (Calcutta: Deep Prakashan, 2001).
153. *ABP*, 25 February 1999, 1.
154. Ibid., 10.
155. *Bartaman*, 25 February 1999, 8.
156. Gautam Bhattacharya, *Dadatantra* (The Big Brother) (Calcutta: Deep Prakashan, 2009), 3.
157. Ibid., 8.
158. Ibid., 4.
159. Chaudhuri, *Calcutta: Two Years in the City*, 109.
160. Ashok Malik, 'A Place Time Forgot', *TOI*, 20 January 2010, 6.

5 Spectators, Gender and Public Space

Suddenly, 'women' are everywhere.[1]

A cartoon published in the *Hindustan Standard* newspaper during the India–England Test match at the Eden Gardens in 1961–62 featured two women. They were seated on the back rows and enjoying themselves, chatting and knitting sweaters, with visible disregard to the innings in progress. The rest of the spectators, all men, were shown absorbed in the game. The caption, speculating what one of the women might have asked her companion, was, 'One sweater and two mufflers. Yours?'[2] The cartoon captured the general attitude to female cricket spectators in Calcutta at the time. Male spectators and journalists, and sometimes female writers too, reproached female spectators for their inadequate knowledge of the sport. Many women challenged the stereotype. One of them reprimanded the author Sankariprasad Basu for considering 'women as ignorant fools when it [came] to cricket', claiming that in her experience 'quite a few women [understood] what cricket [was]'.[3] Women's cricket has since gained in popularity, women have taken to commentary and anchoring shows about men's cricket, and the number of female spectators has multiplied. Yet the conventional understanding of female fandom remains so invested in the familiar stereotype that a historian writing in 2005 characterised female spectators as little more than 'consumers of nationalism and modernity, designer clothes and television advertisements, martinis and the sex appeal of Rahul Dravid'.[4] While the observation may have been valid for a particular company of strangers, no mention is made of any alternative, informed grade of spectatorship, which reveals the persistence of the female fan's negative image.

For a long time, men considered women trespassers in sporting spaces. The opinion on women's unsuitability to sport as athlete and spectator has not radically changed over the twentieth century, as many societies continue to set androgenic boundaries in sports, segregating women from men.[5] The gendered compartmentalisation of the society is conspicuous in stadiums and sport in general. Scholars have drawn our attention to the power and provenance of the transgression of gender and sexual boundaries, usually constituted by acts of women breaching male preserves, that reshapes the gender order in sport and society.[6] The sports media either conservatively position women as objects of 'sexualised humour' in a 'man's world', or acknowledge diversity of body types and images.[7] Women in sport can both dismiss timeless misogynistic divisions, and undergird ideologies of gender and sexual difference. Misogynist representation of women in the press counteract women's claim to new spaces, while the narratives supportive of women constantly re-evaluate the canons of sport.

This chapter brings a historical perspective to the study of women's attachment with sport as a means to understand the restrictive and emancipatory gendering of public spaces. It aims to make two contributions. First, it adds sport as a fresh perspective to understand the problematic connection between women and public space in India, which has so far been examined in mostly colonial contexts and from perspectives of class, caste, marriage, labour, nationalism, migration, and so on.[8] Scholars have emphasised the reflexivity of actors of various sexes in the making of womanhood, paying attention to the differences emerging from the coexistence of primordial, restrictive codes of behaviour and contrarian impulses towards what was popularly called progress.[9] There have been relatively few attempts to trace gender interaction in outdoor leisure activities, public displays of femininity, and male regulatory anxieties in the postcolonial context, and most academic studies in this genre are centred on cinema.[10] The symbolism of women's presence in sports stadiums can reflect the nature of power, authority and hierarchy in urban Indian society in a more nuanced manner than cinema and other popular lenses, the reasons for which are stated later.

Second, this chapter takes the literature on global women's sports fandom forward by offering a historical and South Asian perspective. Women's growing visibility as sports fans, or the 'feminisation' of sports fandom, arguably began in the West in the 1990s. The consumerist role of women as fans has been attributed to women's increased freedom of choice, control over lives and leisure activities, and greater exposure to sport from an early age through schools and the media. The 'female-friendly' atmosphere in the post-hooligan era stadiums has also attracted women with their enhanced comfort and safety.[11] A body of works on the experiences of female fans in the West has developed in the 2010s, focused on how women engage with men's and women's sport, are socialised into fandom, shed the stigma of ignorance, form a community of practice, cope with a hyper-masculine environment, negotiate consumerism and media representations, use digital technologies, and harness sport as a tool for empowerment.[12] These works, except for Stacey Pope's study of female football fans in postwar England, situate fans in the hypercommoditised sports market in the twenty-first century. As a result, they do not reflect on long-term gender relations and the transformation of gender hierarchies in the society and have little insights to offer on the twentieth century.

This chapter considers the sports stadium a useful site for observing the regulatory mechanisms of a male-dominated society. It studies cricket matches in the Eden Gardens in Calcutta as a site where gender structures and social hierarchies were both reinforced and unravelled. With the daily presence of 60,000 spectators on average, with the number reportedly swelling to 100,000 on several occasions, the Eden Gardens has been one of India's largest sites of sustained mass gathering, comparable to pilgrimages, religious festivals and political rallies. It is a highly visible public site where a large number of spectators socially communicate and perform their gender roles through a large part of the day. This is significant for studying not only gender relations in Calcutta and India (embedding Calcutta's ethnic diversity in a broader national context) but also global womanhood on account of the frequent allusions to the impact of Westernisation on Indian women. Thus, the experience of cricket and its mediated representation is an ideal, and the least served by academics, context for making broader inferences on the history of gender relations in public spaces in India, the gendering of global sport fandom, and the politics of marginality in general.

Women's increased presence and participation in the hitherto male domain of spectatorship is framed here as an infrapolitical development in gendered public spaces.[13] It makes the point that the codes of appropriate public behaviour at the Eden Gardens can illustrate the ways in which women embodied the configuration of modernity. Through a reading of the mediated parti pris impressions and interview-generated memories of female spectators, it maps the transition in society's approach to sport from a structured homosocial community activity to a relatively unstructured field of shared experience. In the absence of information on the numbers and categories (age, class, caste, sex, marital status) of spectators, it is not possible to ascertain demographic details such as the proportion of female to male spectators, or the number of single or married women in the galleries. Hence, analysis of published texts and oral interviews remains the only available resource with which to interpret cricket spectatorship and gender structures.

THE BEGINNING OF FEMALE SPECTATORSHIP

Like most other English sports, cricket had a noticeable masculinist agenda since the mid-nineteenth century. Athletic masculinity, propagated vigorously through public schools, became a dominant method of training boys so that they could be turned into useful men in the service of the British Empire. The characteristics of manliness inscribed in the British education system included 'physical courage, chivalric ideals, virtuous fortitude', and so on.[14] As playing cricket became a tool of demonstrating manhood, a sense of hegemonic masculinity pervaded the sport and rendered it a male preserve. Women played cricket, but they were not encouraged or taken seriously by most men when they did. There was rather much hostility towards the women's game, with men calling it pretentious or an outright disgrace.[15] At the turn of the century, the 'respectable urban housewife' was supposed to watch rather than play cricket, and to behave in a certain manner. As sociologist Jennifer Hargreaves has pointed out, women's relegation to spectatorship reinforced men's superiority over women.[16] Such behavioural codes were followed across the British imperial world and were not necessarily specific to cricket. Women in Canada were asked to stay away from the gallery, which was adversely publicised as a site of vices like 'gambling, alcoholism, tobacco chewing, smoking'.[17] Certain sports such as rugby union, the promoters of which were allegedly belligerently anti-women and did not care for the presence of female spectators, perpetuated an 'ungentle' manliness embedded in the Darwinian notion of 'strength through struggle'.[18] Nevertheless, it would be unwise to assume that male dominance alone deterred female spectators. There were factors such as the end of free admission for women, increased violence as part of working-class sociability, and stadiums becoming more crowded and uncomfortable that led to a decline in female spectatorship in British football in the 1880s.[19]

The invisibility and marginal status of women in early cricket are strongly linked to the fact that cricket, self-consciously constructed as 'the gentleman's game', is historically one of the most dogmatic of all sports. Patriarchy was at its height in mid- to late-nineteenth-century Britain when the game assumed its modern character and spread to the colonies.[20] Cricket was identified as the gentleman's code of honour; while female cricketers were considered trespassers into the hallowed field.[21] Giving women equal rights as men would have undermined the male control of sporting spaces and values of Muscular Christianity and the 'imperial mission' upon which the ethos of cricket was based.[22] Female cricketers did not have the resources to claim the denied space and upstage cricket's image as a game dominated and regulated by 'gentlemen', though it must be mentioned that overarm bowling – the bedrock of modern cricket – was invented by a woman. It has also been suggested that they accepted the hierarchy and were careful not to challenge the 'harmonious inequality'.[23] While sportswomen were dismissed for lacking athletic body–mind harmony and other qualifiers of sporting excellence, female spectators were judged by entirely different parameters.

Spectatorship was not supposed to threaten women's domestic, feminine attributes. It offered women a chance to display their feminine aesthetic well within the boundaries of modesty and propriety. Historian Greg Ryan claims that women in the peripheries of the British Empire generally enjoyed a wider range of opportunities and experiences within their prescribed roles as wives, mothers, daughters and sisters. For most of the nineteenth century, women maintained a purely supporting role within the male sporting community, being called upon to 'launch boats, donate trophies and provide victuals for participants'. Some men believed that women's presence as spectators lent a civilising and festive atmosphere to sport.[24] Sports venues also opened up a new possibility for men and women to meet outside the household.[25] In some of the baseball grounds in the United states in the late nineteenth to early twentieth centuries, the authorities granted free entry to ladies accompanied by gentlemen that is, any ticket-holding man, to curb the number of rowdies in the gallery, thereby reducing the possibility of riots.[26] In interwar England, cash-strapped county boards saw women members as an emerging, affluent, independent class who attended games and parties to flaunt themselves as cultured socialites.[27] In India, the European communities and upper-class locals followed the practice of enabling activities that were coded as feminine. Mrs Lemans, wife of the Times group's chairperson, presented the winners' prize for the inaugural Times of India Challenge Shield in 1930.[28] 'Ladies' were particularly invited to the dinner dance in honour of the touring MCC at the Bombay Taj Mahal Hotel's new ballroom, the ticket of which cost a steep 12 rupees.[29] Women performed their domestic role of civilising the family in the extended setting of the community.

The upper-class dimension of colonial female spectatorship was more evident in the bigger cities with greater British influence, where transcultural forms of women's civility had emerged. One of the most notable developments in the nineteenth-century urban Bengali society was the emergence of the *bhadramahila*, conceptualised by the elite patriarchy as a benign confluence of the traditional Hindu woman and the enlightened Victorian lady. A large number of journals and instruction manuals were published for the purpose of training them as good mothers and housewives. The domestic position of these women fluctuated as gender relations were continually modified by identity politics, giving rise to new and uneven agencies, innovations and restrictions. In the transitory sociocultural milieu of Calcutta, women's behaviour became a yardstick of Indian men's social status.[30] Women were given the responsibility of 'producing' the nation by taking care of the family and disseminating moral values and culture in the family as well as in the community.[31] Women's increasing visibility and effective role in the public sphere and in public work did not pertain to upper-class identity or necessarily indicate enhancement of their status. In the late nineteenth century, some communities like Parsis or some cities like Bombay, which was not an 'indigenous' city, appeared to be more inclusive about women's public presence.[32] Parsi women were regularly seen at cricket grounds in the 1890s. There can, however, be no generalisation regarding the class and community female spectators were from, or the extent to which they were encouraged or allowed to be publicly visible.

Female spectatorship evidently increased with the gradual shift of the site of play from open, unpretentious grounds to the built environment of stadiums. Richard Cashman estimated that women made up 25 to 30 per cent of the crowd at the newly built Brabourne Stadium (1938 onwards) whereas they constituted fewer than 5 per cent of the spectators at the erstwhile Bombay Gymkhana ground.[33] Women were usually accompanied by elder men. Aloo Bamjee, a pioneer of women's cricket in India, attended her first cricket match only after marriage since her orthodox father did not consider it proper for a maiden to enter a stadium.[34] The extent of knowledge among these colonial women is difficult to estimate since their voices hardly come through the press and literary texts. In colonial Bengal, most female spectators were from elite families, who sat in special, secluded tents. An impression of female presence can be found in an amusing Bengali short story by Brahmanyabhusan and

Kshama Bandyopadhyay, the title of which translates to 'The Poet Laureate Plays Cricket'. The story is about an imaginary cricket match played at Gomoh sometime in the 1930s at the behest of Rabindranath Tagore.[35] The match was attended by both local women dressed in saris worn the Marathi way and elite women like the dancer Mani Behn, the motor racer Rajkumari Sharmila, the daughters of the Gaekwad royal family, the Rajkumari of Burdwan and women from royal or business families. Sankariprasad Basu's interview with the author Lila Majumdar about how the women in the famous Ray family watched cricket reflects some of the issues with women's public presence in the 1920s–30s.[36]

Majumdar recounted that Saradaranjan Ray, called the father of cricket in Bengal, was opposed to the idea of girls publicly watching cricket matches.[37] His brother Kuladaranjan, who did not believe in such discrimination, would arrive at Majumdar's house before a Sporting Union match and troop every boy and girl off to the Eden Gardens in a bus or taxi. Saradaranjan cordially ushered the women towards comfortable chairs under the tent once they were at the ground. Attendants brought lemonades and young European gentlemen were eager to strike conversations with them. Saradaranjan always snubbed their advances. A pot-bellied, middle-aged gentleman from the Calcutta Club, Birkmeyer, once proposed, pointing to the gaggling ladies, 'Oh god! I shall look after them.' Apprehensive, Saradaranjan grimly said, 'Not with anything strong I hope!'[38] Women in the tent were isolated from the rest of the spectators in the way the inner household separated them from the public sphere. Men were often reluctant to allow women to actively participate in the gatherings or recreations related to cricket matches. Majumdar's cricketer brothers insisted their sisters returned home for lunch and not eat with them and other cricketers.[39] Their inclination to control women's behaviour and mobility, and hide them from sexualised male gaze, prevailed over women's lived experience of cricket. A rapid change can be discerned in the gendered dichotomy of the cricket stadium in the late 1950s.

THE VISIBILITY AND LEGITIMACY OF FEMALE SPECTATORS

Newspaper reports and literary texts suggest two significant developments in the 1950s as a matter of scale: first, women entering territories deemed inappropriate and unnecessary for their kind; second, women's self-sufficiency and independence. With greater access to education and employment, women started questioning their place in long-established customs through what historian Geraldine Forbes describes as the ideology of 'social feminism' – asserting their individual rights while fulfilling familial expectations and obligation.[40] Four acts passed in the 1950s, the Hindu Marriage Act (1955), the Hindu Succession Act (1956), the Hindu Adoption and Maintenance Act (1956) and the Hindu Minority and Guardianship Act (1956), entitled some Hindu women to greater say in divorce, equal inheritance of paternal property as male relatives, a fixed portion of the family's income and more authority as children's guardian.[41] Some of the empowered 'new women' of the 1960s shed stereotypes of domesticity and shared men's social pursuits, sometimes encouraged by men themselves. The number of women's clubs increased, providing women a 'safe space' to socialise and endowing them with the confidence and skill to participate in public activities, and often leading to the creation of larger organisations.[42] Cricket matches provide useful insights into women's discursive experience of accessing leisure and navigating the social legitimacy of these practices.

The reading of the sports press and my interviews with several female spectators revealed how they negotiated patriarchy, public space and leisure choices. Cricket permeated the household to a great extent through vernacular radio commentary that demystified cricket jargon for women (as well as men) and piqued their interest. Some caricatures showed women to have become so attached to radio commentary that the evocative description of police teargassing spectators (in 1967) made listeners cry at home. A young woman on a surgery table purportedly urged the anaesthetist to stand by and let her listen to the score one final time.[43] Exposed to discussion of cricket at home and outside, women could not have been unaffected. The Eden Gardens was centrally located and easily accessible from all parts of Calcutta and the nearest rail stations connecting to the suburbs. The leisurely pace of cricket enabled women to chat with companions, knit sweaters or distribute food among the family without taking their attention away from the game. The uncomfortable restrooms and seats did not discourage them.[44] Few families were comfortable with their women going to watch cricket with a group of friends and going by oneself was rarely an option.[45] Affluent women went to polo matches or the racecourse with their families. Cricket galleries were less class-oriented, and more welcoming than football galleries, which were known for regular and more violent skirmishes between rival fan groups or even fans from the same club than in cricket matches. The image of cricket as a safe, leisurely and festive sport persuaded even the most disinterested women to join their cricket-loving relatives and friends. Many women were genuinely intrigued by cricket and would not have lost an opportunity to watch an international match, while some simply wanted to see their favourite players.

Many women were introduced to the game early in their lives by fathers and brothers, or later by their husbands and children. Some were compelled to take notice of the game since it was the main topic of casual conversation at home.[46] Ila Sinha, sister of Prasad Sinha, the first Bengali umpire to officiate in a Test match, recollected that she first went to the stadium with her father, and later with her brothers and cousins.[47] By interacting with her brothers who played for Sporting Union and reading the cricket books in the family library she amassed great historical and technical knowledge of cricket. She could identify fielders from her seat in the crowd, which even the legendary radio commentator Ajay Basu sometimes failed to do.[48] Sinha's account corresponds to historian Judith Walsh's theory of a shift in family relationships in late colonial India when, inspired by colonial modernity, the younger generation of Indian men conferred greater authority of the household to their wives, undermining the customary exercise of power by the earning male. Walsh further argues that women found this newly conceived romantic, dyadic husband–wife relationship as elevating their position.[49] This companionate household was a significant departure from previous home environments where authority prevailed over affection. In the new, cohesive family units, members shared leisure interest more than at any other previous historical period. While discussing such categorisation of families, one must remember that the changes outlined above were class, space and culture specific. Many families in India still do not operate with egalitarian ideas.

With encouragement and out of their own volition, postcolonial women were gradually drawn into previously denied leisure consumptions. Acknowledgement of women's agency suggests 'democratisation of the family', following historian Indrani Chatterji's formulation about a previous historical period. But gender interaction in public spaces shows that such relationships were ambivalent rather than democratic.[50] In particular, men not used to interacting with unknown women often found themselves in a strange situation in a 'mixed company', and often ended up, both intentionally and unknowingly, embarrassing or humiliating women.[51] Cricket administrator Manindra Dutta Ray said in an interview that he told an inquisitive English woman in 1948 that in India the mother, not the father, bossed over the household. Yet during his administrative career stretching from the 1940s to the 1970s many people considered women's presence in the ground inappropriate.[52] Kabita Sinha, a feminist author, wrote about Test matches from a woman's perspective in her weekly column 'As I See It' for the *Amrita Bazar Patrika*. She explains the position of female spectators with a personal story from the 1961–62 India–England Test match told in retrospect:

> I saw my childhood friend Barin sitting in the same row … About an hour after the start of play, Barin convinced the man sitting next to him to exchange his seat with mine. We were happily watching the game but India soon stumbled. Barin started losing temper. The exchange of seats seemed to have caused the reversal of fortune. People overheard him and gave me murderous stares … People were not in favour of women's presence at the stadium. Now India's poor performance became my doing … Finally, India won, for the first time in Calcutta. People forgot I was there. I tried to take credit for India's victory, but Barin was in no mood to listen. Everyone returned home celebrating. But what if India had not won? The collective fury could have singed me.[53]

Sinha's experience suggests that most men considered women trespassers in a male domain. Unaccustomed to interacting with women in public spaces and unwilling to give up their territory, most men tenaciously held on to their masculine power and privilege. As tickets were in short supply, most cricket-loving men could not enter the stadium. They unleashed their frustration upon women who were able to watch the game. This outrage and women's response expressed the everyday negotiation of patriarchy and paternalism in the postcolonial Bengali society. The small acts of gendered resistance against the dominant ideology of participation in public activity, which usually left little trace in public records outside newspaper reports on spectators, were hidden conflicts occurring outside the realm of politics. Explaining how infrapolitics materialise in Indian society, Douglas Haynes and Gyan Prakash wrote, 'Social structure … appears more commonly as a constellation of contradictory and contestatory processes … neither domination nor resistance is autonomous; the two are so entangled that it becomes difficult to analyse one without discussing the other.'[54] Through an analysis of three problematics that fomented this cycle of contestation of power between sexes – women's knowledge, sexuality and celebrity obsession – this chapter ponders what the operative infrapolitics in public leisure activities tell us about gender relations in the society.

KNOWLEDGE

As mentioned in the introductory paragraph of the chapter, women's knowledge of cricket was lampooned in the press. Historian Sudeshna Banerjee argues that Sankariprasad Basu's comical descriptions of female spectators and radio listeners in *Ramaniya Cricket* represented women as an emerging but unthinking and ignorant category of spectators.[55] According to Banerjee, the idea of informed spectatorship was effectively invested with the discourse representing intellect and knowledge as male traits, as opposed to the supposedly feminine properties of uncontrolled emotion and passion. This male–female dichotomy, she argues, became evident in the 1950s and 1960s when women's unmistakable visibility in the galleries threatened patriarchal monopoly over cricket. Unwilling to let women recast the stadium space, discursive tactics in the form of public comments, literature and newspaper editorials were used to dissuade women from infringing the gender divide in cricket. Banerjee cites a female author, also a cricket follower, who was publicly taunted with technical questions about the game and who overheard remarks that women, invariably ignorant about the game, were unjustifiably blocking tickets and depriving male followers.[56]

In the book under question, as well as in the books preceding and following its publication, Basu wrote hilarious stories about female spectators, especially about their dresses and habits, and indicating women did not have the intellectual capacity to understand cricket. A woman, who mistook the end of the first day's play for the end of the match and asked her female companion about the winner even though the match was far from over, represented the paradigm of women's abject knowledge of cricket.[57] Evidently, Basu's first three books, the contents of which were drawn from the articles he wrote for the *Anandabazar Patrika* in the early 1960s, contained oblique references to women's physicality, or mindless activities such as knitting or eating. Assorting these accounts as a reflection of the period's male discourse, as Banerjee has done, disregards the plurality of public responses to female spectators. A study of Basu's later books, four in number, shows that the author was not complicit in gender politics as believed. Basu did not necessarily believe in men's superiority in matters of cricket appreciation. He quoted an anonymous cricket writer who came up with a tripartite division of female spectators: first, the old and middle-aged upper-class women for whom the stadium was a space to socialise and to sustain social status; second, the few women who actually understood cricket; third, the well-dressed girls who fancied handsome young cricketers, the sort which apparently prompted England captain Peter May to station the good-looking cricketers in the team in the outfield to garner women's support in an away Test match.[58] Basu might have portrayed some women as superficial, cacophonous spectators, interested more in knitting and dressing up seductively, but he chastised ignorant male followers and admired women who understood cricket.

In *Ramaniya Cricket*, in which female spectators are ridiculed the most, Basu sketched one of them as knowledgeable. Banerjee observes that Basu makes certain qualifying remarks about this woman, emphasising her difference in matters of dress and disposition from other women. He possibly implied that this woman had the intellectual ability to control her physicality unlike most women. At the same time, he said, the woman did not masculinise herself by wearing men's clothes and flaunting masculine mannerisms; she was rather a 'human'. Such a certificate from Basu, confirming the woman's knowledge of cricket and portraying her as occupying a higher state of consciousness than purely female, was paternalistic.[59] The woman was shown asking for protection of women's right to watch Test matches much the same way as the Government of India was then protecting new, fledgling industries by limiting the maximum output of bigger enterprises.[60] Women's interest in cricket, the woman persistently argued, should be nurtured rather than ridiculed.[61] Later in the book, Basu admitted that his humorous stories of women were meant to attract reader's attention ('cricket literature cannot flourish without teasing references to women'), confessing to intentional sexism for a primarily male market.[62] It appeared as though he wished to respect the knowledgeable women audience of cricket but could not effectively challenge the market logic which called for women as a whole to be portrayed as somewhat brainless and irrational.

A bizarre story appeared in Basu's final book on cricket, *Sara Diner Khela* (The Day's Cricket). Rain had interrupted the first day's play against Australia in 1964. As the ground staff struggled to dry the waterlogged areas, a woman offered them her hair dryer.[63] The very absurdity of the situation probably shows that Basu simply did not care for political correctness. The woman, as is clearly borne out, was wealthy and fashionable enough to carry the appliance to a cricket match. She might not have breached the soft mud of the outfield to talk to perspiring ground staff, but the story also refers to a possibility that she understood the problem and wanted to expedite the sopping up process so that play could be resumed quickly. The story indicates either a mockery of women's presumptions or, in an unlikely manner, an announcement of the coming of the knowledgeable female spectator. In his later works, Basu conceded that an increasing number of women were being initiated into the game every passing year. Arguably feedback from his female readers had a role in this shift. In 1965, one Rita Mitra, for instance, complained,

> I study in class X. Once during a Duleep Trophy match, I overheard two gentlemen talking among themselves. Either they don't understand cricket or they don't recognise players from this country. One of them asked, pointing at Durani, 'Does this lad bowl good enough to play Tests regularly?' His friend asked him who it was, to which he replied, 'Why? Prakash Poddar?' Why do these people go to the stadium – is it to watch the garnished girls you describe?[64]

One Rina Bose wrote in 1967 about her encounter with an elderly man who blamed the presence of women for the decline in the quality of cricket. She requested Basu to protest against such offensive remarks.[65] In a joint letter, four women students from the Calcutta Medical College in 1968 congratulated Basu for exposing the sham of female cricket followers whose 'stupid' actions maligned the entire community.[66] Basu ridiculed the male chauvinists who scorned at women – calling the scrawny youths who danced in the galleries, not too gender sensitively, more effeminate than the women. Just as unemployed men had no right to question women's capability to work hard, the 'ticketless and cricket-less' fools, he writes, should not mock women's love of cricket.[67] Examples of uninformed 'gentlemen' and a diatribe against ignorant male supporters in his works show Basu was not an archetypal woman-basher. On an overall assessment, Basu seems more intent on building committed spectatorship around cricket than satirising women to increase his marketability. His portrayal of women was certainly complex, if not always entirely gender sensitive. A major point that Banerjee's criticism of male monopoly seems to have missed is that a number of women mocked the lack of knowledge among female spectators too. Monica Bandyopadhyay shared some amusing stories in an essay in the *Mahila* (Woman), a women's magazine, on her experience of watching the India–England Test match in 1961–62. This was highly unusual as women's magazines until the 1990s rarely gave any space for sport. She writes,

> I had no idea that the stadium could be a place to read. After taking my seat, I found quite a few girls with their pretty faces buried in glossy film

magazines for the entire day. Had they decided to read at home, a few cricket lovers would have been able to sit and watch the game.[68]

During the match, she overheard the woman sitting next to her confiding to the latter's brother that Ken Barrington, who was fielding at 'fine leg', should better start bowling instead of hovering at 'mid on'. The two fielding positions are half the ground apart. A Marwari woman, awakened from her siesta by a commotion after Tony Lock caught Mansur Ali Khan Pataudi, whimpered, appalled at the sight of the prostrate fielder, 'Hay Ram! Why is he lying down? Is he hurt?'[69] Then, as Ramakant Desai hit a six, an unusual occurrence in those days, an ageing grandmother started shouting, 'Can't you see where you are hitting? If the ball crushes my head, will you pay the doctor's fee?'[70] A young girl apparently praised Nari Contractor's performance in the match, who had scored merely four and eleven in two innings and drawn criticism from the press.[71] Bandyopadhyay concluded her essay with scathing remarks. The contest to look pretty, she said, betrayed women's lack of knowledge and sophistication. The women who did not understand cricket should not enter a stadium or pretend to be cricket enthusiasts, as they deprive authentic cricket fans who deserved to be there but did not have tickets. She redeemed the 'proper' cricket-woman by attacking the 'improper' ones, in an obviously liberal dichotomous fashion. As it was published in a popular women's magazine, the article could aim its cricket pedagogy at a predominantly female readership.

Even though Basu acknowledged women's legitimacy as spectators in the 1960s, other writers did not and continued to question women for nearly another two decades. One journalist reported a woman asking her companion why the two sets of stumps were erected, sullying the lush green field.[72] An interesting aspect of their criticism was that while the behaviour of female spectators was under continual scrutiny and funny stories about them were offered for public consumption, the ones who stayed at home listening to radio commentary were praised and shown to have often surpassed their husbands in knowledge of cricket. The sister-in-law mentioned by the writer Narayan Gangopadhyay in 'Paribarik Cricket' (Cricket in the Family) is an eminent example of a knowledgeable female follower. The woman shocked the author with her grasp of cricket terms, which was pompous but admirable.[73] Admittedly a revolution brought on by vernacular radio commentary, but the familial embeddedness of the well-informed yet homely woman takes the reader back to the colonial imagery of a desirable traits in a *bhadramahila*.

Women featured prominently in cricket books written in the 1960s–70s, in which they were mainly listeners but carried the narrative forward by asking questions. Jayanta Dutta arranged the chapters in his book *Rupasi Eden-er Rupasi Cricket* (Glorious Cricket at Beautiful Eden) in the form of an ongoing dialogue between a young man with an encyclopaedic knowledge of cricket and his curious girlfriend.[74] The man explains the philosophy of cricket through anecdotes to his attentive and receptive partner. He reels off stories of honesty such as that of Wally Grout, who had once resented being given not out by the umpire and sacrificed his wicket the very next ball to honour the bowler's effort. The girlfriend asks her beau to repeat the story of Jack Hobbs, who had more than once walked away, defying the umpire's decision, simply as the opponent claimed that he was out. She asks keen questions and, in the end, appears to have gained much knowledge. Not once does the author dispute her femininity. Her 'female' traits are rather well documented in her panicky reaction to the 'bodyline' strategy of intimidatory bowling and to Colin Cowdrey's heroic effort to save a Test match batting with a broken right arm.

A chapter in Achintya Kumar Sengupta's book *Mriga Nei Mrigaya* (Hunt without Deer) narrates a similar conversation between a betrothed couple as they watch the Bengal Chief Minister's XI take on the Commonwealth XI.[75] Two other chapters describe the author's conversations with two (Basanti and Anamika) and three women (Ira, Rajashri and Chitrita) about cricket's philosophy.[76] Their relationship to the author is not clear but they appear to have been quite familiar and informal with one another. Here too the man comes up with cricket stories in response to the women's questions. The women listen attentively and pass uninhibited value judgements. Although the women come across as acquainted with cricket, they are not empowered to direct the course of conversations. They discussed the distinction between 'bright cricket' and 'good cricket' and concluded that 'sensible cricket' is what players should practise and spectators learn to appreciate.

The narrative of women's ignorance about cricket, nevertheless, persisted in the sports press. After India defeated England by 28 runs in 1972–73, one journalist wrote in his account of post-match celebrations: 'The girl who ate fries without smudging her lipstick while knitting wool, was overwhelmed by the enormous event of an Indian victory.'[77] In 1978, on the second day of the India–West Indies Test match, a woman started to sing and dance at 10 in the morning in front of gate 23. She wore a *rudraksha* prayer bead and a white sari with red borders. She asked the guards to let her enter. A young man later turned up and whisked her away, saying that it was his mother who was slightly deranged.[78] Such idiosyncratic stories, which could have been tools of dominating women, gradually disappeared in the late 1970s from the major dailies. In 1979, Hariprasad Chattopadhyay suspected that in the near future women might outnumber men in the galleries. He stressed that most of these women were not there to knit, eat or chat; they were quite engrossed in the play. Women discussed cricket among themselves and were quite aware of Gavaskar reaching the milestone 4,000 Test runs. One of them even kept calling Gavaskar by endearing names such as 'Gavu', 'Sani', 'Sunu' and kept advising him to calm down and complete the double century, 'as if she were Gavaskar's mother'.[79] Writing about the next Test match, Umashankar Das reported the presence of fewer women in the galleries, and a complete absence of wool and needles.[80] Probably during this match, a female fan surprised an entire row of people, including a cricket journalist, by telling them that Gundappa Vishwanath's middle name was Ranganath, which nobody else knew.[81]

The very next year, in 1980, a bride-to-be was reported to have refused to marry a man who barely understood cricket. Female students took radios to the university and listened to radio commentary.[82] The Statesman put in the photograph of a disturbed-looking Usha Mukherjea, wife of the former BCCI president J. C. Mukherjea, in its advertisement of the open forum 'Is Cricket Dead?', organised as part of the CAB's golden jubilee celebration to which women were particularly invited. Mukherjea was introduced as an 88-year old woman who had seen more Test matches than most public could remember, and who now listened to radio commentary, being too old to go to the Eden Gardens. Her statement – 'It's disgraceful what they've done to gracious cricket' – was printed in bold and large letters, setting the tone for the concept note, which was concerned with the changing contours of cricket, especially that of the 'Monday of stiff professionalism' replacing the 'Sunday atmosphere'.[83] Finally, when Pakistan came to Calcutta in 1987, one journalist lamented the absence of the woman in 'deep green sari with matched blouse, and bobbed hair, who irritated fellow spectators by pacing to and fro along the narrow passage between two rows, with a radio pinned to her ears'.[84] More than the nod to women using radio as a tool of knowledge, the depiction of a sense of fashion among women aimed at increasing their desirability among men grabs attention. The emphasis on physical appearance rather than knowledge for modernising the female body takes centre stage in the cycle of objectification in the male-dominated sports press. Yet the reference to radios and informed conversations indicate a paradigm shift from the yesteryears, suggesting acknowledgement of some women being able to resist domination. Although the scepticism about knowledge dwindled, discussions about women's physicality noticeably intensified over time.

SEXUALITY

As referenced before, the centrality of male figures to most women's initiation into cricket, travel to the cricket stadium and representation in the press, meant some of the general male sentiments and anxieties regarding women's public presence were reproduced in the context of female spectatorship. A regular male spectator revealed in an interview that a large section of men considered the stadium a place that liberated them from household prohibitions on swearing and smoking. Some people were concerned about their wives spying on their holiday activities, which often violated the norm of 'gentlemanly' behaviour.[85] They unconsciously empowered women as voyeurs who did not directly engage with but subverted the male domain by gaze and physical occupation of space.[86] Women were able to admire male bodies in sport, of both players and fellow spectators, in a socially agreeable manner.[87] There are few references to the female gaze in press reports but conversely these pieces are full of stories about men's attitude to the unfettering of women's cultural choices and authority over social spaces. Working women, relatively autonomous on account of the time spent away from home and income through labour, were nonetheless a problematic category.[88]

Few men, it appears from stories in the press, were appreciative of female spectators and radio listeners in the formerly undisputed male preserve of watching and understanding cricket. In addition to criticism of women's lack of knowledge, remarks were made about the sexuality of female spectators and the waning control over female bodies in public. The concept of the *bhadramahila*, whose 'bearing, dress, speech and access, were insistently interiorised' and whose honour depended on their invisibility in the public domain, was in flux.[89] The publicness of the 'new women' raised confusion about the boundaries of women's respectability. This is evident from the response to the clothes and behaviour of upper-class female spectators. A *Statesman* correspondent declared in 1961 that cricket matches were a social parade of women's fashion.[90] Achintya Kumar Sengupta began his report on the India–England Test match in 1964 with a story of a fictitious group of friends:

> A number of friends, sitting cosily across two rows of benches, were watching the game, equipped with transistor, binocular and Dunlopillo mattress.
>
> 'Do you see that woman?'
>
> 'No, I am looking at the man sitting next to her.
>
> 'Watch the game,' barked the third.
>
> 'All in a game,' said the fourth.
>
> 'See how lovely her eyes are,' the first looked for approval.
>
> 'Don't you stare so often,' grumbled the third again.
>
> 'Don't talk rubbish!' chattered the first. 'A thing of beauty is a joy for ever.'
>
> 'I'm just watching her boyfriend,' quibbled the second. 'A thing of beauty has a boy for ever.'
>
> 'Let him be. Not just him but a bunch of others. Nobody cares. But admit', continued the first, 'she has beautiful eyes.'
>
> The fourth person, in whose opinion everything was a game, bellowed now, 'Can a woman wearing a swimming costume expect people to just look at her eyes?'
>
> Everyone froze for a moment.
>
> 'Watch the game; see how smooth and firm Cowdrey is even amidst the rain.'
>
> A mere 23 runs in one hour …
>
> 'Don't look at her so ridiculously,' the second warned the first.
>
> 'It will be rude not to look at her.'
>
> 'Whatever you say, isn't she feeling cold?' wondered the fourth.
>
> 'Why will she?' He reasoned, 'A Sahara could be burning inside her.'
>
> The first guy recited like a verse, 'Can you lend a shawl to people living in Gobi-Sahara?'[91]

A reputed author writing a misogynist public (male) conversation about female physicality in the form of banter for a newspaper shows that disrespect for female spectators had public approval. Some men made evaluative remarks and ogled at women, while some others tried to restrain them. Male fantasies often took ridiculously exaggerated forms, such as the fourth person's assertion about the woman wearing clothes as revealing as swimsuits, vaguely suggesting the woman invited male gaze. Two in the group quoted a famous line from a poem written by Jatindranath Sengupta in 1923 about the absurdity of romanticism in a stressful life. The poem asked affluent people to share their wealth with the less fortunate, which the friends tweaked to overlay on the girl's behaviour and their sexual desire.[92] It should be noted that in the same month as Sengupta's article was out, one Nabakumar Shil wrote a letter to the *Jugantar* criticising male spectators for insulting the women sitting nearby using obscene language and gestures.[93] In this regard, some press reports could be seen as the mechanism through which violence against women were normalised, and some others were redemptive.

Later in 1964, during the Test match against Australia, presumably the same fictitious group of friends gossiped about a woman named Jayanti who apparently hunted for a partner in the stadium. Clad in sparse clothing, Jayanti's 'tireless efforts' had proven futile so far, prompting one of the friends to advise an 'attireless effort'.[94] Among other instances of pillorying women's putative exhibitionism, Basu wrote about an old man imploring a maiden to put on more clothes to protect herself from the chilly breeze.[95] He also wrote about a woman in the posh 35-rupee season ticket stand changing her *sari* during the lunch and tea breaks, emerging 'brand new' every session, and redoing her hairstyle as frequently as the captain shuffled his bowlers on the field.[96] In the winter of 1966–67, he produced a satire in verse to describe two women in contrasting clothes:

This lady's pullover
Stripped all the Himalayan sheep bare
Another one hover
Like an ascetic, there,
With nominal clothes and no care.[97]

Writing in 1967, humourist Shibram Chakraborty observed an urgency among women to parade the latest fashion, if not to attract men then at least to make other women envious, rather than a zeal for cricket.[98] The text hinted at women's indecisiveness about their adorned bodies. About a decade later, Prafulla Roy, novelist, wrote about seven girls, aged between 18 and 22, sitting three rows down from his seat. He noted that wearing bellbottom, *sari*, cardigan, shawl, sunglasses and binoculars, they looked like 'a shoal of colourful fish in an aquarium'.[99] The girls celebrated the batting performances of Gavaskar and Viswanath and the fielding efforts of Bacchus and Gomes, laughing continuously. Most authors seemed to have reconciled with the fast disappearance of submissiveness as a cultural appendage of womanhood. Women bonding in a public space, in contrast with their prescriptive domestic role, was another symbol frequently referred to in the press. The mediatised reflections on the weakening of the communal mythologies regarding women's public behaviour, albeit from a male viewpoint, highlighted women's greater independence and complexity in social roles.

These images have been discussed to some extent by scholars of cinema and women's work in modern India. An ethnographic research on the gaze of male Hindi filmgoers in 1991 offered a conclusion that while watching female actors in a film, men distinguished between the 'legitimate objects of the gaze' and sacrosanct women who should be spared the gaze. These men reinforced male dominance by objectifying women and, simultaneously, limiting women's public activities in order to protect them from 'corrupt' behaviour.[100] The sexualised depiction of women in most 'commercial' films produced in India operated through suggestive tropes, called 'the erotic promise' by the feminist scholar Jigna Desai, as opposed to full-fledged nudity, leaving a lot to the audience's imagination, all the while conceding little sexual agency to female characters.[101] A confrontation of the so-called conservative and liberal approaches to women's activities runs through the gamut of production and reception of Indian films. The interplay of power and fantasy was so woven into the texture of everyday consumption of leisure that it can be said to have informed changes in behaviour towards women in public. A major difference between the cinema and stadium audience is the normative silence and absence of communication among the former. The extensive interaction among people in the cricket galleries made the sporting public sphere more noticeable and suitable for mediatisation.

In one of his weekly columns for the *Desh* in 1970, the author Narayan Gangopadhyay warned against an epidemic of disrespect towards women in public.[102] Cricketers too were implicated in the rising tide of flippancy, most notably weeks before Gangopadhyay's comment was published. In 1969 the entire Indian team was rumoured to be arrested on the eve of the Test match against New Zealand in Nagpur for having misbehaved with a military officer's daughter. At the team manager's behest, it was said, the chief minister asked the police to release the cricketers so that the match could take place. The BCCI formed a committee to investigate the allegation in which two senior players were particularly implicated, but no more was heard of the incident.[103] In an interview given to Gavaskar for the *Debonair* magazine, the captain, Pataudi, denied the incident, telling him that other cricketers would deny it too.[104] The report of the Committee on the Status of Women in India in 1974 set off debates on inequality and predatory behaviour towards women, animating feminist groups into action. The resentment among feminists was perfectly reflected in a poem by Kabita Sinha:

> What do you want from her body?
> Flesh, fat? Prehistoric fire? Smell of burnt flesh?
> Blood wine? Or nails teeth hair?
> The goddess skull shaped like a rice bowl?
> Or will you filter the best cocktail
> Of talent and loveliness? ...[105]

The question of objectification of female bodies was further illustrated by debates about appropriate clothing for female spectators. Clothes were a significant part of constructing the ideal upper-class and upper-caste woman. In the colonial period, the aesthetic form and moral content of a *bhadramahila*, one scholar has argued, was informed by nationalist discourses of creating the ideal female in response to colonial critiques of 'animality and sensuality of Bengali/pagan women in particular'.[106] One of the outcomes of the Indian intelligentsia's moral reform projects in response to European allegations of their innate incapability to self-improve was the imposition of a restrictive code of honour upon Indian women. Shame was an important aspect of women's behaviour under this patriarchal nationalist enterprise that was carried out chiefly through sex-appropriate clothing. The sexually chastened female body became an icon for the emerging aspirations of Bengali culture and nationalism.[107] The normative assumptions about and restrictions on a woman's body in colonial Bengal were gradually replaced by different sets of norms. Greater autonomy of women over their body and behaviour was widely seen as the result of the corrupting influence of a monolithic, depraved West, especially in films and political ideologies.[108] The fracturing of men's sovereignty over women's subjectivities as social beings has been one of the most publicly discussed topics in modern India and has had an enormous bearing on the gender practices through which the postcolonial nation has been fabricated into existence.

In comparison with the evidences mustered by the Hindu Law Committee in the 1940s, the socio-economic position of middle-class women had changed indubitably by the 1970s.[109] Having acquired equal inheritance and property rights, and the necessary training to obtain relevant jobs, urban women were now in principle uncoupled from their heteronormative familial relationships.[110] Many families started to depend on their earnings.[111] However, sustaining the family did not always give them equal power of decision-making as the male members. The overall attitude to women remained paternalistic.[112] As spaces of recreation continued to open up for more women across class barriers, most notably cinema and theatre, the question of women's autonomy over their body and leisure interest frequently came under criticism.[113] Groups of women in cinemas, sports grounds or political rallies sometimes raised safety concerns. Many families were still alarmed by the sight of a solitary woman in a public assembly, and even as part of a sports team. Some conservative households considered an independent woman immoral. As structural referents to womanhood in public spaces, keeping late nights, smoking, drinking, dressing in Western attire as opposed to Indian outfits and making male friends superficially but powerfully determined a woman's personality. Some women found other women's sartorial conventions as subversive of Indian traditions in a meek surrender to immorality. One of them, Archana Chattapadhyay, said in a letter to the *Khelar Asar* magazine that trousers were for disreputable women.[114]

Some agents of consumption, such as newspaper columnists, fetishised women's body for profit, as Sankariprasad Basu had admitted. Contrary to the usual masculinisation of female sportspersons, female spectators have been invariably portrayed as attractive and elegant components of the galleries, and their femininity utilised to advertise stadium events. The dressed and ornamented body was central to this process. In addition to adorning signs of gender such as clothing, make-up and hairstyle, bodily gestures articulated and affirmed one's gender role.[115] As we have observed, cricket writers used gender stereotypes to describe women's involvement with the game. They exaggerated women's irrationality and often focused on women's transgressive role with the aim to draw both casual and critical male readers. Also, at a time when India lost more matches than they even came close to winning, the descriptions of spectators often elicited more interest than the match itself. Female writers sometimes used satire to counter these judgemental attitudes. In an article for the *Amrita Bazar Patrika*, Sudeshna Barua gloated that she took one hour and a half to dress, keeping her brother and his friends waiting, and strolled into the stadium expecting looks of admiration.[116] Throughout the article Barua feigned conventional attributes of inadequate knowledge, aversion to detail, impatience with the game's pace and fascination with cricketers, all the while evincing her understanding of the game.

Newspapers highlighted female celebrities attending a match to attract male readership. During the India–West Indies Test match in 1966–67, they covered every movement of the actresses Sharmila Tagore and Anju Mahendru, the prospective partners of the India captain, Pataudi, and the West Indies captain, Garry Sobers. The *Dainik Basumati* sent a reporter to Sobers's hotel room to check if Mahendru was around.[117] In 1979, a man fell from the concrete gallery next to the Club House trying to catch a glimpse of Tagore.[118] The media's stratagems of sensationalism, which met with feminist criticism of collusion with patriarchy, continued throughout the later decades. A report about the India–Sri Lanka World Cup semi-final match in 1996 mentioned that the Indian captain Mohammad Azharuddin's fiancé, the former Miss India Sangeeta Bijlani, wore a green full-sleeve t-shirt and black gloves, and Maria, an unmarried foreign tourist, was in a white and green striped t-shirt.[119] The uninvited co-presence of the body images of an Indian celebrity and a tourist identified by her name and esoteric looks represented a new journalistic practice. The history of women's objectification outlined in this section manifest how little had changed, except for a certain degree of refinement in description.

A common tendency among men was to blame women for distracting men. The *Dainik Basumati* distinctly mentioned that many among the 20,000 people who disrupted Australia's net practice in 1969 were women.[120] Most female football fans could not attend important matches because of the violent and hostile atmosphere created by partisan male supporters, so they sometimes went to practice sessions. In a letter to the *Khelar Asar*, one Sanjay De mentioned that at a forum organised by the Left Front government on 29 July 1979 P. K. Banerjee had entreated women to not attend practice sessions. Apparently, the footballer Sabbir Ali had refused to shoot a ball with his weaker left foot in fear of being ridiculed by female onlookers. Finding it his duty to save the game of football, De decided to make Banerjee's grumblings known to a sports magazine so that its female readers stopped attending practice in empathy.[121] Female readers predictably blasted his sexist opinion of women as objects of distraction. Why should women take the blame for a footballer's lack of confidence? Any suggestion of women's attraction to the charisma of footballers rather than a passion for football would have possibly been generated by the actions of one or two women, and generalisation would be a gross misjudgement, they said.[122] When the Calcutta Cricket and

Football Club (CCFC) considered granting membership to women, the noted sport commentator Pearson Surita expressed strong objection in a letter to the club's president. He stated that admitting single or married women would constitute 'a real danger to the physical or other well-being' of male members. He refused to speak at the Annual General Meeting of the club in front of women, afraid that women's presence would 'cramp' his speech delivery.[123] In a hegemonic spatial strategy of marginalising women, men like P. K. Banerjee and Pearson Surita made use of the inegalitarian power relations drawn from their involvement in men's sport to exclude women from the community. The constitution of women as objects of desire was further reinforced by inappropriate behaviour that bordered on violence.

One of men's canonical responses to what they consider recalcitrant femininity is treating women as a legitimate subject of aggression. Inappropriate behaviour towards female spectators probably existed from the very beginning of stadium sport in India, but instances started to be documented in the press in the 1990s, possibly coinciding with the widening of feminist sensibilities. Large-scale 'eve teasing' by people sitting in the CAB member galleries was reported during the India–England Test match in 1993.[124] The accused uttered obscenities at women, insulted a 75-year-old man for protesting, hurled banana and orange skins at bald heads and paper planes at everyone. At the centre of the commotion was a group of men in the annual members' gallery at Block G, which could be accessed from gate 11. They wore decent clothes, came from affluent families and some were students of some of the city's better colleges and universities. During the tea break, they were heard making nasty comments about a boy wearing a cap with an elephant trunk and ears. Some young men sitting in the lower tier started doing the same. In a different block, the correspondent saw a married woman nearly fainting on account of the remarks made about her. Apparently, other spectators were irritated but no one protested.[125] Finally, a police officer grabbed two men by their collars and dragged them away, promising to teach them unforgettable lessons, while his colleagues made several arrests at Block F.[126] This was one of the many instances of heckling women that were published in the press in the 1990s and later. Most women were seen to ignore the reprehensible phrases often used to embarrass them, feigning they had not heard anything, which further rooted a woman's outsider status.

The sociological and anthropological studies of the construction of gender identities in the mass media in the 1990s, especially anthropologist Purnima Mankekar's work on the serials aired on national television, offer important insights that might help understand this surge in violence. In most *Doordarshan* serials, Mankekar argues, women were defined through the contrasting tropes of morality and sexuality. The ideal 'new Indian woman' of the 1990s was educated, working outside home, yet chaste and devoted to the family and nation. The problematic women were wives and lovers with an unabashed sexuality, and that corrupts men and by extension the nation.[127] Elsewhere, Mankekar argues that the spread of erotics through television programmes had extensive influence on personal disposition, if not public behaviour, as television added a tactile dimension to the pleasure of gazing upon and desiring commodities.[128] These studies suggest a proliferation of mediated notions of what counted as acceptable female sexuality. Incidentally, representations in the sports press moved in the opposite direction of becoming more gender sensitive and value neutral. Therefore, no causal link can be drawn between representations of women in the media and men's behaviour towards women in public spaces. Indeed, even leading women's magazines such as *Sananda* avoided discussions of women's sexuality in the 1990s, in an effort to contain women's bodies within discourses of 'Indian culture'.[129] The threat of violence did not deter women from embracing their sexuality as a means of resisting male fantasies and proclaiming the autonomy of their bodies. In the 1980s–90s, having ceased to be unspoken subjects since long, women were seen to shout, wave banners with messages to cricketers and dance in the galleries. The openness and unapologetic nature of female spectatorship were manifest most explicitly in how women behaved around cricketers.

CELEBRITY OBSESSION

On the third day of the third Test between India and Australia in Bombay in 1960, as Abbas Ali Baig trudged his way back to the pavilion at tea 58 not out, a girl from the posh North Stand scaled a fence, ran onto the field, and kissed the batsman on his cheek. At the end of the day's play, a board official told Baig several other girls had asked if they could kiss him too.[130] Notwithstanding the drive for women's liberation, the act was highly unusual in the cultural context of the times, raised a storm of comments in the press, was the subject of a famous novel, and inspired a Cadbury advertisement 30 years later.[131] The kiss symbolised the beginning of the end of women's marginality as spectators, or, to quote feminist scholar Jill Dolan, the parting bell for women's role as a 'tacit support system or as decoration that enhances and directs the pleasure of the male spectator's gaze'.[132] Although female spectators were not able to completely overwrite the narrative of marginality, because meanings of gendered actions are ever fluid, their actions reveal how they understood the cultural meanings of femininity and the representations of womanhood.

Writing about the conjugal fantasies of young Bengali women in the 1950s–60s Calcutta, anthropologist Manisha Roy states that besides Hollywood stars, women were attracted to cricketers and tennis players.[133] In an interview with Roy, a woman admitted her desire for Gregory Peck and added that her friend liked the cricketer Naresh Kumar.[134] The actress Arati Bhattacharya 'fell in love' with Pataudi by just reading about his personality.[135] The actress and politician Jayalalitha, more popularly known as Amma, trained her binoculars on Pataudi.[136] Mala Sinha's character in the film *Love Marriage* (1959) had posters of Vinoo Mankad and Khandu Rangnekar in her room. The journalist Nilima Sen Gangopadhyay wrote that tennis players were popular among elite women, whereas footballers and cricketers were acceptable across social class.[137] A short story by Gour Kishor Ghosh gives us a glimpse into a High Court judge's daughter's fascination with the batsman Budhi Kunderan. Set during the India–England Test match in 1964, the story is about the woman's plan to garland and embrace Kunderan on the cricket field and then collapse on his lap unconscious. Her dream cannot materialise without a ticket, so she goes on a hunger strike to force her father to use his influence to acquire a ticket for her.[138] In Suchitra Bhattacharya's novel *Nil Ghurni*, set in the 1990s, cricketers were as much part of dinner table conversations at girls' hostels as were Bollywood stars and politicians, showing the continuance of enthusiasm about cricket.[139] This degree of enthusiasm among women, evident in real-life incidents as well, expanded cricket's domain by creating new topics of discussion and followers for the game.

In 1972–73, after India defeated England, students from Bethune College beat drums, danced, took out a procession and smeared each other with vermillion. Indian captain Ajit Wadekar evaded a woman's embrace with the 'dexterity of ducking under a bumper', as one newspaper reported.[140] Two young girls fell unconscious in the commotion as followers gathered around the hotel to congratulate the Indian team for their win against West Indies in 1975.[141] The female follower's groupie moment finally arrived in 1979 as a bunch of young girls reportedly invaded the team hotel and banged on the doors of Indian and Caribbean cricketers. The cricketers locked themselves in, trying to prevent the girls from entering, as the employees and the police looked on helplessly.[142] After this incident, female constables were assigned to team hotels and given the power to apprehend female followers, in addition to their duty at the galleries. The press was replete with comments about the 'nuisance' caused by female followers. In two decades, the focus turned from women's illegitimacy as cricket followers to their unacceptable zeal as cricket supporters. One journalist mooted the idea of players bringing their wives on tours, to keep discipline and deter female followers.[143] Reports on incidents like these foregrounded a class dimension, suggesting that women from the lower income groups of society were more prone to effusive displays. The ascription of specific forms of behaviour to one's class position could be seen as the press's tool for both indicating the proliferation of cricket following beyond the upper-middle class and associating trouble with the non-elite section of society. The narratives of the kiss and the judge's daughter, however, undermine the strength of these constructs.

In the 1980s, television brought cricketers closer to the public. Watching cricketers move on the field more clearly from one's room than was possible from the gallery added a new visceral layer and intimacy to the visual appreciation of their craft and bodies. In the opinion of international relations scholar Sankaran Krishna, 'the sight of a sweaty Imran Khan, shirt open a good ways down to the waist, loping in to bowl in his snug flannels set many hearts racing. I can't vouch for this but when Mr Khan was on screen, there certainly seemed to be more women watching raptly'.[144] Using one's senses and emotion to interact with the subject on screen, the audience is able to connect with the moving image of a person, which may lead to a strong emotional attachment.[145] Many scholars have suggested that media coverage has played a significant role in making certain physically attractive male players celebrities, which have had a profound impact on stoking the interest of women in the sport. The media ususally portrayed female fans as strange and ill-behaved. The more knowledgeable female followers of cricket found this an offensive manner of demeaning their struggle to breach sports spectatorship's male domain.[146] In Bengal, with the number of women in employment declining through the 1980s and 1990s, contrary to the general national trend, it can be supposed that most women stayed at home and the television became an important tool for them to engage with the outside world.[147]

Pakistani cricketers and Imran Khan in particular featured the most in stories about female fans and non-Indian cricketers.[148] During the India–Pakistan Test match in 1980, Sadiq Mohammad brought a female guest and demanded a free ticket for her. As the guards refused to let her in without a ticket, he threatened to pull out of the match.[149] The CAB treasurer, Jagmohan Dalmiya, salvaged the situation by offering a guest pass from his personal quota.[150] There were rumours about a Bombay actress calling Imran regularly.[151] During the Test match, he received no less than 200 fan letters, most of which were sent by girls aged 15 to 25, professing love and admiration. Some of the letter writers proposed marriage and wanted to meet Khan.[152] In Madras, a woman masqueraded as the hotel receptionist to get past the security and meet Khan.[153] Sometimes cricketers escorted women to the dressing room. Zaheer Abbas was once seen sitting there surrounded by women.[154] The photojournalist S. S. Kanjilal had an unpleasant encounter with Majid Khan at a party. Taking exception to being photographed in conversation with some attractive girls, Khan started abusing him and demanded the film roll to be handed over. Kanjilal, undeterred, asked him to come to the studio if he needed to see the negative before the photographs were processed.[155] At least two Pakistani cricketers had romantic affairs with Indian women. In 1983, after a six-year courtship, actress Reena Roy quit Bollywood to marry Mohsin Khan. The relationship between Sarfraz Nawaz and Sheetal, actress and producer, became acrimonious soon after it started. Sheetal, suspicious that Nawaz was after her property, broke up with him on the eve of Pakistan's tour of Australia in 1984.[156] Nawaz maintained that Sheetal was no more than a fan who posed with him for a few photographs at a party. When an Indian film magazine published the photographs along with a story about their romantic relationship, the rumours landed him in trouble with his family.[157] Women's visibility, emphasised femininity, and sexualised roles had by now become a resource for journalists to increase their readership.[158]

In 1983, some 'ultramodern' women reportedly heckled the Caribbean cricketers looking for leatherworks and suitcases in the New Market. The women's behaviour was 'disrespectful' and 'humiliating'.[159] Two days later, a flirtatious woman apparently forced Viv Richards to abandon his search for the right pair of shoes and return to his hotel. The report was concluded with an agonised comment that such attitude was not seen elsewhere in the cricket world.[160] During the 1987 World Cup, a squad of disguised detectives were tasked with preventing women from entering team hotels.[161]

These reports written by male journalists, however deprecating of women's behaviour, acknowledged women's resistance against normative behaviour in public spaces. The appellation of 'ultramodern', colloquial for over-Westernised and lacking sexual modesty, expresses a general anxiety with women popularly juxtaposed with 'traditional' women to demonstrate a region's disaffection with change. A reversal of women's representation as a new form of predatory cricket followers was seen in the *Jugantar's* report on the assignment of 'good-looking' assistant sub-inspectors and sub-inspectors to protect the wives of cricketers and administrators, and female travellers.[162] Insinuation of some of the dangers of women working in public spaces was made in a report on the West Indian fast bowler Patrick Patterson ambling over to talk to the hotel receptionist while watching the final match on the television at the foyer.[163] The ambivalence towards women suggested that though the irrational fans among them seemed aggressive, the docile working women who represented the ideal Indian female were still considered vulnerable.

These anonymous women, in all their classless ordinariness, did not camouflage their form of resistance, but openly challenged the line demarcating masculine and feminine behaviour. Such behaviour differs from the infrapolitics we have discussed so far and has more in common with Asef Bayat's formulation of everyday resistance as a flexible and adaptive practice of gaining more autonomy. Bayat's theory is based upon the urban poor's resistance against authority, which starts with individual efforts but becomes collective soon after the powers that be take notice and attempt to quell the resistance. Collective resistance operates through a 'passive network' of people with a unity of purpose. This imagined rather than organised solidarity makes the eagerness for a more permissive society more powerful and persistent.[164] The acts of gatecrashing hotels and interacting with male cricketers liberated cricket-loving women from the conventional and conservative social attitudes regarding women's behaviour in public. By flouting the social injunctions on public etiquette, some women caused a furore. Thronging one's favourite cricketer was a sign of hero worship for men, but an act of sexual transgression for women. The symbolism associated with female spectators' celebrity obsession remained centred on the paradigm of nonconformity, but its representation in the press gradually waned as too many women started sharing the behavioural pattern. This is not to claim that the fear of crime against women and the disadvantage of being a woman in a 'man's world' decreased significantly over the decades. Yet the little acts of intrusion empowered female spectators to resist the social control enacted around participation in sport.

CONCLUSION

This chapter has described women's experience of men's international cricket. How did women respond to women's cricket? It was often argued in the press that women's lack of interest in women's cricket betrayed the real reasons for their fascination with cricket – obsession with male celebrities and the thrill of the festive atmosphere during the more corporatised men's cricket. A litmus test for the city's female spectators was the final of the 1997 Women's World Cup. Earlier, the match between India and England during the 1978 Women's World Cup had gone almost unnoticed, resulting in a few unconnected sentences of match report in some of the major dailies.[165] The final between Australia and New Zealand in 1997, billed as a day for women in Calcutta, was an opportunity to demonstrate women's enthusiasm for women's cricket. Bulbul Gayen, president of the West Bengal Women's Cricket Association, anticipated a turnout of 50,000 women. Sport Minister Subhas Chakraborty expected to see 80,000 spectators but later admitted to his over-ambition.[166] His wish was nearly fulfilled the next day as the stadium seemed to be full. Chakraborty's wife, Ramala Chakraborty, despatched tickets to all over West Bengal through her political network, including Bankura, Purulia, Haldia, Bagnan and Sagardwip. Thousands of members of various women's political groups were mobilised to throng the stands as they did for the CPI(M)'s conventions at the Brigade parade ground. Most of these women were watching cricket for the first time. Anuradha Bharati from Naihati brought 5 persons, while one Namitadi brought 200 persons with her. A tribal band with full musical assortments were brought from Bankura. Tickets were sent to many girls' schools for students and accompanying guardians. Students from St John's Diocesan were asked to cheerlead and dance to English music. As the correspondent of the *Aajkal* noticed, not only were the spectators unable to identify any of the players, the anchor failed to pronounce their exotic names. A few women admitted that this match was an alternative to a trip to the zoo or the Victorial Memorial. Members of other cricket teams were shocked to see such a huge turnout, a gigantic leap from 4,000 in London and 400 in Melbourne for the previous finals.[167] Although the women in attendance made a grand political statement, their understanding of cricket was still under interrogation.

'Outsiders', wrote sociologist Robert K. Merton, are those 'who have been systematically frustrated by the social system: the disinherited, deprived, disenfranchised, dominated and exploited'.[168] The popular discourse of women's presence and interaction with men in and around the Eden Gardens, replete with stories ranging from ridiculing to assaulting women, would suggest a permanent 'outsider' status for women. The chapter's analysis of press reports revealed systemic and symbolic male dominance through routine emphasis and capitalising on the otherness of women. Most female spectators were depicted until the mid-1970s as scarcely having any personal agenda, acting mostly in consort with their family and friends, and with the primary desire to flaunt their sexuality. Cricket writers used abundant gender stereotypes, presumably as a 'profitable provocation' and challenging the boundary of civility, to popularise their work.[169] Their writings reflected a canonical drive for subjugating women, framing them in a distinctly patriarchal manner. The periodic creation and utilisation of 'femininity' certainly failed to regulate the entry and conduct of women within or outside the cricket stadium. Through an exploration of women's representations, the chapter has traced the history of women's marginalisation and resilience. The focus on the diverse audience at a sports stadium has enabled it to study women across class, ethnicity and age. This has helped the article to drive home what people expected out of women of a certain class or group, and what impact this reciprocity of expectation and delivery of specific behaviour had on gender relations in the wider society.

Knowledge of cricket enabled women to unevenly self-habilitate and counter criticism. Parts of the press represented them as a charade of a noble game, initially for lack of knowledge and afterwards for impulsive passion for cricketers. This image was not stabilised as objective, since the liberal feminist aesthetic of women's independence of action was recognised by some of the media outlets. Women's voice worked through either erasing the paradigm of their difference from men or foregrounding their form of spectatorship as unique and acceptable. The sarcasms applied to female spectators were steadily replaced with acknowledgement of new forms of spectatorship as women gradually emerged as potential consumers of newspapers and cricket.[170] Men in general still implicitly regulated the gendered space primarily because they were the agents to create and conduct stadium events. Women's representations recast the stadium as a site of struggle rather than of autonomous existence of actors. The study of questions of gender hierarchy, women's mannerism, social identity and informal resistance through a historical lens has enabled this chapter to understand the trajectory of women's outsider status in urban public spaces.

NOTES

1. Susie Tharu and Tejaswini Niranjana, 'Problems for a Contemporary Theory of Gender', *Social Scientist* 22, nos. 3–4 (1994): 93–117, 93.
2. *Hindustan Standard*, 2 January 1962, 1.
3. Sankariprasad Basu, *Edene Shiter Dupur*, in *Cricket Omnibus I* (Calcutta: Mandal Book House, 1976), 119.
4. Satadru Sen, 'History without a Past: Memory and Forgetting in Indian Cricket', in *Cricket and National Identity in the Postcolonial Age: Following On*, ed. Stephen Wagg, 94–109 (London: Routledge, 2005), 105.
5. Since the 1980s feminist scholars have undertaken substantial empirical and theoretical research into women's experience in sport and similar outdoor activities. Their works epitomise the complexity and diversity of women's experiences of sport, male–female dichotomies and non-binary sporting identities. Historians of gender in sport have moved beyond the boundaries of white middle-class feminism to encompass the sporting experiences of, for example, non-Christian, non-white and non-Western women. For studies of gender and sport in the non-Western world, see Dong Jinxia, *Women, Sport and Society in Modern China: Holding Up More Than Half the Sky* (London: Routledge, 2003); Robin Kietlinski, *Japanese Women and Sport: Beyond Baseball and Sumo* (London: Bloomsbury, 2011); Yunxiang Gao, *Sporting Gender: Women Athletes and Celebrity-Making during China's National Crisis, 1931–45* (Vancouver: UBC Press, 2013); Michelle Sikes and John Bale, eds., *Women's Sport in Africa* (London: Routledge, 2015); Gyozo Molnar, Sara N. Amin and Yoko Kanemasu, eds., *Women, Sport and Exercise in the Asia-Pacific Region: Domination, Resistance, Accommodation* (London: Routledge, 2018); and Brenda Elsey and Joshua Nadel, *Futbolera: A History of Women and Sports in Latin America* (Austin: University of Texas Press, 2019).
6. Fatima Mernissi, 'The Meaning of Spatial Boundaries', in *Beyond the Veil: Male-Female Dynamics in Muslim Society*, 137–47 (London: Al Saqi Books, 1975).

7. Michael Messner, *Taking the Field: Women, Men, and Sports* (Minneapolis and London: University of Minnesota Press, 2002), 98.

8. Gail Minault, ed., *The Extended Family: Women and Political Participation in India and Pakistan* (New Delhi: Chanakya Publications, 1981); Rosalind O'Hanlon, *A Comparison between Women and Men: Tarabai Shinde and the Critique of Gender Relations in Colonial India* (New Delhi: Oxford University Press, 1994); Antoinette Burton, *At the Heart of the Empire: Indians and the Colonial Encounter in Late-Victorian Britain* (Berkeley: University of California Press, 1998); Samita Sen, *Women and Labour in Late Colonial India: The Bengal Jute Industry* (Cambridge: Cambridge University Press, 1999); Tanika Sarkar, *Hindu Wife, Hindu Nation: Community, Religion and Cultural Nationalism* (London: Hurst & Co, 2001); Padma Anagol, *The Emergence of Feminism in India, 1850–1920* (Aldershot: Ashgate, 2005).

9. Dipesh Chakrabarty, 'The Difference – Deferral of (A) Colonial Modernity: Public Debates on Domesticity in British Bengal', *History Workshop Journal* 36, no. 1 (Autumn 1993): 1–34; Sanjay Joshi, *Fractured Modernity: Making of a Middle Class in Colonial North India* (New Delhi: Oxford University Press, 2001), ch. 2.

10. Jyoti Puri, *Woman, Body, Desire in Post-Colonial India: Narratives of Gender and Sexuality* (New York and London: Routledge, 1999); Kenneth Bo Nielsen and Anne Waldrop, eds., *Women, Gender and Everyday Social Transformation in India* (London: Anthem, 2004); Rehana Ghadially, ed., *Urban Women in Contemporary India: A Reader* (New Delhi: Sage, 2007); Rachel Tu, 'Dressing the Nation: Indian Cinema Costume and the Making of a National Fashion, 1947–1957', in *The Fabric of Culture: Fashion, Identity, and Globalization*, ed. Eugenia Paulicelli and Hazel Clark, 28–40 (London and New York: Routledge, 2009); Stephen Putnam Hughes, 'Silent Film Genre, Exhibition and Audiences in South India', in *Explorations in New Cinema History: Approaches and Case Studies*, ed. Richard Maltby, Daniel Biltereyst, and Philippe Meers, 295–309 (Chichester: Wiley-Blackwell, 2011).

11. Stacey Pope, *The Feminization of Sports Fandom: A Sociological Study* (New York and London: Routledge, 2017). Historians such as Tony Collins would argue this was a deliberate stratagem of corporatised sport as subscriber television came to dominate. English football clubs and many other sports sought to broaden their support base beyond male working-class supporters watching games on packed terraces to seeking family audiences, including women and children. Across the world this saw a trend towards all-seater

stadiums and merchandising aimed at men, women and children. Tony Collins, *Sport in Capitalist Society* (London: Routledge, 2013).

12. Katharine Jones, 'Female Fandom: Identity, Sexism, and Men's Professional Football in England', *Sociology of Sport Journal* 25, no. 4 (2008): 516–37; Kim Toffoletti and Peter Mewett, eds., *Sport and Its Female Fans* (New York and London: Routledge, 2012); Souvik Naha, 'Adams and Eves at the Eden Gardens: Women Cricket Spectators and the Conflict of Feminine Subjectivity in Calcutta, 1920–1970', *International Journal of the History of Sport* 29, no. 5 (2012): 711–29; Carrie Dunn, *Female Football Fans: Community, Identity and Sexism* (Basingstoke: Palgrave Macmillan, 2014); Verena Lenneis and Gertrud Pfister, 'Gender Constructions and Negotiations of Female Football Fans: A Case Study in Denmark', *European Journal for Sport and Society* 12, no. 2 (2015): 157–85; Anne Cunningham Osborne and Danielle Sarver Coombs, *Female Fans of the NFL: Taking Their Place in the Stands* (New York and London: Routledge: 2016); Kim Toffoletti, *Women Sport Fans: Identification, Participation, Representation* (New York and London: Routledge, 2017); Gertrud Pfister and Stacey Pope, eds., *Female Football Players and Fans: Intruding into a Man's World* (Basingstoke: Palgrave Macmillan, 2018).

13. James C. Scott introduced the term 'infrapolitics' to denote everyday forms of unorganized resistance against hierarchy and dominant elites that often go unnoticed. Infrapolitics is executed through mundane activities like squatting in public places, feigning ignorance or taking unscheduled breaks at work that are not recognized as political action. Dissent of these sorts usually elude detection and fall outside the threshold of political action because of their small scope, but they are nevertheless effective as discursive practices of protest. The counterhegemonic consciousness of the actors manifested in these actions helps us understand the social condition from which they emerge. James C. Scott, *Weapons of the Weak: Everyday forms of Peasant Resistance* (New Haven: Yale University Press, 1985); *Domination and the Arts of Resistance: Hidden Transcripts* (New Haven: Yale University Press, 1990).

14. J. A. Mangan and J. Walvin, *Manliness and Morality: Middle-Class Masculinity in Britain and America 1800–1940.* (Manchester: Manchester University Press, 1987), 1. See also Anthony Bateman, 'Performing Imperial Masculinities: The Discourse and Practice of Cricket', in *Performing Masculinity*, ed. Rainer Emig and Antony Rowland, 78–94 (Basingstoke: Palgrave Macmillan, 2010).

15. Dominic Malcolm and Philippa Velija, 'Female Incursion into Cricket's "Male Preserve",' in *Tribal Play: Subcultural Journeys Through Sport*, ed. Michael Atkinson and Kevin Young, 217–34 (Bingley: Emerald, 2008).

16. Jennifer Hargreaves, 'The Victorian Cult of the Family and the Early Years of Female Sports', in *The Sports Process: A Comparative and Developmental Approach*, ed. Eric Dunning, Joseph Maguire and Robert Pearton, 71–84 (Champaign, IL: Human Kinetics, 1994), 73.

17. Colin D. Howell, *Blood, Sweat, and Cheers: Sport and the Making of Modern Canada* (Toronto: University of Toronto Press, 2001), 90.

18. Timothy J. L. Chandler and John Nauright, 'Introduction: Rugby, Manhood and Identity', in *Making Men: Rugby and Masculine Identity*, ed. Timothy J. L. Chandler and John Nauright, 1–12 (London: Frank Cass, 1996).

19. Tony Mason, *Association Football and English Society, 1863–1915* (Brighton: Harvester Press, 1980), 152–53.

20. Derek Birley, *A Social History of English Cricket* (London: Aurum Press, 1999); Jack Williams, *Cricket and Race* (Oxford: Berg Publishers, 2001).

21. Kathleen E. McCrone, *Playing the Game: Sport and Physical Emancipation of English Women, 1870–1914* (Kentucky: University of Kentucky Press, 1988), 142–43.

22. Keith Sandiford, *Cricket and the Victorians* (Aldershot: Scolar Press, 1994).

23. Philippa Velija, *Women's Cricket and Global Processes: The Emergence and Development of Women's Cricket as a Global Game* (Basingstoke: Palgrave Macmillan, 2015) 47–49.

24. Greg Ryan, *The Making of New Zealand Cricket 1832–1914* (London: Frank Cass, 2004), 21.

25. Eric Hobsbawm, *The Age of Empire 1875–1914* (New York: Vintage, 1989), 205.

26. Virginia Club in the United States started this practice in 1883. It was later adopted by a few other clubs and evolved into the Ladies Day. W. Harrison Daniel and Scott P. Meyer, *Baseball and Richmond: A History of the Professional Game, 1884–2000* (Jefferson: McFarland & Co., 2003), 14.

27. Jack Williams, *Cricket and England: A Cultural and Social History of the Inter-war Years* (London: Frank Cass, 1999), 106–11.

28. *TOI*, 8 October 1930, 11.

29. Ibid., 1 March 1934, 7.

30. The women's question was one of the most serious public issues in the nineteenth century. It revolved around not what women wanted but how they could be modernised in keeping with contemporary male ideas of civility and modernity. The encounter of precolonial forms of domesticity

with nineteenth-century ideologies recast notions of marriage, family and responsibility in the context of a colonial 'native' public sphere. Meredith Borthwick, *Changing Role of Women in Bengal 1849–1905* (Princeton: Princeton University Press, 1984); Geraldine Forbes, *Women in Modern India* (Cambridge: Cambridge University Press, 1996); Rajat Kanta Ray, *Exploring Emotional History: Gender, Mentality and Literature in the Indian Awakening* (New Delhi: Oxford University Press, 2003).

31. Antoinette Burton, *Burdens of History: British Feminists, Indian Women, and Imperial Culture, 1865–1915* (Chapel Hill: University of North Carolina Press, 1994), 33–44.

32. Burton, *At the Heart of the Empire*, 173.

33. Richard Cashman, *Patrons, Players and the Crowd: The Phenomenon of Indian Cricket* (New Delhi: Orient Longman, 1980), 117.

34. Ibid., 118.

35. Brahmanyabhusan and Kshama Bandopadhyay, 'Kabigurur Cricket Khela' (The Poet Laureate Plays Cricket), reprinted in Sankariprasad Basu, *Cricket Omnibus II* (Calcutta: Mandal Book House, 1976), 370–75.

36. The Ray family, better known to the rest of India and the Western world through the filmmaker Satyajit Ray, were a pioneering influence in education, literature, politics, religious reform, printing technology and book design in colonial Bengal. Chandak Sengoopta, *The Rays before Satyajit: Creativity and Modernity in Colonial India* (New York: Oxford University Press, 2016).

37. Basu, *Not Out* (1965), in *Cricket Omnibus II*, 99.

38. Ibid., 100.

39. Ibid.

40. Forbes, *Women in Modern India*, 7.

41. Chitra Sinha, *Debating Patriarchy: The Hindu Code Bill Controversy in India, 1941–1956* (New Delhi: Oxford University Press, 2012), 198–202.

42. Benjamin Cohen, 'Networks of Sociability: Women's Clubs in Colonial and Postcolonial India', *Frontiers: A Journal of Women's Studies* 30, no. 3 (2009): 169–95.

43. Trilochon Kalamchi, 'Nikat Dur' (Far and Near), *Desh* 35, no. 11 (14 January 1967), 1102.

44. Chanakya, 'Kolkatar Diary', *Desh* 35, no. 11 (14 January 1967), 1074.

45. Basu, *Cricket Omnibus I*, 421.

46. Chitra Narayanan, 'The Indian Spectator: A Grandstand View', in *Cricketing Cultures in Conflict: World Cup 2003*, ed. Boria Majumdar and J. A. Mangan,

198–212 (London: Routledge, 2004), 205. To cite an example from literature, Tara Das, one of the protagonists in Anita Desai's novel *Clear Light of Day*, was a fielder in cricket games played between her brother Raja and his friend Hamid. Anita Desai, *Clear Light of Day* (New York: Mariner, 2000 [1980]), 124. In Shashi Deshpande's novel *The Only Witness*, Minu, Polly and Padma sometimes join their brothers and cousins in cricket. Shashi Deshpande, *3 Novels* (New Delhi: Puffin, 2006).

47. Personal interview with Ila Sinha, 1 July 2011. She criticised the exhibitionism of body painting and jingoistic slogans as inimical to cricket appreciation.

48. Ajay Basu, *Akashe Cricket Bani* (Calcutta: Falguni Prakashani, 1971), 2.

49. Judith Walsh, *Domesticity in Colonial India: What Women Learned When Men Gave Them Advice* (New Delhi: Oxford University Press, 2004).

50. Indrani Chatterjee, ed., *Unfamiliar Relations: Family and History in South Asia* (Ranikhet: Permanent Black, 2004), 5.

51. Burton, *At the Heart of the Empire*, 175.

52. Alok Dasgupta, 'M Dutta Ray: The Kingmaker', *SKA, 1978*, 140.

53. Kabita Sinha, 'Cricket: Kichhu Smriti' (Cricket: Some Memories), *Khelar Asar* 2, no. 33 (29 December 1978), 64.

54. Douglas Haynes and Gyan Prakash, eds., *Contesting Power: Resistance and Everyday Social Relations in South Asia* (New Delhi: Oxford University Press, 1991), 2–3.

55. Sudeshna Banerjee, 'Fleshing out Mandira: Hemming in the Women's Constituency in Cricket', *International Journal of the History of Sport* 21, nos. 3–4 (2004): 481–82.

56. Ibid.

57. Sankariprasad Basu, *Ramaniya Cricket* (Calcutta: Karuna Prakashani, 1961), 53.

58. Ibid, 55.

59. Banerjee, 'Fleshing Out Mandira', 481.

60. The Indian government had set up an elaborate system of regulations to control industrial production. Private companies required licences to start developing their product, and even the extent of investment and production were determined by the state. These restrictions benefitted the Indian business class which had worked in connivance with the Congress since the late colonial period, stalling implementation of development planning in order to control the spaces left vacant by outgoing British capital. Vivek Chibber, *Locked in Place: State-Building and Late Industrialization in India* (Princeton: Princeton University Press, 2003).

61. Basu, *Ramaniya Cricket*, 64.
62. Ibid, 156.
63. Sankariprasad Basu, *Sara Diner Khela*, in *Cricket Omnibus II*, 264–375 (Calcutta: Mandal Book House, 1976), 319.
64. Basu, *Cricket Omnibus I*, 418.
65. Ibid., 421–22.
66. Ibid., 422.
67. Basu, *Not Out*, 253.
68. Monica Bandyopadhyay, 'Mahilader Cricket Preeti' (Women's Love of Cricket), *Mahila*, 1961, collected in Siddhartha Ghosh ed., *Cricket Elo Banglae* (Cricket in Bengal) (Calcutta: Subarnarekha, 2002), 118.
69. Ibid.
70. Ibid.
71. Ibid., 119.
72. *Jugantar*, 15 December 1969, 6.
73. Narayan Gangopadhyay, 'Paribarik Cricket', in *Sunandor Journal*, 487–88 (Calcutta: Mitra O Ghosh, 2002).
74. Jayanta Dutta, *Rupasi Eden-er Rupasi Cricket* (Calcutta: Karuna Prakashani, 1964).
75. Achintya Kumar Sengupta, 'Badurbagan Theke Mohunbagan' (From Badurbagan to Mohunbagan), in *Mriga Nei Mrigaya*, 71–79 (Calcutta: Anandadhara Prakashan, 1965).
76. Achintya Kumar Sengupta, 'Cricketer Darshan' (Philosophy of Cricket), in *Mriga Nei Mrigaya*, 107–17; Achintya Kumar Sengupta, 'Nake Kaj Na Niswase Kaj' (How Important Is the Nose for Breathing), in *Mriga Nei Mrigaya*, 128–38.
77. Siddheswar Mishra, 'Gallery Theke' (From the Gallery), *DB*, 5 January 1973, 5.
78. *DB*, 31 December 1978, 3.
79. Hariprasad Chattopadhyay, 'Eden: Anya Chokhe' (A Different Eden) *KA* 2, no. 34 (19 January 1979), 10.
80. Umashankar Das, 'Gallery Theke' (From the Gallery), *DB*, 27 October 1979, 3.
81. Alok Dasgupta, 'Test Crickete Edener Darshak' (Test Cricket Spectators at Eden), *SKA*, 1984, 141.
82. *Jugantar*, 1 February 1980, 4.
83. *TS*, 30 December 1980, 14.
84. *Jugantar*, 19 February 1987, 8.

85. Personal interview with Soumyen Mallik, 30 June 2011.

86. Woman's gaze started to be talked about as a powerful mechanism of scrutinising the world with the release of Satyajit Ray's *Charulata* in 1964. Throughout the film, the eponymous female lead observes the world around her so intently that, according to one commentator, her gaze controls the film's action. Her gaze was not returned with the same vigour or emotion in the film, thereby refusing her possible empowerment over the subjects of her gaze. Brinda Bose, 'Modernity, Globality, Sexuality, and the City: A Reading of Indian Cinema', *Global South* 2, no. 1 (2008): 35–58, 49.

87. Rob Hess, '"Ladies Are Specially Invited": Women in the Culture of Australian Rules Football', in *Sport in Australian Society: Past and Present*, ed. J. A. Mangan and John Nauright, 111–41 (London: Frank Cass, 2000), 118.

88. Samita Sen has pointed out some of the problems with working women, in particular the question of a working woman's commitment to family, marginalisation in industrial work, and the ideology of women's subservience to men in the family. See Samita Sen, 'Gendered Exclusion: Domesticity and Dependence in Bengal', *International Review of Social History* 42, no. 5 (1997): 65–86.

89. Swati Chattopadhyay, *Representing Calcutta: Modernity, Nationalism, and the Colonial Uncanny* (London: Routledge, 2005), 265.

90. *TS*, 2 January 1961, 12.

91. Achintya Kumar Sengupta, 'Mriga Nei Mrigaya', (Hunt without the Game), *ABP*, 2 February 1964, 1.

92. 'Cherapunjir theke/Ekkhani megh dhar dite paro Gobi-Saharar buke?' in Jatindranath Sengupta, 'Ghumer Ghore' (Half Asleep), in *Jatindranath Sengupter Srestha Kabita*, ed. Sushanta Basu (Calcutta: Bharabi, 2001), 21.

93. *Jugantar*, 19 February 1964, 8.

94. Achintya Kumar Sengupta, 'Uthlo Tara Akash Bhora' (Starry Sky), *ABP*, 21 October 1964, 6.

95. Sankariprasad Basu, *Edene Shiter Dupur* (A Winter Afternoon at Eden) (Calcutta: Bookland, 1960), 122.

96. Basu, *Ramaniya Cricket*, 96.

97. Trans. Anirban Bandyopadhyay. The original four lines are: *Himalaya-meshpal koriya nishesh/Ek nari lomoboti poriache besh/Onyo nari tapaswini pottimatro gaye/Huhu shite hihi hasi thotete goraye.* *ABP*, 7 January 1967, 9.

98. *ABP*, 5 January 1967, 4.

99. Prafulla Roy, 'Joubone Bujhi Kichu Furoe Na' (Nothing Expires in Youth), *Jugantar*, 3 January 1979, 1. The performance of female cricketers was

bracketed with that of spectators. When asked to comment on the Women's World Cup match India and England on 1 January 1978, the only thought two male spectators conveyed was women looked smart in men's clothing. Sudeshna Barua, 'Meyeder Khelata Ki Sudhui Khela?' (Are Women's Sport Merely Sport), *SKA*, 1979, 90.

100. Steve Derné and Lisa Jadwin, 'Male Hindi Filmgoers' Gaze: An Ethnographic Interpretation of Gender Construction', in *Urban Women in Contemporary India: A Reader*, ed. Rehana Ghadially, 46–62 (New Delhi: Sage, 2007).

101. Jigna Desai, *Beyond Bollywood: The Cultural Politics of South Asian Diasporic Film* (New York and London: Routledge, 2004), 98–99.

102. Narayan Gangopadhyay, 'Dhanbad', *Desh* 37, no. 15 (6 February 1970), 115–16.

103. *DB*, 31 October 1969, 6.

104. Pallab Basumallick, 'Dressingroom', *Saradiya Khela*, 1985, 87.

105. Kabita Sinha, 'Deho' (Body), trans. Subhas Saha, in *Women Writing in India: The Twentieth Century*, ed. Susie Tharu and K. Lalita, 332 (New York: Feminist Press at the City University of New York, 1993).

106. Himani Bannerji, *Inventing Subjects: Studies in Hegemony, Patriarchy and Colonialism* (New Delhi: Tulika, 2001), 125–29.

107. Himani Banerjee, 'Attired in Virtue: The Discourse on Shame and Clothing of the *Bhadramahila* in Colonial Bengal', in *From the Seams of History: Essays on Indian Women*, ed. Bharati Ray, 67–106 (New Delhi: Oxford University Press, 1995).

108. A large number of films from Bollywood and other regional industries have thrived on the popular assumption that the East is superior to the West. Similarly, certain political parties, most notably the BJP, routinely invoke the harm wrought by Western culture upon Indian traditions. One cannot reduce these ideologies to cultural atavism, as their proponents are often the proponents of women's rights. Women are also often apprehensive of how elite, bourgeois, Westernised women might reshape their known world. Asha Kasbekar, 'Negotiating the Myth of the Female Ideal in Popular Hindi Cinema', in *Pleasure and the Nation: The History, Politics, and Consumption of Public Culture in India*, ed. Rachel Dwyer and Christopher Pinney, 286–308 (New Delhi: Oxford University Press, 2001); Amrita Basu, 'Hindu Women's Activism in India and the Questions it Raises', in *Appropriating Gender: Women's Activism and Politicized Religion in South Asia*, ed. Patricia Jeffrey and Amrita Basu, 167–84 (London: Routledge, 1998); Kumkum Sangari, 'Violent Acts: Cultures, Structures and Retraditionalisation', in

Women of India: Colonial and Post-Colonial Periods, ed. Bharati Ray, 159–82 (New Delhi: Centre for Studies in Civilizations, 2005); Sikata Banerjee, 'Chaste Like Sita, Fierce Like Durga: Indian Women in Politics', in *India's 2004 Elections: Grass-roots and National Perspectives*, ed. Ramashray Roy and Paul Wallace, 34–57 (New Delhi: Sage, 2007).

109. Sinha, *Debating Patriarchy*, 229.

110. Anupama Roy, *Gendered Citizenship: Historical and Conceptual Explorations* (New Delhi: Orient Blackswan, 2013 [2005]), 217.

111. In the film *Meghe Dhaka Tara* (*The Cloud-Capped Star*, 1960) a refugee family survives on the elder girl child's income. They even refuse to arrange her marriage, afraid that once out of her house she will be unable to contribute as much to the family. Films have been a useful media for studying the shifting notions and configurations of modern women. See Paulomi Chakraborty, 'The Refugee Woman and the New Woman: (En)gendering Middle-Class Bengali Modernity and the City in Satyajit Ray's *Mahanagar* (*The Big City* 1963)', in *Being Bengali: At Home and In the World*, ed. Mridula Nath Chakraborty, 69–91 (London and New York: Routledge, 2014).

112. Malavika Chanda, 'Is There a Generation Gap?' *Hindustan Standard Annual Number*, 1969, 81.

113. Amitav Ghosh narrates the general male tendency to limit women's liberty in the 1960s rather precisely in *The Shadow Lines*. He describes a man's objection to his niece's wish to dance at a night club even though he had accompanied her all the way and even ordered drinks:

> Listen, Ila, Robi said, shaking his head. You shouldn't have done what you did. You ought to know that; girls don't behave like that here.
> What the fuck do you mean? she spat at him. What do you mean 'girls'? I'll do what I bloody well want, when I want and where.
> No you won't, he said. Not if I'm around. Girls don't behave like that here.

Amitav Ghosh, *The Shadow Lines* (London: John Murray, 2011 [1988]), 66.

114. *KA* 3, no. 41 (29 February 1980), 18.

115. Jayne Caudwell, 'Femme-fatale: Re-thinking the Femmeinine', in *Sport, Sexualities and Queer/Theory*, ed. Jayne Caudwell, 145–58 (London and New York: Routledge, 2006), 146.

116. *Amrita Bazar Patrika Sunday Magazine*, 2 January 1977, 1.

117. *DB*, 7 January 1967, 8.

118. Jayanta Dutta, 'Edener Sajghor Theke' (From the Eden Dressing Room), *Jugantar*, 1 January 1979, 3.

119. *ABP*, 14 March 1996, 11.

120. *DB*, 11 December 1969, 6.

121. *KA* 3, no. 17 (31 August 1979), 28.

122. Ibid., 3, no. 19 (21 September 1979), 10.

123. Sujoy Gupta, *Seventeen Ninety-two: A History of the Calcutta Cricket and Football Club* (Calcutta: CCFC, 2002), 96.

124. 'Eve teasing' is a South Asian euphemism used by the press in the 1980s–90s to report sexual harassment of women in public places. First used in legal parlance in the 'Delhi Prohibition of Eve-teasing Bill 1984', the term has been criticised for soft-pedalling the degree of the offence. It has since been largely discarded.

125. *ABP*, 2 February 1993, 12.

126. *TT*, 2 February 1993, 15.

127. Purnima Mankekar, *Screening Culture, Viewing Politics: An Ethnography of Television, Womanhood, and Nation in Postcolonial India* (Durham, NC: Duke University Press, 1999).

128. Purnima Mankekar, 'Dangerous Desires: Television and Erotics in Late Twentieth-Century India', *Journal of Asian Studies* 63, no. 2 (2004): 403–31.

129. Srimati Basu, 'Describing the Body: The Writing of Sex and Gender Identity for the Contemporary Bengali Woman', in *Confronting the Body: The Politics of Physicality in Colonial and Post-Colonial India*, ed. Jim Mills and Satadru Sen, 146–61 (London: Anthem Press, 2004).

130. Rohit Brijnath, 'Opinion: The Kissing of Abbas Ali Baig and Other Stories', *Live Mint*, 15 November 2019, https://www.livemint.com/mint-lounge/features/opinion-i-the-kissing-of-abbas-ali-baig-and-other-stories-11573803307992.html, accessed on 12 January 2020.

131. The kiss also inspired the fictional Aurora Zogoiby to make a painting, in which she rather exaggerated the eroticism of the kiss. While the painting was on display in an art gallery, a reactionary political outfit called Mumbai's Axis (while the city was still called Bombay) threatened to ravage the gallery unless the painting was taken down, which they described as 'a pornographic representation of a sexual assault by a Muslim 'sportsman' on an innocent Hindu maiden'. Salman Rushdie, *The Moor's Last Sigh* (London: Vintage, 1996), 232–33.

132. Jill Dolan, *The Feminist Spectator as Critic*, 2nd ed. (Ann Arbor: The University of Michigan Press, 2012), 2.

133. Manisha Roy, *Bengali Women* (Chicago: University of Chicago Press, 1992 [1970]), 59.

134. Ibid., 69. Roy forgot to mention that Naresh Kumar was a tennis player (fuelling some suspicion about knowledge of sport even among highly educated women).

135. Hariprasad Chattopadhyay, 'Amar Hero' (My Hero), *SKA*, 1981, 128.

136. Ajith Pillai and A. S. Panneerselvan, 'The Life and Times of Jayalalitha', *Outlook*, 4 May 1998, http://www.outlookindia.com/magazine/story/the-life-and-times-of-jayalalitha/205450, accessed on 15 January 2016.

137. Nilima Sen Gangopadhyay, 'Uchchabitto Kishori Fan' (Wealthy Young Fan), *KA* 2, no. 45 (13 April 1979), 22–23.

138. Gour Kishor Ghosh, 'Saptam Gulpo' (Seventh Story), in *Brajadar Gulpo Samagra* (Calcutta: Ananda Publishers, 1996), 40.

139. Suchitra Bhattacharya, *Nil Ghurni* (Blue Whirlpool) (Calcutta: Ananda Publishers, 2000), 7.

140. *Jugantar*, 5 January 1973, 8.

141. Srijayanta, 'Edener Gallery Theke' (From the Eden gallery), *DB*, 2 January 1975, 3.

142. *Jugantar*, 2 January 1979, 3.

143. Ibid., 2 January 1979, 4.

144. Sankaran Krishna, 'The Gender Question', *espncricinfo.com*, 4 March 2014, http://www.espncricinfo.com/blogs/content/story/725123.html, accessed on 12 October 2015.

145. The disembodied bonding between the distant subject and the audience has been discussed in several works, namely Vivian Sobchack, *Carnal Thoughts: Embodiment and Moving Image Culture* (Berkeley: University of California Press, 2004).

146. Jones, 'Female Fandom'; Pope, *The Feminization of Sport Fandom*.

147. Henrike Donner, 'Making Middle-Class Families in Calcutta', in *Anthropologies of Class: Power, Practice, and Inequality*, ed. James G. Carrier and Don Kalb, 131–48 (Cambridge: Cambridge University Press, 2015).

148. Imran Khan has been described as 'a celebrity and a star; an object of desire, tough, sexy, incredibly handsome', with a 'reputation as a playboy, his numerous girlfriends (mostly white), his reputedly dissolute lifestyle and his pukka Oxbridge accent'. Pnina Werbner, 'Anthropology, Cultural Performance and Imran Khan', in *Anthropology and Cultural Studies*, ed. Stephen Nugent and Cris Shore, 34–67 (London and Chicago: Pluto Press, 1997), 48–51.

149. *Jugantar*, 31 January 1980, 1.

150. *AmBP*, 31 January 1980, 8.

151. *Jugantar*, 1 February 1980, 6.

152. *DB*, 1 February 1980, 3.

153. Ashok Kamath, 'Pakistani Tour Diary', *Sportsworld* (30 January 1980), 21.

154. *DB*, 4 February 1980, 3.

155. *Sharadiya Khela*, 1983, 112–13.

156. *IWI*, 4 March 1984, 55.

157. *KA* 7, no. 43 (2 March 1984), 18.

158. Raewyn Connell introduced the term 'emphasised femininity' to describe how women perform the roles ascribed to them by men, therefore surrendering to 'hegemonic masculinity'. R. W. Connell, *Gender and Power* (Cambridge: Polity Press, 1987). Connell's idea of women's submissive role in society has been criticised for its essentialism, contrary to the admiration for her nuanced understanding of masculinity. For a concise account of Connell's criticism, see Carrie Paechter, 'Rethinking the Possibilities for Hegemonic Femininity: Exploring a Gramscian Framework', *Women's Studies International Forum* 68 (May–June 2018): 121–28.

159. *Jugantar*, 14 December 1983, 7.

160. Ibid., 16 December 1983, 7.

161. Ibid., 4 November 1987, 1.

162. Ibid.

163. *AmBP*, 9 November 1987, 11.

164. Asef Bayat, 'Cairo's Poor: Dilemmas of Survival and Solidarity', *Middle East Report* no. 202 (Winter 1997), 2–12; 'Un-civil Society: The Politics of the "Informal People",' *Third World Quarterly* 18, no. 1 (1997): 53–72; 'From "Dangerous Classes" to "Quiet Rebels": Politics of the Urban Subaltern in the Global South', *International Sociology* 15, no. 3 (2000): 533–57.

165. *Jugantar*, 1 January 1978, 4; *Jugantar*, 2 January 1978, 3.

166. *Aajkal*, 29 December 1997, 8.

167. Anilabha Chattopadhyay, 'Anya Edene Galper Rasad Peten Gullivero' (Even Gulliver Would Have Found Stories in a Different Eden), *Aajkal*, 30 December 1997, 7.

168. Robert K. Merton, 'Insiders and Outsiders: A Chapter in the Sociology of Knowledge', *American Journal of Sociology* 78, no. 1 (1972): 9–47, 29.

169. The term 'profitable provocation' has been used in relation to how the media objectifies women to sell their content. William Mazzarella and Raminder Kaur, 'Between Sedition and Seduction: Thinking Censorship in South

Asia', in *Censorship in South Asia: Cultural Regulation from Sedition to Seduction*, ed. Raminder Kaur and William Mazzarella, 1–28 (Bloomington: Indiana University Press, 2009), 3.

170. Female literacy percentage in West Bengal jumped from 20.79 in 1961 to 26.56 in 1971 and to 34.42 in 1981, while the male average grew from 47.69 to 57.03 in the twenty years. No data on the demographics of newspaper readership is available from this period. Considering 'literate' people read newspapers, the number of reading women was now presumably higher than ever, and the press could not risk losing this readership by publishing comical reports. http://www.education.nic.in/cd50years/g/z/EI/0ZEI0401.htm, accessed on 21 December 2011.

6 The Moral Economy of Violent 'Gentlemen'

Calcutta's cricket spectators are known to be volatile and fiercely partisan. In contrast with appreciation of their knowledge and understanding of the game, as outlined in the first two chapters, their violent behaviour in the galleries has undermined their dignity as spectators and cricket followers. Minor skirmishes aside, the Eden Gardens has seen four incidents of major violence that continue to be recounted in sports writings. In 1967, large sections of spectators clashed with the police, vandalised the stadium, and caused the day's play to be abandoned. In 1969, six people died in a stampede as a vast crowd jostled for a limited number of tickets before play started. Match reports from the 1970s and the 1980s are full of incidents of fighting in the gallery and spectators pelting cricketers with food items, though without any serious harm or trouble like before. In two episodes of crowd trouble in 1996 and 1999, with India on the cusp of defeat, spectators threw various substances on the field and interrupted play. The first match was forfeited and the other played to an empty gallery after spectators were ejected out of the stadium. These two incidents led to a two-year ban for Calcutta as an international cricket venue from 1999 to 2001. The local, national and international press have structured these outbursts as reflections of a rapidly degenerating society, and as symbols of a culture of violence in West Bengal. Their reports, however, have reprised what E. P. Thompson called 'a spasmodic view of popular history', explaining problems of violence as 'simple response stimuli' to infringement of the people's entitlements as spectators.[1] This chapter will sift through press reports of these incidents to examine the general culture of violence in postcolonial Calcutta.

In many colonial societies, violence was not just a method of demand but also had an emancipatory value that helped people 'recreate' themselves, restoring the selfhood lost under colonial rule. Colonialism entailed authoritarian rule by violence and power, argues Frantz Fanon, and the colonised subversively appropriated and unified themselves through retaliatory violence. The violence that connected people drawn into the struggle against the colonial state retained its purpose when people protest againsted postcolonial governments. For the individual, Fanon provocatively says, 'violence is a cleansing force' that enlightens and makes them more conscious of their identity and rights.[2] Fanon has been accused of promoting violence as a nation-building force, but Achille Mbembe, in his support, has argued that Fanon's conceptualising of the liberating use of coercion was based on his critique of colonialism as a dehumanising process that begets violence. Mbembe agrees with Fanon that violence was grafted into colonial institutions, and colonialism operated 'outside of law' and was constituted by 'empty' and 'unreserved' force.[3] Bengal had a long history of resisting colonial rule with violence.[4] It was also rife with instances of communal riots, workers' agitations and political actions that were not directly associated with the state.[5] Both organised and spontaneous popular violence were not transitional, but an inescapable materiality of public life in twentieth-century Calcutta, resulting from popular anxieties and angst against state and non-state establishments.[6] Violence was recentred around new issues of politics and identity after independence.

The Nehru-led Congress was ideologically opposed to the use of political violence in independent India. Examining Nehru's idea of appropriate political behaviour for Indians, Dipesh Chakrabarty draws attention to a 1955 speech in which Nehru criticised violence in public life as a sign of political immaturity. Breaking the law was an acceptable form of anticolonial resistance. Violent methods derived their significance and moral legitimation through the stated objective of ending the colonial regime of fear and exploitation. In Nehru's opinion, violence as a political means was undesirable in a democratic and sovereign India, as respect for law should have been a cornerstone of a liberal nation. Chakraborty says that Nehru's vision of debate and discussion rather than disorder as tools of political arbitration failed because violence had been normalised as a resource for demanding political enfranchisements and public utilities.[7] Disaffected Indians, the people of Calcutta in particular, continued with violence as a means of demand.

In a description of scenes of political violence in the 1950s Calcutta, political scientist Myron Weiner wrote that the people's discontent with the government was expressed only to a small degree through organised violence.

Some of the grievances, such as against transport fare going up or salary for school teachers remaining stagnant, stemmed from financial problems for a largely impoverished people. An agitation against question papers in a school-leaving examination, which saw 400-odd students trashing examination centres and even beating up students who chose not to join their cause, however, was symptomatic of a culture of violence in the city. The extent of violence in protests and demonstrations, Weiner writes, depended on how far the organisers, usually the leftist parties, wanted to take the protest. Most agitations were violent, and the middle classes were more likely to be at the centre of the most explosive of public outrages.[8] It has been suggested that political violence of the post-independence middle class had derived its spirit from the long history of anti-colonialism in Bengal.

Popular violence in postcolonial Bengal marked the advent of a new polity in which a long-subjugated people found in brute force the ideal method of persuading an unresponsive government. The uneasy relationship between the coloniser and the colonised was reproduced after India's independence in the form of a government whose reform measures lacked any real substance and delivered a progress that was imperceptible to most citizens. The people could not simply want, but had to demand their entitlements, for the most part encouraged by the government's opposition but also of their own volition. Episodes of violence and a social anxiety of losing out to other states and the propertied elites of one's own state became almost ontological. In the 1950s, the people of Calcutta depended more on the state government than private industry for employment, accommodation, food, medicine and education, which the government could ill-afford to do. The middle class's resentment with the government built up as reforms were inadequate, and the people themselves did little to ameliorate local conditions. Weiner has said that despite having the capacity to organise community events like religious and cultural festivals, Bengalis lacked the inclination to arrange civic activities such as cleaning streets and encouraging queues at bus stops. In his opinion, the people expected too much of the government, and the inevitable heartbreak from first the repressive colonial state and then the deficient postcolonial state led to acts of random violence as pressure tactics.[9] In the mid-1960s, the state was engulfed by riots, eventually leading to a Naxalite uprising and its violent political repression.[10] Once the CPI(M) came into power in 1977, their moderate policies and shift away from revolutionary tactics reduced the extent of violence in the state. Demonstrations and strikes continued to be a part of the state's everyday life, the logic of violence as a cleansing force arguably seeping into the public psyche to such an extent that it became a part of the people's cultural repertoire against the state.

This chapter uses two connected approaches to study the nature of incidents of violence at the Eden Gardens, in particular in connection with politics in the press, state and party politics, communal politics and consumerist politics. First, inspired by historian Gyanendra Pandey's emphasis on treating violence 'not as an isolated fact, or a series of isolated acts, but rather ... a total social phenomenon', it will study crowd disorders outside the routine and remarkable episodes of violence to analyse what these seemingly unorganised, apolitical and yet emotive events tell us about the relationship between violence and the politics of everyday life.[11] Second, it thinks in terms of the conjunctural analysis developed by cultural theorist Stuart Hall, examining specific events as a conjuncture of social classes, forms and relations of power, and political and public interventions that enable us to understand long-term social structures.[12] In a city known for political violence, it asks, did skirmishes in an apolitical venue mean an invasion of politics in every sphere of life? Were the Eden Gardens rioters deriving legitimacy from the everyday experience of resisting authority? Through a study of press reports of cricket riots, this chapter examines the relationship between various kinds of politics of everyday life and violence in Bengal. It is uncertain whether the media prefer to merely share with an audience what they perceive as the incident's authentic account or invite the audience to express opinion and participate in an open discussion about the incident. The media can act as an arbiter of knowledge by sorting and assessing the audience's perspectives on events before circulation. Hence, a study of the media's response to riots needs to probe the intersections of the press, politics and public culture in the topology of spectator violence. In examining the narratives of the four incidents mentioned earlier, the chapter examines contending personal and group experiences of violence that constituted the mediatisation of collective history.

SPECTATOR VIOLENCE AND THE PRESS

Academics consider irresponsible media coverage a catalyst of violence at sports stadiums.[13] It has been alleged that the press provokes disorder by creating unreasonable expectations from a sports event, circulating misleading and instigative impressions about rival teams and their supporters, and trivialising the problems arising from violence.[14] Sociologist Pierre Bourdieu, unhappy with the belligerence of European sports spectators, blamed the television for nurturing a class of incompetent critics with a preposterous understanding of sport.[15] In addition to allegedly influencing public action, the media frames the popular perception of 'deviant behaviour' and 'mythologies of violence' more powerfully than they are willing to admit, consequently causing a moral panic around stadium spectatorship despite their best efforts.[16] In the absence of a consensus about what counts as inappropriate behaviour and provocation, an examination of the mediated public debates raised in the aftermath of stadium riots offers insights into the media's agency in the creation, distribution and appraisal of spectator behaviour as a social aspect of sport.

Much of the literature on sports violence has been inspired by the figurational sociological perspective that prioritises studying the interdependence of social structures. Influenced by Norbert Elias' concept of sportisation as part of the 'civilising process' – which is the compulsion of modern people to discipline and control their affective character – the research by Eric Dunning and broadly the Leicester School have examined football hooliganism as a long-term process patterned by social class and masculinity.[17] Other explanations of fan violence variously emphasise working-class economy, subcultural adherences, the commercialisation of experience and the aesthetic of violence.[18] The debate about methodology and the need to sidestep the despotism of theory produced so comprehensive a body of research into fan behaviour from the late 1980s to the early 2000s that nearly every subsequent case study from Europe and the Americas appositely conformed to one paradigm or the other. Among the logic of violence listed by historian Rob Lynch in 1992 are:

> Resting in a particular malaise of the wider class system of the society, a resistance to dominating ideologies; a result of professionalisation of soccer which severed the socially controlling ties between home crowd and working-class club; influenced by media exaggeration; arising from TV provocation; being an outlet for male aggression; alcohol induced (a common explanation preferred by administrators, police, and media); a reaction against poor facilities; a reflection of the social and economic conditions of the times; a reaction to on-field incidents; and a dynamic interaction of a variety of social processes.[19]

Riots at the cricket ground posed a peculiar problem for scholars who considered the game's tension-reducing slowness and elitism as deterrents to violence. Historian John Ford explained the outbreaks of violence in eighteenth-century English cricket as a result of the increase in gambling and drinking among the lower classes, a category of patrons not usually associated with modern cricket.[20] Wray Vamplew, fully convinced that cricket spectators were far more peaceful than their football counterparts in the late nineteenth century, held a middle class takeover of spectatorship responsible for the decline of aggression. The genteel spectators, who did not gamble on cricket for a livelihood and were content with their class position in the nation, helped to circulate the myth of orderliness among English cricket followers.[21] Vamplew analysed the greater incidence of abusive behaviour in Australia with reference to a greater acceptance of impoliteness in Australian society.[22] Keith Sandiford repudiated the notion of ubiquitous courtesy and amiability among middle-class English spectators, arguing that they were sometimes no less bitter about the society than the working-class population. Nevertheless, continuing the psychosocial justification of class distinction, he assumed that the lore of civility around cricket discouraged the more frivolous public from attending cricket matches.[23] Sociologist Dominic Malcolm rejected each of the explanations based on the 'pastoral myth' and civilising process potential of cricket, suggesting they were inconsistent with evidences from across the world.[24] The riots in Indian stadiums in particular contradict any interpretation based on class, capital and the character of the game and its spectators.

Violence in cricket was not a specific problem for Calcutta. In 1953, the first unofficial Test match between the Commonwealth team and India in Lucknow was postponed as rioters hollowed out the pitch.[25] In 1969, spectators hurled projectiles and set fire to parts of the Brabourne Stadium in Bombay in protest against an umpiring decision.[26] In 1983, members of secessionist groups disrupted the ODI match between India and West Indies in Srinagar. They cheered for West Indies throughout the match and dug up the turf with stumps, leading to the arrest of 120 people.[27] In 1986, a charity match in aid of the Sant Tukaram hospital in Akola, a town 290 kilometres east of Bombay, was abandoned after the crowd inexplicably invaded the ground.[28] Despite the violence in cricket matches being a nation-wide phenomenon, Calcutta emerged as the concourse of rioters, to a large extent owing to the prevalence of football fights in the city.

Historians Paul Dimeo, Boria Majumdar and Kausik Bandyopadhyay have unlocked the logical culminations of various historical processes and events in West Bengal in football-related violence.[29] Spectator violence in Calcutta football goes back to 1907 when, provoked by the aggression of the Dalhousie B footballers during a Trades Cup match, Mohun Bagan supporters invaded the field and assaulted the opposition players and supporters.[30] The Muslim political ascendency in the provincial assembly and communal riots divided football spectators in the 1930s–40s. In a sharp contrast to the celebration of Mohun Bagan's famous IFA Shield win in 1911 by both Hindus and Muslims, the Mohammedan Sporting's unique record of five straight Calcutta League wins between 1934 and 1938 intensified communal polarisation and conflict among supporters.[31] Hindu–Muslim clashes were reported after nearly every match involving Mohammedan Sporting and another major club. Any semblance of control vanished in the 1970s, and the club was threatened with suspension unless the behaviour of its supporters was restrained. The peak of violence was reached on 16 August 1980 when 16 people were killed in a stampede during an East Bengal–Mohun Bagan match.[32] As riots continued in the early 1980s, there were calls from the public to dissolve the big three clubs of the local league.

East Bengal–Mohun Bagan rivalry scaled epic proportions in the post-partition years as the two clubs came to symbolise identities of the migrant refugee *bangal* as opposed to the older resident *ghoti*. The two communities eventually made peace with their differences in accent, food habits, songs and other traditions, but never on the football field.[33] While football victories offered the *bangal* a chance to avenge their territorial dislocation and humiliations in their quest for livelihood, the *ghoti* ostensibly looked forward to chasten the migrants who were becoming a dominant force in local politics and the job market.[34] Although most of the riots were started by specific incidents in matches, it can be said that the history of communitarian tensions had primed spectators for violence since their childhood. This contradicts the feature of riots that Allen Guttmann characterised as 'expressive rather than instrumental'.[35] Incidentally, the aggression with which the two communities fought during football matches was rarely replicated in cricket or hockey matches. The worst riots in Calcutta's domestic cricket took place when Mohun Bagan played against clubs other than East Bengal.

In 1959, as Albert Sporting were cruising at 163 for 4 chasing Mohun Bagan's 233, the Bagan supporters invaded the field, uprooted the stumps, dug up the pitch and demonstrated at the pavilion against what they perceived as an umpiring blunder against their team.[36] As the Bengal and Nagpur Railways beat Mohun Bagan in the CAB knock-out tournament final in 1963, a number of supporters started throwing brickbats into the ground and the pavilion, breaking glass panes and clashing with the police. A baton charge was followed by the arrest of 'young delinquents'.[37] After supporters assaulted an umpire during a match against Sporting Union in 1968, Mohun Bagan's next opponents forfeited their upcoming match and withdrew from the competition.[38] The Mohun Bagan secretary led some supporters into manhandling the umpire for giving a dubious decision in a match against East Bengal in 1983.[39] Crowds have resorted to violence more often in international cricket matches, provoked by either or a combination of India's miserable performance, poor umpiring decisions against India and the CAB's failure to satisfy the entitlements promised against a valid ticket.

Local and international newspapers published different and sometimes contradictory opinions on the circumstances and nature of the cricket riots. Brought into existence by people with different agenda, newspapers are known to present readers with 'a portrayal of contending forces in the world'.[40] The effort to establish their reports as authentic is arguably meant to address the collective sensibility of their readers. With reference to the cricket riots in Calcutta, the press did not treat the rioting public as ludic respondents or irrational, violent and de-individualised as the old theories of crowd behaviour suggested.[41] It created an aesthetic of loss and victimhood, which was defined as a number of interlocked templates – honour, property, sport, tradition and politics – and posed against the perceived insensitivity of organisers. This aesthetic assumed different contours in each newspaper, bringing into question the instrumentality of the news media in the construction of the riot's public discourse.

1967: INDIA VERSUS WEST INDIES

Indeed, Calcutta had never seen quite like what happened at the Eden Gardens on that day.[42]

The riot on 1 January 1967, the second day of the India–West Indies Test match, lasted for a little over an hour. The previous day, obstructions in front of the sightscreen had delayed start. Spectators encroached on the field and sat six rows deep inside the boundary ropes.[43] It was alleged that the police let anybody with a camera and a photographer's pass enter. Some of the ticket inspectors failed to identify valid gate passes and harassed even bona fide pass-holders and journalists.[44] Gates were closed because of overcrowding of the gallery while many people were still queuing for entry. Former Indian cricketer Shute Banerjee found his seat occupied and sat on the turf.[45] CAB officials issued an apology and appealed to stop the misuse of gate passes, which did not seem to have an effect as the same problem occurred the next day.[46] The Eden Gardens could accommodate 57,000 spectators at the time, but 59,020 tickets were issued for the second day.[47] The turnout was far greater. The stadium was visibly overcrowded, with a long queue of ticket holders outside the ground, as the day's play was to begin. Many people could not find their seats or saw people with tickets with the same number occupying their seats. At around 10 a.m., about 150 spectators who could not find their seats in the 25-rupee gallery scaled the American fences and squatted along the boundary line, some in front of the sightscreen. Instead of just asking spectators to disperse as on the previous day, the security personnel charged at them with bamboo staff. A brief skirmish with bricks, crackers and teargas ensued.

Meanwhile, the police beat a middle-aged gentleman named Sitesh Roy who was apparently pleading with them to stop hurling teargas shells in the tiers full of women and children. The sight of about a dozen police constables beating him and then dragging him away infuriated other spectators. At the same time, a rumour circulated that former cricketer Ghulam Ahmed was beaten to death.[48] The spectators retaliated strongly. According to the *Anandabazar Patrika*, they chased the 1,500 police constables and home guards out of the stadium in three minutes, and set fire to piles of chairs and benches.[49] Most of the cricketers ran to the dressing room as the canvas awnings were set alight. Some of them, fearing for their lives, ran towards their hotel, whilst the rest left either in cars or the heavily guarded team bus. The spectators did not attack cricketers, but assaulted security personnel and vandalised state properties. A Gorkha regiment was sent to restore order. Most of the CAB officials, including the president A. N. Ghosh and the secretary N. C. Colay, went into hiding.[50] About 200 persons, including 52 police personnel, were injured.[51] The Relief Welfare Ambulance Corps administered first aid to 158 people, while 36 persons were hospitalised.[52] Commenting on the turn of events, one fan sarcastically wrote,

With a heavy heart we inform you that Indian Cricket, our most venerated goddess, died wilfully at five past eleven on Thursday at the Eden Gardens. Only 35 at the time of her death, she was surrounded by more than 60,000 local and foreign devotees … her pain was not prolonged, lasting for a mere 65 minutes between 10 to 11.05 in the morning … she had been very charitable and forgiving in her lifetime. She is survived by the Board of Control for Cricket, who we expect will tend to her last rites.[53]

The state government realised that Calcutta's future as an international cricket venue and the revenue and goodwill earned from cricket were in jeopardy. It took unprecedented steps to ensure resumption of play.[54] A committee of officials and former cricketers from India and the West Indies persuaded players to continue the match after a rest day. The BCCI announced bonus money for each player to ensure their participation, something Ray Robinson compared to the benefit added to workers' pay packages.[55] Chief Minister Prafulla Chandra Sen instructed the CAB to withdraw 5,000 vendor passes and reduce the number of day tickets. He sent a government official to Sitesh Roy's house to convey his regret.[56] The High Court issued several warrants to confiscate the CAB's accounts registers, ticket distribution lists, passbooks and other documents. The state government set up a commission under Justice Kamlesh Chandra Sen to inquire into the causes of the riot and suggest preventive measures. The commission released a 180-page report along with 4,000 typed pages of evidence, based on 74 interviews and 181 written statements, on 30 August 1967. The press was briefed on 13 September and excerpts from the document were published the next day.

A primary reason for the riot was the inefficient organisation of the match. According to the report of the Commission of Enquiry, in the mid-1960s the Eden Gardens could seat 39,000 persons. The increasing demand for tickets led the CAB to set up new concrete galleries. According to a dispatch sent to S. N. Sen, Deputy Secretary to Government of West Bengal in charge of sport, the CAB planned to seat 52,000 people in the existing and new galleries during the match against West Indies.[57] A year of construction work was hastily wound up only two days before the match.[58] Apparently, the engineers in charge were not satisfied with the design and quality of construction. One of them, S. Bandopadhyay, told the commission that the galleries were built with the objective of packing as many spectators as possible, without any consideration to their comfort.[59] After inspecting the stadium following the riot, B. N. Banerjee, the government architect, said that the seats, aisle space, lavatories and exits in most of the new sections were below standard and inadequate.[60]

A. N. De, the CAB architect, testified that work had started with the plan to provide seats for 34,746 people in the new gallery. But the demand for tickets rose so rapidly as work progressed that he was forced to compromise on quality. With the aim to seat 70,000 people in the same space, the gallery was built haphazardly and as a temporary construction.[61] The CAB allotted 16 inches space to reserved seats (25-rupee season tickets) and 14 inches to unreserved seats (day-tickets).[62] On the basis of the recognised standard of 18 inches seating space per person, B. N. Banerjee estimated that 46,752 people could be possibly seated in the galleries excluding the NCC block, while the CAB's unprincipled construction would have made possible a total accommodation of 55,244 people.[63] As reported by the CAB, excluding daily tickets and including vendors' badges, 51,452 tickets were issued per day. Adding to the number the 8,450 tickets sold daily, a total of 59,922 tickets were distributed, of which 58,122 were supposed to be seated, 3,000 beyond the planned accommodation.[64] About 3,000, or more than half of the badges issued to vendors and staff, were reportedly bought on the black market and used by upper-class spectators. The NCC printed and sold tickets independently. Adding the 3,311 people sitting on the NCC block, the estimated total number of spectators on 31 December 1966 becomes 66,233.[65] Finally, the use of a defective printing machine resulted in duplication of the same ticket and printing of non-existent seat numbers. The commission report concluded that overcrowding was caused by improper printing and distribution of tickets, lack of proper guidance to ticket holders and clumsy checking by the Congress Sevadal volunteers and the police.[66]

The press's response to the riot brought out the political culture in the state and popular resentment against the government and the police in vivid detail. On the one hand, the press placed it as one of the extreme incidents within the chain of political radicalism unfolding for over a year. The political nature of the riot was reflected in popular literature too. In Sunil Gangopadhyay's novel *Sei Samay* (Those Days), two characters discussed how the riot was an outcome of the collective resentment regarding incidents such as the strikes in Presidency College, protests by transport employees and restriction on the sale of rice.[67] On the other hand, the compass of blame veered wildly among the police, the state government, the CAB and team selectors. It was reported that the non-selection of the Bengal cricketer

Subrata Guha, who was expected to make his debut in the Calcutta Test match after stellar performances throughout the domestic season, was one of the reasons behind the outburst. He had bowled well against the West Indies in a practice match, spearheading the visitor's only defeat in the entire tour.[68] The euphoria among local fans collapsed as the young left-arm spinner Bishen Singh Bedi was selected ahead of Guha. A few disappointed supporters took out a protest march in front of the Great Eastern Hotel where the cricketers were staying.[69] The Statesman reported before the Test match that 'rumbles of disappointment' were heard over Guha's exclusion.[70] Spectators cheered when Guha fielded as a substitute on the first day, some even thinking that he was in the team.[71] However, they went home frustrated at yet another lacklustre bowling display from India on the first day.

The next morning, the press reported on various reactions to Guha's non-selection. Former cricketer Dattu Phadkar wrote in the Dainik Basumati that Guha would have done better than any of the bowlers in the team.[72] Journalist Sriamitav shared an apocryphal story of a gentleman telling the captain M. A. K. Pataudi, 'You're going to be our son-in-law in two days; how could you overlook the boy from Bengal for the Test.'[73] Although the selectors justified Guha's non-selection on cricketing grounds, the poor performance of his replacement and the team as a whole stoked the debate over selection politics. Both the Jugantar and the Anandabazar Patrika hinted at a conspiracy, spurring readers to think that India would have played better with Guha in the team.[74] Such reports presumably instilled a sense of deprivation before play started on the day of the riot. The suspicion of Bechu Datta Ray's involvement in the conspiracy made some people torch the Sporting Union tent.[75] Two weeks later, former cricketer Saradindu Sanyal wrote about the role of 'anti-Bengali conspiracy' rumours in the build-up to the riot.[76] The delayed revisit clearly shows how deep-seated the problem was.

The rancour against non-Bengalis found another outlet of expression in the criticism of the Anglo-Indian police officer who had ordered the baton charge on Roy. This accusation was brought forward by the Jugantar, which was generally critical of the police for provoking violence by treating spectators callously.[77] The officer's ethnicity was cited as the reason for his unkind behaviour and abuse of power. Being on the outside of Bengali culture, he failed to empathise with local sentiments.[78] Moreover, the report suggested, none too subtly, that the person embodied the ruthless colonial police officer and the police force the colonial constabulary that prosecuted fellow nationals on orders from a foreign power. Such statements brought to focus the hostility of Indians towards Eurasians in colonial and independent India. Anglo-Indians were known in colonial times for their insistence on close connections with the British and self-assessment as culturally more advanced than the rest of Indians.[79] Although politicians such as Gandhi tried to involve people from all walks of life in the nation-making, the Anglo-Indians had mostly remained outside the ambit of this constructive pluralism. The *Jugantar's* allegations reflected the popular representation of Anglo-Indians as a residue of the unsavoury parts of India's colonial encounter. In general, resentment against the non-Bengali other was on the rise in the late 1960s. There were instances of localised violence against Biharis, Oriyas and Punjabis, who had immigrated to Calcutta at various points in time.[80]

The trope of colonial atrocity informed other reports on the police in the *Jugantar*. It reported that the police had arrested 25 people for their ties with the riot. Among those arrested were an advocate, an income tax officer, a film star and a corporate employee, which indicates that class, education and social status had little bearing on the violence.[81] In a petition for their unconditional release, the defence lawyer argued that the event could have become another Jallianwala Bagh massacre, thus resurrecting the ghost of colonial brutality.[82] The *Jugantar* editorialised the need for a probe into the retreat of the police, expressing doubt over their training to handle critical situations.[83] The *Dainik Basumati* demanded strict disciplinary action against the police, whom it compared to the epic *Ramayana*'s mythical 'monkey army in Lanka' and a frenzied elephant.[84] It too evoked colonial imageries, comparing the police violence with the torture on freedom fighters, and stating how unjust and rare such incidents were in the civilised world.[85] Evoking colonial trauma, these newspapers fulfilled a nationalist duty by recovering a history of colonial violence and criticising the present government for having failed to progress beyond the hateful past.

The police issued an official statement in response to these criticisms, labelling the crowd as vandals. Published in the *Anandabazar Patrika*, the statement praised how the heavily outnumbered police carried out their responsibility with courage. The detailed timeline attached with the statement indicated that the police were in complete control of the situation. The police blamed the CAB for three lapses leading to the riot – sale of excess tickets, failure to stop the unauthorised entry of people wearing various badges, and flawed stadium plan that made parts of the field invisible from the top rows of the gallery, resulting in overcrowding of the lower stands. They claimed to have tried to pacify rioters with folded hands, resorted to tear gas only as a last resort, and rescued people from stampede even when hit with brickbats.[86] Clearly the police projected themselves as victims of crowd violence and unsung heroes of the day.[87] The report did not mention the beating of Roy. The surprisingly precise and chronological summary of the spread of violence gave the police's statement an aura of authenticity. In comparison, the accounts of witnesses and journalists overlapped and contradicted one another like testimonies usually do. The police evidently needed self-vindication against strong public opinion. Nevertheless, despite publishing the police's perspective, the *Anandabazar Patrika* did not moderate its criticism of the police.

Politicians in the opposition treated the riot as a convenient tool to expose the inadequacies of the government and its subsidiaries. The *Anandabazar Patrika* published statements from a variety of associations and people such as the mayor, the High Court Bar Association, members of the opposition in the municipal corporation, the Congress and the Motor Dealers' Association (of which Roy was a member), all of which condemned the CAB's pitiful management and police arrogance for causing the riot. Some of these associations filed petitions or conducted signature campaigns demanding immediate punishment for the guilty. In the *Jugantar*, moderate left leaders such as Nihar Mukherjee, secretary of the Socialist Unity Centre of India, condemned the police action.[88] About 20 councillors of the opposition including the United Citizens' Committee (UCC) secretary Samar Rudra, leader of the Progressive Urban Bloc Kumar Dutta and the Nirdal Bloc's Shyamsundar Gupta protested against police brutality.[89] The *Dainik Basumati* was the mouthpiece for the more radical left-wing leaders such as Prashanta Chattopadhyay, councillor of the municipal corporation; Bhabani Shome, leader of the Communist Party of India; D. Guha, leader of the Socialist Unity Centre; Ashok Dasgupta, leader of the Praja Socialist Party; and Dilip Roychoudhury, leader of the Workers' Party.[90] Furthermore, to show its concern for the common people, the newspaper published a total of nine letters from aggrieved readers from 11 to 13 January.

The political profiles of each of these newspapers came out in sharp relief through the political statements and peoples they represented. The *Anandabazar Patrika* criticised the police as a failed organ of the state but not the state itself as such. The *Jugantar* and the *Dainik Basumati* held the ruling Congress government responsible. One reader mentioned in a letter to the *Dainik Basumati* that tickets of 45–60 rupees were distributed through Congress party offices in exchange for a donation of 200–300 rupees to the party fund. A number of the CAB officials who were also Congress nominees in the upcoming election had reportedly dispensed tickets among their henchmen, leading to a ticket shortage.[91] An editorial in the newspaper disapproved the government's decision of calling the army to control the rioters, stating that:

> The Congress leaders have regularly summoned army machine guns instead of police rifles to stifle the Language movement and other political demonstrations. The army should be called into action as the last resort when the police fail to safeguard public life and property ... the police actually aggravated the crisis by exerting undue force in the name of control ... Therefore calling the army was not only ridiculous, but could have broken people's trust in the army.[92]

Beyond these reflections of power politics, journalists created a sense of loss using witness accounts and reports on damage to the stadium. They brought alive the riot's psychological and social impact, creating expectations and demands for action to prevent its repetition. Generally, the extent to which these expectations are fulfilled, and the force with which they are demanded, depends very much on the political circumstances of the tragedy and those affected.[93] The state government's urgency to resume the match met with some favourable comments, but the CAB's apathetic behaviour, in particular that of the absconding officials, continued to be criticised after the match. Sympathy for the victims became a journalistic agenda. After the riot, the *Anandabazar Patrika* poignantly reported about Aalo Majumdar crying while talking about her 12-year old brother Pradip and sisters Anupama, Nilima and Swapna, all missing in the commotion. Three other teenagers, namely Prakash Kumar Jaini (15), Swapan Ghosal (16) and Santimoy Chatterjee, were reported missing.[94] Dhiren Deb's car was stolen from the parking space.[95] Stories of police brutality, missing persons, theft, and so on, were part of the people's everyday reading experience of newspapers, especially in the period of turmoil in the 1960s. Repetition of these stories in the context of a cricket match drove home the permanence of the state of disorder and the incursion of politics into every sphere of public activity. The newspapers fulfilled their public commitment by empathising with the victims of violence. However, years later, a correspondent revealed that some of the spectators wanted to beat journalists too. One of them apparently yelled, 'We have burnt the CAB, let's burn the reporters now.'[96] The anger was probably informed by suspicion of the major newspapers on the grounds that they were controlled by political and affluent elites, who used the press to circulate self-serving ideological messages. It could also have signalled the people's disaffection with the press's role in creating unreal expectations from cricket, which came under further scrutiny when a stampede claimed six lives in 1969.

1969: INDIA VERSUS AUSTRALIA

When the tickets for the Test match against Australia went on sale in 1969, cricket followers started their hunt with renewed enthusiasm. The people thronged practice sessions before the match, and the crowd grew so large in number one day that the teams found it difficult to practise. The CAB's circulation of false timings of net practice to prevent the gathering of over-enthusiastic followers did not work. As the police tried dispersing the crowd, the latter counter-attacked, breaking benches and pipes and tearing down the wire nettings around the practice pitches. Both the teams were very critical of the rowdy behaviour; Australia manager Frederick Bennet called it unsporting.[97] The Australian cricketer Ashley Mallett wrote in his 1973 autobiography that around 15,000 attended the practice sessions, while in his biography of Doug Walters published in 2008, Mallett put the number at 20,000.[98] It is understandable that the number was meant to convey his culture shock at the large gathering and with Indian people in general rather than to accurately represent the situation. Alarmed by the possibility of disorder during the Test match, the government requisitioned the services of nine magistrates to conduct military deployment if need be. An Eastern Frontier Rifles brigade was asked to be ready for emergency.[99]

Spectatorship at this Test match was pervaded with militancy, which can be attributed to the broader climate of discontent among the people. Groups of young men were seen to stop passing cars and pedestrians and grab season tickets as the match began.[100] The division between enthusiasm and mania was now so blurred that one newspaper editorialised, 'The real cricket lover derives a frisson from the game, a frisson consisting partly of cricket literature and partly of memories ... A cricket lover is really an auld lang syner, for whom the scores, however exciting, are not particularly relevant.'[101] However, the sermon had little effect on the public. A section of the crowd that failed to get tickets stormed the team hotel to see the cricketers in person. On being stopped by the hotel authorities, they threw brickbats and smashed many windows and glass doors.[102] Finally, a stampede in front of gates 12 and 13 resulted in six deaths by suffocation and about 100 injuries on the fourth morning of the match. Two persons died on the spot and the rest on their way to the hospital.

The deceased were identified as Pradip Ghosh (25, Inspector at Post and Telegraph) Manish Nandy (25, Overseer of the Port Commissioners, son of a school headmaster), Anil Hoogan (20, student, son of a Police Inspector), Pinaki Chatterjee (22, student, son of a Police Inspector) and Arun Chakravarty (25, radio mechanic and cricketer, son of the Superintendent of George Telegraph).[103] The victims, all young and middle class, fit the description of the ardent spectators the press so intently empathised with. The disturbance spread throughout central Calcutta like in 1967, leading to the arrest of 25 persons. A major difference from 1967 was the increasing temerity of people about open violence. Not content with vandalising shops and police vehicles, groups of people without tickets searched random passers-by for season tickets and tore their passes as a means of avenging their inability to watch cricket.[104] The cricket match, in hindsight, gestured the wanton Naxalite and state violence that started gripping Calcutta from the beginning of 1970. The police had by now gained more notoriety than before as the repressive arm of the state, and retaliation against the police at the practice session was only the beginning of a youth upsurge against the state.[105] The constabulary in charge of maintaining order was evidently not prepared to manage a passionate and violent crowd.

Most of the journalists and eyewitnesses criticised the police's failure to effectively regulate the crowd leading to the stampede. In the wider political climate of the state, Home Minister Jyoti Basu and the CPI(M) were challenged by their United Front allies for misusing the police to embed their power in state administration.[106] Some journalists showed a surprising turnaround in their assessment of law enforcement. A correspondent of the *Dainik Basumati*, G. Shankar, wrote before the incident that the police were very efficient in crowd control.[107] Afterwards, he criticised the police, the CAB and politicians for lack of remorse – Sports Minister Ram Chatterjee for first absconding from ticket-hunters and next for taking 36 hours to come up with a statement of apology, Jyoti Basu for calling the deaths an accident instead of ensuring proper crowd control, and the governor and four ministers for having lunch at the stadium despite knowing about the deaths. He also attacked the morality of the youth for not protesting against injustice as they did in colonial times.[108] The *Jugantar* maintained its practice of giving voice to the moderate left by publishing the Praja Socialist Party's demand for investigation and the Sanjukta Socialist Party's lack of faith in the executive investigative committee and request for judicial intervention. The newspaper exhorted the public to pressurise the government for taking proper actions.[109] The law minister, Bhakti Bhusan Mullick, supported the newspaper's perspective.[110]

After the stampede, the *Saptahik Basumati* published the tales of a number of eyewitnesses, all of which incriminated the police. One Nantu Bagchi reached the stadium at 4 a.m. on the back of a truck loaded with sand. The queue for the 6-rupee ticket was already so long that he shifted to the less crowded queue for the more expensive 15-rupee ticket. Jostling started and queues broke down as more people milled in, swelling to around 15,000 in an informal estimate. The mounted police remained on standby as they were not given any order to handle the crowd. Pradip Kumar Ghose said he was in the middle of the 6-rupee queue when the ticket counter opened. As people surged forward, the single column broke in the commotion and a throng formed in front of the counter. The mounted police finally intervened to restore order, but the people at the back of the queue, unable to see this, continued to press forward, causing a melee in the middle. Bhanu Saha recounted narrowly escaping being trampled by quitting the queue in time.[111] After six deaths were announced, the sports minister promised compensation and job for family members of the deceased. The CAB made a promise of 6,000 rupees to the families. However, after several trips to the CAB office over the next month, the bereaved family members received nothing. Meanwhile the commission of investigation headed by K. K. Sen, former Indian Civil Service officer and member of the Board of Revenue, exonerated the police from the alleged lapse of duty.[112] One of the injured, Shyamal, woke up in the hospital showing signs of cognitive problems. According to a report published in 1996, he never recovered even after psychiatric treatment at several hospitals. His father unsuccessfully sued the state government and the CAB in 1982 for compensation. Shyamal refused the CAB's offer of 10,000 rupees, too paltry a sum considering his monthly medical bill was around 4,000–5,000 rupees.[113] The sense of tragedy was kept alive by newspapers long after the incident.

Many political commentators have written about the general erosion of political trust in the late 1960s. This was expressed through infighting among United Front allies and the people's growing envisioning of politics as an exercise in opportunism.[114] The interviews conducted by the journalists pointed to the people's lack of faith in the government's ability to ensure order and protection. The profile of the deceased and injured indicated the youth were the perpetrators and victims of the disorder. The violence itself had little to do with politics, though it could have been part of the pseudo-political and anti-social disorder usually practised by gangsters, or *mastans*, as they were more popularly known. They were usually young people, mostly school dropouts whose defiant attitude came from disappointment with the education system, and lack of employment and social mobility. Gangsters became more prominent in politics in the 1970s, when anti-social activities and political action could no longer be separated. Gangsters had no class character. Many among them were known to have joined gangs simply to ensure their families were respected in the neighbourhood and not harmed in those lawless times when the state's control over the society slackened.[115] Just as these restive youth were involved in ticket blacking, they swarmed to see cricket too. The violence associated with the 1969 Test match, resulting from the grievance of being deprived from watching cricketers either in practice or in the match, was never again repeated in the same degree. This probably shows the state no longer felt safe leaving cricket to organisers and spectators for self-regulation of safety. Before the incidents of 1967 and 1969, the state, the press and the CAB downplayed minor accidents at the stadium as what inevitably happened at a large gathering of an excited crowd. The change in attitude after 1969 was evident from the press's criticism of the CAB as a body run by businessmen with no training in sport management and interest to employ professional event managers. The managerial inadequacies were never fully resolved, mainly due to the organisers' lack of commitment to spectators.

1996: INDIA VERSUS SRI LANKA

After years of minor skirmishes, hurling food items at cricketers, and disrespect towards female spectators, the Eden crowd were at the centre of ignominy when they disrupted a men's cricket World Cup match. The culture of violence prevalent in the late 1960s–early 1970s was by now replaced by a centralised political intimidation led by the CPI(M) government. Virtually smothering all opposition and imposing the party's will over people's initiatives and mobilisations, the CPI(M) established an authoritarian rule that was widely feared, but which also chipped away at its electoral legitimacy.[116] In the 1990s, other political parties in the state were considered too weak to mount any meaningful challenge to the ruling dispensation. The number of riots and murders had decreased, but the 'decades of chaos' were still so fresh in public memory that occasional inter-party or horrific episodes of violence acted as a throwback to more unsettled times and elicited strong disapproval from the people.[117] If there was one site of immense significance that the CPI(M) was not yet able to imprint its monopoly upon, it was the Eden Gardens. Lorded over by Jagmohan Dalmiya, who kept state politics separate from cricket to the best of his ability, cricket at the Eden Gardens remained remarkably free of political intervention unlike the state's other cultural institutions. Yet it was not entirely free of political muscle-flexing, which came to the fore on the occasion of two riots in 1996 and 1999.

India started as favourites against Sri Lanka in their 1996 World Cup semi-final match in Calcutta. Victory against Pakistan in the quarter-finals raised the country's hope for a second World Cup trophy. Sri Lanka was considered a minor obstacle between India and the final in Lahore. The excitement was palpable all over the city. Over 100 people including civil servants, company executives and four Rapid Action Force (RAF) commandoes, armed with either recommendation letters or verbal assurance from CPI(M) councillors and ministers, reportedly queued outside the sport and youth affairs minister Subhas Chakraborty's office for tickets. They all returned empty handed as Chakraborty had disappeared. Tickets worth 300 rupees were peddled at 3,000 rupees or more in the black market.[118] The Crime Investigation Department accepted that the tickets priced at 1,700 rupees and 1,800 rupees were sold at 600 dollars to Bangladeshi citizens who had come to Calcutta for medical treatment.[119] Dalmiya received several phone threats for not sending enough tickets to political parties; one of them was confirmed to have been made from the Pradesh Congress headquarters while Dalmiya was in a press conference.[120] The CPI(M) MP Mohammad Selim negotiated with the Indian Airlines managing director, P. C. Sen, to arrange for a special flight for dignitaries from New Delhi.[121] The state declared a half day's holiday for people to watch the match on television from home if they could not be at the stadium. Luminaries from the world of entertainment, including the Rolling Stones lead singer Mick Jagger, were seen sitting in the Club House as the match was to begin.[122]

The city's newspapers built up a tense atmosphere around the match, using headlines full of martial imageries such as 'Battlelines Drawn, City Bays for Blood'.[123] Sri Lanka batted first and posted a score of 251 for 8. Sachin Tendulkar powered India to a good start but the rest of the batting imploded soon after his dismissal. As India slumped to 120 for 8, staring at a humiliating defeat to the underdog, spectators started hurling water and liquor bottles, rotten eggs, tomatoes, food packets and burning crackers onto the field. While RAF commandoes escorted the teams out, the police cleared the missiles and baton-charged spectators to bring order. The match referee Clive Lloyd declared the match abandoned and Sri Lanka the winner. The spectators went home applauding Sri Lanka and abusing Indian cricketers.[124] Twenty-one people were injured in the melee, and 38 were arrested.[125] Alistair, a tourist from South Africa, was so impressed by the crowd's passion that he told the media that such fans were a blessing for any team.[126]

It was reported in the Bengali press that some people in Pakistan burst crackers, distributed sweets and chocolates, and launched motorcades, relishing the revenge for their quarter-final defeat.[127] The Sri Lankan team was garlanded and showered with rose petals on arrival in Lahore for the final. Their captain, Arjuna Ranatunga, was thanked for beating India. Some people blank fired to celebrate the revenge in Rawalpindi.[128] In Calcutta, people clashed in the neighbourhoods of Dumdum and Rajarhat; as a group burnt a poster of Azharuddin, another group tried to stop them and started fighting.[129] Someone hurled a flower tub and an iron rod at the CAB office, breaking a glass window, and fled in a waiting taxi.[130] Violence was reported from other cities too. The police fired several rounds in the air to disperse a mob in Ahmedabad and used teargas in Daryapur. Hindus and Muslims clashed across the country, leading to several injured, one of them being the 25-year old Kalu Gautam in Mumbai. Ashok Roy, 32, could not take the defeat and hung himself from a tree.[131] The 20-year-old computer trainee Sunil Kar poisoned himself, leaving behind a suicide note saying he would like to be born as the next Tendulkar and win the trophy in 2012.[132] As a mark of protest, 10 students from the Harijan Hostel in Raipur shaved their heads.[133] The families of several cricketers received phone threats. Azharuddin was apparently the central figure of abusive messages and gestures from fans.[134]

The press mentioned that the state government did little to alleviate the public's grievance and let the CAB pick up the pieces. The CPI(M) stalwarts present at the Eden, Jyoti Basu, Prashanta Sur, Subhas Chakraborty, Somnath Chattopadhyay and Prashanta Chattopadhyay, did not come forward to placate the crowd.[135] Health Minister Sur, who was the first Left Front member to become the mayor of Calcutta in 1969, said the riot was the handiwork of a small number of spectators. The Left Front chairman Shailen Dasgupta told the press that the Eden spectators were usually well behaved, and it was unfortunate that they vented their frustration in a way that tarnished the state's image.[136] Chakraborty blamed the police, and Basu the criminals among the spectators. The state government issued a statement that the emotional outburst of 200–300 people was beyond the police's control.[137] When asked what they thought of the overcrowding of galleries and taps running out of drinking water, the ministers censured the CAB. The *Ganashakti*, the CPI(M)'s mouthpiece, reported that Chakraborty convened a meeting at the Netaji Indoor Stadium on 17 March to discuss the riot. The meeting was chaired by sheriff Abirlal Mukhopadhyay, but nothing more was heard of it.[138] The CPI(M) blamed the CAB for their rift with the police before the match, which had apparently soured their relationship and understanding. It was revealed that the CAB refused to pay the police 1,500,000 rupees for purchasing cars, vans and apparatus for security. Dalmiya and Police Commissioner Dinesh Bajpeyi, then president of the State Hockey Federation, argued about whose duty it was to stop the riot. Bajpeyi claimed to have brought 50 crates of Coca Cola to assuage people when water was in short supply. Furthermore, he accused the CAB of ignoring allegations of alcohol consumption in the Club House before the match started.[139] Years later, in 2006, Bajpeyi contested the CAB elections against Dalmiya as a candidate openly supported by the CPI(M) and lost. The history of acrimony between Dalmiya and the ruling party, which controlled the police and therefore security arrangement at the Eden Gardens, indicates the police might have been less proactive in managing the crisis than one would expect.

In a similar vein to the introspection after the 1967 riot, the press showed more sympathy to the spectators than to the cricketers or the police. Journalist Manas Chakraborty wrote that cricketers did not seem affected by the shocking defeat. He was shocked to see Ajay Jadeja eating an apple and Venkatesh Prasad savouring a sweatmeat without any sign of remorse, while Tendulkar seemed to be shaken even a long time after the defeat.[140] The lack of conciliatory gestures, especially from the cricketers, none of whom came out to pacify the crowd, came under much criticism.[141] Rupak Saha wrote that cricket's new status as a money-spinner had made cricketers too arrogant to care for cricket or its spectators. Cricketers flirted with girls in training camps and spent time with air hostesses in hotel rooms during tours.[142] Journalists in general characterised spectators as victims of inefficient event management and the sport's commercialisation. Cricket fans launched an apology campaign in response to the incident. They wrote in an open letter:

Dear Arjuna, we Calcuttans have earned a reputation over the years of being excellent hosts, who have always received guests with warmth and affection. We are also very proud of the fact that we understand and care for sport better than most. Sadly, we lost our composure and with it, our reputation that night at Eden Gardens. We are extremely ashamed of our behaviour and wholeheartedly apologise to you and your wonderful team.[143]

A public survey conducted by the market analyst organisation MODE showed overwhelming repentance among the people, corroborating the media's argument that spectators were forced into the outburst. The results of the five-set questionnaire filled by 253 men and 47 women revealed the following trends:

1. Are you upset that India lost? Yes: 90 per cent, No: 10 per cent.
2. If Calcuttans were to say sorry to the Sri Lankan team, will you join them? Yes: 82 per cent, No: 18 per cent.
3. How do you feel about yesterday's incident at Eden Gardens?
   - What happened cannot be called unexpected, given yesterday's conditions: 25 per cent.
   - A thing like this should not have happened: 20 per cent.
   - It was a shameful incident: 55 per cent.
4. As an individual, do you wish to congratulate the Sri Lankan team? Yes: 93 per cent, No: 7 per cent.
5. What was the root for yesterday's trouble?
   - Disappointment with India's performance: 100 per cent.
   - Resentment with Sri Lankan performance: 0 per cent.
   - Others: 0 per cent.[144]

The survey showed that the people admitted the rioting was wrong and crystallised by India's poor performance. The readers' letters published by *The Statesman* maintained that spectators meant no disrespect to Sri Lankan players; the centre of fury were Indian players.[145] Several authors went beyond the political pale and drew attention to the changing attitudes of cricket fans towards victory, ushered largely by the commoditisation of cricket in the wake of the popularity of One-day cricket. Sumon Chattopadhyay criticised politicians for their tendency to pass the blame, and the media pundits and 'so-called sociologists' for offering weak explanations for the disorder.

As he wrote, while some of these commentators had 'dipped their felts into the ink of nostalgia' and lamented Calcutta's urban decay, other self-styled Greek Oracles found in the incident a reflection of the general lumpenisation of society. Some criticised the excesses of the sports media and advertising companies for having corrupted basic values. In Chattopadhyay's opinion, the riot was not simply a manifestation of corrupted social values. Spectators acted out of the desolation of watching India collapse after tolerating the inhuman gallery conditions. Their entitlement to showing grievance, he said, was spurred to a large extent by changes within the sport itself, which now paid more attention to results than aesthetics.[146] His parting argument relapsed into a criticism of cricket's commercialism, something he was initially unwilling to accept as a major reason for the riot.

The hyper-marketing of cricket, 'to a public beyond the frame of recognised consumer behaviour' as professor of English literature Sukanta Chaudhuri wrote, had made the sport just another commodity. Marketing strategies had entwined cricket matches and entertainment. Hence, fans were now consumers who demanded compensation as they would claim for a malfunctioning household utility item. The admiration for cricketers was like the consumer's response to overproduced disposable items – valued when new and functional but discarded once they outlive their usefulness – which even cricketers often failed to realise before coming in for huge criticism.[147] Despite its limitation, this rationale of commodity fetishism was frequently to describe contemporary cricket. The change in cricket's character on account of commercialism, the alleged detachment of cricketers from their expected patriotic duty, and the blasé attitude of the organisers constituted a problem for fans. Hence, in some accounts of the riot, crowd violence was reduced to the customer's dissatisfaction with a product. More than politicking and criticism of the police, representations of the riot in 1996 focused on the success of commodity fetishism in changing cricket. In doing so, they revealed a systemic shift in the crowd's mediatised image from the spectator to the consumer.

1999: INDIA VERSUS PAKISTAN

The incident of 1996 so vitiated the image of Calcutta's cricket spectators that the local press considered the first match of the inaugural Asian Test Championship, against Pakistan in 1999, as both a high-risk undertaking and a shot at redemption. The political hostility between India and Pakistan since 1947 has had a profound impact on their cricket rivalry, which has become an exemplar of communal polarisation and a test of patriotism in the subcontinent.[148] The belligerent atmosphere that comes to mind when thinking of India–Pakistan matches almost belies the fact that the BCCI had moved the motion of Test status to Pakistan in an International Cricket Council (ICC) meeting in 1952.[149] Pakistan's first-ever cricket series was against India in the same year. Cricketers were provided high security and asked to stay alert to trouble. During the tour, when the train carrying Pakistani cricketers stopped at 2 a.m. in Surat, a city with an 87 per cent Hindu population, knocks on the windows alarmed everyone in the team. As one of the cricketers opened the window in response, he saw a crowd thronging the platform. The people had waited for several hours to garland the players. The adulation was reversed a few days later as some Hindu Mahasabha cadres welcomed the touring party to Nagpur with anti-Pakistan slogans.[150] The politically motivated behaviour of cricket followers was manifest most visibly during the India–West Indies ODI match in Srinagar, Kashmir, in 1983. Thousands of spectators waved the Pakistani flag in the gallery, cheered every Indian dismissal and shouted anti-India slogans throughout the match.[151] The crowd became so hostile that Sunil Gavaskar, the Indian captain, wanted to abandon play and forfeit the match. Later, in his autobiography, he wrote of having felt that the match could well have been taking place outside India.[152]

Cricketers, too, were drawn into the surrogate war of establishing national supremacy. Several incidents affirm the percolation of political propaganda among cricketers. Fazal Mahmood made an impassioned speech at a dinner during the Calcutta Test match in 1954 in support of British India's partition, notwithstanding the misery it had brought to millions. Aftab Gul refused to sign a charity bat that was to be auctioned to raise funds for the cholera-affected people of Bangladesh in 1971.[153] Most of the Test matches played between the countries were drawn as cricketers, allegedly, were unwilling to risk losing and hence resorted to defensive play. During the 1979–80 series, Pakistani cricketer Majid Khan controversially commented that Indian Muslims would sacrifice their lives during a war between the two countries but in cricket they would always support Pakistan.[154] During the 1987 World Cup, a heated argument between two young Muslim boys in Gwalior, 11-year old Qadir and 13-year-old Nasir, ended in a mishap. As Qadir had predicted India's win in the tournament, and Nasir Pakistan's, the boys started to fight to settle the score, resulting in Nasir's death and Qadir's arrest by the police.[155] The increasing tension and violence among spectators prompted the two cricket boards to use neutral venues in the 1990s. The Test series in 1999 marked the return of Indo-Pak cricket series after 13 years, and coincided with the undertaking of several confidence-building measures between the countries in February 1999.

The right-wing extremist group Shiv Sena's threat to disrupt matches cast a shadow over the series before it began. Shiv Sena demonstrators vandalised the BCCI's office and had the Test match shifted out of Bombay. They dug out the pitch and threatened to unleash snakes in New Delhi. Pakistan's captain, Wasim Akram, dismayed by such intimidation, said, 'We are going there to better the relations between the two countries, and I hope the Indian government will not allow a handful of people to deprive cricket lovers of some action and tension-packed cricket.'[156] The CPI(M), finding a political opportunity to upstage other states, offered to host the entire Test series in Calcutta, dismissing the Shiv Sena's threat of backlash.[157] The Shiv Sena appeared to have sent them a letter, which could have been a hoax as it was posted in Calcutta rather than Mumbai. A reader from Nadia district sent a poem to the *Aajkal*, the first stanza of which read: 'Diyechhile onek badha/dal niye tumi Thakre/seshkalete bujhle kemon/porle hoye eka re' (You and your goons/Spared not a single trick/But Thackeray the cartoon/It's you who now squeak).[158] Anti–Shiv Sena posters were plastered round the Eden Gardens, which the *Aajkal* presented as a statement of the city's secular outlook.[159] The *Ganashakti* was understandably appreciative of the state government for having stood up to the Shiv Sena's threat. It said the chief minister's eagerness to organise the Test series was admired throughout the cricket world, and asked the people to cooperate with the state to dispel the myth of the playing field as a site of proxy war.[160] Test matches in Chennai and New Delhi were not shown on Doordarshan, but MP Gurudas Dasgupta arranged for the BCCI to pay for live telecast of the Calcutta match through a separate stream for the state.[161] Other newspapers were not so congratulatory of the government; instead, they asked spectators to behave well.

The excitement generated by the match was evident in the presence of a record-breaking 465,000 spectators over five days, negating premonitions of the weekday schedule, the state board examination, the high price of tickets and people's growing preference for watching cricket on television.[162] The police arrested 53 people on various charges on the first day. The Calcutta Improvement Trust's lawyer requested the Green Bench to postpone the hearing on pollution at the Rabindra Sarobar area, saying he was too distracted by cricket to continue pleading.[163] A patient, admitted to hospital for a heart attack, released himself on a personal bond to watch the second day's play. He suffered another attack while sitting in Block B and was taken back to the hospital.[164] In the midst of this madness, on the fourth day, with the game evenly balanced, Sachin Tendulkar collided with Shoaib Akhtar while attempting an easy third run. Tendulkar might have made his ground before the collision, but television replays showed him outside the crease when the ball hit the stumps. As he left the ground grumpily, the public thought this run-out was unfair and hurled bottles on the ground in protest. Tendulkar came out to pacify the crowd. It took 67 minutes for the match to resume. Nobody was hurt or threatened to further disrupt the match.

The day's play closed with India in a precarious position. The hope of victory was pinned on local boy Sourav Ganguly's performance the next day. Within half an hour's play on the final day, Ganguly fell cheaply, followed by the rest, leaving India on the brink of defeat. A gesture from Yousuf Youhana reportedly provoked the disappointed spectators, who now started to burn newspapers in the gallery and threw stones, fruits and plastic bottles onto the field.[165] Some people tried in vain to stop others.[166] Spectators at Block B taunted the police, calling them traitors. Block C hurled a volley of fruits, which the police blocked with shields. Spectators set fire to Blocks J, K and L. It took the police three hours to eject 65,000 people. One spectator claimed that the police chased them even as they were dispersing peacefully. Some people fell into drains near the Raj Bhavan, some slipped on the road trying to evade mounted police, and some regrouped near the Mayo Road–Red Road crossing and stoned the police.[167] Around 200 people were left to witness Pakistan's 46-run victory.

The sports diplomacy exercise ended in a huge embarrassment for India. Among the 250 persons arrested, 49 came under civil prosecution. Home Minister Buddhadeb Bhattacharjee denied the charge of police atrocity, maintaining that people were evacuated without the use of force or panic. He added that a similar incident in Madras or Bombay would have turned worse since the Calcutta police were better prepared than their counterparts from other states to maintain security and order.[168] The tension between Dalmiya and the police did not reach the boiling point of 1996, as the former did not eventually blame the police.[169] The *Bartaman* implicated him as well as the sponsors and betting syndicates for plotting the riot. Sujoy Chakraborty, Additional Superintendent of Police, denied every accusation against the police, and admired the courage and diligence shown by the constabulary in controlling the crisis.[170] Other newspapers such as the *Anandabazar Patrika* asserted that the police treated people like cattle.[171] *The Telegraph* reported that the CAB's medical room treated 17 people, a record since the unit started functioning in the 1980s; but its sister publication, the *Anandabazar Patrika*, put the number at 33.[172] The *Ganashakti* gave credit to the Social Welfare Service for admirably treating 34 persons, administering first aid to a further 50 and sending 2 to be admitted to PG Hospital.[173] The home secretary was asked to probe the crowd's behaviour and submit a report to the state government within three months.[174] Seventy-two-year old Sanjib Dey, however, thought that the events were shameful but not as volatile as in 1967.[175]

Historians have drawn attention to the role played by the media in intensifying India–Pakistan rivalry by drawing 'battlelines', highlighting the history of military conflict and strained diplomatic relations between the countries. This martial imagery polarised Hindus and Muslims even further, at times provoking clashes. The organisation of the bilateral series resonated more with diplomatic initiatives than any positive measure towards achieving peace. Hence, the proclaimed unity remained a pipe dream; the cloak of harmony often slipped to reveal the underbelly of political motive and national sentiment.[176] The media's connivance in provoking the public during Indo-Pak cricket matches was accentuated during the riots in 1999. A part of the local media was apprehensive of communal tension boiling over to the cricket field. *The Statesman* summed up the popular mood before the match, writing, 'A cricket match is a cricket match. But a cricket match against Pakistan is the cricket match.'[177] A correspondent of the daily wrote, displaying a misguided understanding of cultural citizenship:

[The spectators] are 'sane' in their self-professed intent but fret, fume and are not averse to frothing at the mouth in the event they notice someone waving an 'enemy flag' ... [They] won't much stand for any revelry indulged in by the supporters of the Pakistan cricket team. Of course, as excuse for their ire, they will say these supporters are Indian citizens ... Can't someone love a country of his choice, however vague the inherency factor may seem, and yet remain faithful to the nation he is a citizen of? In fact, had there been an aberration or two in the behaviour of these people, it is due chiefly to the fear psychosis they are forced to live in.[178]

The state government's assurance about the non-communal nature of the Calcutta crowd proved to be unfounded as spectators at Block B were heard shouting *Pakistan hai hai* on the second day. When some people objected, they were told that it was a protest against Wasim Akram bouncing Harbhajan Singh and nothing communal was intended.[179] The *Aajkal* reported that the city's Muslims seemed to be unhappy that spectators did not vigorously applaud good performances by Pakistani cricketers, hinting that Indian Muslims sided with Pakistan.[180] As an implication without explanation as to why Indian Muslims empathised with Pakistani cricketers, the news supported the long-standing allegation against the supposedly anti-national behaviour of Muslims in cricketing matters. Soumya Bhattacharya in *The Telegraph* wrote of the hypocrisy of spectators in Block C waving a placard that read, *Indi-Pak pyar to ho na thi tha* (Indo-Pak Love Was Bound to Happen), when the camera zoomed in, but as soon as it panned away shouted *Pakistan murdabad* (Death to Pakistan).[181] He pointed out that the general standard of spectatorship had declined, writing, 'Only one stereotype is missing in that steamy cauldron, among the screaming, flag-waving, foot-stamping multitude: Calcutta's characteristic cricket-lover, that well-informed, well-read person ...' A college student in Block D boasted that the people of Calcutta were not weak, unlike their counterparts in Chennai who had applauded Pakistan's victory. The spectators had come to celebrate India, and Pakistan would not be allowed to win at any cost. Following Tendulkar's run-out, screams were heard that the Pakistanis were cheaters. An angry father taught his four-year old son to extract the maximum noise from two empty bottles by banging them together. Bhattacharya later reminisced about the clamour around him: 'Butchers, cheats, Pakistan *murdabad*!' 'Fucking Muslims, go back to own country.' 'Cheats! Bastards! *Hai hai*! Go back!'[182]

The headline of the *Anandabazar Patrika* on the fourth day was 'Chap Thele Swargajayer Bhar Aj Sachineri' (It Is Sachin's Task to Conquer Paradise), fuelling expectations that were cruelly crushed.[183] It continued its quest of reclaiming Bengal's lost supremacy on the morning of the fifth day, titling its main match report 'Banglar Hate Aj Bharater Bhagya' (Bengal Holds the Key to India's Success), which announced that it was time for Ganguly to prove that he was a hero.[184] One of its journalists lambasted Azharuddin for raising his bat to acknowledge the clapping Pakistan players on reaching 6,000 Test runs. There was no reason for the captain's grandstand, whereas the opposition was not playing cricket but had launched a battle. Pankaj Roy wrote that Akram's professionalism vandalised cricket's tradition. A number of other former cricketers said that Tendulkar was obstructed and wrongfully given out. It was reported that Gavaskar urged Pakistan's coach, Javed Miandad, to revoke the appeal, arguing that such a gesture would be remembered as a landmark in the peace process of the subcontinent.[185] Ganguly's failure was explained as a lapse in concentration having come to know that Raj Singh Dungarpur had just stripped him of the team's vice-captaincy.[186]

Soumya Bhattacharya later criticised *The Telegraph*, which he wrote for during the match, for its inflammatory match report entitled, 'Akram Loses India, May Win Test.' He saw supporters coming to the stadium on the fifth day, brandishing the morning newspapers and angrily discussing the injustice done to Tendulkar.[187] The newspaper wrote that Akram could have offered Pakistan Prime Minister Nawaz Sharif the heart of all of India had he called Tendulkar back, but instead he tried to win the match.[188] Its editorial stated that though the batsman was technically out, Akram violated the spirit of cricket by appealing, which was symptomatic of the declining moral standards of players and spectators.[189] Next day, it published the comments of British journalist Peter Deeley in response to the daily's perturbing reports, countering that he was mistaken about the newspaper's intention; the journalist concerned had not blamed Akram for crowd trouble but had merely reflected public mood without any judgement. Akram apparently said after the match, 'It is all because of you people and your reports. You have held them [the crowd] responsible for the wrongdoings but I will never blame them.'[190] The *Ganashakti* downplayed the fourth-day incident, considering the outburst to be quite regular, given India's precarious position in the match.[191] It admitted to the city's disgrace, but declared that the behaviour of spectators had improved so much that the match was merely suspended, not abandoned, as in 1967 and 1996.[192] However, the fifth day's incident so changed the position of every newspaper that no clear editorial policy could be discerned from the contents.

The main report in *The Telegraph*, under the headline 'At Eden, Cricket Hangs Its Head in Shame', noted that the spectators were no different from the Jamaat-e-Islami fundamentalists who had hurled stones at Indian Prime Minister Atal Bihari Vajpayi's motorcade the same day, during his visit to Lahore Fort for peace talks. Both groups were people with no sense of history, engaged in the common effort of subverting history. The cricket field was now a site in which jingoism had official sanction for a parade.[193] Rupak Saha reported that the CAB ought not to organise any match for the next three years.[194] The editor of the *Ganashakti* was more critical of spectators, having written that cricket was now ruled by commerce and that spectators of this changed cricket were false fans.[195] No longer envisioning the people of Calcutta as an anti-communal brigade who had foiled the Shiv Sena's plan, he accused a section of the spectators of instigating communal hatred and raising hate posters in the galleries. The newspaper defended the police against allegations of brutalising spectators, arguing that a group of young people taunted the police into beating them and later incriminated the government by showing their wounds to the media.[196] Nevertheless, it remarked that most of the public were victims of communal propaganda that had flung cricket, religious identity and the Kashmir situation into a crisis. It claimed that the incident was not spontaneous, but rather was orchestrated by political opposition to discredit the state government.[197] Not so supportive of the government's role, *The Statesman* wrote:

Jyoti Basu's and Buddhadeb Bhattacharjee's interpretation of Calcutta – a culturally sophisticated island nurtured on Marxist values – is a fantasy; no other Indian city erupts so easily at the tiniest non-excuse; nowhere else is civic freedom held in such contempt. But it has taken the ultimate bourgeois pastime – Test cricket – for the point to be rammed home ... Calcutta cannot comprehend that there's more to lose in cricket than merely a match ... [The behaviour of spectators] indicate a pattern of lumpenism, which is activated whenever the home team slips at a crucial stage of the game. Since Mr. Dalmiya cannot ensure the Indian players always come up trumps, and since the apology placards some Calcuttans displayed after the India-Sri Lanka match have been proved to be a mere PR stunt, for the sake of cricket, and for the sake of this country's reputation, the city that reaches for plastic bottles every time Sachin or Sourav is dismissed, must be considered beyond the pale.[198]

The Trinamool Congress organised a protest march, demanding Buddhadeb Bhattacharjee's resignation, which ended in the arrest of 59 members, including 32 women.[199] Basu remarked that such incidents of violence were common in sport, especially when ruffians had access to the stadium as ticket holders. His efforts at self-exoneration failed to influence his political rivals. The BJP general secretary Rahul Sinha demanded an investigation.[200] Trinamool leader Mamata Banerjee demanded an apology from the state, insinuating that Basu had masterminded the disturbances to hinder the peace process.[201] The Youth Congress president Paresh Pal asked for a refund against the fifth day's ticket.[202] The demonstrations fell well short of their target. The sports press stopped its criticism all too suddenly and focused on the next Test match. Dalmiya used his clout to save the Eden Gardens from being blacklisted by the ICC. While the blemish of communalism did not entirely fade, it never returned with the same vengeance during the Indo-Pak matches played later in the city.

The riot, caused by a combination of antagonism towards Pakistan and resentment at coming up second best, brought to light one of the threadbare circuits of the nation's machine. Indo-Pakistan matches have, in this way, generated an idea of nationalist loyalty that needs to be explicit and compliant to a certain political discourse of nationhood. This discourse asserts that one's legitimacy as a citizen depends on one's adherence to a national symbol, that is, cricket. Such an articulation of legitimation, arguably, helps a group to take a majoritarian position and dominate nonconformists. Journalists have inaccurately compared this test of nationalism that is often asked of Muslims to the infamous Tebbit Test in Britain, which was about asking resident South Asian–origin people to prove their right to be British citizens by supporting English cricket teams against India and Pakistan. These are fundamentally different contexts, as the British test was about ethnic South Asians growing out of their traditional group loyalty, and the Indian test has been about ethnic Indians being asked to support their country, irrespective of their religion. Indians who question this arrangement open themselves to allegations of harbouring anti-national sentiment. They are seen by a majority to be inimical to the establishment of a unitary nationalism. Their actions symbolise simultaneously the shortcomings of a nation that fails to inculcate a sense of national belonging in its citizens, and the problem of alienation of a community from Indian society, prompted by a mutual unease between religions. The shared mistrust between India and Pakistan seemed to have been removed on the occasion of the 'Friendship' tour in 2003–04, but later events resulted in another suspension of all bilateral sporting contact.

CONCLUSION

The accounts of the episodes of violence across decades highlight several aspects of political development in Calcutta. Perhaps the most striking was the growing autonomy of journalists within newspapers. It appears that newspapers from the 1960s followed a definitive editorial stance, consistent with the political ideology of their management, subscribing to a set of opinions without much internal diversity. The editor's control over the content in some newspapers seemingly diminished in the 1990s, evidenced by the co-presence of independent voices. Journalists working for the same newspaper expressed distinct opinions – if one of them censured the state government, the other targeted spectators. Journalists working for the mouthpieces of political parties were not able to exercise free will like their counterparts from the more autonomous newspapers. It was a precursor to the emergence of individually generated content in the digital age. A mistrust of journalists as manipulative intermediaries between incidents and readers, however, seemed to have remained embedded, if not worsened, over the decades.

The chapter has also sought to examine the spectators' defiance of social order and expected behaviour at the cricket stadium in the context of the political climate of the state. It has shown that the extent of violence had reduced through the 1960s to the 1990s, which was consistent with the increased political stability and monopolisation of violence in the state. The people had little expectation of benevolence from political parties, and the police never ceased to be considered the repressive arm of the state. They were known to have demonstrated against the CAB for organisational incompetence, and vandalised state properties such as public transports during the riots in the 1960s. Damaging the stadium was their language of protesting against problems in the larger society. Used to violence in their everyday lives, spectators rarely needed organisation or leadership to remonstrate against the CAB and political strifes in general. The show of discontent in the 1990s was targeted at cricketers for poor performance, beginning only when India were on the brink of defeat. Perhaps a watershed in this changed attitude to cricket came in 1984–85, when spectators abused captain Sunil Gavaskar and his wife for the delay in declaring India's innings against England. The creative possibilities of cricket were thus effaced by a stubborn yearning for victory. The rising tide of consumption and outcome-driven mentality, alongside a surge in nationalism in the 1990s, replaced cricket's aesthetic significance as a synecdoche of life with an emphasis on success at all costs, marking a transition in the sport's public culture. Transformed into service providers, cricketers no longer commanded the respect they had in the 1960s, when spectators would not harm them in their protests. Later, they became the reason for the public's outburst. No amount of coming out to pacify the consumers seemed to work after a disappointing performance. The people's pleasure and sense of power in humiliating the government as a revenge for state violence, manifested in strikes and demonstrations, now worked in the context of cricket.

NOTES

1. E. P. Thompson, 'The Moral Economy of the English Crowd in the Eighteenth Century', *Past and Present* 50 (1971): 76–136.

2. Frantz Fanon, *The Wretched of the Earth*, trans. Richard Wilcox (New York: Grove Press, 2004), 51.

3. Achille Mbembe, *Necropolitics*, trans. Steven Corcoran (Durham, NC: Duke University Press, 2019), 26.

4. See Amales Tripathi, *The Extremist Challenge: India between 1890 and 1910* (Bombay: Orient Longman, 1967); Sumit Sarkar, *The Swadeshi Movement in Bengal, 1903–1908* (New Delhi: People's Publishing House, 1973); David Laushey, *Bengal Terrorism and the Marxist Left: Aspects of Regional Nationalism in India, 1905–1942* (Calcutta: Firma K.L. Mukhopadhyay, 1975); Rajat Kanta Ray, *Social Conflict and Political Unrest in Bengal, 1875–1927* (Delhi: Oxford University Press, 1984); Tanika Sarkar, *Bengal 1928–1934: The Politics of Protest* (Delhi: Oxford University Press, 1987); Hiren Chakrabarti, *Political Protest in Bengal: Boycott and Terrorism 1905–18* (Calcutta: Papyrus, 1992); Peter Heehs, *The Bomb in Bengal: The Rise of Revolutionary Terrorism in India, 1900–1910* (Delhi: Oxford University Press, 1993); Shukla Sanyal, *Revolutionary Pamphlets, Propaganda and Political Culture in Colonial Bengal* (New Delhi: Cambridge University Press, 2014); Durba Ghosh, *Gentlemanly Terrorists: Political Violence and the Colonial State in India, 1919–1947* (Cambridge: Cambridge University Press, 2017); Michael Silvestri, *Policing 'Bengali Terrorism' in India and the World: Imperial Intelligence and Revolutionary Nationalism, 1905–1939* (Cham: Palgrave Macmillan, 2019).

5. For histories of communal violence, see Suranjan Das, *Communal Riots in Bengal, 1905–1947* (Delhi: Oxford University Press, 1991); Joya Chatterji, *Bengal Divided: Hindu Communalism and Partition 1932–47* (Cambridge: Cambridge University Press, 1995); Patricia A. Grossman, *Riots and Victims: Violence and the Construction of Communal Identity among Bengali Muslims, 1905–1947* (London: Routledge, 1999); Suranjan Das, 'The 1992 Calcutta Riot in Historical Continuum: A Relapse into 'Communal Fury'?' *Modern Asian Studies* 34, no. 2 (2000): 281–306;

Sekhar Bandyopadhyay, *The Minorities in Post-Partition West Bengal: The Riots of 1950* (New Delhi: Sage, 2011); Anwesha Roy, *Making Peace, Making Riots: Communalism and Communal Violence, Bengal 1940–1947* (Cambridge: Cambridge University Press, 2018).

6. Suranjan Das, 'The Crowd in Calcutta Violence, 1907–1926,' in *Dissent and Consensus: Social Protest in Pre-Industrial Societies*, ed. Basudev Chattopadhyay, Hari S. Vasudevan and Rajat Kanta Ray, 233–72 (Calcutta: K.P. Bagchi, 1989).

7. Dipesh Chakraborty, '"In the Name of Politics": Democracy and the Power of the Multitude in India,' in *From the Colonial to the Postcolonial: India and Pakistan in Transition*, ed. Dipesh Chakrabarty, Rochona Majumdar and Andrew Sartori, 31–54 (New Delhi: Oxford University Press, 2007).

8. Myron Weiner, 'Violence and Politics in Calcutta', *Journal of Asian Studies* 20, no. 3 (1961): 275–81, 275–77.

9. Weiner, 'Violence and Politics in Calcutta', 278–79.

10. Atul Kohli, *Democracy and Discontent: India's Growing Crisis of Governability* (Cambridge: Cambridge University Press, 1991); Ranabir Samaddar, ed., *From Popular Movements to Rebellion: The Naxalite Decade* (London and New York: Routledge, 2019).

11. Gyanendra Pandey, *Routine Violence: Nations, Fragments, Histories* (Stanford, CA: Stanford University Press, 2006), 7.

12. Stuart Hall and Doreen Massey, 'Interpreting the Crisis', *Soundings* 44 (Spring 2010): 57–71. A foundational text in the development of this kind of analysis was Stuart Hall, Charles Critcher, Tony Jefferson, John Clarke and Brian Roberts, *Policing the Crisis: Mugging, the State, and Law and Order* (London: Macmillan 1978).

13. John Williams, 'Having an Away Day: English Football Spectators and the Hooligan Debate', in *British Football and Social Change: Getting into Europe*, ed. John Williams and Stephen Wagg, 160–84 (Leicester: Leicester University Press, 1991).

14. Kurt Weis, 'How the Print Media Affect Sports and Violence: The Problems of Sport Journalism', *International Review for the Sociology of Sport* 21, no. 2–3 (1986): 239–52.

15. Pierre Bourdieu, *In Other Words: Essays towards a Reflexive Sociology*, trans. Matthew Adamson (Stanford, CA: Stanford University Press, 1990), 165.

16. Kevin Young, '"The Killing Field": Themes in Mass Media Responses to the Heysel Stadium Riot', *International Review for the Sociology of Sport* 21, no. 2–3 (1986): 253–66.

17. Norbert Elias and Eric Dunning, *Quest for Excitement: Sport and Leisure in the Civilizing Process* (Oxford: Blackwell, 1986); Eric Dunning, Patrick Murphy and John Williams, *The Roots of Football Hooliganism: A Historical and Sociological Study* (London: Routledge, 1988); Eric Dunning, *Sport Matters: Sociological Studies of Sport, Violence and Civilization* (London: Routledge, 1999). For a summary of the Leicester School's contribution and critiques, see Alan Bairner, 'The Leicester School and the Study of Football Hooliganism,' *Sport in Society* 9, no. 4 (2006): 583–98. For a criticism of Dunning's thesis, see Christian Koller and Fabian Brändle, *Goal! A Cultural and Social of Modern Football* (Washington D. C.: Catholic University of America, 2015), 274–75.

18. Richard Giulianotti, Norman Bonney and Mike Hepworth, eds., *Football, Violence and Social Identity* (London and New York: Routledge, 1994); Gary Armstrong, *Football Hooligans: Knowing the Score* (Oxford: Berg, 1998); Richard Giulianotti, *Football: A Sociology of the Global Game* (Cambridge: Polity Press, 1999); Eric Dunning, Patrick Murphy, Ivan Waddington and A. E. Astrinakis, eds., *Fighting Fans: Football Hooliganism as a World Phenomenon* (Dublin: University College of Dublin Press, 2002); Ramón Spaaij, *Understanding Football Hooliganism: A Comparison of Six Western European Football Clubs* (Amsterdam: Vossiuspers UvA, 2006).

19. Rob Lynch, 'A Symbolic Patch of Grass: Crowd Disorder and Regulation on the Sydney Cricket Ground Hill', in *Crowd Violence at Australian Sport*, ed. John O'Hara, 10–48 (Cambelltown, NSW: Australian Society for Sports History, 1992), 10.

20. John Ford, *Cricket: A Social History, 1700–1835* (Newton Abbot: David and Charles, 1972).

21. Wray Vamplew, 'Sport Crowd Disorder in Britain, 1870–1914: Causes and Controls', *Journal of Sport History* 7, no. 1 (1980): 5–20.

22. Wray Vamplew, 'It's Not Cricket and Perhaps It Never Was: An Historical Look at Australian Crowd and Player Behaviour', *Sport in History* 14, no. 1 (1994): 3–12.

23. Keith Sandiford, *Cricket and the Victorians* (Aldershot: Scolar Press, 1994).

24. Dominic Malcolm, 'Cricket Spectator Disorder: Myths and Historical Evidence', *Sport in History* 19, no. 1 (1999): 16–37.

25. 'Riots Stop India Test', *Sydney Morning Herald*, 4 November 1953, 16.

26. *TOI*, 9 November 1969, 1.

27. *Jugantar*, 18 October 1983, 7; *Jugantar*, 19 October 1983, 1.

28. *TOI*, 6 April 1986, 7.

29. Paul Dimeo, '"Team Loyalty Splits the City into Two": Football, Ethnicity and Rivalry in Calcutta', in *Fear and Loathing in World Football*, ed. Gary Armstrong and Richard Giulianotti, 105–18 (Oxford: Berg, 2001); Boria Majumdar and Kausik Bandyopadhyay, *Goalless: The Story of a Unique Footballing Nation* (New Delhi: Penguin/Viking, 2006); Kausik Bandyopadhyay, *Scoring Off the Field: Football Culture in Bengal, 1911–1980* (New Delhi: Routledge, 2011).

30. Bandyopadhyay, *Scoring Off the Field*, 214.

31. Paul Dimeo, '"With Political Pakistan in the Offing ...": Football and Communal Politics in South Asia, 1887–1947', *Journal of Contemporary History* 38, no. 3 (2003): 377–94.

32. Bandyopadhyay, *Scoring Off the Field*, 193–95.

33. Dipesh Chakraborty, *Habitations of Modernity: Essays in the Wake of Subaltern Studies* (Chicago: The University of Chicago Press, 2002), 139. The author was hit by a stray brickbat the last time he attended a football match before the book's publication.

34. Boria Majumdar, '*Ghati–Bangal* on the Maidan: Subregionalism, Club Rivalry and Fan Culture in Indian Football,' in *Football: From England to the World*, ed. Dolores P. Martinez and Projit B. Mukharji, 120–33 (London and New York: Routledge, 2009).

35. Allen Guttmann, *Sport Spectators* (New York: Columbia University Press, 1986), 8.

36. *IWI*, 12 April 1959, 53.

37. *TOI*, 16 April 1963, 10.

38. 'CAB Cricket Pratijogita', *Amrita* 7, no. 48 (5 April 1968), 400.

39. *KA* 6, no. 41 (18 February 1983), 28.

40. James W. Carey, *Communication as Culture: Essays on Media and Society* (Boston: Unwin Hyman, 1989), 20.

41. For theories of crowd disturbance, see Christian Borch, *The Politics of Crowds: An Alternative History of Sociology* (Cambridge: Cambridge University Press, 2012), 16.

42. Saroj Chakrabarty, *With West Bengal Chief Ministers: Memoirs 1962 to 1977* (Calcutta: Orient Longman, 1978), 184.

43. The sightscreen is an extremely important piece of the cricket ground. It secludes the batsman from the ambient distractions and helps him to concentrate on the bowler. If spectators obstruct the batsman's line of vision by moving around the sightscreen, the police are entitled to evacuate them.

44. *TS*, 1 January 1967, 16.

45. *ABP*, 2 January 1967, 3.

46. Ibid, 1 January 1967, 9.

47. Ibid., 6 January 1967, 10. The *Anandabazar Patrika* published a break-up of how many tickets were issued to which group. The Inquiry Commission enumerated a larger audience. The cricketer Garry Sobers wrote that the stadium had seating arrangements for 30,000 while 40,000 people turned up on that day, which was 20,000 less than the figure quoted in the investigation report. Garry Sobers, *Twenty Years at the Top* (London: Macmillan, 1988), 117.

48. *Jugantar*, 5 January 1967, 4.

49. Ibid., 2 January 1967, 3.

50. *ABP*, 2 January 1967, 1.

51. *HT*, 3 January 1967, 4.

52. *Jugantar*, 2 January 1967, 6.

53. A letter from the 'cricket-lovers of Calcutta' to the editor, *ABP*, 7 January 1967, 9.

54. Garry Sobers wrote that local officials threatened the West Indies cricketers when they failed to persuade them to play. As the players mulled abandoning the match and returning home, a local official said, 'If the people know where you are going, the bus might be stopped on the way to the airport and set on fire with you inside.' Sobers, *Twenty Years*, 118. The statement cast the spectators in an image completely different from their contemporary representation as topophilic people. This falsification for the sake of forcing cricketers to play brings out the apathy of the organisers towards spectators.

55. Ray Robinson, *The Wildest Tests* (Sydney: Cassell, 1979), 77. The bonus of 100 rupees lifted the Indian players' Test match fee to 600 rupees.

56. *ABP*, 3 January 1967, 1.

57. *Report of the Commission of Inquiry*, 24.

58. Ibid., 32.

59. Ibid., 33.

60. Ibid., 35.

61. Ibid., 37.

62. Ibid., 36.

63. Ibid., 46.

64. Ibid., 46.

65. Ibid., 47.

66. Ibid., 51.

67. Sunil Gangopadhyay, *Sei Samay* (Those Days) (Calcutta: Ananda Publishers, 1988), 550.

68. *TS*, 28 December 1966, 16.

69. *ABP*, 31 December 1966, 1.

70. *TS*, 31 December 1966, 10.

71. Chiranjib, 'Darshak Charit' (The Spectators), *ABP*, 26 January 1967, 12.

72. *DB*, 1 January 1967, 1.

73. Ibid., 1 January 1967, 6.

74. *Jugantar*, 1 January 1967, 1; *ABP*, 1 January 1967, 1.

75. *ABP*, 2 January 1967, 3.

76. *HT*, 15 January 1967, 12.

77. *Jugantar*, 2 January 1967, 4.

78. Ibid., 2 January 1967, 6.

79. Noel P. Gist and Roy Dean Wright, *Marginality and Identity: Anglo-Indians as a Racially-Mixed Minority in India* (Leiden: E. J. Brill, 1973); Lionel Caplan, *Children of Colonialism: Anglo-Indians in a Postcolonial World* (Oxford: Berg, 2001).

80. Sajal Basu, *Politics of Violence: A Case Study of West Bengal* (Calcutta: Minerva Publishers, 1982), 62.

81. This feature of the Calcutta public was consistent with the football rioters from the north of Italy, where people from upper-class backgrounds have been shown to be much involved in violence. Carlo Podaliri and Carlo Balestri, 'The Ultràs, Racism and Football Culture in Italy', in *Fanatics! Power, Identity and Fandom in Football*, ed. Adam Brown, 88–100 (London: Routledge, 1998).

82. *Jugantar*, 3 January 1967, 3. For an account of the Jallianwala Bagh massacre, see Kim Wagner, *Amritsar 1919: An Empire of Fear and the Making of a Massacre* (New Haven: Yale University Press, 2019).

83. *Jugantar*, 6 January 1967, 4.

84. *DB*, 3 January 1967, 4.

85. Ibid., 2 January 1967, 1.

86. *ABP*, 3 January 1967, 7.

87. Ibid, 3.

88. *Jugantar*, 2 January 1967, 6.

89. Ibid, 3 January 1967, 1.

90. *DB*, 2 January 1967, 1.

91. Ibid., 2 January 1967, 4.

92. Ibid.

93. Martin Johnes, 'Heads in the Sand: Football, Politics and Crowd Disasters in Twentieth-Century Britain,' in *Soccer and Disaster: International Perspectives,* ed. Paul Darby, Martin Johnes and Gavin Mellor, 10–27 (London: Routledge, 2005), 10.

94. *ABP,* 2 January 1967, 3.

95. *Jugantar,* 5 January 1967, 4.

96. Chiranjib, 'Khabar Sangraher Nana Jhuki' (The Dangers of Sourcing News), *SKA,* 1979, 17.

97. *AmBP,* 11 December 1969, 8.

98. Ashley Mallet, *Rowdy* (Blackwood: Lynton, 1973), 54; Ashley Mallet, *One of a Kind: The Doug Walters Story* (Crows Nest: Allen & Unwin, 2008), 172.

99. *AmBP,* 12 December 1969, 1.

100. *TOI,* 17 December 1969, 1.

101. *AmBP,* 14 December 1969, 6.

102. *TOI,* 17 December 1969, 1.

103. 'The Trail of Tragedy They Left Behind', *TOI,* 18 December 1969, 12.

104. *DB,* 16 December 1969, 5.

105. A chronological account of the Naxalite revolution can be found in Sumanta Banerjee, *India's Simmering Revolution: The Naxalite Uprising* (London: Zed Books, 1980).

106. The criticism of CPI(M)–police brutality increased in 1970 after the fall of the second United Front government. A booklet of the CPI said, 'public opinion must be organized against police repression', which could not be done effectively to end the repression. Bhupesh Gupta, Ranen Sen and Prabhat Das Gupta, *CPM Terror in West Bengal* (Calcutta: Communist Party Publication, 1970), v. Accounts of the United Front government's history and dissolution can be found in Sankar Ghosh, *The Disinherited State: A Study of West Bengal, 1967–70* (Calcutta: Orient Longman, 1971); and Dhruba Jyoti Bhaumik, *Political Movements in India (A Study of the United Front Experiment in West Bengal)* (Delhi: Anmol Publications, 1987).

107. G. Shankar, 'Edener Gallery Theke' (From the Eden Gallery), *DB,* 16 December 1969, 6.

108. *DB,* 18 December 1969, 6.

109. *Jugantar,* 18 December 1969, 1; *Jugantar,* 19 December 1969, 1.

110. *Jugantar,* 20 December 1969, 7.

111. 'Abhisopto Mangalbar: Ja Dekhechi Ja Dekhini' (Cursed Tuesday: What I Saw and What I Didn't), *Saptahik Basumati* 74, no. 27 (1 January 1970), 1727–28.

112. Santipriyo Bandopadhyay, 'Khela Dhula' (Sports), *Saptahik Basumati* 74, no. 34 (19 February 1970), 2174.

113. *Aajkal*, 2 March 1996, 8.

114. Basu, *Politics of Violence*, 92.

115. Sajal Basu, *West Bengal: The Violent Years* (Calcutta: Prachi Publications, 1974), ch. 4.

116. Jyotiprasad Chatterjee and Suprio Basu, *Left Front and After: Understanding the Dynamics of Poriborton in West Bengal* (New Delhi: Sage, 2020).

117. Subrata K. Mitra, *The Puzzle of India's Governance: Culture, Context and Comparative Theory* (London and New York: Routledge, 2006), 150.

118. 'Oh! For a Ticket to the Garden of Eden,' *TT*, 12 March 1996, 14. The newspaper referred to the 'Garden of Eden' imagery throughout the 1990s to describe the craze for tickets: 'Oh! For a Ticket to the Garden of Eden' (when seven people suffered head injuries as the police charged the disorderly queue), 27 November 1993, 16; and 'Oh! For a Ticket to the Eden', 2 November 1994, 16. The copywriter(s) were probably a fan of Arnab Ghose's article 'Ticket for the Garden of Eden', *AmBP*, 10 December 1969, 10.

119. *TS*, 12 March 1996, 1.

120. *Ganashakti*, 12 March 1996, 1.

121. Ibid., 8.

122. *ABP*, 14 March 1996, 10.

123. *TT*, 13 March 1996, 1.

124. Ibid., 1.

125. *ABP*, 15 March 1996, 4.

126. Ibid., 14 March 1996, 11.

127. Ibid., 14 March 1996, 10.

128. Ibid., 15 March 1996, 1.

129. *Ganashakti*, 14 March 1996, 7.

130. Ibid., 15 March 1996, 8.

131. *ABP*, 15 March 1996, 5.

132. *Aajkal*, 20 March 1996, 1.

133. *ABP*, 16 March 1996, 8.

134. Ibid., 15 March 1996, 12.

135. Suman Chattopadhyay, 'Edene Oshanti: Kathgawrae Sudhu Dorshok Keno' (Eden Disorder: Why Blame Only the Spectator), *ABP*, 19 March 1996, 4.

136. *ABP*, 14 March 1996, 10.

137. Ibid., 15 March 1996, 1.

138. *Ganashakti*, 15 March 1996, 8.

139. *ABP*, 14 March 1996, 12.
140. Ibid., 14 March 1996, 10.
141. Ibid., 15 March 1996, 4.
142. Ibid., 14 March 1996, 12.
143. 'Calcutta Seek to Make Amends, Draft Apology to Arjuna', *TT*, 15 March 1996, 14.
144. Ibid., 15 March 1996, 14.
145. *TS*, 21 March 1996, 8.
146. Chattopadhyay, 'Edene Oshanti'.
147. Sukanta Chaudhuri, 'The Playing Fields of Eden', in *View from Calcutta*, 175–78 (New Delhi: Chronicle Books, 2002).
148. Kausik Bandyopadhyay, 'Feel Good, Goodwill and India's Friendship Tour of Pakistan, 2004: Cricket, Politics and Diplomacy in Twenty-First-Century India,' *International Journal of the History of Sport* 25, no. 12 (2008): 1654–70, 1656.
149. *Minutes of the Imperial Cricket Conference*, 28 July 1952.
150. Fazal Mahmood, with Asif Sohail, *From Dawn to Dusk: Autobiography of a Pakistan Cricket Legend* (Karachi: Oxford University Press, 2003), 32.
151. *Jugantar*, 18 October 1983, 7.
152. Sunil Gavaskar, *Runs n' Ruins* (New Delhi: Rupa, 1984), 76.
153. Mahmood, *From Dawn to Dusk*, 77–78; 'Gul Refuses to Autograph Bat', *TOI*, 20 June 1971, 14. Gul was quoted having said, 'This is an excuse, I believe, to provide money for India after India has raised the bogey of cholera to give us a bad name.'
154. *AmBP*, 3 February 1980, 8.
155. *TS*, 20 October 1987, 14.
156. Rahul Bhattacharya, *Pundits from Pakistan: On Tour with India, 2003–04* (New Delhi: Picador, 2005), 12.
157. *Aajkal*, 12 February 1999, 8.
158. Ibid., 14 February 1999, 4, translated by Anirban Bandyopadhyay.
159. Ibid., 15 February 1999, 7.
160. *Ganashakti*, 15 February 1999, 4.
161. *ABP*, 16 February 1999, 1.
162. Rob Steen, *Floodlights and Touchlines: A History of Spectator Sport* (London: Bloomsbury, 2014), 35.
163. *Bartaman*, 18 February 1999, 1.
164. Ibid., 19 February 1999, 8.
165. *ABP*, 21 February 1999, 7.

166. *TT*, 21 February 1999, 15.

167. Avijit Nandi Majumdar, 'Mob, Police Sweep fair Play Out of Eden', *TT*, 21 February 1999, 8.

168. *Ganashakti*, 21 February 1999, 6.

169. Ibid., 8.

170. *Bartaman*, 21 February 1999, 1.

171. *ABP*, 21 February 1999, 1.

172. Indranil Majumdar and Atreyo Mukhopadhyay, 'Paradise Lost at the Garden of Eden', *TT*, 21 February 1999, 15; *ABP*, 21 February 1999, 7.

173. *Ganashakti*, 21 February 1999, 1.

174. *TOI*, 24 February 1999, 29.

175. *TT*, 21 February 1999, 15.

176. Jishnu Dasgupta, 'Manufacturing Unison: Muslims, Hindus and Indians during the India–Pakistan Match', in *Sport in South Asian Society: Past and Present*, ed. Boria Majumdar and J. A. Mangan, 239–48 (London: Routledge, 2005); Jishnu Dasgupta, 'Exploring Politics and Sports: Towards a Disaggregated Understanding,' in *People at Play: Sport, Culture and Nationalism*, ed. Amitava Chatterjee, 51–85 (Kolkata: Setu Prakashani, 2013).

177. *TS*, 15 February 1999, 16.

178. Arunava Das, 'The Hypocrisy Is Galling', *The Statesman Midweek*, 17 February 1999, 1.

179. *Aajkal*, 18 February 1999, 1.

180. Ibid., 19 February 1999, 7.

181. Soumya Bhattacharya, 'Passions, All but Bottled Up', *TT*, 20 February 1999, 10.

182. Soumya Bhattacharya, *You Must Like Cricket? Memoirs of an Indian Cricket Fan* (London: Yellow Jersey Press, 2006), 128.

183. *ABP*, 19 February 1999, 1.

184. Ibid., 20 February 1999, 1.

185. Ibid., 20 February 1999, 10.

186. Ibid., 22 February 1999, 12.

187. S. Bhattacharya, *You Must Like Cricket?* 132.

188. *TT*, 20 February 1999, 1.

189. Aveek Sarkar, 'Satan at the Garden of Eden', *TT*, 20 February 1999, 12.

190. S. Bhattacharya, *You Must Like Cricket?* 132.

191. *Ganashakti*, 20 February 1999, 1.

192. Ibid., 20 February 1999, 7.

193. *TT*, 21 February 1999, 1.
194. *ABP*, 23 February 1999, 10.
196. *Ganashakti*, 21 February 1999, 2.
196. Ibid., 21 February 1999, 1.
197. Ibid., 2.
198. 'Editorial', *TS*, 21 February 1999, 8.
199. *ABP*, 22 February 1999, 12.
200. *Bartaman*, 22 February 1999, 1.
201. After a long struggle against the CPI(M), Mamata Banerjee won the state elections and became the chief minister in 2011. For an analysis of Banerjee's political career, see Kenneth Bo Nielsen, 'Mamata Banerjee: Redefining Female Leadership', in *India's Democracies: Diversity, Co-optation, Resistance*, ed. Arild Engelsen Ruud and Geir Heierstad, 101–34 (Oslo: Universitetsforlaget, 2016).
202. Ibid., 24 February 1999, 1.

Conclusion

A short story by Sunil Bose in the autumn annual of the *Khelar Asar* in 1980 well summarises the culture of cricket described in the book. The author stitched a patchwork of incidents on the field, the attitude of spectators and practices of the press. The story begins with Bengalis deciding to give the Hindu goddess Durga respite from her annual task of battling the demon Mahisasur, instead asking the male gods to confront a team of demons in a three-day game of cricket at the Eden Gardens in 1977.[1] Tickets vanished from the counters in no time. The 150,000 complimentary tickets sent to heaven were not enough for the 3.3 billion gods, so Mahadeb, one of the holy trinity, asked for additional 2 million complimentary tickets as ministers were known to demand. As the CAB could not fulfil his demand, he replaced the current secretary with a person named Biswanath, much like how Biswanath Dutt was appointed the CAB secretary in 1977. The treasurer god organised a lottery for ticket distribution. Millions of enthusiastic gods queued for two days to buy coupons. The police commissioner among the gods ordered baton charge to discipline the troublemakers. Mahadeb used his clout as Durga's husband to lead the team like the Indian Maharajas of yore often enough abused their role as sponsors and would lead the team themselves. He unabashedly included one of his less athletic sons in the team ignoring a more deserving candidate, mirroring the very signs of the favouritism among Indian selectors that allegedly went against Bengal for generations.

The football matches organised in the stadium in summer had left the ground in poor condition, damaging the pitch, which was going to deteriorate as the match progressed. The team batting second was for sure at a disadvantage. Durga, like a typical female spectator, was knitting a new tiger skin for Mahadeb. As one of the demons reached his century, a young girl invaded the field with a garland in hand, mirroring the behaviour of star-struck female followers. The centurion's behaviour towards fielders was appalling, which the umpires overlooked just as they did in real life out of deference for the foreigner. Spectators heckled the less agile fielders. The demon captain complained against one of the god bowlers for using Vaseline to get a prodigious swing, reminding readers of the controversy surrounding England's John Lever's use of Vaseline to shine the ball in 1977. The umpire acceded and sent off the bowler. One of the demons failed to show up to bat as he was fast asleep, but the team manager acted like his Western counterparts and blamed the local food for his indisposition. The press speculated about certain umpiring decisions and presented the first day's play from various perspectives. Durga criticised Mahadeb's captaincy and defended his son's use of Vaseline, reflecting the irrational comments made by former cricketers, whereas a demon cricketer's wife wrote a newspaper column as companions of Western cricketers often did for the local press. The goddess of learning wrote a critical match report like most vernacular correspondents, convincingly defending God XI and her family's performance, not giving credit where it was due and praising undeserving candidates.

The quick dismissal of one of the demon cricketers on the second day was celebrated with a barrage of 3,000 oranges, 5,000 bananas and 10,000 flower bouquets on the ground. The last demon, known for his cycle of six month's sleep followed by a day's wakefulness, was uproariously greeted by government employees notorious for their aversion to work. As the gods were about to begin their innings, the stadium overflowed with people, with the ends of the queue reaching Chowringhee on one side and Babughat on the other. Radio commentators set up the match so thrillingly that the public could not stay at home and wanted to be a part of the atmosphere. The umpire warned the leading demon bowler for running on the pitch and creating footmarks to assist spinners. Mahadeb got out trying to score briskly, and returned to the pavilion amid of the popular 'Bolo Hori Hori Bol' chant. The demon known for sleeping reprised Tony Greig's act of eating the fruits thrown at him. In disapproval of the god of engineering's gratis service as a night watchman, Calcutta's labour unions called a strike the next day.

The third day's play started on an acrimonious note as one of the demon bowlers kicked down the stumps like Michael Holding in New Zealand to show his displeasure as the umpire turned down two appeals and was promptly given a warning. Spectators branded god Krishna as a stooge of the capitalists for his defensive batting, which was consistent with his emphasis on service without desire. A big hit landed on a spectator, nearly killing him, which incensed other spectators into launching a riot. As the gods were hurtling towards defeat, the crowd started abusing them, particularly the captain for his dubious team selection and poor performance. Much like real-life commentators, those in the story made several faux pas. One of them choked with grief while the other minced no words to criticise the gods. However, the god of water (Varun) came to the rescue of his friends by starting a downpour, ending the match in a draw. The story comprehensively captured the traits of spectators and players until 1980, summarising the conventions of the experience of cricket as a parable of gods and demons.

A number of Indians criticised cricket as an alien import and hence unsuitable for the people of the emerging nation, dismissing it as a futile pastime and as a sedative for the masses. In response to these critics, journalist Soumya Bhattacharya wrote,

> There's a general assumption that sport is a childish, frivolous pursuit. That it is not worthy of the degree of emotional and intellectual engagement that politics, classical music or Estonian films merit. I'm often told that cricket is basically twenty-two grown men meeting in a park to throw things at each other. (Imagine being interested in *that*.) But in these terms Mozart was messing around with doh ray me; Shakespeare was juggling twenty-six letters.[2]

This book has hopefully developed a more sophisticated method of exploring the significance of cricket, integrating with the history of the sport and its reception the multiple histories of culture, media, politics and gender in the context of Calcutta, and, by extension, modern India. It showed that in addition to providing substance to Bengal's idea of culture, cricket produced intersectional identities in spectatorship and readership. The sociability generated by spectators transcended the curious spectacles of office employees malingering to watch cricket, students furtively listening to radio commentary in classrooms or crowds going berserk over disappointing results. In their efforts to legitimise cricket as a pursuit, Bengali journalists and authors synchronously embraced the sport's English traditions and local innovations, and bred new imagined communities. They protected the invented tradition from criticisms made by antagonistic Indians and non-Indians, who objected to the indigenous cricket culture for various ideological reasons. This book explored the spectrum of mediated perceptions of cricket, rehabilitating spectators from the periphery of history to the fold of Indian society as a crucial segment. It analysed the nature of people's participation in cricket through a reading of press reports and literature.

The first chapter showed the contradictory attitude of Indians towards cricket. While a section of people welcomed cricket as an entertaining sport, another invoked the critical task of nation-building and social responsibility to downplay the popular indulgence in it. A third section that was politically averse to British colonialism respected the Englishness of cricket's tradition and patronised the sport due to personal and group affinity. The mutually incompatible perspectives, implanted in conflicting systems of belief as they were, underline the fragmentary nature of cricket's imagined community in Calcutta, and possibly elsewhere too. The chapter uses cricket to qualify historian Benedict Anderson's postulate about the role of the circulation of motifs in nation-building, by arguing that neither did cricket speak, or spark, a 'national language' nor did the community woven around it acquire a stable identity or cadre of subscribers at any point in time, and yet it emerged as one of the most popular symbols of the society. The chapter contends, moreover, that an exhaustive understanding of the history of cricket requires a combined study of its supporters and adversaries. The press played an important role in cricket's circulation among the more intellectual sections of the sport's audience by positioning it, tantalisingly, as an answer to aesthetic yearnings. However, regional publications often ran counter to one another depending on the language and readership, and there is only so much discursiveness that a book can adequately explore. Hence, the next chapters exclusively focused on Calcutta.

The second chapter explored the mediatisation of the public's attachment to cricket. It pondered the appropriate questions to ask of the primary sources to review the illusion of textual mimesis. The reading of sources is an important part of understanding cricket's community of sentiment since the agenda of newspapers and periodicals alternated between decades, change of ownership and editorship, and narrative agency of journalists. The sources hardly allow for an examination of the function of individual spectators partly owing to the difficulty in testing authenticity and primarily since it was only in a group context and an aggregated perspective that singular routines made sense as part of a public history. Nevertheless, press reports highlighted the instrumentality of journalists as actors in the process of popularising cricket. The chapter did not inspect the reflexive awareness and careers of individual journalists and authors, preferring to place them next to their readers as part of the sporting public.

In the third chapter, narratives of the people's craving for the Eden Gardens and match tickets illuminate how the press constructed the cricket follower. The chronicles of the agonies and ecstasies of potential spectators elicited a multitude of responses from the readers – a testimony about how the attributes of narration serviced the culture of cricket as a public pursuit. The mediation of the ticket crisis was a double bind for the press as its attention to detail was simultaneously admired by readers and accused of encouraging frenzied behaviour. The mediated descriptions of spectators, sedimented in public memory over the years, created a continuous cultural narrative. A match at the Eden Gardens was a locally enacted national phenomenon – a public ceremony of Bengali and Indian sensibilities. In the form of international cricket, Bengali culture performed its conflicts with wider forces of identity in the nation. This social drama enabled the people of Bengal to define and contest, rationally and irrationally, the ways in which the state and the nation sought to control public activities. This public collective kindled a growing sense of cultural identity that resonated with Bengali insularity rather than provincialism.

The exploration into the correlated public spheres of politicians and politicised civilians in the fourth chapter yielded a rich discourse of the dialectic of identity. It showed Indian and Bengali politicians to have been involved in cricket as patrons and players irrespective of their class and political position. The CPI(M) in particular set aside its ideological incompatibility with the bourgeois mode of ticket acquisition, celebration and commodity consumption. Although it transcended the tyranny of theory, by surrendering to populist politics it emerged more as an opportunist than a nonconformist group. The non-selection of cricketers from West Bengal in the Indian national team proved to be an affective crossroads of local, insular and dissident sentiments, which contradicted the universalism shown by Bengali authors when constructing a tradition for cricket in the state. The allegations of discrimination practised by national cricket selectors which were coextensive with Bengal's complaints against the nation demonstrated the vulnerability of nationalism in contrast with provincial-cultural citizenship. The CPI(M) turned a new leaf in 2006 by protesting in parliament against Sourav Ganguly's sacking from the India team, threatening to reconsider its support for the government unless the cricketer was reinstated. Seldom were the performances of administrative and cultural politics so seamlessly integrated and subnational identity discursively apportioned for the sake of sport as in the context of Bengal cricket.

The book took a closer look at the communities of sentiment by mapping the performance and perception of gendered bodies in the cricket gallery. The mediation of the misunderstood and violated representative space of female following extended the question of the press's impact on the making of subjecthood. Considered out of place by a group of men and women, female spectatorship became a topic of intense discussion in the press. Initially, the female cricket followers were challenged to prove their knowledge of the game. The test soon turned out to be a hoax, however, as the disputers had already objectified feminine subjectivity in their own terms. Whether or not the press influenced the negative attitude towards female spectators by exaggerating the latter's deficiencies is a moot question. The shifting sand of press reports illustrates, despite all the circumlocution, how the mediatised inspection of female spectatorship constituted its objects in terms relevant to Calcutta's cultural specificities. It is tempting to conceptualise the image of female cricket followers as easily manipulable, dependent as they were on the rhetorical provenance of authors. However, subversion being a necessary condition of power, some women claimed their ground by strategically and self-consciously articulating their standpoints. Although it was evident from the gender dialectic that possession of more resources did not necessarily empower one public to prevail over another, the lack of a proper dialogue meant that the medium of representation mostly acted as a one-way mirror of social relationships.

The discussion of four incidents of crowd disorder and their transitory effects on the public in the final chapter brought out several layers of internal contradiction in the sports press. The common aspect of the mediatisation of the disturbances in the 1960s was the tendency of the sports press to maintain a consistent political approach, a highly subjective distribution of blame, and strong justification of public action. The letters to the editor showed that the stand against the infraction of spectatorial rights earned the press the public's admiration and the respect of an arbiter. The internal uniformity of the sports press was arguably replaced by a more decentred sort of journalism throughout the intermediate period before the next spurt of spectator violence in the 1990s. The complexity of the spectators grew enormously in the meantime, leading to the introduction of new subjectivities such as those formed around communal tension and obdurate nationalism. The vicissitude of cricket was both reflected and aggrandised in press reports. The mediation of the riots in the 1990s exhibited the often-overlooked facet of journalists both participating in and representing the sporting public. It was regular for journalists to produce different, and often conflicting, narratives while surrogating public sentiments into texts.

The book identified several underexplored issues as avenues of future research. Analysis of the setting and narrative structure of cricket fiction, especially of the sport's significance in the life of the protagonist and other people, would enrich the understanding of cricket in everyday life. Moti Nandi's novels have the capacity to illuminate the mundane interplay of cricket and society outside the context of international cricket matches. In-depth studies of cricket broadcast on radio and television offer other possible openings to extend our knowledge of the quotidian. This book deliberated the problems of reading indeterminate sources, stressing the conflation of reality and appearance in media texts and the need to consider these as more than sprouts of information. Taking an aggregated approach to the content of press reports and other texts, the chapters have revealed the contest for legitimacy and authenticity among contending opinions. An interpretation involving analysis of the organisation, function and performance of language, or development of a taxonomy of writings, would certainly enrich future research.

An examination of representation must synthetically analyse discourses to illustrate its context. Examining the social life of media narratives in South Asia in around mid-twentieth century is arduous in the absence of definitive data on audience and reception. This book circumvented the problem by taking the cultural theorist Stuart Hall's approach to consumption as part of circulation.[3] The importance of ethnography cannot be ignored while pondering the question of what, why and how some agents of consumption observe others perform the very same functions in an utterly different manner. While this book focused on the internal diversity of production and circulation of discourses, it recommends a closer reading of consumption.

Likewise, it is necessary to study the strategic innovations in cricket's marketing in the media as a consumer item and the representation of cricket and cricketers in advertisements of consumer commodities such as cosmetics, apparels, beverages, transport vehicles, insurance plans, watches, television sets, telephone networks, and so on. The processes of cultural self-projections, nationalism and glocalisation woven into advertisements reveal much about the preferences of cricket fans. As media texts, these advertisements construct elegant images of the body and consumer items, and propagate methods to optimise the efficiency of both. The shifts in the representation of the body images of cricketers explain the course of cricket's discourse over the years. Whereas some advertisements portray cricketers as sophisticated, alert and yet only moderately aggressive male figures, some others epitomise the disembodiment of these paradigms from a cricketer. An assessment of the context of publication, syndication and translation of the captions, use of cricketers as models, and possible reception would supplement the present reading of cricket's consumption through press reports.

Many journalists such as Raju Bharatan have described the Calcutta spectators as Bengali and emotional while writing about their passion for cricket.[4] In contrast with the characterisation of cricket as a cultural sector dominated by Bengalis, this book showed how misplaced this ethnic determinism is, considering the involvement of non-Bengalis as players, administrators, spectators and black marketeers. A study of the Hindi newspapers published from Calcutta would reveal the life worlds of non-Bengali journalists, readers and spectators, adding another group of actors alongside Bengalis and non-Indians into the cricket cauldron. The Bengali press mocked the city's non-Bengalis as uncultured people who were unable to understand cricket, caricaturing them as discussing business ventures without paying attention to cricket and disrupting the gallery's decorum with their penchant for mindless music and dance. A consideration of this angle would facilitate a better understanding of the social history of ethnic minority communities in a state.

The search for patterns in the maze of meanings and attitudes, iconography and sociability, and agency and structure led this book's analysis of the complex of actions surrounding a cultural form. Cricket assembled people, who developed practices of appropriation, which in turn intensified through repetition and evolved into cultures. Despite the global media's difference in opinion about the character of cricket's public culture, specifically in reference to the distinction around Test and ODI cricket, certain value judgements such as cricket being a 'gentleman's game' retain their currency. Though the media acknowledges the hybridity of sporting encounters, it understands its full complexity only to an extent. The overlap of media and publics with state and non-state politics has for long informed cricket's panoply of meanings. Indeed, this ensemble convergence shaped public culture, or, as the book shows, how Calcutta became experienced as a distinct cultural region.

NOTES

1. Sunil Bose, 'Rabon Run Out', *SKA*, 1980, 104–23.
2. Soumya Bhattacharya, *You Must Like Cricket? Memoirs of an Indian Cricket Fan* (London: Yellow Jersey Press, 2006), 172.
3. Stuart Hall, 'Encoding/Decoding', in *Culture, Media, Language*, ed. Stuart Hall, Dorothy Hobson, Andrew Lowe and Paul Willis, 128–38 (London: Hutchinson, 1980).
4. Raju Bharatan, *Indian Cricket: The Vital Phase* (New Delhi: Vikas, 1977), 147.

Select Bibliography

PUBLISHED OFFICIAL RECORDS

Crime in India: 1960, the National Crime Records Bureau.
Proceedings of the West Bengal Legislative Assembly 57 (November 1974).

UNPUBLISHED OFFICIAL RECORDS

Minutes of the Imperial Cricket Conference, 28 July 1952. MCC Archives.
Report of the Commission of Inquiry, prepared by Justice Kamalesh Chandra Sen,
    1967. Copy in author's personal collection.

NEWSPAPERS

Aajkal
Amrita Bazar Patrika
Anandabazar Patrika
Bartaman
Daily Mercury
Dainik Basumati
Ganashakti
Hindustan Standard
Hindustan Times
Jugantar
New York Times
Sunday Times

Sydney Morning Herald
The Guardian
The Observer
The Scotsman
The Star
The Telegraph
The Times
Times of India
Washington Post

PERIODICALS

Amrita
Amrita Bazar Patrika Sunday Magazine
Desh
Hindustan Standard Annual Number
Hindustan Standard Puja Annual
Indian Cricket
Illustrated News
Illustrated Weekly of India
Khelar Asar
Outlook
Sandesh
Saptahik Basumati
Sharadiya Dainik Statesman
Sharadiya Khela
Sharadiya Khelar Asar
Sportsweek
Sportsworld
Telegraph Magazine

PRIMARY SOURCES

FICTION

Anand, Mulk Raj. *Two Leaves and a Bud*. New Delhi: Arnold Associates, 1981 [1937].

Bhattacharya, Suchitra. *Nil Ghurni* (Blue Whirlpool). Calcutta: Ananda Publishers, 2000.

Brahmanyabhusan and Kshama Bandopadhyay. 'Kabigurur Cricket Khela' (The Poet Laureate Plays Cricket). In Sankariprasad Basu, *Cricket Omnibus II*, 370–75. Calcutta: Mandal Book House, 1976.

Camus, Albert. *The Outsider*. Harmondsworth: Penguin, 2000 [1942].

Chakravarti, Nirendranath. *The King without Clothes*. Translated by Sukanta Chaudhuri. New Delhi: Sahitya Akademi, 2010 [1989].

Chaudhuri, Amit. *A New World*. London: Picador, 2000.

———. *Calcutta: Two Years in the City*. New York: Alfred A. Knopf, 2013.

Desai, Anita. *Clear Light of Day*. New York: Mariner, 2000 [1980].

Deshpande, Shashi. *3 Novels*. New Delhi: Puffin, 2006.

Frater, Alexander. *Chasing the Monsoon: A Modern Pilgrimage Through India*. London: Picador, 2005.

Gangopadhyay, Sunil. *Sei Samay* (Those Days). Calcutta: Ananda Publishers, 1988.

Ghosh, Amitav. *The Shadow Lines*. London: John Murray, 2011 [1988].

Ghosh, Gour Kishor. *Brajadar Gulpo Samagra* (Collected Stories of Brajada). Calcutta: Ananda Publishers, 1996.

Hughes, Thomas. *Tom Brown's Schooldays*. Oxford: Oxford University Press, 1989.

Jatindranath Sengupta. 'Ghumer Ghore' (In Trance). In *Jatindranath Sengupter Srestha Kabita*, edited by Sushanta Basu, 21. Calcutta: Bharabi, 2001.

Lapierre, Dominique. *City of Joy*. London: Arrow, 1992 [1986].

Majumdar, Samaesh. *Kalpurush* (Orion). Calcutta: Ananda Publishers, 1985.

Mehta, Suketu. *Maximum City: Bombay Lost and Found*. New York: Vintage, 2005.

Mujtaba Ali, Syed. 'Obishyashya' (Unbelievable). In *Syed Mujtaba Ali Rachanabali V*, 1–107. Calcutta: Mitra O Ghosh, 1954.

Mukhopadhyay, Shirshendu. *Golmal* (Trouble). Calcutta: Dey's Publishing, 2002 [1989].

———. *Gosain Baganer Bhut* (Ghost of the Gosain Garden). Calcutta: Ananda Publishers, 2005 [1979].

Nandi, Moti. *Nanida Not Out*, in *Dashti Kishor Upanyas*, 9–49. Calcutta: Ananda Publishers, 2000 [1973].

———. 'Shot, Cut, Ebong Nanida' (Shot, Cut, and Nanida). *Saradiya Khela* 1987, 10–24.

Pinter, Harold. *Collected Poems and Prose*. New York: Grove Press, 1996.

Roy, Falguni. 'Tinti Kabita' (Three Poems). In *Hungry Generationer Srastader Khudhartha Sankalan*, edited by Saileshwar Ghosh, 551–52. New Delhi: Sahitya Academy, 1995.

Rushdie, Salman. *The Moor's Last Sigh*. London: Vintage, 1996.

———. *The Satanic Verses*. London: Vintage, 1988.

Sankar. *Kata Ajanare* (So Much Unknown). Calcutta: New Age, 1954.

Seth, Vikram. *A Suitable Boy*. London: Phoenix House, 1993.

Sinha, Kabita. 'Deho' (Body), translated by Subhas Saha. In *Women Writing in India: The Twentieth Century*, edited by Susie Tharu and K. Lalita, 332. New York: Feminist Press at the City University of New York, 1993.

Subrahmanyan, K. V. V. 'In Defence of Cricket". In *'A Breathless Hush ...': The MCC Anthology of Cricket Verse*, edited by David Rayvern Allen, 143. London: Methuen, 2004.

Wordsworth, William. 'Composed in the Valley, Near Dover, on the Day of Landing'. *Poems II*, 208. London: Longman, 1815.

AUTOBIOGRAPHIES AND BIOGRAPHIES

Ali, Mushtaq. *Cricket Delightful*. New Delhi: Rupa, 1960.

Baden-Powell, Robert. *Indian Memories*. London: Herbert Jenkins, 1915.

Bhattacharya, Soumya. *You Must Like Cricket? Memoirs of an Indian Cricket Fan*. London: Yellow Jersey Press, 2006.

Bose, Gopal. *Soja Byate* (Straight Bat). Calcutta: Sristi, 2001.

Brookes, Christopher, *His Own Man: The Life of Neville Cardus*. London: Methuen, 1985.

Cardus, Neville. *Autobiography*. London: Hamish Hamilton, 1984 [1947].

Chakrabarty, Saroj. *With West Bengal Chief Ministers: Memoirs 1962 to 1977*. Calcutta: Orient Longman, 1978.

Chaudhuri, Nirad C. *Thy Hand, Great Anarch! India, 1921–1952*. London: Hogarth Press, 1990.

Compton, Denis. *End of an Innings*. Calcutta: Rupa, 1962.

Cowdrey, Colin. *MCC: The Autobiography of a Cricketer*. London: Hodder & Stoughton, 1976.

Denness, Mike. *I Declare*. London: Arthur Barker, 1977.

Doshi, Dilip. *Spin Punch*. Calcutta: Rupa, 1991.

Gavaskar, Sunil. *Runs n' Ruins*. New Delhi: Rupa, 1984.

———. *Sunny Days*. Calcutta: Rupa, 1976.

Guha Neyogi, Runu. *Sada Ami Kalo Ami* (Myself in Black and White). Calcutta: Jinia Publishers, 1997.

Grass, Günter. *Show Your Tongue*. Translated by John E. Woods. London: Secker & Warburg, 1989.

Howat, Gerald. *Len Hutton: A Biography*. London: Kingswood Press, 1988.

Kanhai, Rohan. *Blasting for Runs*. Calcutta: Rupa, 1977.

Lele, Jaywant Y. *I Was There: Memoirs of a Cricket Administrator*. Mumbai: Marine Sports, 2011.

Mahmood, Fazal, with Asif Sohail. *From Dawn to Dusk: Autobiography of a Pakistan Cricket Legend*. Karachi: Oxford University Press, 2003.

Mallett, Ashley. *One of a Kind: The Doug Walters Story*. Crows Nest, NSW: Allen & Unwin, 2008.

———. *Rowdy*. Blackwood: Lynton, 1973.

Mitra, Ashok. *Apila Chapila*. Calcutta: Ananda Publishers, 2003.

Mukherjee, Sujit. *Autobiography of an Unknown Cricketer*. New Delhi: Ravi Dayal, 1996.

Robinson, Ray. *The Wildest Tests*. Sydney: Cassell, 1979.

Sarbadhikary, Berry. *My World of Cricket*. Calcutta: Cricket Library, 1964.

———, ed. *Presenting Indian Cricket*. Calcutta: A. Mukherjee, 1946.

Sobers, Garry. *Twenty Years at the Top*. London: Macmillan, 1988.

Thompson, Harry. *Penguins Stopped Play: Eleven Village Cricketers Take on the World*. London: John Murray, 2006.

Walters, Doug. *The Doug Walters Story*. Adelaide: Rigby, 1981.

MISCELLANEOUS

Basu, Ajay. *Akashe Cricket Bani* (Cricket on the Radio). Calcutta: Falguni Prakashani, 1971.

———. *Phire Phire Chai* (Looking Back). Calcutta: Aajkal, 2005.

———. *Hater Bat Hatiyar* (Bat Becomes a Weapon). Calcutta: Ruprekha, 1969.

———. *Math Theke Bolchhi* (From the Field). Calcutta: Ruprekha, 1968.

Basu, Sankariprasad. *Ball Pore Bat Nare* (The Clash of Ball and Bat). Calcutta: Karuna Prakashani, 1962.

———. *Cricket Sundar Cricket* (Cricket Lovely Cricket). In *Cricket Omnibus II*. Calcutta: Mandal Book House, 1976 [1963].

———. *Edene Shiter Dupur* (Winter Afternoon at Eden). Calcutta: Bookland, 1960.

———. *Not Out*. In *Cricket Omnibus II*, 84–262. Calcutta: Mandal Book House, 1976.

———. *Ramaniya Cricket* (Beautiful Cricket). Calcutta: Karuna Prakashani, 1961.

———. *Sara Diner Khela* (The Day's Cricket). In *Cricket Omnibus II*, 264–375. Calcutta: Mandal Book House, 1976.

Bharatan, Raju. *Indian Cricket: The Vital Phase*. New Delhi: Vikas, 1977.

Bhattacharya, Gautam. *Dadatantra* (The Big Brother). Calcutta: Deep Prakashan, 2009.

Bhattacharya, Rahul. *Pundits from Pakistan: On Tour with India, 2003–04.* New Delhi: Picador, 2005.

Cardus, Neville. *English Cricket.* London: Prion, 1997.

Dasgupta, Amitabho, *Bhalo Acho, Calcutta?* (How Are You, Calcutta?). Calcutta: Dey's Publishing, 2000.

Dasgupta, Biplab. 'Tin Kingbadanti' (Three Legends). In *Kolkata Betar, 1927–1977,* edited by Bhabesh Das and Prabhatkumar Das, 487–94. Calcutta: Purbanchal Sanskriti Kendra, 2011.

Downing, Clement. *A Compendious History of the Indian Wars.* London: T. Cooper, 1737.

Dutta, Amal. *Ghera Math Chharano Gallery* (Enclosed Ground, Unbound Gallery). Calcutta: Bishwabani Prakashan, 1972.

Dutta, Jayanta. *Rupasi Eden-er Rupasi Cricket* (Beautiful Cricket at Beautiful Eden). Calcutta: Karuna Prakashani, 1964.

Gangopadhyay, Narayan. 'Paribarik Cricket' (Cricket in the Family). In *Sunandor Journal,* 487–88. Calcutta: Mitra O Ghosh, 2002.

Gupta, Sujoy. *Seventeen Ninety-two: A History of the Calcutta Cricket and Football Club.* Calcutta: CCFC, 2002.

Haigh, Gideon. *Spheres of Influence: Writings on Cricket and Its Discontents.* London: Simon & Schuster, 2011 [2010].

Hoult, Nick, ed. *The Daily Telegraph Book of Cricket.* London: Aurum Press, 2009.

Lohia, Rammanohar. *Language.* Hyderabad: Rammanohar Lohia Samata Vidyalaya Nyas, 1986.

Lucas, E. V. 'The English Game'. In *Cricket All His Life,* 213–15. London: Pavilion Library, 1989 [1950].

Mukherjee, P. L. 'Cricket in Calcutta: Its Growth and Development'. In *Indian Cricket through the Ages: A Reader,* edited by Boria Majumdar, 275–81. New Delhi: Oxford University Press, 2005.

Mukherjee, Sujit. *Between Indian Wickets.* New Delhi: Orient Paperbacks, 1976.

Nandi, Moti. 'Cricket Ke Mukti Dewa Hok' (Liberate Cricket). In *Khelasangraha,* 38–40. Calcutta: Deep Prakashan, 2015.

Preston, Hubert. 'From Russia with a Dropped Catch', in *Wisden Cricketers' Almanack 1951.* In *The Essential Wisden: An Anthology of 150 Years of Wisden Cricketers' Almanack,* edited by John Stern and Marcus Williams, 40–41. London: Bloomsbury, 2013.

Raha, Sujata et al., eds. *Sankariprasad: Byakti O Sristi* (Sankariprasad: The Man and His Creation). Calcutta: Sankariprasad Basu Sambardhana Samiti, 2000.

Ramaswami, N. S. *Winter of Content*. Madras: Swadesmitran Limited, 1967.

Rice, Jonathan, ed. *Wisden on India: An Anthology*. New Delhi: Penguin, 2011.

Sarkar, Sabyasachi, *Lords Theke Taunton* (From Lords to Taunton). Calcutta: Ananda Publishers, 2000.

———. *Sobar Sachin Amader Sourav* (Everyone's Sachin, Our Sourav). Calcutta: Deep Prakashan, 2001.

Sengupta, Achintya Kumar, *Mriga Nei Mrigaya* (A Hunt without Deer). Calcutta: Anandadhara, 1965.

INTERVIEWS

Anonymous cricketer, 28 June 2013, Kolkata.

Chakraborty, Ajita. 26 October 2011, Kolkata.

Mallik, Soumyen. 30 June 2011, Kolkata.

Sinha, Ila. 1 July 2011, Kolkata.

SELECT SECONDARY SOURCES

A.M. 'Calcutta Diary'. *Economic and Political Weekly* 9, no. 50 (14 December 1974): 2041–42.

Addy, Premen and Ibne Azad. 'Politics and Culture in Bengal'. *New Left Review* 1, no. 79 (May–June 1973): 71–112.

Agur, Colin. 'A Foreign Field No Longer: India, the IPL, and the Global Business of Cricket'. *Journal of Asian and African Studies* 48, no. 5 (2013): 541–56.

Ahmed, Akbar S. *Postmodernism and Islam: Predicament and Promise*. London: Routledge, 2004.

Allison, Lincoln. 'Sport and Politics'. In *The Politics of Sport*, edited by Lincoln Allison, 1–26. Manchester: Manchester University Press, 1986.

———. 'The Changing Context of Sporting Life'. In *The Changing Politics of Sport*, edited by Lincoln Allison, 1–14. Manchester: Manchester University Press, 1993.

Anagol, Padma. *The Emergence of Feminism in India, 1850–1920*. Aldershot: Ashgate, 2005.

Anand, Sirivayan. *Brahmans and Cricket: Lagaan's Millenial Purana and Other Myths*. Chennai: Navayana, 2003.

Anderson, Benedict. *Imagined Communities: Reflections on the Origins and Spread of Nationalism*. London: Verso, 1991.

Ankersmit, Frank. *Meaning, Truth, and Reference in Historical Representation*. Ithaca, NY: Cornell University Press, 2012.

Ansari, Sarah and William Gould. *Boundaries of Belonging: Localities, Citizenship and Rights in India and Pakistan*. Cambridge: Cambridge University Press, 2020.

Appadurai, Arjun. 'Disjuncture and Difference in the Global Cultural Economy'. *Public Culture* 2, no. 2 (1990): 1–23.

———. 'Playing with Modernity: The Decolonization of Cricket'. In *Modernity at Large: Cultural Dimensions of Globalization*, 89–113. Minneapolis: University of Minnesota Press, 1996.

Appiah, Kwame Anthony. 'Is the Post- in Postmodernism the Post- in Postcolonial?' *Critical Inquiry* 17, no. 2 (1991): 336–57.

Archetti, Eduardo P. 'The Meaning of Sport in Anthropology: A View from Latin America'. *European Review of Latin American and Caribbean Studies* 65 (1998): 91–103.

Armstrong, Gary. *Football Hooligans: Knowing the Score*. Oxford: Berg, 1998.

Arumugam, M. *Socialist Thought in India: The Contribution of Rammanohar Lohia*. New Delhi: Sterling Publications, 1978.

Bag, Kheya. 'Red Bengal's Rise and Fall'. *New Left Review* 70 (2011): 69–98.

Bairner, Alan. 'National Sports and National Landscapes: In Defence of Primordialism'. *National Identities* 11, no. 3 (2009): 223–39.

———. 'The Leicester School and the Study of Football Hooliganism'. *Sport in Society* 9, no. 4 (2006): 583–98.

Bala, Rajan. *The Covers Are Off: A Socio-Historical Study of Indian Cricket*. New Delhi: Rupa, 2004.

Bale, John. 'Anti-Sport: Victorian Examples from Oxbridge'. *Sport in History* 34, no. 1 (2014): 34–48.

———. *Anti-Sport Sentiments in Literature: Batting for the Opposition*. London and New York: Routledge, 2007.

———. *Landscapes of Modern Sport*. Leicester: Leicester University Press, 1994.

———. *Sport, Space and the City*. London and New York: Routledge, 1993.

———. *Sports Geography*, 2nd ed. London and New York: Routledge, 2003.

Bandyopadhyay, Kausik. 'Feel Good, Goodwill and India's Friendship Tour of Pakistan, 2004: Cricket, Politics and Diplomacy in Twenty-First-Century India'. *International Journal of the History of Sport* 25, no. 12 (2008): 1654–70.

————. *Scoring Off the Field: Football Culture in Bengal 1911–80*. New Delhi: Routledge, 2011.

Banerjee, Himani. 'Attired in Virtue: The Discourse on Shame and Clothing of the *Bhadramahila* in Colonial Bengal'. In *From the Seams of History: Essays on Indian Women*, edited by Bharati Ray, 67–106. New Delhi: Oxford University Press, 1995.

Banerjee, Sikata. 'Chaste Like Sita, Fierce Like Durga: Indian Women in Politics'. In *India's 2004 Elections: Grass-roots and National Perspectives*, edited by Ramashray Roy and Paul Wallace, 34–57. New Delhi: Sage, 2007.

Banerjee, Sudeshna. 'Fleshing Out Mandira: Hemming in the Women's Constituency in Cricket'. *International Journal of the History of Sport* 21, nos. 3–4 (2004): 478–501.

Banerjee, Sumanta. *India's Simmering Revolution: The Naxalite Uprising*. London: Zed Books, 1980.

Bannerji, Himani. *Inventing Subjects: Studies in Hegemony, Patriarchy and Colonialism*. New Delhi: Tulika, 2001.

Barlow, Tani E. 'Introduction: On Colonial Modernity'. In *Formations of Colonial Modernity in East Asia*, edited by Tani E. Barlow, 1–20. Durham, NC: Duke University Press, 1997.

Baruah, Sanjib. *India against Itself: Assam and the Politics of Nationality*. Philadelphia: University of Pennsylvania Press, 1999.

Basu, Amrita. 'Hindu Women's Activism in India and the Questions It Raises'. In *Appropriating Gender: Women's Activism and Politicized Religion in South Asia*, edited by Patricia Jeffrey and Amrita Basu, 167–84. London: Routledge, 1998.

Basu, Sajal. *Politics of Violence: A Case Study of West Bengal*. Calcutta: Minerva Publishers, 1982.

————. *West Bengal: The Violent Years*. Calcutta: Prachi Publications, 1974.

Basu, Srimati. 'Describing the Body: The Writing of Sex and Gender Identity for the Contemporary Bengali Woman'. In *Confronting the Body: The Politics of Physicality in Colonial and Post-Colonial India*, edited by Jim Mills and Satadru Sen, 146–61. London: Anthem Press, 2004.

Bateman, Anthony. 'Performing Imperial Masculinities: The Discourse and Practice of Cricket'. In *Performing Masculinity*, edited by Rainer Emig and Antony Rowland, 78–94. Basingstoke: Palgrave Macmillan, 2010.

————. *Cricket, Literature and Culture: Symbolising the Nation, Destabilising Empire*. Farnham: Ashgate, 2009.

Bayat, Asef. 'Cairo's Poor: Dilemmas of Survival and Solidarity'. *Middle East Report* no. 202 (Winter 1997): 2–12.

———. 'From "Dangerous Classes" to "Quiet Rebels": Politics of the Urban Subaltern in the Global South'. *International Sociology* 15, no. 3 (2000): 533–57.

———. 'Un-civil Society: The Politics of the 'Informal People''. *Third World Quarterly* 18, no. 1 (1997): 53–72.

Bayly, C. A. *Recovering Liberties: Indian Thought in the Age of Liberalism and Empire.* Cambridge: Cambridge University Press, 2012.

Benjamin, Walter. 'Paris, Capital of the Nineteenth Century'. In *The Arcades Project*, translated by Howard Eiland and Kevin McLaughlin, 8–9. Cambridge, MA: Belknapp Press, 1999.

———. *Reflections: Essays, Aphorisms, Autobiographical Writings.* Translated by Edmund Jephcott. New York: Schocken Books, 1986.

———. 'The Work of Art in the Age of Mechanical Reproduction'. In *Illuminations*, translated by Harry Zohn, 217–51. New York: Schocken Books, 1968.

Berkhofer, Robert. *Beyond the Great Story: History as Text and Discourse.* Cambridge, MA: Harvard University Press, 1995.

Bernstein, Alina and Neil Blain, eds. *Sport, Media and Culture: Global and Local Dimensions.* London: Routledge, 2002.

Bhaumik, Dhruba Jyoti. *Political Movements in India (A Study of the United Front Experiment in West Bengal).* Delhi: Anmol Publications, 1987.

Birley, Derek. *A Social History of English Cricket.* London: Aurum Press, 1999.

———. *Land of Sport and Glory: Sport and British Society 1887–1910.* Manchester: Manchester University Press, 1995.

Birrell, Susan and John W. Loy. 'Media Sport: Hot and Cool'. *International Review for the Sociology of Sport* 14, no. 5 (1979): 5–18.

Blackburn, Kevin, *War, Sport and the Anzac Tradition.* Basingstoke: Palgrave Macmillan, 2016.

Blain, Neil, Raymond Boyle and Hugh O'Donnell, eds. *Sport and National Identity in the European Media.* Leicester: Leicester University Press, 1993.

Booth, Douglas. 'Sport History: Modern and Postmodern'. In *Making Sport History: Disciplines, Identities and the Historiography of Sport*, edited by Pascal Delheye, 71–99. London and New York: Routledge, 2014.

Borch, Christian. *The Politics of Crowds: An Alternative History of Sociology.* Cambridge: Cambridge University Press, 2012.

Borthwick, Meredith. *Changing Role of Women in Bengal 1849–1905.* Princeton: Princeton University Press, 1984.

Bose, Brinda. 'Modernity, Globality, Sexuality, and the City: A Reading of Indian Cinema'. *Global South* 2, no. 1 (2008): 35–58.

Bose, Mihir, *The Magic of Indian Cricket: Cricket and Society in India*. London: Routledge, 2006.

———. *A History of Indian Cricket*. New Delhi: Rupa, 1990.

Bose, Sumantra, *Transforming India: Challenges to the World's Largest Democracy*. Cambridge, MA: Harvard University Press. 2013.

Bourdieu, Pierre. *In Other Words: Essays towards a Reflexive Sociology*. Translated by Matthew Adamson. Stanford, CA: Stanford University Press, 1990.

Boyle, Raymond and Richard Haynes, *Power Play: Sport, the Media and Popular Culture*, 2nd ed. Edinburgh: Edinburgh University Press, 2009.

Brass, Paul. *The Politics of India since Independence*. Cambridge: Cambridge University Press, 1990.

Brohm, Jean-Marie. *Sport: A Prison of Measured Time*. Translated by Ian Fraser. London: Ink Links, 1978.

Brookes, Rod, *Representing Sport*. London: Arnold, 2002.

Burton, Antoinette. *At the Heart of the Empire: Indians and the Colonial Encounter in Late-Victorian Britain*. Berkeley: University of California Press, 1998.

———. *Burdens of History: British Feminists, Indian Women, and Imperial Culture, 1865–1915*. Chapel Hill: University of North Carolina Press, 1994.

———, ed. *Gender, Sexuality and Colonial Modernities*. London and New York: Routledge, 1999.

Carey, James W. *Communication as Culture: Essays on Media and Society*. Boston: Unwin Hyman, 1989.

Cashman, Richard. 'Cricket and Colonialism: Colonial Hegemony and Indigenous Subversion?' In *Pleasure, Profit, and Proselytism: British Culture and Sport at Home and Abroad 1700–1914*, edited by J. A. Mangan, 258–72. London: Frank Cass, 1988.

———. *Patrons, Players and the Crowd: The Phenomenon of Indian Cricket*. New Delhi: Orient Longman, 1980.

Caudwell, Jayne. 'Femme-fatale: Re-thinking the Femme-inine'. In *Sport, Sexualities and Queer/Theory*, edited by Jayne Caudwell, 145–58. London and New York: Routledge, 2006.

Chakrabarti, Rajesh, ed. *The Other India: Realities of an Emerging Power*. New Delhi: Sage, 2009.

Chakrabarty, Dipesh. 'The Difference – Deferral of (A) Colonial Modernity: Public Debates on Domesticity in British Bengal'. *History Workshop Journal* 36, no. 1 (Autumn 1993): 1–34.

———. *Habitations of Modernity: Essays in the Wake of Subaltern Studies*. Chicago: The University of Chicago Press, 2002.

———. '"In the Name of Politics": Democracy and the Power of the Multitude in India'. In *From the Colonial to the Postcolonial: India and Pakistan in Transition*, edited by Dipesh Chakrabarty, Rochona Majumdar and Andrew Sartori, 31–54. New Delhi: Oxford University Press, 2007.

———. 'Modernity and Ethnicity in India: A History for the Present'. *Economic and Political Weekly* 30, no. 52 (1995): 3373–80.

Chakraborty, Abin. 'The Peasant Armed: Bengal, Vietnam and Transnational Solidarities in Utpal Dutt's *Invincible Vietnam*'. In *Cultures of Decolonisation: Transnational Productions and Practices, 1945–70*, edited by Ruth Cragge and Claire Wintle, 109–25. Manchester; Manchester University Press, 2016.

Chakraborty, Paulomi. 'The Refugee Woman and the New Woman: (En) gendering Middle-Class Bengali Modernity and the City in Satyajit Ray's *Mahanagar* (*The Big City* 1963)'. In *Being Bengali: At Home and In the World*, edited by Mridula Nath Chakraborty, 69–91. London and New York: Routledge, 2014.

Chakroborty, Chandrima. 'Subaltern Studies, Bollywood and Lagaan'. *Economic and Political Weekly* 38, no. 19 (2003): 1879–84.

Chanda, Asok Kumar. *Federalism in India: A Study of Union–State Relations*. London: Allen & Unwin, 1965.

Chartier, Roger, *Cultural History: Between Practices and Representations*. Translated by Lydia Cochrane. London: Polity, 1988.

———. 'Intellectual History or Sociocultural History? The French Trajectories'. In *Modem European Intellectual History: Reappraisals and New Perspectives*, edited by Dominick LaCapra and Steven L. Kaplan, 13–46. Ithaca, NY: Cornell University Press, 1982.

Chatterjee, Indrani, ed. *Unfamiliar Relations: Family and History in South Asia*. Ranikhet: Permanent Black, 2004.

Chatterjee, Jyotiprasad and Suprio Basu. *Left Front and After: Understanding the Dynamics of Poriborton in West Bengal*. New Delhi: Sage, 2020.

Chatterjee, Partha. *The Nation and Its Fragments: Colonial and Postcolonial Histories*. Princeton: Princeton University Press, 1993.

Chattopadhyay, Swati. *Representing Calcutta: Modernity, Nationalism, and the Colonial Uncanny*. London: Routledge, 2005.

———. *Unlearning the City: Infrastructure in a New Optical Field*. Minneapolis and London: University of Minnesota Press, 2012.

Chaudhuri, Rosinka. 'Modernity at Home: The Nationalization of the Indian Drawing Room, 1830–1930'. In *Interpreting Homes in South Asian Literature*, edited by Malashri Lal and Sukrita Paul Kumar, 221–40. New Delhi: Pearson Longman, 2007.

Chaudhuri, Sukanta. 'The Playing Fields of Eden'. In *View from Calcutta*, 175–78. New Delhi: Chronicle Books, 2002.

Chibber, Vivek. *Locked in Place: State-Building and Late Industrialization in India*. Princeton: Princeton University Press, 2003.

Cohen, Benjamin. 'Networks of Sociability: Women's Clubs in Colonial and Postcolonial India'. *Frontiers: A Journal of Women's Studies* 30, no. 3 (2009): 169–95.

Colley, Linda. *Britons: Forging the Nation 1707–1837*. London: Pimlico, 1994.

Collier, David. 'Translating Quantitative Methods for Qualitative Researchers: The Case of Selection Bias'. *American Political Science Review* 89, no. 2 (1995): 461–66.

Collins, Tony. *Sport in Capitalist Society*. London: Routledge, 2013.

Connell, R. W. *Gender and Power*. Cambridge: Polity Press, 1987.

Cunningham Osborne, Anne and Danielle Sarver Coombs. *Female Fans of the NFL: Taking Their Place in the Stands*. New York and London: Routledge: 2016.

Daniel, W. Harrison and Scott P. Meyer. *Baseball and Richmond: A History of the Professional Game, 1884–2000*. Jefferson: McFarland & Co., 2003.

Das, Hari Hara and Sanjukta Mohaptra. *Centre–State Relations in India (A Study of Sub-national Aspirations)*. New Delhi: Ashish Publishing House, 1986.

Das, Suranjan. 'The Crowd in Calcutta Violence, 1907–1926'. In *Dissent and Consensus: Social Protest in Pre-Industrial Societies*, edited by Basudev Chattopadhyay, Hari S. Vasudevan and Rajat Kanta Ray, 233–72. Calcutta: K.P. Bagchi, 1989.

Dasgupta, Jishnu, 'Exploring Politics and Sports: Towards a Disaggregated Understanding'. In *People at Play: Sport, Culture, and Nationalism*, edited by Amitava Chatterjee, 51–85. Calcutta: Setu Prakashani, 2013.

———. 'Manufacturing Unison: Muslims, Hindus and Indians during the India–Pakistan Match'. In *Sport in South Asian Society: Past and Present*, edited by Boria Majumdar and J. A. Mangan, 239–48. London: Routledge, 2005.

Dasgupta, Probal. *The Otherness of English: India's Auntie's Tongue Syndrome*. New Delhi: Sage, 1993.

Dasgupta, Shamya. 'Sachin Almighty'. *Sport in Society* 16, no. 1 (2013): 33–44.

De Certeau, Michel, *The Practice of Everyday Life*. Translated by Steven Rendall. Berkeley: University of California Press, 1984.

Debord, Guy, *The Society of the Spectacle*. Translated by Donald Nicholson-Smith. New York: Zone Books, 1994.

Derné, Steve and Lisa Jadwin. 'Male Hindi Filmgoers' Gaze: An Ethnographic Interpretation of Gender Construction'. In *Urban Women in Contemporary India: A Reader*, edited by Rehana Ghadially, 46–62. New Delhi: Sage, 2007.

Derrida, Jacques. *Writing and Difference*. Translated by Alan Bass. London: Routledge and Kegan Paul, 1978.

Desai, Manali. 'Party Formation, Political Power, and the Capacity for Reform: Comparing Left Parties in Kerala and West Bengal, India'. *Social Forces* 80, no. 1 (2001): 37–60.

Dimeo, Paul. 'Cricket and the Misinterpretation of Indian Sports History'. *Historical Studies* 24 (2005): 98–111.

———. 'Sporting and the 'Civilizing Mission' in India'. In *Colonialism and Civilising Mission: Cultural Ideology in British India*, edited by Harald Fischer-Tiné and Michael Mann, 165–78. London: Anthem, 2004.

———. "Team Loyalty Splits the City into Two': Football, Ethnicity and Rivalry in Calcutta'. In *Fear and Loathing in World Football*, edited by Gary Armstrong and Richard Giulianotti, 105–18. Oxford: Berg, 2001.

———. "With Political Pakistan in the Offing …': Football and Communal Politics in South Asia, 1887–1947'. *Journal of Contemporary History* 38, no. 3 (2003): 377–94.

Dirks, Nicholas. *Castes of Mind: Colonialism and the Making of Modern India*. Princeton: Princeton University Press, 2001.

Dissanayake, Ellen. *Homo Aestheticus*. New York: Free Press, 1992.

Dodson, Michael and Brian Hatcher, eds. *Trans-Colonial Modernities in South Asia*. New York: Routledge, 2012.

Dolan, Jill. *The Feminist Spectator as Critic*, 2nd ed. Ann Arbor: The University of Michigan Press, 2012.

Donner, Henrike. 'Making Middle-Class Families in Calcutta'. In *Anthropologies of Class: Power, Practice, and Inequality*, edited by James G. Carrier and Don Kalb, 131–48. Cambridge: Cambridge University Press, 2015.

Dube, Saurabh and Ishita Banerjee-Dube, eds. *Unbecoming Modern: Colonialism, Modernity, Colonial Modernities*. New Delhi: Social Science Press, 2006.

Dunn, Carrie. *Female Football Fans: Community, Identity and Sexism*. Basingstoke: Palgrave Macmillan, 2014.

Dunning, Eric. *Sport Matters: Sociological Studies of Sport, Violence and Civilization*. London: Routledge, 1999.

Dunning, Eric, Patrick Murphy and John Williams. *The Roots of Football Hooliganism: A Historical and Sociological Study*. London: Routledge, 1988.

Dunning, Eric, Patrick Murphy, Ivan Waddington and A. E. Astrinakis, eds. *Fighting Fans: Football Hooliganism as a World Phenomenon*. Dublin: University College of Dublin Press, 2002.

Eco, Umberto. 'Sports Chatter'. In *Travels in Hyperreality: Essays*. Translated by William Weaver, 159–65. San Diego: Harcourt, Inc: 1986.

Edelman, Robert. *Serious Fun: A History of Spectator Sports in the USSR*. New York: Oxford University Press, 1993.

Edensor, Tim. *National Identity, Popular Culture and Everyday Life*. Oxford and New York: Berg, 2002.

Elias, Norbert and Eric Dunning. *Quest for Excitement: Sport and Leisure in the Civilizing Process*. Oxford: Blackwell, 1986.

Elsey, Brenda and Joshua Nadel. *Futbolera: A History of Women and Sports in Latin America*. Austin: University of Texas Press, 2019.

Fabian, Johannes. *Time and the Other: How Anthropology Makes Its Objects*. New York: Columbia University Press, 1983.

Famaney-Lamon, A. and F. Van Loon. 'Mass Media and Sports Practice'. *International Review for the Sociology of Sport* 13, no. 4 (1978): 37–45.

Fanon, Frantz. *The Wretched of the Earth*. Translated by Richard Wilcox. New York: Grove Press, 2004.

Farred, Grant. 'The Double Temporality of Lagaan: Cultural Struggle and Postcolonialism'. *Journal of Sport and Social Issues* 28, no. 2 (2004): 93–114.

Ferguson, Niall, *Empire: How Britain Made the Modern World*. New York: Penguin, 2004.

Forbes, Geraldine, *Women in Modern India*. Cambridge: Cambridge University Press, 1996.

Ford, John. *Cricket: A Social History, 1700–1835*. Newton Abbot: David and Charles, 1972.

Foucault, Michel, *The Order of Things: An Archaeology of the Human Sciences*. London and Routledge: 2002.

Franda, Marcus. *West Bengal and the Federalizing Process in India*. Princeton, NJ: Princeton University Press, 1968.

Freitag, Sandria. *Action and Community: Public Arenas and the Emergence of Communalism in North India*. Berkeley: University of California Press, 1989.

Gaffney, Chris. *Temples of the Earthbound Gods: Stadiums in the Cultural Landscapes of Rio de Janeiro and Buenos Aires*. Austin: University of Texas Press, 2008.

Gaffney, Chris and John Bale. 'Sensing the Stadium'. In *Sites of Sport: Space, Place, Experience*, edited by Patricia A. Vertinsky and John Bale, 25–38. London: Routledge, 2004.

Gao, Yunxiang. *Sporting Gender: Women Athletes and Celebrity-Making during China's National Crisis, 1931–45*. Vancouver: UBC Press, 2013.

Gaonkar, Dilip Parmeshwar, ed. *Alternative Modernities*. Durham, NC: Duke University Press, 2001.

Geertz, Clifford. *Local Knowledge: Further Essays in Interpretive Anthropology*. New York: Basic Books, 1983.

Gemmell, Jon. 'All White Male? Cricket and Race in Oz'. In *Cricket, Race and the 2007 World Cup*, edited by Jon Gemmell and Boria Majumdar, 23–39. London and New York: Routledge, 2008.

Gems, Gerald. *Sport and the American Occupation of the Philippines: Bats, Balls, and Bayonets*. Lanham: Lexington Books, 2016.

Ghadially, Rehana, ed. *Urban Women in Contemporary India: A Reader*. New Delhi: Sage, 2007.

Ghosh, Amitav. *In an Antique Land*. London: Granta Books, 1992.

Ghosh, Sankar. *The Disinherited State: A Study of West Bengal, 1967–70*. Calcutta: Orient Longman, 1971.

Ghosh, Siddhartha, ed. *Cricket Elo Banglae* (Cricket in Bengal). Calcutta: Subarnarekha, 2002.

Gikandi, Simon. *Maps of Englishness: Writing Identity in the Culture of Colonialism*. New York: Columbia University Press, 1996.

Ginzburg, Carlo. *Threads and Traces: True False Fictive*. Translated by Anne C. Tedeschi and John Tedeschi. Berkeley: University of California Press, 2012.

Gist, Noel P. and Roy Dean Wright. *Marginality and Identity: Anglo-Indians as a Racially-Mixed Minority in India*. Leiden: E.J. Brill, 1973.

Giulianotti, Richard. *Football: A Sociology of the Global Game*. Cambridge: Polity Press, 1999.

Giulianotti, Richard, Norman Bonney and Mike Hepworth, eds. *Football, Violence and Social Identity*. London and New York: Routledge, 1994.

Gopal, Sarvepalli. 'The Spell of Cricket'. In *Imperialists, Nationalists, Democrats: The Collected Essays*, 408–15. Ranikhet: Permanent Black, 2013.

Greenblatt, Stephen. 'Invisible Bullets'. In *The Greenblatt Reader*, edited by Michael Payne, 121–60. Malden, MA: Blackwell, 2005.

Gruneau, Richard and David Whitson. *Hockey Night in Canada: Sport, Identities, and Cultural Politics*. Toronto: Garamond Press, 1993.

Guha, Ramachandra. *A Corner of a Foreign Field: The Indian History of a British Sport*. London: Picador, 2002.

———. 'The Gentleman Scholar: Sujit Mukherjee'. In *The Last Liberal and Other Essays*, 229–36. Ranikhet: Permanent Black, 2003.

———. *The States of Indian Cricket: Anecdotal Histories*. Ranikhet: Black Kite, 2005.

———, ed. *Makers of Modern India*. New Delhi: Penguin Viking, 2010.

Guha, Ranajit. *History at the Limit of World-History*. New York: Columbia University Press, 2002.

Gupta, Amit. 'India and the IPL: Cricket's Globalized Empire'. *The Round Table* 98, no. 401 (2009): 201–11.

———. 'The Globalization of Cricket: The Rise of the Non-West'. *International Journal of the History of Sport* 21, no. 2 (2004): 257–76.

———. 'The IPL and the Indian Domination of Global Cricket'. *Sport in Society* 14, no. 10 (2011): 1316–25.

Gupta, Bhupesh, Ranen Sen and Prabhat Das Gupta. *CPM Terror in West Bengal*. Calcutta: Communist Party Publication, 1970.

Gurry, Meg. 'Leadership and Bilateral Relations: Menzies and Nehru, Australia and India, 1949–1964'. *Pacific Affairs* 65, no. 4 (Winter, 1992–1993): 510–26.

Guttmann, Allen. *Sport Spectators*. New York: Columbia University Press, 1986.

Habermas, Jürgen. *The Structural Transformation of the Public Sphere: An Inquiry into a Category of Bourgeois Society*. Translated by Thomas Burger. Cambridge, MA: The MIT Press, 1989.

Hall, Stuart. 'Encoding/Decoding'. In *Culture, Media, Language*, edited by Stuart Hall, Dorothy Hobson, Andrew Lowe and Paul Willis, 128–38. London: Hutchinson, 1980.

Hall, Stuart and Doreen Massey. 'Interpreting the Crisis'. *Soundings* 44 (Spring 2010): 57–71.

Hall, Stuart, Charles Critcher, Tony Jefferson, John Clarke and Brian Roberts. *Policing the Crisis: Mugging, the State, and Law and Order*. London: Macmillan 1978.

Haqqi, Anwarul Haque. *Union–State Relations in India*. Meerut: Meenakshi Prakashan, 1967.

Hardiman, David. 'Indian Medical Indigeneity: From Nationalist Assertion to the Global Market'. *Social History* 34, no. 3 (2009): 263–83.

Hargreaves, Jennifer. 'The Victorian Cult of the Family and the Early Years of Female Sports'. In *The Sports Process: A Comparative and Developmental Approach*, edited by Eric Dunning, Joseph Maguire and Robert Pearton, 71–84. Champaign: Human Kinetics, 1994.

Hariman, Robert. 'Political Parody and Public Culture'. *Quarterly Journal of Speech* 94, no. 3 (2008): 247–72.

Harvey, Andy. 'Team Work? Using Sporting Fiction as an Historical Archive and Source of Developing Theoretical Approaches to Sport History'. *International Journal of the History of Sport* 30, no. 2 (2013): 131–44.

Haseler, Stephen. *The English Tribe: Identity, Nation and Europe*. Basingstoke: Palgrave Macmillan, 1996.

Haynes, Douglas and Gyan Prakash, eds. *Contesting Power: Resistance and Everyday Social Relations in South Asia*. New Delhi: Oxford University Press, 1991.

Haynes, Douglas, Abigail McGowan, Tirthankar Roy and Haruka Yanagisawa, eds. *Towards a History of Consumption in South Asia*. New Delhi: Oxford University Press, 2010.

Haynes, Douglas E. *Rhetoric and Ritual in Colonial India: The Shaping of a Public Sphere in Surat City, 1852–1928*. Berkeley: University of California Press, 1991.

Hess, Rob. '"Ladies are Specially Invited": Women in the Culture of Australian Rules Football'. In *Sport in Australian Society: Past and Present*, edited by J. A. Mangan and John Nauright, 111–41. London: Frank Cass, 2000.

Hill, Jeffrey. 'Anecdotal Evidence: Sport, the Newspaper Press, and History'. In *Deconstructing Sport History: A Postmodern Analysis*, edited by Murray G. Phillips, 117–30. Albany: State University of New York Press, 2006.

———. 'Rite of Spring: Cup Finals and Community in the North of England'. In *Sport and Identity in the North of England*, edited by Jeffrey Hill and Jack Williams, 85–111. Keele: Keele University Press, 1996.

———. *Sport and the Literary Imagination: Essays in History, Literature, and Sport*. Oxford: Peter Lang, 2006.

Hill, Jeffrey and Jean Williams. 'Introduction'. *Sport in History* 29, no. 2 (2009): 127–31.

Hoberman, John. *Sport and Political Ideology*. London: Heinemann, 1984.

Hobsbawm, Eric. *The Age of Empire 1875–1914*. New York: Vintage, 1989.

Holt, Richard. 'Cricket and Englishness: The Batsman as Hero'. *International Journal of the History of Sport* 13, no. 1 (1996): 48–70.

———. *Sport and the British: A Modern History*. Oxford: Clarendon, 1989.

Holt, Richard and Tony Mason, *Sport in Britain 1945–2000*. Oxford: Blackwell, 2000.

Horne, John. *Sport in Consumer Culture*. Basingstoke: Palgrave Macmillan, 2006.

Howell, Colin D. *Blood, Sweat, and Cheers: Sport and the Making of Modern Canada*. Toronto: University of Toronto Press, 2001.

Hughes, Stephen Putnam. 'Silent Film Genre, Exhibition and Audiences in South India'. In *Explorations in New Cinema History: Approaches and Case Studies*, edited by Richard Maltby, Daniel Biltereyst and Philippe Meers, 295–309. Chichester: Wiley-Blackwell, 2011.

Hughson, John. 'The Postmodernist Always Rings Twice: Reflections on the "New" Cultural Turn in Sports History'. *International Journal of the History of Sport* 30, no. 1 (2013): 35–45.

Jackson, Steven, David Andrews and Jay Scherer. 'Introduction: The Contemporary Landscape of Sport Advertising'. In *Sport, Culture and Advertising: Identities, Commodities and the Politics of Representation*, edited by Steven Jackson and David Andrews, 1–23. London and New York: Routledge, 2005.

Jago, Michael. *Clement Attlee: The Inevitable Prime Minister*. London: Biteback, 2014.

Jain, Sumitra Kumar. *Party Politics and Centre-State Relations in India*. New Delhi: Abhinav Publications, 1994.

Jarvie, Grant. *Sport, Culture and Society: An Introduction*. London and New York: Routledge, 2006.

Jha, Rajani Ranjan and Bhavana Mishra. 'Centre–State Relations, 1980–90: The Experience of West Bengal'. *The Indian Journal of Political Science* 54, no. 2 (1993): 209–37.

Jhally, Sut. 'The Spectacle of Accumulation: Material and Cultural Factors in the Evolution of the Sports/Media Complex'. *Insurgent Sociologist* 12, no. 3 (1984): 41–57.

Jinxia, Dong. *Women, Sport and Society in Modern China: Holding Up More Than Half the Sky*. London: Routledge, 2003.

Johnes, Martin. 'Heads in the Sand: Football, Politics and Crowd Disasters in Twentieth-Century Britain'. In *Soccer and Disaster: International Perspectives,* edited by Paul Darby, Martin Johnes and Gavin Mellor, 10–27. London: Routledge, 2005.

Jones, Katharine. 'Female Fandom: Identity, Sexism, and Men's Professional Football in England'. *Sociology of Sport Journal*, 25, no. 4 (2008): 516–37.

Jones, Stephen G. *Sports, Politics and the Working Class: Organised Labour and Sport in Inter-War Britain*. Manchester: Manchester University Press, 1988.

Joshi, Sanjay. *Fractured Modernity: Making of a Middle Class in Colonial North India*. New Delhi: Oxford University Press, 2001.

Kaplan, Sam. 'Documenting History, Historicizing Documentation: French Military Officials' Ethnological Reports on Cilicia'. *Comparative Studies in Society and History* 44, no. 2 (2002): 344–69.

Kasbekar, Asha. 'Negotiating the Myth of the Female Ideal in Popular Hindi Cinema'. In *Pleasure and the Nation: The History, Politics, and Consumption of Public Culture in India*, edited by Rachel Dwyer and Christopher Pinney, 286–308. New Delhi: Oxford University Press, 2001.

Kaviraj, Sudipto. 'The Imaginary Institution of India'. In Subaltern Studies VII, edited by Partha Chatterjee and Gyanendra Pandey, 1–39. New Delhi: Oxford University Press, 1992.

Kennedy, Eileen and Laura Hills. *Sport, Media and Society*. Oxford and New York: Berg, 2009.

Kidambi, Prashant. *Cricket Country: An Indian Odyssey in the Age of Empire*. Oxford: Oxford University Press, 2019.

———. 'Hero, Celebrity and Icon: Sachin Tendulkar and the Indian Public Culture'. In *The Cambridge Companion to Cricket*, edited by Anthony Bateman and Jeffrey Hill, 187–202. Cambridge: Cambridge University Press, 2011.

Kietlinski, Robin. *Japanese Women and Sport: Beyond Baseball and Sumo*. London: Bloomsbury, 2011.

Kohli, Atul. *Democracy and Discontent: India's Growing Crises of Governability*. Cambridge: Cambridge University Press, 1991.

———. *The State and Poverty in India. The Politics of Reform*. Cambridge: Cambridge University Press, 1987.

Koller, Christian and Fabian Brändle. *Goal! A Cultural and Social of Modern Football*. Washington D.C.: Catholic University of America, 2015.

Krüger, Arnd and James Riordan, eds. *The Story of Worker Sport*. Champaign, IL: Human Kinetics, 1996.

Kumar, Krishan. 'Varieties of Nationalism'. In *The Victorian World*, edited by Martin Hewitt, 160–74. London and New York: Routledge, 2012.

Kurian, K. Mathew and P. N. Varughese, eds. *Centre–State Relations*. New Delhi: Macmillan, 1981.

Lal, Vinay and Ashis Nandy. 'Introduction'. In *Fingerprinting Popular Culture: The Mythic and the Iconic in Indian Cinema*, edited by Vinay Lal and Ashis Nandy, xi–xxvii. New Delhi: Oxford University Press, 2006.

Lefebvre, Henri, *The Production of Space*. Translated by Donald Nicholson-Smith. Oxford: Blackwell, 1991.

Lenneis, Verena and Gertrud Pfister. 'Gender Constructions and Negotiations of Female Football Fans: A Case Study in Denmark'. *European Journal for Sport and Society*, 12, no. 2 (2015): 157–85.

Lévi-Strauss, Claude. *Structural Anthropology*. Translated by Claire Jacobson and Brooke Grundfest Schoepf. New York: Basic Books, 1963.

Lu, Zhouxiang and Hong Fan. *Sport and Nationalism in China*. London and New York: Routledge, 2014.

Lynch, Rob. 'A Symbolic Patch of Grass: Crowd Disorder and Regulation on the Sydney Cricket Ground Hill'. In *Crowd Violence at Australian Sport*, edited by John O'Hara, 10–48. Cambelltown, NSW: Australian Society for Sports History, 1992.

MacLean, Malcolm. 'Ambiguity within the Boundary: Re-reading C.L.R. James's *Beyond a Boundary*'. *Journal of Sport History* 37, no. 1 (2010): 99–117.

Maguire, Joseph. 'The Global *Media-Sport* Complex'. In *Global Sport: Identities, Societies, Civilizations*, 144–75. Cambridge: Polity Press, 1999.

Major, John. *More Than a Game: The Story of Cricket's Early Years*. London: Harper, 2007.

Majumdar, Boria. '*Ghati–Bangal* on the Maidan: Subregionalism, Club Rivalry and Fan Culture in Indian Football'. In *Football: From England to the World*, edited by Dolores P. Martinez and Projit B. Mukharji, 120–33. London and New York: Routledge, 2009.

———. *Lost Histories of Indian Cricket: Battles Off the Pitch*. London and New York: Routledge, 2006.

———. 'Soaps, Serials and the CPI(M), Cricket Beats Them All: Cricket and Television in Contemporary India'. In *Television in India: Satellites, Politics and Cultural Change*, edited by Nalin Mehta, 124–39. London and New York: Routledge, 2008.

———. *Twenty-Two Yards to Freedom: A Social History of Indian Cricket*. New Delhi: Penguin, 2004.

Majumdar, Boria and Kaushik Bandyopadhyay. *Goalless: The Story of a Unique Footballing Nation*. New Delhi: Penguin Viking, 2006.

Majumdar, Boria and Sean F. Brown. 'Why Baseball, Why Cricket? Differing Nationalisms, Differing Challenges'. *International Journal of the History of Sport* 24, no. 2 (2007): 139–56.

Malcolm, Dominic. *Globalizing Cricket: Englishness, Empire and Identity*. London: Bloomsbury, 2013.

——. 'Cricket Spectator Disorder: Myths and Historical Evidence'. *Sport in History* 19, no. 1 (1999): 16–37.

Malcolm, Dominic and Philippa Velija. 'Cricket: The Quintessential English Game?' In *Sport and English National Identity in a 'Disunited Kingdom'*, edited by Tom Gibbons and Dominic Malcolm, 19–33. London: Routledge, 2017.

——. 'Female Incursion into Cricket's "Male Preserve"'. In *Tribal Play: Subcultural Journeys Through Sport*, edited by Michael Atkinson and Kevin Young, 217–34. Bingley: Emerald, 2008.

Mallick, Ross. *Development Policy of a Communist Government: West Bengal since 1977.* Cambridge: Cambridge University Press, 1993.

Mangan, J. A. 'Ethics and Ethnocentricity: Imperial Education in British Tropical Africa'. In *Sport in Africa: Essays in Social History*, edited by William J. Baker and J.A. Mangan, 138–71. New York and London: Africana Publishing Co., 1987.

——. *The Games Ethic and Imperialism: Aspects of the Diffusion of an Ideal.* Harmondsworth: Viking, 1985.

Mangan, J. A. and James Walvin, eds. *Manliness and Morality: Middle-class Masculinity in Britain and America, 1800–1940.* Manchester: Manchester University Press, 1987.

Mankekar, Purnima. 'Dangerous Desires: Television and Erotics in Late Twentieth-Century India'. *Journal of Asian Studies* 63, no. 2 (2004): 403–31.

——. *Screening Culture, Viewing Politics: An Ethnography of Television, Womanhood, and Nation in Postcolonial India.* Durham, NC: Duke University Press, 1999.

Mannathukkaren, Nissim. 'Reading Cricket Fiction in the Times of Hindu Nationalism and Farmer Suicides: Fallacies of Textual Interpretation'. *International Journal of the History of Sport* 24, no. 9 (2007): 1200–25.

——. 'Subalterns, Cricket and the "Nation": The Silences of Lagaan'. *Economic and Political Weekly* 36, no. 49 (2001): 4580–88.

Marcus, George E. and Michael F. Fischer. *Anthropology as Cultural Critique: An Experimental Moment in the Human Sciences.* Chicago: University of Chicago Press, 1986.

Marqusee, Mike. *Anyone but England: An Outsider Looks at English Cricket*, 3rd ed. London: Aurum Press, 2005.

Mason, Tony. 'All the Winners and the Half Times …'. *Sport in History* 13, no. 1 (1993): 3–13.

——. *Association Football and English Society, 1863–1915.* Brighton: Harvester Press, 1980.

Mazzarella, William and Raminder Kaur. 'Between Sedition and Seduction: Thinking Censorship in South Asia'. In *Censorship in South Asia: Cultural Regulation from Sedition to Seduction*, edited by Raminder Kaur and William Mazzarella, 1–28. Bloomington: Indiana University Press, 2009.

Mbembe, Achille. *Necropolitics*. Translated by Steven Corcoran. Durham, NC: Duke University Press, 2019.

McCrone, Kathleen E. *Playing the Game: Sport and Physical Emancipation of English Women, 1870–1914*. Kentucky: University of Kentucky Press, 1988.

McDonald, Ian. 'Between Saleem and Shiva: The Politics of Cricket Nationalism in 'Globalising India''. In *Sport in Divided Societies*, edited by John Sugden and Alan Bairner, 213–34. Aachen: Meyer and Meyer Sport, 1999.

McGarr, Paul M. '"The Viceroys are Disappearing from the Roundabouts in Delhi': British Symbols of Power in Post-colonial India'. *Modern Asian Studies* 49, no. 3 (2015): 787–831.

McGuigan, John. 'The Cultural Public Sphere'. In *Festivals and the Cultural Public Sphere*, edited by Liana Giorgi, Monica Sassatelli and Gerard Delanty, 79–91. London and New York: Routledge, 2011.

McLuhan, Marshall. *Understanding Media: The Extensions of Man*. New York: McGraw-Hill.

McPherson, Barry D., James E. Curtis and John W. Loy. *The Social Significance of Sport*. Champaign, IL: Human Kinetics, 1989.

Mehta, Nalin. 'Batting for the Flag: Cricket, Television and Globalization in India'. *Sport in Society* 12, no. 4 (2009): 579–99.

———. 'The Great Indian Willow Trick: Cricket, Nationalism and India's TV News Revolution, 1998–2005'. *International Journal of the History of Sport* 24, no. 9 (2007): 1187–99.

Mernissi, Fatima. 'The Meaning of Spatial Boundaries'. In *Beyond the Veil: Male–Female Dynamics in Muslim Society*, 137–47. London: Al Saqi Books, 1975.

Merton, Robert K. 'Insiders and Outsiders: A Chapter in the Sociology of Knowledge'. *American Journal of Sociology* 78, no. 1 (1972): 9–47.

Messner, Michael A. *Power at Play: Sports and the Problem of Masculinity*. Boston: Beacon Press, 1995.

———. *Taking the Field: Women, Men, and Sports*. Minneapolis and London: University of Minnesota Press, 2002.

Middell, Matthias. 'Is There a Timetable when Concepts Travel? On Synchronicity in the Emergence of New Concepts Dealing with Border-Crossing Phenomena'. In *The Trans/National Study of Culture: A Transnational*

Perspective, edited by Doris Bachmann-Medick, 137–54. Berlin: De Gruyter, 2014.

Minault, Gail, ed. *The Extended Family: Women and Political Participation in India and Pakistan*. New Delhi: Chanakya Publications, 1981.

Mink, Louis O. 'The Autonomy of Historical Understanding'. *History and Theory* 5, no. 1 (1966): 24–47.

Mitra, Shakya. 'The IPL: India's Foray into World Sports Business'. *Sport in Society* 13, no. 9 (2010): 1314–33.

———. 'The IPL Post-2010: An Uneasy Transition Phase?' *South Asian History and Culture* 3, no. 1 (2012): 116–25.

Mitra, Subrata K. *The Puzzle of India's Governance: Culture, Context and Comparative Theory*. London and New York: Routledge, 2006.

Molnar, Gyozo, Sara N. Amin and Yoko Kanemasu, eds. *Women, Sport and Exercise in the Asia-Pacific Region: Domination, Resistance, Accommodation*. London: Routledge, 2018.

Mukharji, Projit Bihari. '"Feeble Bengalis" and "Big Africans": African Players in Bengali Club Football'. *Soccer and Society* 9, no. 2 (2008): 273–85.

Munslow, Alan. *The Routledge Companion to Historical Studies*, 2nd ed. London and New York: Routledge, 2006.

Naha, Souvik. 'Adams and Eves at the Eden Gardens: Women Cricket Spectators and the Conflict of Feminine Subjectivity in Calcutta, 1920–1970'. *The International Journal of the History of Sport* 29, no. 5 (2012): 711–29.

———. 'Cricket, Film, Glamour Industry and Promotional Culture in India, 1913–2013'. *Sport in History* 35, no. 3 (2015): 464–89.

———. 'No One Plays with Nehru: Sport, Games Ethic and Postcolonial Nationhood in India' (unpublished article).

———. 'Visually Playing Politics: Use of Sports as Political Critique in Newspaper Cartoons'. In *Visual Histories of India: New Methodologies and Perspectives on South-Asian History*, edited by Annamaria Motrescu-Mayes and Marcus Banks, 209–29. New Delhi: Primus, 2018.

Nalapat, Abilash and Andrew Parker. 'Sport, Celebrity and Popular Culture: Sachin Tendulkar, Cricket and Indian Nationalisms'. *International Review for the Sociology of Sport* 40, no. 4 (2005): 433–46.

Nandy, Ashis. 'Introduction: Indian Popular Cinema as a Slum's Eye View of Politics'. In *The Secret Politics of Our Desires: Innocence, Culpability and Indian Popular Cinema*, edited by Ashis Nandy, 1–18. New Delhi: Oxford University Press, 1998.

————. *The Intimate Enemy: Loss and Recovery of Self under Colonialism*. Delhi: Oxford University Press, 1983.

————. *The Tao of Cricket: On Games of Destiny and the Destiny of Games*, 2nd ed. New Delhi: Oxford University Press, 2000.

Narayanan, Chitra. 'The Indian Spectator: A Grandstand View'. In *Cricketing Cultures in Conflict: World Cup 2003*, edited by Boria Majumdar and J.A. Mangan, 198–212. London: Routledge, 2004.

Nauright, John and Timothy J. L. Chandler, eds. *Making Men: Rugby and Masculine Identity*. London: Frank Cass, 1996.

Nielsen, Kenneth Bo. 'Mamata Banerjee: Redefining Female Leadership'. In *India's Democracies: Diversity, Co-optation, Resistance*, edited by Arild Engelsen Ruud and Geir Heierstad, 101–34. Oslo: Universitetsforlaget, 2016.

Nielsen, Kenneth Bo and Anne Waldrop, eds. *Women, Gender and Everyday Social Transformation in India*. London: Anthem, 2004.

Nielsen, Niels K. 'The Stadium in the City'. In *The Stadium and the City*, edited by John Bale and Olof Moen, 21–44. Keele: Keele University Press, 1995.

Nilekani, Nandan. 'The Phoenix Tongue'. In *Imagining India: Ideas for the New Century*, 83–102. New Delhi: Penguin Allen Lane, 2008.

O'Hanlon, Rosalind. *A Comparison between Women and Men: Tarabai Shinde and the Critique of Gender Relations in Colonial India*. New Delhi: Oxford University Press, 1994.

Olson, Gary A. and Lynn Worsham. 'Staging the Politics of Difference: Homi Bhabha's Critical Literacy'. *JAC: A Journal of Composition Theory* 18, no. 3 (1998): 361–91.

Oriard, Michael, *Reading Football*. Chapel Hill: University of North Carolina Press, 1993.

Paechter, Carrie. 'Rethinking the Possibilities for Hegemonic Femininity: Exploring a Gramscian Framework'. *Women's Studies International Forum* 68 (May–June 2018): 121–28.

Pandey, Gyanendra. *Routine Violence: Nations, Fragments, Histories*. Stanford, CA: Stanford University Press, 2006.

Peatling, G. K. 'Rethinking the History of Criticism of Organized Sport'. *Cultural and Social History* 2, no. 3 (2005): 353–71.

Perelman, Marc. *Barbaric Sport: A Global Plague*. Translated by John Howe. London and New York: Verso, 2012.

Pfister, Gertrud and Stacey Pope, eds. *Female Football Players and Fans: Intruding into a Man's World*. Basingstoke: Palgrave Macmillan, 2018.

Podaliri, Carlo and Carlo Balestri. 'The Ultràs, Racism and Football Culture in Italy'. In *Fanatics! Power, Identity and Fandom in Football*, edited by Adam Brown, 88–100. London: Routledge, 1998.

Ponsford, Megan. 'Frank and Bhupinder: The Odd Couple of Indian Cricket'. *Sport in Society* 18, no. 5 (2015): 565–76.

Pope, Stacey. *The Feminization of Sports Fandom: A Sociological Study*. New York and London: Routledge, 2017.

Prakash, Gyan. 'Civil Society, Community, and the Nation in Colonial India'. *Etnográfica* 6, no. 1 (2002): 27–39.

———. 'The Colonial Genealogy of Society: Community and Political Modernity in India'. In *The Social in Question: New Bearings in History and the Social Sciences*, edited by Patrick Joyce, 81–96. London and New York: Routledge, 2002.

Prakash, Gyan, Michael Laffan and Nikhil Menon. 'Introduction: The Postcolonial Moment'. In *The Postcolonial Moment in South and Southeast Asia*, edited by Gyan Prakash, Michael Laffan, and Nikhil Menon, 1–10. London: Bloomsbury, 2018.

Prasad, Anirudh. *Centre–State Relations in India*. New Delhi: Deep and Deep Publications, 1985.

Puri, Jyoti. *Woman, Body, Desire in Post-Colonial India: Narratives of Gender and Sexuality*. New York and London: Routledge, 1999.

Ray, Manas. 'Growing Up Refugee'. *History Workshop Journal* 53, no. 1 (2001): 149–79.

Ray, Rajat Kanta, *Exploring Emotional History: Gender, Mentality and Literature in the Indian Awakening*. New Delhi: Oxford University Press, 2003.

———. *The Felt Community: Commonalty and Mentality before the Emergence of Indian Nationalism*. New Delhi: Oxford University Press, 2003.

Ray, Raka, *Fields of Protest: Women's Movements in India*. Minneapolis: University of Minnesota Press, 1999.

Ray, Somshankar. '"The Wood Magic": Cricket in India – A Postcolonial Benediction'. *International Journal of the History of Sport* 25, no. 12 (2008): 1637–53.

Ray, Utsa. *Culinary Culture in Colonial India: A Cosmopolitan Platter and the Middle-Class*. New Delhi: Cambridge University Press, 2015.

Renton, Dave, *C.L.R. James: Cricket's Philosopher King*. London: Haus, 2007.

Rigauer, Bero. 'Marxist Theories'. In *Handbook of Sports Studies*, edited by Jay Coakley and Eric Dunning, 28–47. London: Sage, 2002.

Rineart, Robert. 'Poetic Sensibilities and the Use of Fiction for Sport History: Map-making in Representation of the Past'. In *Examining Sport Histories: Power, Paradigms, and Reflexivity*, edited by Richard Pringle and Murray Phillips, 184–201. Morgantown, WV: Fitness Information Technology, 2013.

Riordan, James. *Sport, Politics and Communism*. Manchester: Manchester University Press, 1991.

Rowe, David. *Popular Cultures: Rock Music, Sport and the Politics of Pleasure*. London: Sage, 1995.

———. *Sport, Culture and the Media: The Unruly Trinity*, 2nd ed. Maidenhead: Open University Press, 2004.

Roy, Anupama. *Gendered Citizenship: Historical and Conceptual Explorations*. New Delhi: Orient Blackswan, 2013 [2005].

Roy, Manisha. *Bengali Women*. Chicago: University of Chicago Press, 1992 [1970].

Roy, Parama. *Indian Traffic: Identities in Question in Colonial and Postcolonial India*. Berkeley, Los Angeles, London: University of California Press, 1998.

Ryan, Greg. *The Making of New Zealand Cricket 1832–1914*. London: Frank Cass, 2004.

Sahni, Sati, ed. *Centre–State Relations*. New Delhi: Vikas Publishing House, 1984.

Samaddar, Ranabir, ed. *From Popular Movements to Rebellion: The Naxalite Decade*. London and New York: Routledge, 2019.

Sandiford, Keith. 'Cricket and the Victorian Society'. *Journal of Social History* 17, no. 2 (1983): 303–17.

———. *Cricket and the Victorians*. Aldershot: Scolar Press, 1994.

Sandvoss, Cornel. 'Public Sphere and Publicness: Sport Audiences and Political Discourse'. In *Media and Public Spheres*, edited by Richard Butsch, 58–70. Basingstoke: Palgrave Macmillan, 2007.

Sangari, Kumkum. 'Violent Acts: Cultures, Structures and Retraditionalisation'. In *Women of India: Colonial and Post-Colonial Periods*, edited by Bharati Ray, 159–82. New Delhi: Centre for Studies in Civilizations, 2005.

Sarkar, Tanika. *Hindu Wife, Hindu Nation: Community, Religion and Cultural Nationalism*. London: Hurst & Co, 2001.

Scott, Anne Firor. 'On Seeing and Not Seeing: A Case of Historical Invisibility'. *Journal of American History* 71, no. 1 (1984): 7–21.

Scott, James C. *Domination and the Arts of Resistance: Hidden Transcripts*. New Haven: Yale University Press, 1990.

———. *Weapons of the Weak: Everyday Forms of Peasant Resistance*. New Haven: Yale University Press, 1985.

Sedlatschek, Andreas. *Contemporary Indian English: Variation and Change.* Amsterdam and Philadelphia: John Benjamins, 2009.

Sen, Bhowani. *CPM's Fight against United Front in West Bengal.* New Delhi: Communist Party Publication, 1969.

Sen, Ronojoy. 'Divided Loyalty: Jaipal Singh and His Many Journeys'. *Sport in Society* 12, no. 6 (2009): 765–75.

Sen, Samita. 'Gendered Exclusion: Domesticity and Dependence in Bengal'. *International Review of Social History* 42, no. 5 (1997): 65–86.

———. *Women and Labour in Late Colonial India: The Bengal Jute Industry.* Cambridge: Cambridge University Press, 1999.

Sen, Satadru. 'History without a Past: Memory and Forgetting in Indian Cricket'. In *Cricket and National Identity in the Postcolonial Age: Following On*, edited by Stephen Wagg, 94–109. London and New York: Routledge, 2005.

———. 'How Gavaskar Killed Indian Football'. *Football Studies* 5, no. 2 (2002): 27–37.

Sengoopta, Chandak. *The Rays before Satyajit: Creativity and Modernity in Colonial India.* New York: Oxford University Press, 2016.

Sikes, Michelle and John Bale, eds. *Women's Sport in Africa.* London: Routledge, 2015.

Sinha, Aseema. *The Regional Roots of Developmental Politics in India: A Divided Leviathan.* Bloomington and Indianapolis: Indiana University Press, 2005.

Sinha, Chitra, *Debating Patriarchy: The Hindu Code Bill Controversy in India, 1941–1956.* New Delhi: Oxford University Press, 2012.

Sobchack, Vivian. *Carnal Thoughts: Embodiment and Moving Image Culture.* Berkeley: University of California Press, 2004.

Spaiij, Ramón. *Understanding Football Hooliganism: A Comparison of Six Western European Football Clubs.* Amsterdam: Vossiuspers UvA, 2006.

Steen, Rob. *Floodlights and Touchlines: A History of Spectator Sport.* London: Bloomsbury, 2014.

Stoddart, Brian. 'Sport, Cultural Imperialism, and Colonial Response in the British Empire'. *Comparative Studies in Society and History* 30, no. 4 (1988): 649–73.

Szymanski, Stefan. 'A Theory of the Evolution of Modern Sport'. *Journal of Sport History* 35, no. 1 (2008): 1–32.

Tadié, Alexis. 'Heroes, Fans and the Nation: Exploring Football in Contemporary Fiction'. *International Journal of the History of Sport* 29, no. 12 (2012): 1774–90.

Tarlo, Emma. *Clothing Matters: Dress and Identity in India.* Chicago: University of Chicago Press, 1996.

Thapar, Romila. 'Syndicated *Moksha*'. *Seminar* 313 (September 1985): 14–22.

Tharu, Susie and Tejaswini Niranjana. 'Problems for a Contemporary Theory of Gender'. *Social Scientist* 22, nos. 3–4 (1994): 93–117.

Thompson, E. P. 'The Moral Economy of the English Crowd in the Eighteenth Century'. *Past and Present* 50 (1971): 76–136.

Thompson, John B. *The Media and the Modernity: A Social Theory of the Media.* Cambridge: Polity Press, 1995.

Toffoletti, Kim. *Women Sport Fans: Identification, Participation, Representation.* New York and London: Routledge, 2017.

Toffoletti, Kim and Peter Mewett, eds. *Sport and Its Female Fans.* New York and London: Routledge, 2012.

Tomlinson, Alan and Christopher Young. 'Sport in Modern European History: Trajectories, Constellations, Conjunctures'. *Journal of Historical Sociology* 24, no. 4 (2011): 409–27.

Trouillot, Michel-Rolph. *Silencing the Past: Power and Production in History.* Boston: Beacon Press, 1995.

Tu, Rachel. 'Dressing the Nation: Indian Cinema Costume and the Making of a National Fashion, 1947–1957'. In *The Fabric of Culture: Fashion, Identity, and Globalization*, edited by Eugenia Paulicelli and Hazel Clark, 28–40. London and New York: Routledge, 2009.

Tuan, Yi-Fu. *Space and Place: The Perspective of Experience.* Minneapolis, MN: University of Minnesota Press, 1997.

———. *Topophilia: A Study of Environmental Perception, Attitudes and Values.* Englewood Cliffs, NJ: Prentice-Hall, 1974.

Vamplew, Wray. 'It's Not Cricket and Perhaps It Never Was: An Historical Look at Australian Crowd and Player Behaviour'. *Sport in History* 14, no. 1 (1994): 3–12.

———. 'Sport Crowd Disorder in Britain, 1870–1914: Causes and Controls'. *Journal of Sport History* 7, no. 1 (1980): 5–20.

Vaugrand, Henri. 'Pierre Bourdieu and Jean-Marie Brohm: Their Schemes of Intelligibility and Issues towards a Theory of Knowledge in the Sociology of Sport'. *International Review for the Sociology of Sport* 36, no. 2 (2001): 183–201.

Velija, Philippa. *Women's Cricket and Global Processes: The Emergence and Development of Women's Cricket as a Global Game.* Basingstoke: Palgrave Macmillan, 2015.

Wagg, Stephen, '"Time Gentlemen Please": The Decline of Amateur Captaincy in English County Cricket'. In *Amateurs and Professionals in Post-War British*

Sport, edited by Adrian Smith and Dilwyn Porter, 31–59. London and New York: Routledge, 2000.

Wagg, Stephen and Sharda Ugra. 'Different Hats, Different Thinking? Technocracy, Globalization and the Indian Cricket Team'. *Sport in Society* 12, nos. 4–5 (2009): 600–12.

Wagner, Kim. *Amritsar 1919: An Empire of Fear and the Making of a Massacre.* New Haven: Yale University Press, 2019.

Walsh, Judith. *Domesticity in Colonial India: What Women Learned When Men Gave Them Advice.* New Delhi: Oxford University Press, 2004.

Wann, Daniel, Christina Bayens and Allison Driver. 'Likelihood of Attending a Sporting Event as a Function of Ticket Scarcity and Team Identification'. *Sport Marketing Quarterly* 13, no. 4 (2004): 209–14.

Warner, Michael. *Publics and Counterpublics.* New York: Zone Books, 2002.

Washbrook, David. 'Towards a History of the Present: Southern Perspectives on the Nineteenth and Twentieth Centuries'. In *From the Colonial to the Postcolonial: India and Pakistan in Transition*, edited by Dipesh Chakrabarty, Rochona Majumdar and Andrew Sartori, 332–57. New Delhi: Oxford University Press, 2007.

Webster, Wendy. *English and Empire 1939–1965.* Oxford: Oxford University Press, 2005.

Weiner, Myron. 'Violence and Politics in Calcutta'. *Journal of Asian Studies* 20, no. 3 (1961): 275–81.

Weis, Kurt. 'How the Print Media Affect Sports and Violence: The Problems of Sport Journalism'. *International Review for the Sociology of Sport* 21, nos. 2–3 (1986): 239–52.

Wenner, Lawrence, ed. *Media, Sports, and Society.* Newbury Park, CA: Sage, 1989.

Wenner, Lawrence A., ed. *MediaSport.* London and New York: Routledge, 1998.

Werbner, Pnina. 'Anthropology, Cultural Performance and Imran Khan'. In *Anthropology and Cultural Studies*, edited by Stephen Nugent and Cris Shore, 34–67. London and Chicago: Pluto Press, 1997.

Williams, Jack. *Cricket and England: A Cultural and Social History of the Inter-war Years.* London: Frank Cass, 1999.

———. *Cricket and Race.* Oxford: Berg Publishers, 2001.

Williams, John. 'Having an Away Day: English Football Spectators and the Hooligan Debate'. In *British Football and Social Change: Getting into Europe*, edited by John Williams and Stephen Wagg, 160–84. Leicester: Leicester University Press, 1991.

Williams, Raymond. 'Culture Is Ordinary'. In *Resources of Hope: Culture, Democracy, Socialism*, 3–18. London: Verso, 1989.

———. *Marxism and Literature*. Oxford: Oxford University Press, 1977.

———. *The Long Revolution*. Harmondsworth: Penguin, 1965 [1961].

Wilson, Adrian. 'Foundations of an Integrated Historiography'. In *Rethinking Social History: English Society 1570–1920 and Its Interpretation*, edited by Adrian Wilson, 293–335. Manchester and New York: Manchester University Press, 1993.

Windschuttle, Keith. *The Killing of History: How Literary Critics and Social Theorists Are Murdering Our Past*. New York and London: Encounter Books, 1996.

Young, Kevin. '"The Killing Field": Themes in Mass Media Responses to the Heysel Stadium Riot'. *International Review for the Sociology of Sport* 21, nos. 2–3 (1986): 253–66.

Žižek, Slavoj. *For They Know Not What They Do: Enjoyment as a Political Factor*. London: Verso, 1991.

UNPUBLISHED PHD THESIS

Westall, Claire, 'What Should We Know of Cricket Who Only England Know? Cricket and Its Heroes in English and Caribbean Literature' (PhD thesis, Warwick University, 2007).

WEBSITES

Education.nic.in
Espncricinfo.com
India-seminar.com
Livemint.com

Index